Proceedings of the American Gas Light Association
by American Gas Light Association

Address:
HardPress
8345 NW 66TH ST #2561
MIAMI FL 33166-2626
USA
Email: info@hardpress.net

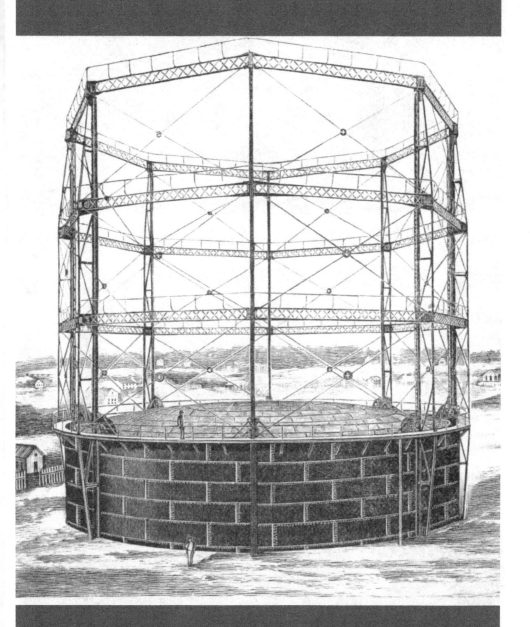

Proceedings of the American Gas Light Association ...

American Gas Light Association

THE

American Gas Light Association.

83299

Report of Proceedings

OF THE

Fifteenth Annual Meeting, Held at New York,

OCTOBER 19, 1887,

AND THE

Sixteenth Annual Meeting, Held at Toronto, Canada,

OCTOBER 17, 1888.

APRIL, 1889.

PUBLISHED BY ORDER OF THE ASSOCIATION.

C. J. Russell Humphreys, Secretary.

Press of A M. Callender, & Co., 42 Pine St., New York.

The American Gas Light Association is indebted to the courtesy of the AMERICAN GAS LIGHT JOURNAL for the stenographic report of the Fifteenth Annual Meeting, gratuitously furnished for publication in this volume.

C. J. RUSSELL HUMPHREYS,
Secretary.

CONTENTS.

INDEX TO SPEAKERS.

INDEX TO SUBJECTS DISCUSSED.

FIFTEENTH ANNUAL MEETING

OF THE

AMERICAN GAS LIGHT ASSOCIATION,

HELD AT

DOCKSTADER'S HALL, NEW YORK CITY,

OCTOBER 19, 20 AND 21, 1887.

FIRST DAY, MORNING SESSION—WEDNESDAY, OCTOBER 19.

The Convention was called to order by the President, M. S. Greenough, Esq., of Boston, Mass.

On motion of Mr. Slater, the reading of the minutes of the last annual meeting was dispensed with, the same having been published in the *American Gas Light Journal*.

ROLL CALL.

The following members were present:

Honorary Members.

Prof. H. Morton, Hoboken, N. J.; Prof. E. G. Love, New York, N. Y.; Robert P. Spice, London, England.

Active Members.

Allen, A. L.,	-	Poughkeepsie, N. Y.
Amory, Dr. R.,	-	Brookline, Mass.
Andrew, J.,	-	Chelsea, Mass.
Atwood, H. A.,	-	Plymouth, Mass.
Balmore, J.,	-	New York, N. Y.
Baumgardner, J. H., -	-	Lancaster, Pa.
Baxter, I. C.,	-	Evansville, Ind.
Baxter, R., -	-	Halifax, N. S.
Baxter, W. H.,	-	Petersburg, Va.
Benson, F. S.,	-	Brooklyn, N. Y.
Beal, W. R.,	-	New York, N. Y.
Blodget, C. W.,	-	Brooklyn, N. Y.
Boardman, A. E., -	-	Macon, Ga.
Borgner, C., -	-	Philadelphia, Pa.

Bradley, W. H., - -	New York, N. Y.
Bredel, F., - - -	New York, N. Y.
Brown, T. R., - -	Philadelphia, Pa.
Bush, J. S., - - -	New York, N. Y.
Butterworth, W. C., -	Rockford, Ills.
Byrne, T. E., - -	Brooklyn, N. Y.
Cadwell, W. D., - -	Nashua, N. H.
Cartwright, J., - -	Poughkeepsie, N. Y.
Cartwright, M., - -	Rochester, N. Y.
Cartwright, W., - -	Oswego, N. Y.
Clark, Walton, - -	Chicago, Ills.
Coggshall, H. F., - -	Fitchburg, Mass.
Cole, T. W., - -	Altoona, Pa.
Connelly, J. S., - -	New York, N. Y.
Connelly, T. E., - -	New York, N. Y.
Copp, A. M., - - -	Boston, Mass.
Corbett, C. H., - -	Brooklyn, N. Y.
Cornell, T. C., - -	Yonkers, N. Y.
Cowdery, E. G., - -	Milwaukee, Wis.
Coyle, P., - - -	Boston, Mass.
Crafts, D. W., - -	Northampton, Mass.
Cressler, A. D., - -	Fort Wayne, Ind.
Curley, T., - -	Wilmington, Del.
Cushing, O. E., - -	Lowell, Mass.
Davis, F. J., - -	Waltham, Mass.
Dell, J., - - -	St. Louis, Mo.
Denniston, W. H., -	Pittsburg, Pa.
Diall, M. N., - -	Terre Haute, Ind.
Dickey, C. H., - -	Baltimore, Md.
Dickey, R. R., - -	Dayton, Ohio.
Dingee, F. A., - -	Philadelphia, Pa.
Down, W. H., - -	New York, N. Y.
Edgerton, H. H., - -	Philadelphia, Pa.
Edwards, G. B., - -	New York, N. Y.
Elkins, W. L. Jr., - -	Philadelphia, Pa.
Faben, C. R., Jr., - -	Toledo, Ohio.
Fay, W. J., - -	Denver, Col.
Findlay, J. H., - -	Ogdensburg, N. Y.
Flemming, D. D., -	Jersey City, N. J.

Floyd, F. W.,	- -	New York, N. Y.
Floyd, H. E.,	- -	New York, N. Y.
Floyd, J. R., -	- -	New York, N. Y.
Foster, T. G.,	- -	Montgomery, Ala.
Fowler, J., -	- -	Philadelphia, Pa.
Frost, W. H.,	- -	Baltimore, Md.
Gardner, J., Jr.,	- -	Pittsburg, Pa.
Gates, F. W.,	-	Hamilton, Ont., Can.
Geggie, D. H.,	- -	Quebec, Can.
Gerould, C. L.,	- -	Brooklyn, N. Y.
Gerould, L. P.,	- -	Manchester, N. H.
Gilbert, T. D.,	- -	Grand Rapids, Mich.
Goodwin, W. W.,	- -	Philadelphia, Pa.
Gordon, J. J.,	- -	Cincinnati, O.
Graeff, G. W., Jr.,	- -	Philadelphia, Pa.
Greenough, M. S.,	-	Boston, Mass.
Gribbel, J., -	- -	New York, N. Y.
Griffin, J. J.,	- -	Philadelphia, Pa.
Hallett, J. L.,	- -	Springfield, Mass.
Harbison, J. P.,	- -	Hartford, Conn.
Helme, Wm.,	- -	Philadelphia, Pa.
Hookey, G. S.,	- -	Augusta, Ga.
Hopper, W. H.,	- -	Germantown, Pa.
Horry, W. S.,	- -	Philadelphia, Pa.
Humphreys, A. C.,	- -	Philadelphia, Pa.
Humphreys, C. J. R.,	-	Lawrence, Mass.
Huntington, P. W.,	- -	Columbus, Ohio.
Isbell, C. W.,	- -	New York, N. Y.
Jones, E. C., -	- -	Boston, Mass.
Jones, S. L.,	- -	Philadelphia, Pa.
King, E. J., -	- -	Jacksonville, Ills.
Kitson, A.,	- -	Philadelphia, Pa.
Kraft, G. W.,	- -	Philadelphia, Pa.
Kreischer, G. F., -	-	New York, N. Y.
Lansden, T. G.,	- -	Washington, D. C.
Leach, H. B.,	- -	Taunton, Mass.
Learned, E. C.,	- -	New Britain, Conn.
Learned, W. A.,	- -	Newton, Mass.
Lindsley, E.,	- -	Cleveland, O.

Loomis, B.,	Hartford, Conn.
Lowe, L. P.,	Philadelphia, Pa.
Ludlam, E.,	Brooklyn, N. Y.
Mayer, F.,	Baltimore, Md.
McCullough, E. H.,	Philadelphia, Pa.
McDonald, W.,	Albany, N. Y.
McElroy, J. H.,	Pittsburg, Pa.
McIlhenny, J.,	Pniladelphia, Pa.
McMillin, E.,	Columbus, O.
Merrifield, P. S.,	New York, N. Y.
Merrick, S. V.,	Philadelphia, Pa.
Monks, R. J.,	Boston, Mass.
Murphy, H.,	Sing Sing, N. Y.
Neal, G. B.,	Boston, Mass.
Nettleton, C. H.,	Birmingham, Conn.
Nettleton, C.,	New York, N. Y.
Norton, A. M.,	Nashua, N. H.
O'Brien, W. J.,	Philadelphia, Pa.
Page, G. S.,	New York, N. Y.
Gardner, Wm.,	Pittsburg, Pa.
Park, W. K.,	Philadelphia, Pa.
Parrish, W.,	Seneca Falls, N. Y.
Pearson, W. H.,	Toronto, Ont.
Perkins, J. D.,	New York, N. Y.
Pratt, John C.,	Boston, Mass.
Prichard, C. F.,	Lynn, Mass.
Ramsdell, G. G.,	Vincennes, Ind.
Richardson, F. S.,	N. Adams, Mass.
Robinson, W. L.,	Uniontown, Pa.
Roots, D. T.,	Connersville, Ind.
Seaverns, F.,	New York, N. Y.
Sherman, F. C.,	New Haven, Conn.
Slade, J.,	Yonkers, N. Y.
Slater, A. B.,	Providence, R. I.
Smallwood, J. B.,	Baltimore, Md.
Smedberg, J. R.,	Baltimore, Md.
Smith, M.,	Wilkesbarre, Pa.
Spaulding, C. S.,	Brookline, Mass.
Sprague, C. H.,	Boston, Mass.

Stanley, I. N.,	- -	Brooklyn, N. Y.
Stedman, W. A.,	- -	Newport, R. I.
Stein, E.,	- - -	Philadelphia, Pa.
Stiness, S. G.,	- -	Pawtucket, R. I.
Taber, R. B.,	- -	New Bedford, Mass.
Townsend, S. S.,	- -	New York, N. Y.
Turner, T.,	- -	Charleston, S. C.
Vanderpool, E.,	- -	Newark, N. J.
Warmington, G. H.,	- -	Cleveland, O.
Watson, C.,	- -	Camden, N. J.
Watrous, V. S.,	- -	Little Falls, N. Y.
Weber, A.,	- -	New York, N. Y.
Weber, O. B.,	- -	New York, N. Y.
White, C. A.,	- -	New York, N. Y.
White, W. H.,	- -	New York, N. Y.
Willetts, C. A.,	- -	Flushing, N. Y.
Wood, A. C.,	- -	Syracuse, N. Y.
Wood, G.,	- -	New Bedford, Mass.
Zolikoffer, O.,	- -	New York, N. Y.

Applications for active membership from the following gentlemen, were read by the Secretary :

Bierce, F.,	- -	Memphis, Tenn.
Brown, E. C.,	- -	Philadelphia, Pa.
Frost, E. I.,	- -	New York City.
Glasgow, A. G.,	- -	Philadelphia, Pa.
Howard, E.,	- -	New York City.
Houston, W. B.,	- -	Rahway, N. J.
Jackson, W. M.,	- -	New York City.
Krumholz, J.,	- -	Buffalo, N. Y.
Lucas, Jr., P.,	- -	Mt. Vernon, N. Y.
Lenz, E.,	- - -	New York City.
Morgans, W. H.,	- -	Pontiac, Mich.
Milsted, M. N.,	- -	New York City.
Murphy, J. M.,	- -	Chicago, Ill.
Mooney, W.,	- -	New York City.
Peters, M.,	- -	Brockton, Mass.
Quinn, A. K.,	- -	Newport, R. I.
Russell, D. R.,	- -	St. Louis, Mo.

Snow, W. H.,	-	-	Holyoke, Mass.
Stephens, G.,	-	-	Tarrytown, N. Y.
Scriver, J. F.,	-	-	Montreal, Can.
Stacey, W.,	-	-	Cincinnati, Ohio.
Scrafford, W. H.,	-	-	Bath, N. Y.
Tilden, W. D.,	-	-	New York City.
Wagner, L., -	-	-	Philadelphia, Pa.
Whittier, C. R.,	-	-	New York City.
Ward, G. M.,	-	-	New York City.
Wilcox, W. K.,	-	-	Middletown, N. Y.
Waldo, J. A.,	-	-	Boston, Mass.
Zimmermann, W. F.,	-		Pittsburg, Pa.

The names were referred for consideration to a committee, consisting of Messrs. A. M. Norton, T. C. Connell and G. B. Neal. The committee subsequently reported in favor of the election of the gentlemen whose names were read, and the Secretary was instructed to cast the ballot of the Association for their election. The Secretary cast the ballot, and the gentlemen were declared duly elected members of the Association.

On motion of Mr. McMillin, the regular order of business was modified so as to bring the reports of officers and standing committees ahead of the President's address.

REPORT OF THE TREASURER AND SECRETARY.

Secretary and Treasurer Humphreys presented the following annual report for the year ending September 30, 1887.

RECEIPTS.

Initiation fees	-	-	-	-	-	$	410.00
Dues for year 1883		-	-	-		10.00
" " 1884	-	-	-	-		20.00
" " 1885	-	-	-	-		85.00
" " 1886	-	-	-	-		260.00
" " 1887	-	-	-		1,080.00
" " 1888, in advance	-	-		5.00
Sale of " Proceedings "	-	-	-		12.00
Interest	-	-	-	-		87.79
	Total receipts	-	-	-	$1,969.79
Cash brought forward from last year	-		2,202.59
	Total amount to debit	-	-		$4,172.38

EXPENDITURES.

Printing Vol. 7 of " Proceedings " and mailing same - - - -	$918.35	
Salary of Secretary and Treasurer -	500.00	
Expenses of Philadelphia meeting -	81.35	
Printing, stationery, postage and sundries - - - - -	234.96	
Total expenditures - -	$1,734.66	
Cash carried forward to next year	2,437.72	
Total amount to credit -		$4,172.38

Memo. of cash on hand:

Deposit in South Brooklyn Savings Inst. - -		$1,194.71
" Williamsburg Savings Bank - - -		805.60
" Lawrence Savings Bank - -		368.08
" Nat. Pemberton Bank, of Lawrence -		61.15
Cash in Treasurer's hands - - -		8.18
Total - - - - - - -		$2,437.72

Due from members, including year 1888 - $1,915.00

Examined and found correct.

C. H. NETTLETON,
A. E. BOARDMAN,
Finance Committee.

The roll call for the year shows as follows :

HONORARY MEMBERS.

Number on the roll Sept. 30, 1886 - -		6
Admitted Oct., 1886 - - - - -		1
On roll Oct. 1, 1887 - - -		7

ACTIVE MEMBERS.

Number on the roll Oct. 1, 1886 - -	281	
Admitted Oct., 1886 - - - -	41	
		322
Resigned - - - - - -	10	
Died - - - - - - -	2	
Number on roll Oct. 1, 1887 - -	310	
		322

DECEASED MEMBERS.

H. H. Fish, Utica, N. Y.; J. H. Walker, Sr., Tonawanda, N. Y.
The report was accepted and ordered placed on file.

REPORT OF THE EXECUTIVE COMMITTEE.

NEW YORK, October, 18, 1887.

To the Members of the American Gas Light Association :

GENTLEMEN :——Your Executive Committee would respectfully offer the following report :

The following papers, to be read at the present Convention, have been approved by the Executive Committee:

"Fuel Gas," by Emerson McMillin, of Columbus, O.; Illumination *vs.* Candle Power," by Alex C. Humphreys, of Philadelphia, Pa.; " Utilization of Residual Products," by C. H. Nettleton, of Birmingham, Conn.; "The Advantages of Gas Companies Engaging in the Electric Light Business," by E. J. King, of Jacksonville, Ill.; " Water Gas," by Walton Clark, of Chicago, Ill.; "Development of the Half-Depth Regenerative Furnace and Some of the Results," by O. B. Weber, of New York ; "The Comparative Illuminating Power of Gas Purified with Lime *vs.* Oxide of Iron," by C. W. Blodget, of Brooklyn, N. Y.; " Disadvantages Occasioned by Fluctuations of Candle Power in Gas Furnished to Consumers," by Richard J. Monks, of South Boston, Mass.; "The Advantages of Regenerative Furnaces for Large and Small Gas Works," by Fred. Bredel, of New York City ; "Purification Puzzles," by Thomas Turner, of Charleston, S. C.; " The Relation of Intensity of Light and Visual Perception," by E. C. Jones, of Boston, Mass.; " The Use and Value of Coke for Generating Steam," by J. L. Hallett, of Springfield, Mass.

Your Committee would recommend that at the present meeting the President's address be read after the reports of officers and committees.

At the last meeting of the Association the following amendment to the Constitution was offered, namely, to amend Article IV., by striking out the words " or engaged in industries relating thereto." Under the rule, this proposed amendment was referred to the Executive Committee. Your Committee recommends that the amendment be adopted.

A resolution was also passed at the last meeting requiring the Executive Committee to submit to the Association such other amendments to the Constitution as might be thought wise. Your Committee, therefore, submits to the meeting the amended form of the Constitution accompanying this report, as a basis upon which a more perfect Constitution can be built up.

In regard to the resolution upon the matter of Gas Commissions, which was considered at the last meeting of the Association, and referred to the Executive Committee, your committee would report that it is inexpedient to take action upon the subject.

(The Committee submitted a form of a new Constitution.)

THE PRESIDENT—The recommendations of the Executive Committee will now be taken up separately. The first recommendation is that referring to the proposed amendment to Article IV., of the Constitution. On motion of Mr. Harbison the recommendation was adopted.

THE PRESIDENT—The draft of the new Constitution submitted by the Executive Committee is now before the meeting. On motion of Mr. Harbison, the matter was referred back to the Executive Committee, they to report thereon at the next annual meeting.

THE PRESIDENT—We now come to the recommendation of the Executive Committee in regard to Gas Commissions. On motion of Mr. Harbison the recommendation was adopted.

REPORT OF THE FINANCE COMMITTEE.

NEW YORK, October 19, 1887.

To the Members of the American Gas Light Association:

GENTLEMEN:—Your Finance Committee would respectfully report that they have examined the books and accounts of the Secretary and Treasurer, C. J. R. Humphreys, for the year ending September 30, 1887, and find the same to be correct.

Very respectfully,   C. H. NETTLETON,
                        A. E. BOARDMAN,
                                Finance Committee.

The report was received and ordered placed on file.

REPORT OF THE COMMITTEE ON UNIFORMITY OF METER COUPLINGS.

Mr. F. C. Sherman, on behalf of the Committee, presented the following report :

The Committee to whom was referred the matter of uniformity in meter connections, respectfully recommend that the members of this Association adopt the unions of the American Meter Company, of New York City, as their standard. The Committee would take this time to express their obligation to the meter manufacturers for their samples of unions and valuable suggestions.

The report was laid upon the table, and on motion of Dr. Amory, it was voted that a new committee be appointed, consisting of representatives of the various meter manufacturing firms ; the committee to report, if possible, at the present meeting.

The President appointed the following as such committee :

Messrs. W. H. Down, W. W. Goodwin, J. J. Griffin, Wm. Helme, J. B. Smallwood and Nathaniel Tufts.

PRESIDENT'S ADDRESS.

President Greenough then delivered the following address :

Gentlemen of the American Gas Light Association :—The first and most agreeable duty which falls to your presiding officer is that of welcoming you all to another meeting, and congratulating you upon the year's prosperity which the companies that we represent have almost without exception enjoyed. There are few industries in existence which for so many years in the past have afforded a safer investment to the capitalist and trustee. Whether this will be so in the future depends to a great extent upon the members of our profession here and abroad.

If we accommodate ourselves to the new demands which are now made upon us, and meet with cheaper or better light our various competitors in the race for public favor, then gas will continue to yield a fair profit to the genuine investor. If we do not, the consequences can easily be foreseen. The time has gone by when a gas company could charge such a price as would yield them the profit they desired, and collect it without difficulty. The time has come when the price must be fixed to get the business, and the profit looked for afterwards. By dilligent searching, however, I think we shall be able to find it.

It is also a matter for congratulation that during the past year the inroads of death have been so small among us. We have left but few of our friends by the wayside, in our march through life this year. With but two exceptions, the Association remains intact, and I speak, I know, the general sentiment, when I express my great and thankful satisfaction that our friend, Mr. Denniston, was not killed in that recent terrible disaster in Ohio. The gentlemen who have gone from among us, Mr. Fish, of Utica, and Mr. Walker, of Tonawanda, will be much regretted, and I trust the Association will take suitable action at this meeting in regard to them.

The second duty, which I shall try to perform, will be that of briefly reviewing various matters which have been brought prominently to our attention during the past year, and I shall then devote a few minutes to some subjects directly concerning our Association.

Undoubtedly the question which has been more than any other in the minds of most of us, is the future of electric lighting, and the policy of gas companies with regard to it. We are all familiar with numbers of patents which have each promised to wholly revolutionize existing methods of gas making, and which gradually subsided like heaving waves of the sea, leaving no more effect upon our method of doing business than has been produced upon a rocky coast by the waves breaking against it. We have also seen an unreasoning terror of electric light seize with panic the holders of gas stock, and cause them to part for a low price with stock which to-day is more valuable than ever. As a result of these experiences the stockholder has grown, perhaps, too bold, and after an uncalled for fear of the threats of his electric rival, he has not unnaturally passed into a defiant frame of mind, with entire confidence in the stability of his investment. It was, however, calculated to somewhat startle the strongest believer in gas to receive the circular from the Westinghouse Electric Lighting Company, which was sent a year ago to the gas companies of the country. In that document we were invited to abandon our business altogether, so far as gas lighting was concerned, to turn our mains into conduits for fuel, and to furnish our customers with incandescent electric light as being the light of the future. Mr. Westinghouse is a man so well known throughout the world, of such indomitable energy, and such financial success, that his name is a host in itself to the scheme he favors, and can command from his friends and followers the requisite capital to push it. You are to hear at this meeting a paper on the subject of the combination of gas and electric lighting, from a gentleman well versed upon the question, and I do not wish to say too much, or I may be trenching upon his ground. You will also hear a paper on fuel gas, from one to whom we always listen with interest, so that that branch of the subject will require no detailed treatment at my hands. At the same time I should be unwilling to pass over this reference to the proposition of Mr. Westinghouse without expressing my disapproval of it. Far be it from me to underrate the value of the incandescent electric light. On the contrary, I am well known to have been favorably disposed to it for some time, and many gentlemen here will remember the criticism which I received at Providence, R. I., in 1886, for the advice* on the subject which I ventured to offer the New England Association. But there is a wide difference between supplying electric light to those who want it, and supplying nothing else. Before gas can be abandoned some other light must appear which is equally reliable and either better or cheaper. How are these requisitions filled by electricity? Better? yes; in some places. Cheaper? no; hardly anywhere. Equally reliable? not yet.

We hear a great deal of wiring new buildings for electric light, and we certainly see a great deal of it going into stores and theatres; but I fail to hear of buildings being erected without gas pipes, also, nor is it customary to order out a gas meter when the wires are put up. People must have something to fall back upon which will not fail them. Perhaps the same may some day be said of electricity, but it will only happen when the wires are as securely buried and insulated as a gas main, and when a sufficient number of amperes are stored in various parts of the town, to prevent the lights going out in case of an accident to the generating station. It is perfectly true that people bear with some degree of equanimity an accident to their electric lights at present. They say that too much must not be expected of a new system, and cheerfully light their

*See AMERICAN GAS LIGHT JOURNAL, Vol. XLIV., March 2, 1886, p. 123.

gas. Suppose, however, that the gas company abandoned its supply and turned over its pipes wholly to fuel, relying upon wires for light, and that then there should be the troubles which we occasionally have brought to our notice. I think the company and the public would both regret the change. So far the electric lamp has hardly penetrated the walls of private houses. From time to time I hear of some financial magnate who has put in a separate installation for his exclusive benefit, and I know of one station where a small number of neighbors are supplied from a storage battery into which the dynamo is continually working. Practically, however, the domestic lighting business is still untouched. To get this a light must be cheaply produced, which must either have less of that intense brilliancy which characterizes the ordinary lamp, or which must be so pleasantly shaded as to largely detract from its illuminating power. Still more important, however, is the question of reliability. It is all very well to attach as a novelty to a chandelier, the glass globes containing the electric light, but when a steady and permanent use of a light is considered, it must be one for which gas can be abandoned. Now, this can unquestionably be done by the use of storage batteries upon a direct current, at a price. Whether it can be done at all upon an alternating current, such as the Westinghouse, remains to be proved. Perhaps so; but so far as I know it has not been. Upon a direct current it is feasible under certain conditions. In the first place the storage batteries are very expensive, considering the uncertainty of their duration; and in the second, I am informed that they still are unsatisfactory. A battery should be like a gas holder. It should fill or empty itself as rapidly as may be desired, without injury or inconvenience; it should certainly give up in five hours the accumulations of the other nineteen, without any deleterious effects; but this, I am informed, has not yet been accomplished in practice. Probably it will be done—nothing seems impossible to an electrician, but when it is it will be at no trifling expense. In other words, putting aside the question of the quality of the light, which needs improvement, my conclusion is this—that if you want cheapness you lose reliability, and if you insist on reliability you lose cheapness. Now some people want cheapness, some reliability, most people both. It has been said that literature is a good stick, but a poor crutch—very well to help along, but bad to depend upon in a pinch. So with incandescent electricity.

If there is a demand for electric light of one kind in stores and of another in houses, I know no reason why the same gas company should not furnish both ; but I think there are very good reasons why it should continue to furnish gas as well. And let it not be understood that when I talk of cheapness in regard to electric light I believe that it can be supplied as cheap as the same amount of light is furnished by gas in most of our larger cities. It can certainly be furnished cheaper than at first, and the use of high tension alternating currents with reducers has undoubtedly been a step in that direction ; but I do not see my way to believing that it can as yet approach the cost of gas in this city, light for light, nor even that in towns where gas costs somewhat more than here. If there is an incandescent electric lighting company which sells its light at a price equivalent to gas at $1.50 per thousand, and which pays dividends out of its earnings, I can only say that I have not heard of it. Gas, at that price, however, is unfortunately the exception and not the rule, and in very many of our smaller cities it is in the power of an electric lighting company to play the part of dog in the manger. It can prevent the gas company's making money without doing so itself. As in many other operations, the cost of running electric lights does not increase proportionately to the number in use, and it is, therefore, the policy of a small company to increase its business at almost any price, even at rates which not only exclude competition from gas, but which cannot return a new dollar for an old one. Under these circumstances the same alternative is presented as in the case of a competing gas company. The old one must settle or fight, and its policy must be governed to some extent by the character of the men who control the electric lighting company. If they act as did a company recently brought to my notice—put in a plant for $30,000, and ask $100,000 for it, the course of the gas company is plain ; but if they are sensible men, then I think a union of interests advisable. I am aware that this view is not universally held, but we are here for the purpose of comparing our ideas, and I trust that Mr. King's paper may elicit a full discussion.

Many members of our profession have been in hopes that they would be assisted in their business by an incandescent gas burner. The statement has been made, on good authority, that of the heat units in a gas flame only about five per cent. are utilized in light. I confess to having some doubts about the fact, but there is no doubt that if it is incorrect it is only a question of percentage, and that undoubtedly there is much more light in a foot of gas than has ever yet been got out of it. The development of the Siemens and other high-power burners is a step in this direction, though by a different road. By utilizing some of their own waste heat they greatly develop brilliancy ; in fact, a brilliancy so great as to make the light unsuitable for domestic lighting. It has been, then, in an attempt to get the same amount of light from less gas, and not more light from the same amount of gas, that the work has been done that has attracted so much attention, both here and abroad, during the past six months. A steady light, almost white, producing much less heat than an ordinary gas flame, perhaps because only half the amount is burnt, seems a very attractive investment and a very powerful ally ; but an examination of all the facts is sure to greatly dampen any premature enthusiasm.

It has been found in the Welsbach burner that the light, though beautiful when the incandescent mantle was new, deteriorated rapidly, and it was not very long before the gas with which it was heated yielded hardly more light per cubic foot than could be obtained from ordinary burners. It was also found that the mantle was so extremely friable as to render its domestic use almost out of the question, and as a result of these two radical defects it has practically been a failure in Germany, except that in Vienna it can be seen in limited use. It is fair to say that some of the people interested in this and kindred burners admit its defects, and are busily experimenting with a view to their removal ; and when we remember how boundless are the limits of human ingenuity, and against what seemingly insurmountable difficulties our electric rivals have successfully struggled, it would be a foolish prophet who would undertake to say what can or cannot be done in this direction. It has become evident that success in this business means a fortune to all concerned, and many brains have been set working at it. Without much faith in the present burners on the market, I am not without some hope of the future ; and when the day shall come that an incandescent gas burner shall burn 1,000 hours and still give a light of eight candles per foot of gas, and that with this shall be combined a toughness which shall defy ordinary jars, then I shall feel that the gas companies have really found a friend.

In this connection also should be mentioned the efforts of Mr. Lowe, Mr. Fahnehjelm, and others, to utilize for incandescent light the heat-giving powers of pure fuel gas. Personally I have grave doubts about the success of such a gas, both on economical and sanitary grounds. I may, however, be wrong. The fuel of the future may turn out to be artificially-scented hydrogen and carbonic oxide, at least in factories; and if this shall prove to be the case there will certainly be a great opening for somebody, who shall succeed in satisfactorily meeting the demand for cheaper light as well as heat. Whether it has yet been met or not by the inventions now on the market, I am not prepared to say ; but I confess to considerable skepticism at present.

There is only one more practical question on which I wish to speak. That is regenerative furnaces. It is a subject which will be discussed in two papers at this meeting ; but I wish to express my opinion to the effect that the tendency is to spend less money to save waste heat. Since the attention of engineers has been called to the possibility of heating retorts with ever-decreasing percentage of fuel, they have steadily persevered in that direction, piling up ever-increasing quantities of tile, and making the systems more complete, but at the same time more complicated. Every additional air flue brought in close contact to the outgoing gases for the purpose of extracting heat from them furnishes another opportunity for leakage also ; and nothing can be more exasperating, as well as costly, than the failure of elaborately constructed settings to do their work. Suppose that in a comparatively simple system the percentage of fuel is not over twenty-five per cent. by volume or seventeen by weight, and that in an elaborate setting it is cut down to twelve, the cost of one being double that of the other, then it is apparently a question only of the value of fuel in each locality. But if the simple system works more reliably than the other, and with the exercise of much less care and intelligence, then I think another factor is introduced which is well deserving attention. It is probably the case that this audience contains men who can assure us of the entire success in their works of the most elaborate systems yet devised; but I think that if human nature were as willing to avow its failures as its good fortunes, they would be outnumbered by other men who would tell a totally different story. A very little thing can spoil any system yet invented. Only the greatest care can insure the perfect construction and working of a first-class regenerative setting. I was in Europe for a short time this summer, and visited one day one of the largest stations on the Continent. The engineer informed me that they had used there several of the best systems of elaborate firing with good results. He also said that they had used one of the unpatented systems of half-regenerative work with so great comparative success that he doubted very much their building any more of the other kind. This of course is only a straw showing how the breeze is blowing on other people as well as myself, but as such it is worth something; and I am inclined to the opinion that the furnace which will eventually come into general use will be one which does not aim at the highest possible results.

The number of new processes for making gas which are devised by inventive and not too scrupulous men has become so great that it is no wonder that interest has been taken by the managers of so many companies in the formation of what Mr. Egner has tentatively christened by the name of the Gas Institute. He has called my attention officially to the scheme, that I might recommend it, if I saw fit, to the favorable consideration of this Association. Upon mature reflection I am unable to do this; first, because I doubt very much its satisfactory working, and, second, because if combined action is advisable for the gas companies I think it can be obtained in a simpler and less expensive way. I think also that the name proposed for the enterprise is not a happy one. It would, I think, be much better to select one which had not already been chosen by the largest association of gas managers in the world, to describe an institution so wholly different from that which it is now proposed to establish. The name, however, is of minor consequence, though

I trust some other one will be selected if the scheme proposed should become an established fact.

Granting, then, that combined action by gas companies is advisable, is there no way of obtaining it save by the appointment of a high-class expert and a corps of assistants, and their establishment with offices and laboratory in Washington or elsewhere? If this expert is to be of value, his judgment must be of the best, and his character so high that no possible suspicion may rest upon him of possessing interested motives when he recommends or disapproves of any particular scheme. There are such men to be found in this country, of course; but they are all busily engaged at good salaries, and I think it would be by no means easy to induce one of them to leave his present assured position and take at any reasonable salary a place of which the permanency seems so dubious, for I doubt there being business enough to occupy a man for more than half his time; and I do not believe that the plan, if put in operation, would prove sufficiently profitable to gas companies to induce them to subscribe for many years.

I think, however, that by the medium of this Association the same result may be obtained, and in a better way. The plan which I would suggest would be the election of a permanent Investigating Committee, who should be nominated after careful consideration of localities, and who should be assisted when called upon to act by such of their neighbors as should put their names on the Secretary's list as willing to serve as volunteers. Let us suppose that Mr. Slater was the New England member. Mr. Wood the New York, Mr. McMillin the Ohio, or anybody else you please. Suppose also that myself and a dozen other gas engineers of New England had signified our willingness to assist Mr. Slater whenever called on. Suppose again, that the manager of some town in our neighborhood was approached by the representative of some patent process, valuable or otherwise, but on which he is unwilling to trust his own judgment. He calls upon Mr. Humphreys, who refers him to Mr. Slater. If Mr. Slater himself is in doubt, he calls in turn upon such of the nearest volunteers as he desires, and they jointly make an examination of the process, make their report to the manager of the gas company interested, send a copy of it to the Secretary of this

Association, and draw from him the amount of their expenses incurred. Transfer the locality to New York or Ohio, and with different people a similar scene would be enacted. In this way the member of this Association in need of advice would not only get the best to be had in his neighborhood, but the Association would also get at the end of the year a valuable and interesting mass of information, from which a useful report might be extracted. The expense might be $500 to this Society, though I should doubt it. If it were more it might be necessary to raise the assessment a trifle, if the value of the plan did not increase our members sufficiently to counterbalance it. As to serving on the committee, I think it would not be difficult to find candidates. Every man wishes to keep posted, and is desirous to learn about any new plan of making. distributing, or burning gas better. The number of occasions which he would be called upon would probably be small, and, I think, he could well afford the time. The number of volunteer aids whom he could summon, would be, I think, nearly that of the Association.

I commend then, this plan to the committee, which I presume will be appointed to consider the President's address. Although in a crude form, and perhaps not fulfilling every requisite as a substitute for Mr. Egner's, I think it can be whipped into such a shape as to sustantially do the work desired.

It is not remarkable that a demand should exist for educated assistance from the managers of smaller companies, for it is the experience of every person who has to do with engaging such, that it is hard to select, at the salary which can be paid, men who are competent to attend to all the varied details of a gas manager's work.

Although our large technical schools in Hoboken, New York, Troy, Boston and elsewhere are annually turning out scientifically educated young men, yet few of them know anything worth mentioning about gas; and when called upon to choose between the practical gas maker who works by rule of thumb, and the man of science who knows nothing in particular of the gas business, the employer is sure to select the former. Now, if there is any profession in the world that needs educated brains, it is ours; and yet there are not enough of them in it. The amount of money invested in our business exceeds, I believe, that in any other, except railroads, and yet its management is largely in the hands of men who lack a strictly technical education.

Often have I regretted myself, when listening to some glib scientific talker, that my education had not been thorough enough to enable me to detect what I believed to be his errors. A perfectly equipped gas manager should be both engineer and chemist, and besides that should have that technical knowledge of his profession for which many years of experience are the best teacher, but which a hard course of study can, to some extent, replace. When it has been sufficiently realized by the public that there is money in it, then very likely a special course may be given in some technical school, but at present I doubt that it would be appreciated, and I have been turning over in my head the possibility of some similar scheme to that adopted by the association of London Guilds. These ancient bodies have joined together for the purpose of technical examinations, not only for the trades which they once represented, but also for others. They do not teach, they simply examine; and workers in every industry come to London to get, or fail to get, a diploma, which they can show anywhere as a proof of their efficiency. Among the other examinations held is one for the office of gas manager. It is held by Mr. Robert Morton, formerly engineer of the London company, and the papers are prepared and examined by him. It is by no means easy to pass, and a considerable number of those offering are rejected. A young man who should come to me with a certificate that he had passed with honor, would impress me in the same way as would a young physician. His natural common sense could not, of course, be determined by any examination, and his information would be increased by a little experience; but a man possessed of thorough theoretical knowledge acquires experience rapidly. If there were some institution in this country of high repute, which would take up this matter, I think very few holders of its diplomas would find themselves long out of work. I have nothing to suggest yet, for my only effort in this direction has been but a failure; but perhaps something may occur to one of my hearers, from which results may eventually grow, and with that hope I commend it to your thoughts.

Among the other papers which we shall listen to at this meeting, will be one on water gas. Although I know nothing of its contents, we shall undoubtedly be interested in hearing it. Because this Association was founded by the representatives of the older and more conservative companies, and because many of our members are still skeptical of some of the virtues attributed to water gas, yet we are all of us open to conversion. I probably am reputed myself to be as stubborn an opponent of it as there is, but I am none the less bent on acquainting myself with the details of every new process brought out—its advantages and its weak points. Although the merit of economy can in many places be no longer claimed, yet some most ardent objectors to its use have received a change of heart, owing to the influence of the Knights of Labor. No company can tell when they may be forced into its use, either wholly or as a supplementary system; and with this possibility before us I know no better place than the meetings of this Association to discuss all questions pertaining to the various processes. If the enthusiastic adherents of water gas—first, last and always—insist on withdrawing from their benighted fellows and getting up an association of their own, of course, the rest of us cannot help it; but I am sure I speak the sentiments of this body when I say that we should regret their action, and no matter where they go, or what society they found, I doubt their ever finding more interested auditors than here.

One thing more before I close. One of the weaknesses of human nature is a desire for decoration, and one of the evidences of this fact is the way in which most organized bodies take pleasure in ornamenting themselves with badges. To provide a simple and yet tasteful emblem of membership is always a tax upon the ingenuity and the pockets of those who arrange our meeting. If it is the desire of the Association to continue the custom of wearing something at our annual gatherings by which members can be distinguished from outsiders, then I would suggest that a committee be formed to whom shall be committed the preparation of designs for a permanent badge, and that they be requested to submit these designs to the Secretary, with estimates of their cost, and that he then take the sense of the society as to the one to be adopted, and order for the next meeting that number which the individual members agree to take and pay for. The only real necessity for conspicuous badges is upon the persons of the Committee of Arrangements, at our annual excursion, and perhaps upon our Secretary. These might be easily provided. The rest of us can use some simple decoration, emblematic of our profession, and which I have full faith that we have among us sufficient ingenuity to design.

Gentlemen of the American Association—" United we stand, divided we fall." The man who manages the business of his company, relying solely upon his individual experience and intelligence, can never keep up with the times. It is only by imparting to each other the results of our efforts to do better, no matter whether successful or not, and putting all our information into a common fund, that we can expect to prosper in the struggle before us. Hundreds of millions of dollars are invested in the business we represent, which it is our chief aim to protect. Nor can I better conclude than by reiterating my belief that if we are true to our duty the supply of gas will continue to be the chief source of modern light, and will yield a safe profit to the judicious investor. Strong in this opinion, I feel, of course, a firm confidence in the future of this Association, and a great desire for its prosperity.

Captain White moved that a committee of three be appointed to consider the President's address, and report to the Association recommendations respecting such matters as are contained in the address which they might deem of special interest to the Association. The motion prevailed, and the Chair appointed as such committee Messrs. R. B. Taber, A. E. Boardman and G. G. Ramsdell.

APPOINTMENT OF SPECIAL COMMITTEES.

The following special committees were appointed : *On Nomination of Officers*—Messrs. F. C. Sherman, A. C. Wood, T. G. Lansden and W. A. Stedman. *On Place for Holding Next Meeting*—Messrs. W. Clark, D. H. Geggie and T. G. Lansden.

MR. HARBISON—Mr. Barker, a member of the Massachusetts Gas Commission is with us. I suggest that he be requested to occupy a seat on the platform during the meeting of the Association.

THE PRESIDENT—We shall be glad to have Mr. Barker take a seat on the platform.

MR. BARKER—Thanking you, Mr. President and members of the Association, for the courtesy you have been pleased to extend to me, I trust I may not seem discourteous if I ask to be excused from appearing on the platform. I can assure you that I am very much pleased to be here. We have come to look upon the meetings of this Association with a great deal of interest; and I am sure that my associates in the Gas Commission would be pleased to be present with you were they not detained by other engagements. (Applause.)

Mr. Walton Clark then read the following paper on

WATER GAS.

There are before the American gas public many systems of water gas making. As to their individual peculiarities and merits or demerits, I have nothing to say here. I desire simply to give to the Association some of the conclusions to which my efforts after economy in water gas making have brought me, hoping they will be of use to some member about to enter this comparatively new branch of our business.

The possible economies may be grouped under two heads, entitled respectively, plant construction and operation. Granting that a proper design has been selected, there is little to be said about construction. As in coal gas or any other manufacturing plant, so in water gas, the apparently cheap is often the really dear, and the saving of dollars in construction may result in the waste of eagles in operation and repairs. The importance of a good construction in water gas plant is even greater than coal gas, because every portion of the apparatus is necessary to the manufacture. A coal gas works can lay off a bench for repairs at almost any time, without danger of landing the holder. With a water gas plant, except in the largest works, where they may be in duplicate, all repairs in the busy season must be made in the shortest possible time—for the night's supply of gas depends upon one generator; hence the importance of first-class construction and readiness of access for repairs can hardly be exaggerated. There is no difficulty about constructing a plant which will need no repairs extensive enough to cause any delay during the winter, but it takes more iron and brick than another may which will make as much gas per day while in operation, but is liable to fail at a critical time. The take-off pipes are subject to occasional stoppage from careless working, and it is important that they should be put up with crosses and hand plates. All parts of the apparatus, in fact, should be made easily and quickly accessible by the use of plates and doors.

In locating a generator the most important point to be considered is the ease with which coal can be handled to it; yet it is one which must yield in part in extensions of old works to the location of the boilers. When an entirely new plant is erected the generator is best located where the handling of coal to it and ash from it will be easiest, and the rest of the plant made to conform. A generator requires either a cellar or a firing floor, and the coal or the ash must be elevated, unless the works are on rising ground, where one may be wheeled in and the other out without elevation. Unless the necessity of using an old building with a low roof, or some other local complication arises, I should not hesitate to adopt the elevated firing floor. The cost of raising the coal is slight, and the advantage of a well-ventilated and lighted clinkering floor is great.

Under the head of operating expenses are three important items, viz., fuel, oil and labor; and upon the way the first is manipulated will depend in great part the cost of purification.

As the boilers, engines and pumps of a water gas plant have no features distinguishing them from those in use for other purposes, I will not consider them; therefore the first part of the apparatus to be noticed in connection with fuel economy is the blast pipes. All blast furnace experience shows the importance of having them large with long bends. On this point I have no comparative figures, but it is self-evident that reduced resistance to the blast will result in reduced consumption of fuel under the boilers.

Passing to the generators the question meets us—and upon it there has been, and may still be, a difference of opinion—shall the fuel bed be deep, five feet and upward, or shallow, three feet and under? One objection to a shallow bed is that there is danger that an opening in the fuel, or a heavy clinker, will so far reduce the available depth of hot carbon that steam will escape undecomposed, or converted only to carbonic acid and hydrogen. Many experiments have convinced me that the possible rate of make of a certain standard purity (freedom from carbonic acid), or the degree of purity with a certain rate of make, is less with a shallow than with a deep fuel bed. Steam in the presence of incandescent carbon is decomposed, the oxygen uniting with the carbon. In the presence of an excess of oxygen carbonic acid is formed, to be converted into carbonic oxide by further contact with hot fuel. The larger part of the carbonic acid is almost immediately converted, but a certain quantity requires further contact, and the last portion, being more diluted, requires more depth of fuel for its conversion than any other equal portion. Experiments have shown me that the best gas is made at the beginning of a run, or when the depth of hot fuel was greatest. From these experiments, all made with apparatus on a working scale, I have come to the conclusion that a deep bed of fuel is desirable. One, and the principal, objection known to me is that in blasting, the escaping gases from a deep fuel bed will be almost entirely nitrogen and carbonic oxide, the latter carrying off more carbon than would the carbonic acid made with a less depth of fuel. Where there are, as in making carburetted water gas, opportunities of utilizing the carbonic oxide to heat a fixing chamber, superheating steam, or preheating oil or blast, this objection disappears.

It is obvious that the arrangement of grate should be such as to bring the blast and steam into contact with every possible piece of fuel, and that there should be no ledges or offsets upon which coal could lodge away from their direct action. Fuel in such positions will gradually burn away in the eddies made by the blast, but will aid little in the manufacture of gas.

In burning the producer gas in the fixing chamber or superheaters, I often find that too much or too little air (generally the former) is admitted. Either will result in loss of heat, and delay in bringing the vessel to a proper temperature. The perfect point is where neither free oxygen nor carbonic oxide is present in the escaping gases; but it takes a chemical test to determine this. The practical way is to admit just air enough to keep the blue flame from showing at the outlet.

The introduction of steam into the generator at as high a

temperature as possible is of advantage in two ways : It restores to the generator some of the heat given off in blasting, and prevents in part the quenching of the hot fuel with the consequent shortening of the period of gas making. An extensive experiment with a cupola blasted with a jet blower has shown that the amount of ash and cinder taken from it, when using steam at about 300° F., was fifty per cent. in excess of the amount taken from the same cupola, doing the same work, with steam at 650° F., about. As the ash in each instance must have been the same, the excess in one case must have been due to fuel quenched by wet steam.

The benefit derived from using superheated steam was in part neutralized by the fact that the generator required clinkering twice as often, with a consequent loss of time and consumption of fuel for heating. Experience has convinced me, however, that the advantage is decidedly upon the side of hot steam. Mr. Carroll, of New Orleans, La., has made many experiments upon this point, and he agrees with me. Several months' running of two sets of water gas apparatus standing in the same building, and exactly similar, except that one had steam superheaters, showed a saving of two pounds of fuel per 1,000 cubic feet for the superheaters, which, in this case, were not large enough to utilize all the available so-called " waste heat."

One of the difficulties experienced in the use of retort coke in generators has been the rapid quenching of the fuel by the steam. Coke, being light, has less storage capacity for heat than has anthracite, and is more rapidly cooled. In my experience increasing the temperature of steam from 300° to 700° has enabled me to use soft coke with greater success. There is no difficulty in bringing steam to a temperature of over 600° before sending it into the generator, and with the " waste heat." After the first run, in blasting, the fixing chamber is heated before the generator is in condition to make gas, and a part of the " waste heat " can be stored in brickwork, to be absorbed by the steam during the succeeding run.

Gas issues from a fixing chamber at a high temperature, the heat it carries away being absorbed by water in the condensers. In a large plant now building it is sought to utilize this heat for the volitilization of oil before sending it into the apparatus. I believe this will be accomplished and good will result in two ways—heat otherwise wasted will be utilized, and the cooling effect of sending cold oil upon hot fuel will be avoided. The bad effect of this cold oil is greater than would appear at first thought. I have known of its cooling a path for itself through a shallow fuel bed, and actually reaching the ashpit as a liquid. I believe that if no " waste heat " is available for vaporizing the oil, it would pay to do it with steam. Cold oil chills the fuel and shortens the run, to prolong which is worthy the most earnest efforts of the gas maker. It is the period of production, and as it is long or short compared to the alternate period of blasting, so is the producing power of the plant greater or less.

I will speak of one more point in connection with fuel economy, and I know that my opinion upon it is different to that held by some water gas constructors. I refer to the proper direction in which to blast; whether it is the same as followed by steam in making gas, or, as in my opinion, the reverse? The effect of making water gas is to cool the fuel. Only through the decomposition of steam, which absorbs a large quantity of heat, can water gas be produced, and the first layers of fuel operated upon are rapidly lowered in temperature until they reach that of the incoming steam. Where the blast is directly applied some of this fuel does not reignite thoroughly, for the cold air passes through it before reaching the still heated mass above. This is especially the case with coke, which, from its porosity, becomes more thoroughly cooled by the steam. Where the direction is reversed and the steam enters at the top of the fuel, its cooling effect is entirely overcome at the next blasting, for the air, before reaching the cooled portion, passes through the heated mass below it. I have knowledge of an experiment which illustrates the good effect of this way of working. A plant in which the direction of steam and blast had been different was changed for a time to work on the other plan. The result was an increase of seven pounds per 1,000 cubic feet of gas in the fuel account. There was no superheater connected with this plant. It should be mentioned that introducing steam at the top of a deep fuel bed has the effect of increasing the clinker, as does the superheating of the steam. This effect can, however, be overcome. I know of a plant which works in this way, and has not in six months had its fires drawn. At the end of every twelve hours wet steam is admitted at the bottom of the fire for one run. The effect is to soften the clinker, which is then easily broken and removed.

Upon the question of oil economy there are few points to be observed; but these few are of great importance to the water gas maker. If the temperature of the mixing chamber is such that the condensation contains only traces of lampblack or light oil, I think the manager need not worry about his oil account. I believe the best temperature to be a cherry red, but this depends upon the quality of the oil, and the area and height of the fixing chamber compared to the rate of make. I try to run as near to the lampblack limit as possible without touching it. While, as coal gas makers, we have given time and labor to solve the problem how best to shorten the stay of gas in the retort, as water gas makers we seem hardly to have thought of the effect of long contact with hot bricks upon our enriching material. Reasoning from analogy, I believe that we should shorten the stay of our product in the fixing chamber to the least possible period consistent with the thorough gasification of the oil. The fact that we may find no deposit of carbon proves nothing; for, upon blasting, the deposit would be carried off unless very heavy.

To economize labor in water gas making it is necessary, as in all manufacturing, that everything the men have to handle should be convenient to them. The boiler can be on the firing floor; a double-cylinder engine on the floor below can always be started from above; and, by arranging these things thus conveniently, in a small works one smart man can make all the gas in hours of daylight. A works sending out 20,000 cubic feet per day, with a storage capacity of 50,000, can be safely run by two men, who shall make gas but a part of one day in two, and can give the rest of their time to services, meter setting, etc.

I have so far treated of water gas as made by the cupola process only. To go into the question of the relative efficiency and economy of this and other systems of making carburetted water gas would make my contribution to this meeting too long. Before closing, however, I desire to compare the candle power developed per gallon of oil in pure oil gas; in a mixture of oil gas made in retorts with water gas made in cupolas; and in carburetted water gas made at one operation in cupolas.

Mr. J. Desha Patton has said that commercial benzine will yield, in regular working in a retort, seventy cubic feet of seventy-candle gas, or 4,900 candle-feet per gallon. In the Pintsch system the yield is, from crude oil, about seventy cubic feet of fifty-candle gas, or 3,500 candle-feet per gallon. The best result I have been able to obtain in clay retorts is seventy cubic feet of sixty-candle gas, or 4,200 candle-feet per gallon of naphtha. I have the results obtained from mixtures of oil and water gases in different proportions upon a commercial scale, the gases being made separately. At a small works in New England, where gas is made in this way of thirty-five-candle power, the yield per gallon of naphtha, in 1883, was 3,509 candle-feet. At New Orleans, La., in June, 1885, the yield, making a 33⅓-candle gas, was 4,432 candle-feet per gallon; and though I have made many experiments with different mixtures, this is the best result I ever obtained.

The following results, representing, I think, fairly what can be done with the cupola system, are based upon information obtained by me directly from the books of companies, or the statements of engineers in charge. They vary considerably, and represent five different so-called "processes," the names of which, for obvious reasons, I do not give. The highest yield per gallon of which I have a record is 6,302 candle-feet. From that the figures range down thus: 5,647, 5,526, 5,471, 5,467, 5,251, 5,000, to 4,687 candle-feet per gallon. Here we have the material for a comparison of the results obtained from oil in regular working under three systems:

First, with pure oil gas...4,900, 4,200, 3,500 candle-feet.
Secondly, with gases mixed
    after generation...... 4,432, 3,509 candle-feet.
Thirdly, with carburetted
    water gas made at one
    operation in cupolas...6,302 down to 4,687 candle-feet.

I believe the advantage in the cupola system to consist in the almost complete conversion of the oil into gas. In the retort process as I have worked it the tar made equals nearly ten per cent. of the oil used. In the cupola system it is only about two per cent.

DISCUSSION.

THE PRESIDENT—As our membership numbers many water gas people, we ought to hear from them with regard to their experience in relation to some of the facts stated by Mr. Clark. Mr. Clark's paper contains a great deal of valuable information, which must be deliberately studied to be fully appreciated. Is not Mr. Lansden using a Granger generator, with a thin body of fuel?

MR. LANSDEN—We were, but are not now.

THE PRESIDENT—We would like to hear from you on that subject.

MR. LANSDEN—A year ago we had two large Granger machines in the Washington (D. C.) works. Mr. McIlhenny had one of the machines lengthened out. In our original Granger machines the generators carried about $5\frac{1}{2}$ to 6 feet of fuel, and the machines were fed by several small tanks, probably 5 feet in height by $2\frac{1}{2}$ feet in diameter, the oil passing into each generator through four little cocks, fitted with glass gauges showing the oil while running. We took these out and dismantled the tanks, replacing them with a tank located some 300 or 400 feet from the works, elevated sufficiently to give us a supply for the whole machinery from one receptacle. I brought that into the works, attached a box with a float ball in it similar to an ordinary closet. I then attached, for each machine, an inch pipe, bringing it up through the floor to the height of about three feet, and put on that a one-inch stopcock. The inch pipe then ran to the machine, and the machine was divided into four sections. The stopcock has a lever handle to it twelve inches long. Under that is the segment of a circle, by which the cock can be turned to the same point every time. That system enabled a machine that had been making 600,000 cubic feet to produce 750,000 cubic feet in the same time. We are running right along with it at that rate, and have even done better. I claim that the main thing secured is that we now have a regular feed of oil supplied all the time, insuring perfect uniformity.

MR. LOWE—I would like to ask Mr. Lansden what, if any, advantage they found in increasing the fire below their generator.

MR. LANSDEN—We found, just as Mr. Clarke stated in his paper, that when using the blast from the bottom the fire would go out. Although the generators were of the same diameter, we were able to increase the capacity of the machine a little over fifty per cent.

MR. LOWE—I am decidedly in favor of deep fires in generators. In fact, I think you cannot get them much too deep. I have used twelve-feet fires, and found great advantage in them. It does not take any more coal to keep a deep than a shallow bed going; in fact, I think it takes considerably less. I think Mr. Clark's paper is a very able one. I have made many experiments, and my results closely coincide with what he has told us. I am a great advocate of using superheated steam, and believe we can make a third more gas from the same amount of coal with superheated steam than when wet steam is used. I never found much difference in the clinkering of a generator fire, using superheated steam, over wet steam; and when clinkers did appear I adopted the remedy of introducing wet steam, which rapidly softens the clinkers and causes them to fall. If more than usually obstinate, I put in oyster shells, fluxing them down as you would in a blast furnace, and found it to be a very satisfactory plan.

THE PRESIDENT—The Association would like to hear from Mr. A. C. Humphreys on this subject, as he has had much experience in it.

MR. A. C. HUMPHREYS—I do not find myself in a position to discuss Mr. Clark's paper, chiefly for the reason that I agree almost entirely with his every statement. There is no doubt that a deep fuel bed is the proper thing. Although in the past we have perhaps been identified with the shallow fuel bed, we have now rather eliminated that from our drawings. We are to-day putting in nothing less than five-feet beds. With regard to superheated steam, there can be no question about the accuracy of Mr. Clark's position, because we want the heat in the steam for two purposes—as a matter of economy, and also for the better operation of the generator after it is admitted. From our experience, the question of where to admit the oil is not very important, provided we admit it in the right way when we get it there. The whole point is to bring it to the temperature required, and the temperature to which it should be superheated is entirely governed by the quality of the oil. We can handle naphtha without trouble by simply raising the temperature of the steam to the ordinary boiler pressure as we run the works. When using the heavy oil, which we do largely in many works, we have to bring about other methods for superheating it, and there comes in the question of using the waste products from the generator, or from the superheater, or perhaps the waste heat in the illuminating gas as it is made. I think Mr. Clark touched on that method in his paper. In regard to the exact proportion of superheater, and in relation to the generator, much yet remains for solution. In the past no doubt a great mistake was made in having the superheater entirely too small for the generator. Our practice now is this: Say, for instance, that with the generator five feet in diameter, there is a fuel bed five feet in depth, the superheater being of the same diameter, and probably twenty-two feet high. A few years ago this would have been looked upon as absurd. We do not find, however, and have no reason yet to believe, that that superheater is too large, or that we subject the gas to contact with too great a heated surface, providing our temperatures are right. I am a very firm believer in having surface enough, and so being able to run at low temperatures. That is the only point in which I differ from Mr. Clark. I do not believe in keeping our temperature very high, if we can get our result without. Our experiments go to show that we can, provided we have surface enough. Especially is this the case in the use of heavy oils—I mean oils having a gravity of twenty-seven to thirty-three, which we are using with entire success. We also class, under heavy oils, crude petroleum; and the treatment for those oils is entirely different from the treatment for naphtha. In a number of cases our superintendents have sent back word it was impossible to use the oil—that it could not be done. We have, in such cases, by following it up and insisting upon its use, and sending directions, and perhaps a special engineer to look after the thing, been so far successful, finally, in every case. One or two cases exist in which we are still having trouble, but no doubt it will be remedied. The whole question is one as to temperature and heated surface.

Mr. Lansden—I will say, with reference to the size of the

superheater spoken of, that we have one twenty-four feet high ; and I know that it works better than those which are only eighteen. I would like to ask Mr. Clark what he considers the fair amount of coal to the thousand feet of gas, for all purposes.

MR. CLARK—That is rather a pointed question. The answer depends, of course, on the size of the works. I do not know of anything better than forty pounds per thousand, all round. If there is anything better than that I am not aware of it.

THE PRESIDENT—The Association would like to hear from Mr. Edgerton, of New Orleans, on this question.

MR. EDGERTON—I have nothing to say with regard to this, except to ask Mr. Clark how his comparison of the yield and quality of gas is based. I do not understand the comparison. I have ordinarily seen it stated that so many gallons of oil will make a thousand feet of a certain standard. I must confess to a little confusion, and I do not understand exactly what results he arrives at. I would like to inquire the number of gallons of oil and pounds of fuel used per 1,000 cubic feet of gas.

MR. CLARK—My comparison was simply regarding the illuminating power of oil as used in the two different methods. First, the mixture of oil and water gas and then carburetted, and water gas made at one operation, I put into candle feet, as being the simplest way of showing the amount of light that we got from a gallon of oil. In the case of pure oil I multiplied the yield per gallon by the candle power of the oil. In the case of the mixture of oil and water gas I multiplied the candle power by 1,000 feet, and divided by the number of gallons used in making the 1,000 feet, which gave the number of light units as expressed in candle feet which we got from one gallon of oil. I am aware this is not the most scientific way of doing it, yet, it is the best way I can think of presenting it to coal gas men, who are familiar with Mr. Farmer's candle feet theory.

MR. EDGERTON—What style of burner did you use in testing the water gas ?

MR. CLARK—In testing the water gas I employed the simple burner in every day use, and a Scotch tip burner, consuming from one to two feet per hour of the pure oil gas.

MR. EDGERTON—I must confess, if I understand it correctly in candle feet, you show that in one process, or by my regenerator and superheater system, there is some thirty per cent. difference than when manufactured separately. Is that correct?

MR. CLARK—I think so. I did not work out the percentage any higher.

MR. EDGERTON—That statement contains something entirely novel. I cannot discuss it in candle feet, because my results are not translated into candle feet. But in the plan of manufacturing water gas at one operation, and then carburetting and manufacturing again, and passing through the superheater, there is no published result which shows any such discrepancy. I should be very glad to know where such statements can be found, so that I may look into them. I do not doubt the result stated; but still I would like to examine further.

MR. CLARK—The results, with reference to gases made separately and mixed afterwards, were, as stated, obtained in one case from the New Orleans works, the other being the result of a year's work accomplished in a New England gas plant. Regarding the results obtained in making the gas at one process, these were obtained, as stated, with five different processes. I do not give their names, because I do not want to introduce civil war into this Association; but I either have the figures myself from the books of the companies, or obtained them from statements of the engineers in charge.

MR. EDGERTON—Do they not largely exceed any public statement.

MR. CLARK—I do not think so. I took them as being a fair average. Some of those figures were obtained from members of this Association.

MR. PEARSON—You have given the number of candle feet to the gallon of oil. Can you give the figures as to the pounds of coal and amount of water and steam; and can you tell us what percentage of carbonic oxide is present in the highly superheated steam as compared with the wet steam?

MR. CLARK—The proportion of carbonic oxide would be greater, because the gas would be washed with less carbonic acid.

MR. PEARSON—Can you give the relative proportion?

MR. CLARK—In the finished gas I suppose there is thirty per cent.

MR. E. C. JONES—I was pleased to hear Mr. Clark state his

reduction of gas in candle feet. There is a wide diversity of opinion with regard to the amount of oil used per thousand feet to produce a given candle power of gas. I am very much in favor of hourly or half-hourly observation of the photometer in connection with the amount of gas made. If it can be demonstrated that there is 4,200 candle feet in a gallon of oil of certain quality, I think that the measure of the production of gas in candle feet will tell us what we are doing with our oil—whether we are making gas with it or making lampblack of it.

On motion of Mr. Boardman, a vote of thanks was tendered Mr. Clark for his paper.

FIRST DAY—AFTERNOON SESSION.

Mr. A. C. Humphreys, M.E., Philadelphia, Pa., read the following paper, entitled:

ILLUMINATION VS. CANDLE POWER.

I have undertaken to prepare for this meeting a paper under the title of "Illumination *vs.* Candle Power." The subject of measurement of light is a large one, and I cannot hope to more than touch upon certain special features of the subject. The title will suggest that I have in mind some of the papers recently written in this line, namely: The paper by Mr. Boardman,* at our last year's meeting; the papers by Messrs. Prichard† and Taber,‡ at the last meeting of the New England Association; and the paper by Mr. Chollar,§ at the last meeting of the Western Association.

Mr. Boardman told us, you will remember, of the increase from sixteen to twenty-two candle power he obtained by substituting a student's Argand chimney, for a regular Argand chimney, but that while he obtained this apparent advantage the "illumination" was actually less, as shown by applying the chimney to an Argand at his house. In the paper and the following discussion you were told that a white light would not "diffuse" as well as a yellow light. It was also stated during the discussion, and with great confidence, that a sixteen candle coal gas gave as much light, on account of this "extra diffusibility," as a twenty-candle water gas—the twenty-candle

---

* Vol. VII., p. 301 of Proceedings. † ‡ AMERICAN GAS LIGHT JOURNAL, vol. XLVI., March 2, pp. 130, 140. § Vol. XLVII., July 2, '87, p. 7.

water gas being whiter than the coal gas ; and in explanation of this it was suggested that the whiter light from water gas " was intense, local, but not diffusive like coal gas."

In Mr. Prichard's paper considerable stress is laid upon a law of the intensity of light to the effect that " rays *emitted* obliquely from a surface are less intense in proportion as they were more inclined to the surface which emits them," and then, that by this law, " the rays of light from a flame as they leave the horizontal and approach the vertical, leave the maximum measured candle power, and approach the minimum of zero." We were also told that flames must be of the same size and same color to enable us to measure their lighting power correctly. The old question of the opal globe was also brought up prominently. It was also proposed that *daylight should* be regarded as the standard—that is, a white light. Also that a sixteen-candle gas, which was whiter than the richer twenty-candle, on account of its increased " temperature per unit of flame areas," produced a better light than the richer gas—of Boston. A disagreement from what has gone before is here to be noted.

By Mr. Taber's paper we were reminded of the uncertainty of our photometrical measurements. The varying quality of the so-called standard candle, the necessity of bars of varying length according to the strength of the light, the lack of accurate formula for correction of candle and gas consumption, the question as to how to read the disc, the color trouble, the abnormal condition of atmosphere—fog, for instance—entering as a disturbing element. And also, the opinion is expressed that the subject is one for the physicist, instead of the gas engineer. Then, by a carefully prepared table, it is to be noticed that the candle power does not follow the amount of bromine illuminants, and that CO is a positive evil. In the discussion which followed, the example of the illumination from a bull's-eye lantern is used to demonstrate the varying power of the rays emitted by a gas flame, according to the angle they make with the surface of the flame. Also, we were told that candle-power "means nothing." Mr. Taber found that Mr. Boardman's experiment gave him an increase in candle-power of from 16 to 19.44. Mr. Prichard had found no difference whatever.

Mr. Thomas spoke of the relative values of oil lights and gas lights—compared directly, I presume—and that the "illuminating duty" of one eighteen-candle gas flame was found to be far in excess of two twelve-candle oil lamps. This was the result of a careful test—presumably with a bar photometer. The experience of Dr. Morton in measuring so-called 2,000-candle electric lights is referred to, and we are reminded that he only found them to be from 500 to 1,100 candles; and the opinion is expressed that if a photometer had been used in these experiments, the light would have largely exceeded 1,100 candles. Also that an observer looking at a thirty-six-candle and a nineteen-candle gas as ordinarily burned, would have difficulty in distinguishing between them; and, still further, the belief was expressed that a nineteen-candle gas would afford a better illumination than a thirty-six-candle gas. Parenthetically, I would here like to say that if the gentlemen would guarantee to convince our consumers on this point, I should be only too glad to accept the theory, anyway during business hours, and let the statement go unchallenged.

At the close of this discussion Messrs. Prichard and Taber were appointed as a committee to continue their investigations and experiments during the following year.

In Mr. Chollar's paper we are told to beware how we put our faith in the law which says that the light from a luminous body decreases in proportion to the square of the distance—that is, the law on which photometry is based; and he also refers to Professor Tait's statement of the law, namely: "If the medium be transparent, the intensity of illumination which a luminous *point* can produce on a *white* surface *directly* exposed to it is inversely as the square of the distance."

Attention is then drawn to the fact that the well-known law is simply following out the principle that the surfaces of spheres are to each other as the squares of their diameters. Then, the proof is attempted of the proposition that, "irrespective of intensity, the quantity of light from a luminous body at any particular point is independent of the distance of the body, and is in direct proportion to its diameter;" and it is stated "The rule governing the value of lights, therefore, would be something like this: The light from a luminous body is inversely as the square of the distance, and directly as its projected area." We are also advised in the study of the subject to drop empiricism and go at the matter as thoroughly and systematically as the electricians do in their measurements; and we are encouraged to believe that we shall be able, by means of high candle power lamps, to compete with the 1,200 and 2,000-candle power electric lights.

These papers you have doubtless all read, and it may seem that it was unnecessary for me at this time to refer to them at such length. My object has been to bring clearly before you the fact that there is in the minds of the gas engineers of America much uncertainty on the subject of light and its measurement, and to demonstrate the necessity of a special consideration of this subject on the part of this Association. I take it for granted that we are all gas engineers—not coal gas engineers, or water gas engineers, or oil gas engineers, or wood gas engineers, or any other special kind of gas engineers. Perhaps it would be better if we said we were light engineers. If we cannot go this far, it is high time we went far enough to be able to say that in this Association we are gas engineers, and that we are ready to study any subject in connection with our business, so as, as far as possible, to get at the exact truth, let it strike where it will. I believe most of the members will acknowledge there is room for improvement in this direction, though I am, for one, glad to acknowledge there is every appearance of a movement toward the overthrow of prejudice. I cannot expect to try to meet all the points raised in the papers referred to, and I know you would be sorry to have me attempt it. I believe, however, that I have been able to make certain experiments which will tend to clear up some of the questions raised.

It certainly is very deplorable if we must acknowledge to the public that we can tell actually nothing as to the value of the light we offer to them; and that is what we must practically acknowledge if we leave the subject at this point. Of course, the foundation laws of intensity of light which have governed us in our photometric work are:

I. The intensity of illumination on a given surface is inversely as the square of the distance from the source of light.

II. The intensity of illumination which is received obliquely is proportional to the cosine of the angle which the luminous rays make with the normal to the illuminated surface.

It is with the first law we are chiefly concerned, for we can provide against the second law interfering in our photometric work by having the disc at right angles to the rays from the light to be measured; and this can be practically done, even if two candles are used, by the use of a bar of sufficient length.

I think that Mr. Prichard, where in his paper he refers to the rays *emitted* obliquely, has this law in mind, and most of his troubles appear to come from a misconception of this law. The law has nothing to do with the emission of light from an oblique luminous surface, but refers to the illumination of a surface oblique to the rays, and simply shows that mathematically, by reason of the incline of the surface, a greater area is exposed to the rays. Therefore we spread a certain number of rays over a greater area than in the case of a perpendicular surface, and consequently the intensity of illumination is diminished. And the exact measure of this inclined surface, as compared with the perpendicular surface, is found to be proportional to the cosine of the angle made by the ray with the normal to the illumined surface. This, therefore, need not come in to bother us. We only have to take account of it so far as to see to it that our photometer is adjusted to reduce the error from this source practically to zero. Part of the confusion on this point may have come from the fact that a flame is not entirely transparent to its own light, as shown by the difference in readings shown between the flame on edge and the flame on the flat. On this point there has been great diversity of opinion, and the rule, I believe, somewhat generally followed has been to take the reading from the flame at 45° as giving the average.

In my past experiments I very quickly satisfied myself of the incorrectness of this as a general rule, and, therefore, in connection with this work I assigned to one of my assistants a somewhat elaborate set of experiments to determine what angle gave the mean reading, and this with different qualities of gas. The following table, prepared by the assistant referred to (Mr. C. Russell Collins, M. E.), shows the *average* of the *mean* readings, or the mean angle of mean light to be 4.68°, and that this mean angle varies with the candle power of the gas. The differences of candle power were obtained by mixing different percentages of fuel (non-illuminating) water gas and illuminating water gas.

By this *table we find the angle of mean illumination, or mean candle power for the whole series of experiments, is 4.68° In the case of the mixture which gave 24.45-candle power on the flat, the mean angle was 7.25°. The largest mean angle was in the case of the six-candle power on the flat, in which case it was 10.25°. In two cases of very low candle power no difference from edge to flat was observable. This question of the mean angle is an important one, and the table given goes to show that, taking the average, our flat flame burner is doing its best for about 280° out of the 360°. It is also worthy of note that at 45° we have practically reached the maximum in every case. The percentage of difference in candle power between the edge and flat runs from zero to 21.67. This difference increases apparently with the candle power of the gas. Intensity of combustion no doubt enters in also to affect the transparency of the flame. The different mixtures were burned with the same burner. Had a burner been carefully selected for each mixture, a different candle power would have been obtained, and no doubt a different result as to variation of candle power from edge to flat.

The importance of adjusting a burner for a particular gas, especially in comparative tests, is, I believe, often lost sight of. For instance, we have the table showing loss of light by mixing air with twelve-candle power gas, one per cent. of air destroying six per cent. of light, and so on up to forty per cent., where the light is entirely destroyed.

Some years ago I had occasion to test this matter with Pintsch gas. A full set of experiments was made, and of course I at once saw that while there was a very serious loss if the same burner was used, there was no such loss with this rich gas as in the case of the twelve-candle power gas. By very carefully selecting a burner for each mixture, I finally succeeded in mixing in forty per cent. of air in a fifty-candle gas, and was still able to get as high a result per foot of gas used, as I obtained by the unmixed gas burned in the small burner selected therefor.

I bring this point out also to emphasize the fact that in making our experiments and drawing our conclusions therefrom, we must bear in mind that to compare two gases we must have a burner properly adjusted for each. For instance, Mr. Boardman

* For tables and accompanying diagram, see Drawing.

with his student argand chimney varied his candle power from 16 to 22; Mr. Taber raised his from 16 to 19.4; Mr. Prichard was unable to observe any difference. In my first experiments with gas varying from 24.78 to 12.70, and under different consumptions, I obtained varying results, sometimes there being a gain for student argand chimney, and sometimes a loss. In my last series of experiments, the candle power of the coal gas fell from 16.47 to 14.37. I do not doubt I could have obtained different results in both cases by different adjustments as to height of flame alone.

This suggests, did Mr. Boardman get the same adjustment at his house that he got in his photometer room; and did he allow in his practical test at his house (where he was vainly trying to read, and his wife to thread her needle) for the fact that, when his argand with the ordinary chimney had been consuming probably seven feet, with the student argand chimney he was only consuming about 3.8 feet?

Say 7 feet 16-candle power gas = 22.4-candle power.
Say 3.8 feet 22-candle power gas = 16.72-candle power.

The fact of smaller consumption being necessary to avoid smoke in the case of student argand chimney, and also the fact that these experiments were made ten years previous to the reading of his paper, Mr. Boardman informed me of by letter.

Coming back to the first law—this is a law entirely dependent upon mathematical principles, and I was surprised to find an intimation in Mr. Chollar's paper that the law was supposed by some to be based upon something outside of mathematics. The law is easily illustrated by supposing a light coming from a point situated at the geometrical center of a hollow sphere—the total illumination from this point will be spread over the inside of this sphere and every part of the surface will be equally illuminated. Suppose now that the sphere is increased in size until its radius is just twice the radius in the first case; as the areas of surfaces of spheres vary as the squares of their diameter or radii, the sphere in the second case will have an area just four times as great as in the first case, and as the amount of light has not been changed, the same amount will have to be spread over four times as great an area—that is, the intensity of illumination is one-fourth as great, or inversely as the square of the distance from the source of illumination.

The law, as stated by Professor Tait, and which Mr. Chollar thinks so much preferable, is the law as it is generally understood; but it is stated more fully than is usual, and includes a reference to the second law. We all know that the calculations are based upon the supposition of the light coming from a point. We also understand that the medium through which the light is to be transmitted must be transparent; we do not expect a law that will apply alike to all conditions in this direction—for instance, the interposition of a red or blue globe, a globe full of steam, to represent fog, etc. We also expect results to vary as to illumination of objects different in color. We do not expect to get the same effect if our walls are black as if they were white; and, as before stated, we do not expect to measure lights against each other, unless we provide for the rays in both cases being practically normal to the disc, or illuminated object. Mr. Chollar then attempts to prove a new law, in place of our old friend which has stood by us so many years, to the effect that irrespective of intensity, the quantity of light is independent of the distance. The second diagram of the article is intended to prove this; but if any of you will study this diagram and bear in mind that every point of the line emits rays in every direction, you will find that the diagram affords no such proof. As in all other laboratory work, we must in the application of the laws involved, take account of the sources of error that naturally come in, and see to it that the instrument is used as designed to reduce the error from these sources to a minimum. For instance, length of bar—if the light at one end of the bar is very intense we must expect to lengthen our bar, for obvious reasons. A man's eye should suggest the necessity at once, for if he uses a short bar for a light of even 200 candle-power he must expect to so partially paralyze his eye as to render his results valueless. This lengthening of the bar also takes care of the trouble from the varying angle of incidence. Difference of color does not interfere much, except in the case of a very bright light at one end; then, by lengthening your bar, this is so reduced that by considering only the edges of the disc—that is, trying to keep in mind the definition of the disc—a man in moderate practice should arrive at a practically accurate result. The use of a standard burner, such as the Methven or Edgerton, is of great assistance, reducing the trouble from both foregoing sources of error and also overcoming the candle trouble.

As to varying quality of candle—get good candles, and if you find after careful handling they are running much out of the way, reject them. As to corrections of gas, set your meter to consume five feet, or almost exactly five feet, if it is a gas proper for such an adjustment. Any correction then necessary to introduce can be safely made by the usual rule. If the gas is, say, a 45-candle oil gas, use the burner that will burn it properly, and then figure it to the five-foot basis, if you wish to do so, for comparison. As that is the proper adjustment for that gas, that is the way to consider its value as a light-giver—namely, direct proportion.

Let us now consider for a moment some of the points which have puzzled us all, and which I believe have led to this discussion. We say an arc light is not so diffusive as a large gas flame, and that we do not get the same duty from it, comparatively. Why should we expect to? Here is an arc light sending out the light of 500 to 1,200 candles, and all practically from a point—the light-giving surface is not bigger than that of one candle. Does it not necessarily follow that we have a very defective distribution? and does not the very law of inverse squares demand that the distribution be uneven—intense around the light source and falling off so rapidly following the square of the distance?

Bear in mind what this falling off of candle power means—a 2,000-candle power arc light is, at a distance of twenty feet, only giving the illumination of five candles at a distance of one foot. Take the 2,000-candle power and distribute it around in 400 gas flames, and we necessarily get a more even illumination and a better working result. Then, again, the eye must seek the light, and it is partially paralyzed by its brilliancy and the contrasts. If we go from a dark room to where there is sunlight on snow, are we not blinded for the time being? The same principle applies to the case of the eye and the arc light. It is a physiological effect and has absolutely nothing to do with the laws regarding the intensity of illumination. Again, the arc light comes from a point, and hence intense shadows are made; whereas, in the case of a light-giving surface, the shadows are toned down by the rays from the wide-apart portions of the surface getting behind portions of the object which are in the shadow of other rays. We are familiar with this under the name of penumbra. For instance, if we had a light-giving surface which extended all around the object, we should have no shadow at all.

Take the case of the opal globe. A certain percentage of the light is cut out as claimed, but the distribution of the light which remains is much better by reason of the enlarged light-giving surface, and as the flame is entirely hidden from view the eye is not subjected to any marked contrast, and is so better able to do its duty. That is all there is in that, for the cases referred to of more brilliant cones of light are simply cases of reflection, as in the instance of the bull's-eye lantern referred to. Of course, we cannot concentrate our light upon any one set of lines and still have its full value elsewhere. Another point which enters in to confuse is obstruction of light, as in the case of the arc light. We must expect the arc light to give more light in the horizontal, for the light above and below is obstructed by the carbon pencil. We must bear in mind what is the *unavailable* light-giving surface in each case and for each position reached by the rays. We have this obstruction in the case of gas flames, as shown, due perhaps to the opacity of the carbon particles, or, perhaps, if they are transparent, to their power of refraction; and if we find in higher candle power lights this difference increases we should not be surprised, for it is reasonable to suppose as the carbon particles increase in number or the flame becomes more dense, this interference will be increased, whatever its exact character. You will remember, the lighthouse authorities find they can use to great advantage animal and vegetable oils for argands made up of concentric rings of flame. They can also economically do so in case of gas; but with the dense flame of the mineral oil lamp they soon reach a point where it is no longer economy to increase the number of flames, because so much of the light from the inner flames is obstructed by the outer flames.

Mr. Thomas, you will remember, speaks of the results obtained

by Dr. Morton in measuring arc lights, and he draws the conclusion from the fact that the results obtained were so much
less than those claimed by the electric light men, that the photometer in the first place must have been at fault. Do we not
go out of our way to mislead ourselves by such arguments?
Because the electric light men have overstated the value of their
light (bear in mind their so-called French method), is that any
reason we should discredit the photometer? Mr. Thomas also
says: "If the intensity of this light had been measured on a
photometer it would have largely exceeded the maximum figure
given." I presume Dr. Morton's experiments at Bridgeport are
the ones referred to. In these experiments Dr. Morton used a
photometer box on wheels, with two candles at one end and the
electric light thirty feet away. That is, the length of the box
was re-enforced by a steel tape-line thirty feet long. These
results were obtained by a photometer, and I venture to assert
Dr. Morton would have been puzzled to proceed other than by
means of a photometer. Of course, as we should expect, Dr.
Morton selected a photometer of proper length, etc., for the
special work in hand. In passing, and to show how carefully
all of our steps in experimental work have to be guarded, it is to
be noted it was here shown that there is a certain amount of
error introduced by reason of the unequal reflection of the light
along the inside of the box, in case of lights far away compared
with those near; the angle of incidence as to the sides of the
box in the case of the near light being smaller, and so leading
to a greater number of reflections. But of course if the box is
blackened very "flat," this source of error is slight. Again, as
to the illuminating duty of two oil lamps of twelve candles, each
being less than that of one gas flame of eighteen candles,
how did this experimenter arrive at these results? Was the
despised photometer the instrument by which these results were
obtained? In regard to the effect of CO in gas as a diluent,
which has been referred to, do we not make the mistake of comparing it with CH_4, calling CH_4 a neutral, and so by comparison proving that CO is an actual negative? I know that CH_4
has been generally classed as a neutral, but Dr. Morton, in some
experiments made some time ago, proved that in chemically
pure CH_4 he had a gas of certain illuminating value. He even

deposited soot from the flame upon a cold metal surface ; hence while CH_4 may, as stated, be a more valuable diluent than CO, we probably get a more correct understanding of the question of illuminants and diluents by recognizing this double value of the CH_4.

The following experiments were designed to cover the questions in regard to diffusiveness, lack of diffusiveness, local intensity, etc., etc.

I felt that while such experiments ought not to be necessary, if made they would be conclusive.

The idea was to have a long photometer room, and so arranged that two lights could be supplied with water gas and coal gas, respectively, through separate meters, the connections to be so made that the lights could be shifted out step by step from the center of the bar, so that the bar could be varied in length, say from six feet to twenty or thirty feet. If, then, the lights were adjusted in the first place at three feet each from the center, and the quantity of gas adjusted so that the illumination on the disc should be equal, the question of local intensity could be settled by taking readings at four feet each from the centre, five feet, six feet, etc., and if the equal illumination was still obtained with the original consumption of the gases, then we could claim that local intensity was effectually disproved.

This experiment I assigned to two of my assistants especially selected for this work, A. G. Glasgow, M.E., and J. M. Rusby, M.E. The proper arrangements were made, and experiments made which went to show that the lengthening of the photometer bar did not change the results. Having checked up the results and provided for still greater exactness in the readings. I made a series of experiments myself, Messrs. Glasgow and Rusby assisting, as follows :

EXPERIMENT NO. I.

Dist. from center.	Water Gas. Bat-Wing Burner.		Coal Gas. "D" Sugg Argand.		
	Sight Box.	Consumption, feet per hour	Consumption, feet per hour	Sight Box.	Dist. from center.
3 feet	=	3·7	4·9	=	3 feet
5 "	=	3·7	4·9	=	5 "
7 "	=	3·7	4·9	=	7 "
9 "	=	3·7	4·9	=	9 "
10 "	‡ 1-8	3·7	4·9	‡ 1-8	10 "
11 "	‡ 3-8	3·7	4·9	‡ 3-8	11 "
12 "	‡1 1-4	3.675	4.875	‡1 1-4	12 "

EXPERIMENT NO. II.

Dist. from center.	Water Gas. Bat-Wing Burner.		Coal Gas. "D" Sugg Argand with Student's Argand Chimney, Flame 4 in.		
	Sight Box.	Consumption.	Consumption.	Sight Box.	Dist. from center.
3 feet	=	3.075	4·4	=	3 feet.
5 "	=	3.075	4·4	=	5 "
7 "	=	3.075	4·4	=	7 "
9 "	‡3-4	3.100	4·4	‡3-4	9 "
			N. B.		

N.B.—Five feet consumption (with student argand chimney) gave smoke.

EXPERIMENT NO. III.

Water Gas. Welsbach Burner.			Coal Gas. " D " Sugg Argand.		
Dist. from center.	Sight Box.	Consumption.	Consumption.	Sight Box.	Dist. from center.
3 feet	═	2.01	4.65	═	3 feet
5 "	═	2.04	4.65	═	5 "
7 "	═	1.97	4.65	═	7 "
9 "	‡1-4 in.	2.05	4.65	‡1-4 in.	9 "
11 "	+1-4 "	1.99	4.65	—1-4 "	11 "

Each of these three experiments conclusively proves that the white light is diffused exactly as well as the yellow, there not being a particle of difference in favor of either. These are facts behind which we cannot go.

The coal gas used was of 16.47 candle-power. With the student argand chimney the candle-power was 14.37. Candle-power of the water gas, 23.

It will be noticed that I used a Welsbach burner also. This was done to make a still more severe test of the question, for the Welsbach burner used was as much whiter than the water gas, as the water gas was whiter than the coal gas. It will also be noticed that there was more variation in the consumption of gas in the case of the Welsbach. This was because a small variation in consumption in this burner makes no appreciable difference in amount of light, and as I determined this fact before, I did not take so much time to adjust the consumption as I did in the other cases.

In conclusion, I beg to offer the opinion that a *white* light will be the best light for actual illumination, apart from considerations as to warmth of color, etc. The definitions both of color and line will be more accurate. Unfortunately, the white light is also generally the more intense light, and, therefore, more concentrated—comes from a smaller surface—and if so, is, therefore, open to the objections referred to. Let us understand the matter, though, and not confuse the subject by ascribing the trouble to the *whiteness* of the light. If we had a white light and a yellow light from an equal area in each case, the white light would be the best illuminator. We have some rooms so equipped that we can light by means of the flat-flame burner (New York city gas), by means of the Welsbach burner consuming the same gas, or by means of the incandescent electric light. Comparing the two latter we find the Welsbach to be much the whiter, but still not so distressing to the eye as the electric. The reason is obvious. The light from the latter is from a surface of hardly appreciable size, whereas the Welsbach light comes from a surface about equal to that from an ordinary argand burner.

I agree with one of the gentlemen quoted that in the study of this subject empiricism should be dropped and the subject studied scientifically and thoroughly. I do not think that we shall be following the proposed line of investigation, however, by going out of our way to attack well-established laws. Do not let us attempt this until we are sure of our ground. One of the counts made against the established laws of light was that they were 150 years old. The law of gravitation, as determined by Newton, is still older, but we are not yet in a position to pronounce it false on that account.

That there is room for much further study in this direction on our part I do not doubt, as it might be well for this Association to provide, perhaps, by the appointment of a committee, as in the case of the New England Association, for gathering together the results obtained by different experimenters during the coming year, the results to be properly prepared and presented to the Association at its next meeting.

THE PRESIDENT—As we have another paper on this subject, I think it would be better to read it now and discuss them jointly afterwards.

In accordance with this suggestion, Mr. Edward C. Jones, of South Boston, Mass., read his paper on

THE RELATION OF INTENSITY OF LIGHT AND VISUAL PERCEPTION.

Mr. President and Gentlemen of the Association :—In presenting for your consideration a few humble thoughts, I trust that my unfinished work may be taken up and treated in a more comprehensive manner by some of the master minds of our Association.

In the various discussions of the questions of candle-power and illumination, as well as the cause of the increase in consumption of gas from year to year, one of the most important factors has been almost ignored—the human eye—that wonderful organ through which we receive all impressions of either candle-power or illumination.

It may be said that the physiology of vision is not pertinent to the gas business, which we are here to discuss, yet it bears the same relationship to it as the judge on the bench to a criminal on trial. To it we must plead our cause, and on its judgment depends the success of our industry.

A large proportion of the companies manufacturing gas at the present time style themselves gas light companies—that is, they morally carry the gas beyond the meter to the burner of the consumer, where it is decomposed by heat, and produces that subtle, vibrating substance, light—described by some as "undulations of the ether," and by others as simply "effect."

The eye may be compared to the photographic camera. It consists of a series of lenses and media, arranged in a dark chamber, the iris acting as a diaphragm, to govern the quantity of light admitted, and the object of the apparatus is to form a distinct image of external objects on the retina, which is the sensitive plate; and it is with the retina we must become best acquainted, for we furnish the stimulant to which this retinal plate is sensitive.

The retina is the termination of the optic nerve in the eye, and is shaped something like an umbrella turned inside out, the handle representing the optic nerve. The retina is the true terminal organ on which light exerts a specific action, and the impression conveyed to our minds of intensity of light depends wholly on the condition, or, we may say, excitability of the retina.

The sunlight—proceeding as it does from one source, and thoroughly diffused and toned for our use, and dealt out to us in healthful allowance—is, of course, the natural light. Its action on the retina is stimulating to the proper degree, and the rest we obtain during the hours of darkness is tonic in effect on the retina. But we must work overtime, and supply a substitute for sunlight. We take a candle, light it, place the source of light in close proximity to our eyes, and to work. The light seems sufficient, but soon the retina becomes hardened to the light of one candle, and we must provide *two*. We gradually increase the number of hours of work of the retina by artificial light, and provide for its stimulation fluid lamps, twelve-candle gas, kerosene, twenty-candle gas, electric arc lights, and an innumerable quantity of incandescent electric lamps, until finally we use regenerative gas burners, and place two or three sixteen-candle incandescent electric lamps inside of our roll-top desks.

As the intensity of light is increased, it seems that the excitability of the retina is diminished, for all sensory nerves bear a strong relationship to each other. Now, we all know how a *little* mustard will burn the tongue, but, as we persist in using it, we may increase the amount gradually until a spoonful will have no more effect on the nerves of taste than so much yellow ochre. The same is true of the sense of smell. For instance, as we enter a room strongly perfumed with a delightful odor, it reaches our sense of smell, but after remaining a few minutes under its influence we are wholly oblivious to the presence of any odor.

In the introduction of large regenerative burners to store windows, we explain to the consumer the increase of candle power developed from the gas and the mumber of times brighter it will be than the adjoining window provided with two four-foot lavatip burners. The consumer looks with expectant eyes for a wonderful illumination, but a shade of disappointment crosses his face as he says: " There may be four times as much candle power, but the window does not seem twice as light as the other one."

The difference between the theoretical increase of intensity of light and the practical impression produced on the retina induced me to search for authority on the subject, and, among others, appears, in the *Encyclopedia Britannica*, under the subject, " Eye," the following :

" Fechner's law regulates the relation between the stimulus and the sensational effect in sensory impressions. This law is that the sensational effect does not increase proportionally to the stimulus, but as the logarithm of the stimulus. Thus, supposing the stimulus to be 10, 100, or 1,000 times increased, the sensational effect will not be 10, 100, or 1,000 times, but only one, two, and three times greater." You understand that where I have made use of the word "stimulus" it means "light," and sensational effect "the impression of the light on the retina."

The law of Fechner explains the disappointment of the shopkeeper, and, aside from the diminished excitability, or hardening of the retina, produced by long exposure to intense light and repeated fatigue, presents the following facts for our consideration.

A sixteen-candle gas produces an impression equal to the logarithm 1.204120, while a twenty-candle gas produces an impression equal to the logarithm 1.301030. Thus the candle power is increased twenty-five per cent., but the impression of brightness on the retina is increased only 8.4 per cent.

The doubling of candle power from twenty to forty candles causes simply an increase of twenty-three per cent. of stimulation of the retina, while a 100-candle light will produce only twice the effect on the retina of that exerted by a ten-candle light, notwithstanding the intensity of light is increased ten-fold. This ratio holds good until the retina is exposed to light so intense that we cannot distinguish any increase in brightness.

The gas engineer and the interior decorator should combine their efforts to please the public eye—the one, to supply a mellow and thoroughly diffused light, with no dark shadows lurking about to strain the eyes; the other, to provide pleasing effects on our vision by proper reflection of light and by ingenious devices to prevent the eyes from meeting the glare of the source of light, without materially diminishing the illuminating effect.

DISCUSSION.

THE PRESIDENT—We have in these two papers food for a good deal of discussion. Some of the other gentlemen who have previously considered and made experiments in this matter ought now to be heard from. We would like to hear from Mr. Boardman about his experiments.

MR. BOARDMAN—When I presented that experiment it was with a view to place this matter before you, so that if you wanted you could think over it and work it out. If I had done no more than to call forth the experiments presented here by Mr. Humphreys, I would have been more than repaid for the trouble taken in bringing the subject to your attention. My statement was simply a *recollection* of the experiment. When Mr. Humphreys wrote to me, asking for further explanations, I had to tell him that it was an experiment made some ten years previous. I also told him that, in the experiments with regard to the candle power determined by the student chimney, of course the actual candle power shown by the photometer was not that of twenty-three but of twenty-two candles, the result secured after making the necessary corrections for the decreased amount of gas burned by the argand chimney. The same amount of gas cannot be burned in the argand burner with the student chimney as with the straight chimney. But, even with the lesser amount of gas, I got a much higher intensity in the light, and it struck my eye so pleasantly that I thought I must have gained very largely in the illuminating power of the gas. The paper called to mind that I did not make that statement clear in my paper. I think I was on the right track when I cautioned the Association against searching for an intense white light of small size, and giving up the broad flame, with its warm, yellow light. Doubtless Mr. Humphreys' experiments have impressed that fact more fully upon you than did my statement. I think you will all agree that the water gas flame, as generally burned, is of smaller area than the coal gas flame as usually burned. I would like to have Mr. Humphreys carry his experiments further, and compare the area of the flame of the water gas in the star burner with the area of the coal gas flame of the argand burner, exposed to the disc, showing the approximate sizes of the flame, so as to determine if there would be any difference. I would suggest, if this matter is carried further, that experiments of that character be made. I trust the subject will be pursued to as great length as possible.

THE PRESIDENT—We have with us to-day one of our Honorary Members, and one whom we do not see very often—a gentleman who has given the subject a great deal of attention, not only with regard to the gas flame, but also with regard to the electric light. I know I express the wish of every member when I say that we shall all be glad to hear from President Morton on this subject. (Applause.)

PRESIDENT MORTON—There are one or two points that have occurred to me in connection with the papers just read which it may be of interest to draw the attention of my fellow-members to. These are, in the first place, the very common misconception as to what we mean when we speak of a light ray. People very often speak of a light ray as if the source of light were giving out certain lines of something. Now, the real meaning of a light ray is the direction in which the action of the light is propagated. There is nothing there. In other words, the light ray is not a thing. It is not true that something in the form of a right line, or a straight line, is passing out from the source of light, any more than it would be true to say that the path of the cannon-ball is a line consisting of anything, or being constituted of anything. It is the direction in which the cannon-ball goes.

What, then, is light, so far as we know it? It is a vibratory motion in the elastic medium pervading all space and most bodies. Now, when we have a source of light (suppose for the moment that it is a point), and we say that it emits rays of light, what we really mean is, and what is the fact, is that that point is in effect expanding and contracting, or moving in such a way as to produce successive waves or shells of motion—little spheres, as it were, or a series of spheres. Imagine for a moment that the luminous point suddenly grew large and then small again, whereby it produced a wave or shell of motion. Now, that minute shell of motion produced around this point acts upon the medium outside of it, producing a larger shell of motion; and that again upon the medium outside of it, and so on, just as you might imagine a soap-bubble blown from a point expanding and growing larger and larger as it spreads out. So this first momentary action of the light produces a shell, as it were, of motion, which spreads out equally in all directions. If the source is a point, it spreads in every direction, getting attenuated as it spreads. This illustration is, of course, not intended to be exact as expressing in detail the motions of light waves, but as a rough physical illustration it strikes me that it is not, perhaps, a bad one—if you will bear in mind that it is not to be carried too far, and that I do not want to say that a light wave is a substance at all. Imagine a bubble produced from the end of a little pipe, and expanding until it fills the whole room. Now, that bubble, at the first instant, contains only a certain amount of substance, and that amount has got to be spread thinner and thinner as it grows larger and larger; so, that if it is twice as large in diameter, a given area of it will only have a quarter as much substance in it. Now, in the case of light, the motion is not in the line in which the force proceeds, but at right angles with it. In other words, if a light ray were passing from this light overhead down on the stage, the motion of the light (the vibrations) would not be in that line, but would be at right angles to it. The particles would be moving at right angles to the direction in which the ray traveled. But that is immaterial in any general consideration. It only becomes important in connection with some recondite subjects, as, for example, that of polarization of light; but in the present case it is immaterial, since we are only considering the subject with reference to the diffusion of light.

Now let us see if we can get a clear idea of what is taking place where light is being emitted by a luminous body. Suppose, for example, that the luminous source is a point emitting these successive shells of motion one after the other, just as if it were a little bubble which was able to expand and spread through the whole building, and then another bubble came right after it, and so on, following each other so quickly that they followed each other at a distance of a quarter of an inch, one bubble within another, and each one expanding continuously through space. That being the condition of things, it follows, as a physical necessity (as a thing, the contrary of which is not supposable), that the intensity of that action should diminish with the square of the distance; or, for example, that if the distance is double the intensity or the amount of action on a given area should be one-fourth at the double distance, or at treble distance one-ninth, and so on. This is as necessary as the conclusion that the half of a thing is equal to the other half, or that if a thing is divided into fifty equal parts, each one of those parts will be one-fiftieth of the whole thing. There is no getting away from that reasoning, and if we find that the result of an experiment seems to differ from this, we must be quite sure that there is some error in the experiment. Some time ago there was a very curious trick with a chess-board, which consisted in cutting the chess-board in a certain way and then so putting it together again that out of the sixty-four squares which exist in a chess-board, you could get sixty-six or sixty-two, according to the way in which the pieces are arranged. Any one looking at that, although they could not explain how the trick was done, yet could be perfectly certain that the two squares were not created or destroyed. So, in this case, if it seems to us that the law of inverse squares in the case of light is not fulfilled, we may be sure we have misunderstood the experiment, or that there is something which we have not taken into account.

Now, suppose that instead of being a point, the source of light were a surface. Then, in the first place, it is manifest that surface may be divided into an infinitude of points, and that what is true of each one of the points must be substantially true of the entire thing. We cannot have a thing true of each one of a number of individuals and not true of them altogether. Therefore, if this law is true as to points, it is true of the surface ; but in the case of a surface this difference would come in. While each point is giving out rays in this way, in various directions, if we are supposed to look obliquely at this surface, then it is possible that its area is fore-shortened, and in effect made smaller than if we were looking at it at right angles. On that account this area will seem to produce less light under certain conditions. If it is a broad, transparent surface, which is giving light, and if there is no obstruction of the light by the luminous particles themselves, then there will be no difference whether we look at the surface point-blank or otherwise, for we will still get the same amount of light from it. That is illustrated in certain flames of thin, transparent character which will give us the same amount of light, whether looked at sidewise or frontwise. A number of the experiments just described by Mr. Humphreys illustrates this very admirably. But if we are dealing with an opaque surface so that one point can obstruct the light coming from another point, then the light will appear less when looked at obliquely. But that will be only under those peculiar conditions, and it will not be in violation of the general laws of light, but will only be a result of special condition of the particular source of light under discussion, which introduces a new factor, or element— that of the obscuration of the light from one point by the presence of some other point of the luminous substance. Let us now consider light emanating from a central source in another way—namely, as a series of waves moving at right angles to their direction of progress. Such waves would be represented by a wave-shaped line, or, more properly speaking, by a sinusoid curve. They have two prominent characteristics—wave length and wave amplitude or intensity. Wave length depends upon the number produced in a given period of time. That is to say, if they are producing red light, it is because there are about four hundred million millions of up and down movements to the second. Four hundred million of million would make the light red. If the motions of all of them were about eight hundred million millions to the second, they would then be producing violet; and between these limits there would be all the various colors, according to the number of vibrations. Now, whether there are four hundred million millions or eight hundred million millions of vibrations produced in each second, they will travel at the same rate. The first one produced will be carried in a second to the distance of about two hundred thousand miles. Whether this motion is made at the rate of four hundred million millions a second, or eight hundred million millions it will equally soon get to this distance. At the end of a second, therefore, the wave produced at the beginning of the second will be 200,000 miles off, and between that distant point and the source of light there will be about four hundred million millions of other waves which had been produced and started out after the first, one after the other, during the second, if the source of light was red; or in other words, if the light emitted was red light. If there were four hundred million millions of waves in a length of 200,000 miles, this would make each wave about one-forty-thousandth of an inch long. If the color of the light was violet there would be about twice as many vibrations produced in the second, and thus twice as many waves in the length of 200,000 miles, and so each wave would be about half as long. The distance longitudinally between one wave and the next is the wave length of light. That is what makes the difference in color. If there are so many to the inch, or each is such a fraction of an inch, it is one color; if it is a different number, then it is another color.

Now comes the question of intensity. If we say that a light is a very bright one we do not mean that it throws out more waves to the inch, or that the motions are given with more or less rapidity ; but we mean that each one swings further up and down, and the intensity of the light would be represented by the extent of this motion up and down. In other words, by the height of the waves. We may say that a dim light would be represented by a motion going up and down, say the one hundred-thousandth of an inch. A picture of this would be a line almost straight, but waving up and down a very little way every forty-thousandth of an inch. If it was a bright light of the same color it would be represented by a curve, with just as many bends in it to the inch, but they would go up and down much more than the other. It would be a steep wave, as distinguished from the other. This also leads us to the same conclusion, that as this motion spreads outward from the center, it must decrease in intensity. That is to say, the height and fall of these waves will diminish. A certain amount of something is put in motion in the first instance, and as that motion is spread and goes outward, it acts upon a larger and larger area of the substance, and must, therefore, produce less and less effect. Thus the little ring, or sphere, whose atoms are moving up and down through a large distance, will become a great sphere, whose particles are moving up and down through very small distance.

What I wish especially to bring to your attention is this idea that if we want to represent a light wave philosophically, as coming from a source, we will represent it as a curve which begins steeply up and down, but with a given length between the convolutions, and goes on with this constant longitudinal length, but decreases in amplitude, or the height and depth to which it goes, and so decreases very rapidly—in fact so that this amplitude, or height of the wave varies inversely as the square of the distance from its source. The length of the wave, however, or the distance between one bend and another in this sinuous line, will be constant for each color. White light being a mixture of all colors, we have it in the result of the combined action of a great many wave lengths ; and, therefore, it becomes a very complex thing to think of or discuss. We need not, however, go into this at present, but may rest in the broad conclusion that what is true of each wave length or color is true of the compound of all colors, namely, white light.

There is one point in the last paper read to which I think it would be interesting to draw your attention, and which was no doubt thought of by the reader of the paper, but not mentioned by him ; and that is this :   Why is it that with greatly increased intensity of light the visual impression is so little increased ?   In the first place, the law of Fechner referred to could not have been in reference to the illumination of a surface, because Fechner and others, among them Dr. G. W. Draper, of New York, had proved that the eye can detect a difference of illumination equal to the one-sixty-fourth of the greater light, but must have been in relation to the effect of intense light upon the eye—of a brilliant point or area of light examined directly.   In fact, he could not assert that by having two candles instead of one you only light up the table, or the book you are looking at with a slight increase, (say twenty-five per cent. more) of illumination ; but that if you doubled the actual luminous intensity of a candle flame and looked at it, you would not be aware that it was doubled, but its effect upon the eye would only be an increase of twenty or twenty-five per cent., as the case might be.   What is the reason of that ?   I believe it to be as follows :   The reader of the paper spoke of the pupil of the eye as a diaphragm through which the light passes into the eye.   Let me now add that this pupil of the eye is an *adjustable* diaphragm.   When you expose the eye to a strong light the aperture in the pupil shrinks up.   You can see this action with the aid of a mirrror even in your own eyes.   You can see it better by looking at the eyes of another person.   If you bring a bright candle near the eye the opening of the pupil grows smaller.   This is very marked in the eye of a cat, where the closing is only from two sides.   In the human eye it closes all around.   It merely makes a smaller circular aperture.   The pupil in the cat's eye spreads out in the dark, making a round aperture, and then closes up to a narrow slit as it contracts in the light.   The result is that, while you are looking at a dim light this aperture is wide open, letting a great amount of light get in through the open pupil and fall upon the retina.   As the light becomes brighter and brighter the aperture shrinks up, and correspondingly closes out the light.

The resultant effect is merely the difference between the two. If the closing up was as rapid as the increase there would be no difference perceptible between a dim and a bright light. In judging of amounts of illumination in apartments we must not forget this physiological action just noticed, by reason of which the eye, if exposed to a very brilliant light, will become less able to perceive a feebler illumination, and, as a consequence, the brighter light will appear to illuminate things more dimly, because the eye has changed its capacity of perceiving. But this should not discredit the quality of the light, but only indicate that we have not been judicious in our location of it.

THE PRESIDENT—I would like to ask President Morton whether he would give us to understand that all lights which on the photometer would measure equally would really be equal illuminants in a room? In other words, whether you would get as much light from a sixteen-candle Edison light as from a sixteen-candle bat-wing burner. Theoretically, I suppose you would.

PRESIDENT MORTON—Theoretically, and as matter of fact " objectively," using that word in its technical sense. That is, there would be as much light in the room; but to a person coming into the room it would not appear so well illuminated, and for this reason : If the room were illuminated with ten Edison sixteen-candle lamps, then there would be scattered around in that room a number of very minute spots of light, of intense whiteness. Wherever the images of those struck the retina of the eye they would have a relatively paralyzing effect upon it, and would also cause the pupil to contract. If that same room were illuminated with ten gas flames of large size, then, as one came into that room, he would not find such intense local spots of light; for although there would be the same amount of light from each lamp, it would come from a larger area, and would be correspondingly less intense, and the nerve located in those parts of the eye on which the images of these flames fell, instead of being violently shaken by the intense vibration, as they would be in the case of the Edison light, would be more gently vibrated, and this paralyzing or diminishing effect, this dulling of the nerves, would not take place to the same degree, nor would the contraction of the pupil be so great. It is just as it is in coming into a room with the naked gas flames all about you, as compared with the light from the same flames in globes. We all have noticed the pleasant effect of the light upon the room when globes are used. The illumination seems much better with globes than with the more intense light from naked burners. I remember a case where the principle here considered was made strikingly manifest.

In Philadelphia, many years ago, in the Academy of Music, it was found that the stage, which was an extremely wide one, was not sufficiently lighted in the middle by the border lights. Some one suggested that the trouble would be very easily corrected by getting two movable chandeliers, and setting them up on either side of the stage, with a number of gas lights on them. This was done, but only with the result of making the stage appear much darker than before, the reason being that as people looked at the stage their eyes were dazzled by the brilliant light coming from those two great chandeliers; the pupils of their eyes contracted, so that a person standing in the middle of the stage was not so easily seen as before the great lights were put on.

Mr. Gilbert—I would like to ask President Morton a question with regard to the probable practical effect upon the eye of continuous changes in the strength of illumination to which people are exposed nowadays by the necessity of living in extremely brilliant lights; and whether turning the back and then the face to brilliant lights of any kind, and so producing rapid, constant, and unnatural changes in the pupil of the eye, does not tend ultimately, practically, to destroy it?

President Morton—There is no question but that such changes are very trying to the eyes. No one can realize that better than while passing through the tunnel of the New York Central Railroad. If one sits with his eyes open while going rapidly through the tunnel, the effect, as they pass the light shafts, of the rapid changes from light to darkness, is, with most persons, extremely painful. That, of course, is an exaggerated case; but any sudden and rapid change must be very injurious to the eyes. Burners that flicker, from which the flame jumps up and down, are undoubtedly very severe and dangerous things to the eye. There is no doubt that the present generation are risking their eyesight by the use of so many brilliant lights.

MR. GRAEFF—Does President Morton mean when stating that the candle power of the Edison light is equal to the candle power of the gas lamp, if there were a dozen Edison lights at our back they would illuminate the space in front of us as well as would a dozen gas burners ? In other words, what I wish to ask is, whether candle power is exactly the same, without consideration of its effect upon the retina of the eye.

PRESIDENT MORTON—If this candle power, properly measured, is the same, then undoubtedly the illumination of a surface would be identical. In other words, it would be almost stating the same thing in two ways. When we say that the candle power is the same we mean that, on testing with the photometer, and allowing the light to fall on a white surface, we get equal illumination of that surface. If it is true in the photometer it cannot be otherwise than true out of the photometer. It is not the photometer that makes the light.

MR. BOARDMAN—I would like to speak on that point one moment, because of the evident misapprehension which seems to be in the minds of some with regard to the transmission of illumination, as indicated by the photometer. While practically, as President Morton says, the illuminating effect on the space must be the same, still I must contend that the illumination of space, as we usually inhabit it, is somewhat different. I must contend that as we inhabit space we are certainly all objects of three dimensions; and that any light proceeding from a fixed point does not illuminate so much of the surface—of a column, for instance—as it does if that light proceeds from a plain surface of two dimensions. And, therefore, that the space which is partly illuminated by reflection from that column is not so well illumined as it would be from a surface throwing light upon it, and lighting a larger surface than that, and then reflecting from that to other surfaces. That is the point that I wish to bring out in respect to the use of large surfaces for illuminating the space which we usually inhabit. That is what we have to contend with. We are to light the rooms that we occupy, and the halls in which we meet. We want those lights so distributed that there shall be as little shadow as possible, and that each object in the room shall be as nearly as possible illumined all around, so that the reflection from them may help to illumine other objects which do not get the direct rays. For this reason I respectfully contend that the illumination of the space we inhabit is greater with the flat-flame burner than with the Edison light.

MR. CLARK—I think the proceedings of this year will be very rich in information concerning light—both theoretical and practical. I think we should be specially grateful to Mr. Humphreys for having settled this question of diffusion, as it is one which has vexed us a good deal. The papers are of such a character that it is hard to discuss them off-hand. We will enjoy them very much when reading them, but we cannot readily discuss them on short notice. They are too deep for us.

MR. LOWE—I would like to ask President Morton a question. If you were to take two flames of equal intensity—for instance, a yellow flame of twenty-candle power and a white flame of twenty-candle power, and take a given area of each, say one square inch—what would be the difference, if any, in the illumination at equal distances?

PRESIDENT MORTON—If they were equal at one distance they would be equal at all other distances. That is to say, if they were tried, as in the experiment described by Mr. Humphreys. If we had a yellow flame here, and a white flame there, and so adjusted their relative strengths that they gave equal illumination upon a surface intermediate between the two, then if we moved them both equally away from the surface, the illumination would remain equal on that surface.

MR. LOWE—Notwithstanding the color of the light?

PRESIDENT MORTON—Notwithstanding the color.

MR. LOWE—Then you do not think that a sixteen-candle coal gas is better than a twenty-candle power water gas?

PRESIDENT MORTON—No; I should not think so, as a matter of mere illumination.

MR. BOARDMAN—In testing the candle power of different

flames, did you ever observe the relative size of those flames necessary to give the candle power?

PRESIDENT MORTON—Yes.

MR. BOARDMAN—Then I should like to ask whether the yellow flame requires a larger surface or a smaller one, or a surface of the same size, in order to give the same candle power by the photometer?

PRESIDENT MORTON—The yellow flame undoubtedly requires a larger surface to give the same amount of light as compared with a white flame. In other words, a white flame, from the nature of things, has a more intense action. And that reminds me of a point which I think will interest you. A great many years ago Prof. John W. Draper, of this city (now dead), who was one of the most original of American scientists, went into this subject and investigated it thoroughly. He found that where a body was rendered luminous by heat, as, for instance, a platinum wire, this was the order in which the colors appeared: When it first became luminous the rays were entirely red; as it became more luminous, there were added, to those red rays, yellow rays; but the red rays were also increased. There came more red light than before with the yellow light added to it. Then, as the heat was increased still more, the red was increased, the yellow was increased, and there was added to them green rays. As the heat was still further increased there was added to the green, blue; and to the blue, violet; but, with each addition of the higher colors, the amount of the light of the lower colors was increased. In other words, we find that in order to get up to such a compound of colors as will give us the white light—that is, a compound which must have in it blue, and violet, as well as the others—we must have a great amplitude of motion or intensity of the lower ones as well as of the higher. In still other words, when we get the white light it is by having a very intense or very powerful vibratory action, or the amplitude of the longer waves must be great in order to bring the shorter waves out so as to produce white light.

THE PRESIDENT—I do not see that there is very much left for the adherents of coal gas, theoretically; but I think that some of us are still unconverted. It seems to me to put the thing in this way, that, theoretically, if you will take five feet of thirty-candle gas, you ought to get from it as much light as you would from a larger burner, burning ten feet of fifteen-candle gas; or as you would get from the same amount of gas, or from two of these Edison burners. Now, as matter of fact, I believe that if you should compare the light upon a surface which was lighted by a large flame burning ten feet of coal gas, with that lighted by a flame which was burning five feet of thirty-candle gas, you would find the room would be better lighted by the ten-foot burner. It seems to me there would be more diffusion in the room; although theoretically, I do not know that I have any reason to give for it except the size of the flame.

PRESIDENT MORTON—I think you are correct, theoretically as well as practically, up to a certain limit. In order that a gas with half the intensity of illumination should produce the same total amount of light, there must be a double area by which the light is produced. That, of course, will diminish the sharpness of the shadows. When we are speaking of single lights it is manifestly true that if you have a light which is one square inch in area, and are getting from that a certain total amount of light and then get the same number of candles from two square inches of light, the intensity must be diminished proportionately; half the intensity involves double the area. With this double area you are getting a better diffusion; it will go more around the columns; it will better light up spaces that otherwise would be shaded; it will diminish sharpness of the shadows, etc. That is undoubtedly true. In practical illumination, however, we are dealing generally with a number of lights. It is very rarely that we attempt to light a room from an absolutely single source. Where we are dealing with a number of lights, and multiply the number of lights when you reduce the intensity, then we are gaining in both ways, because, of course, it is easier to light a space by putting two lights a quarter way from each end than by lighting with one light in the middle, for this law of decrease in proportion to the square of the distance makes it disadvantageous to light from a single source. In any case in which distribution by breaking up one light into several comes in, of course there is great advantage in a number of sources of light as compared with a single one. But I do not think, aside from this, that there is a difference if a given area (say a square inch) is given, of twenty candle-power, and that light is falling on a plain surface, and another of two square inches, which is also giving off a twenty-candle light, which falls on that same surface. Then I cannot conceive that there can be a difference of illumination, except such as may be due to the different colors of the lights. One may illuminate with a pure white light; another may illuminate with a yellow or reddish light; and one or the other may be agreeable; and one or the other may light a surface, if it is a colored surface, very much better than the other. If a majority of the objects are of yellow color, a yellow light will illumine them much better than any other color. If those same objects were blue, then a yellow light would be feebler in its illumination. If we had a room of more chromatic color, all red or all yellow, we could then best light that room with a light of a corresponding color; but, if a room is decorated with all sorts of colors, then the whitest light that we can get—the nearer in fact we can approach to daylight—the more distinctly all the colors will equally appear.

Mr. Edgerton—I understood that the starting point of this discussion was the assertion that sixteen-candle coal gas illumined as well as twenty-candle water gas. I desire to call your attention to a practical illustration—a case of illumination in London, England, where they have a twenty or twenty-one-candle cannel coal gas and a nominally sixteen-candle common gas; and yet, as a practical test, the cannel gas is sold at four shillings, whereas the common gas is sold at two shillings and three pence.

On motion of Mr. Clark, a vote of thanks was tendered to Messrs. Humphreys and Jones for their papers.

Mr. A. C. Humphreys—I wish to say, before moving a vote of thanks to President Morton, and before the discussion on this subject is closed, that last night I made a practical experiment, not a scientific one, in my room, with two light-giving surfaces; two Welsbach mantles, one being perfectly white and the other being a very mellow yellow. So far as I could see they were of the same size, made from the same materials, and practically the same. I have no doubt that, tested on the photometer, they would have been found of the same candle-power. The lighting effect in the room, as we speak of it, from the yellow flame appeared superior, as it was more pleasant to the eye; but when I asked some of those with me to read print at a certain distance from the light, they could read it from the white light the best.

I move the thanks of the Association to President Morton for his very interesting remarks upon this subject. I regard them as a practical lecture, covering some very important features, and I think that, if we deserve thanks for our papers, President Morton most certainly deserves our thanks for his address.

THE PRESIDENT—I understood that in voting the thanks of the Association, we included all three of the gentlemen whom we had the pleasure of hearing, but I am very happy to put a motion tendering a special vote of thanks to President Morton for his entertaining remarks.

The motion was passed.

Mr. C. H. Nettleton, of Birmingham, Conn., then read his paper on the

UTILILZATION OF RESIDUAL PRODUCTS.

Unfortunately the committee appointed by your Association to appoint certain members to prepare papers for this meeting, selected the speaker as one of the victims. It was unfortunate in a double sense for the Association, as a better selection could easily have been made and a far better paper been listened to than the one you will now hear; and unfortunate for the speaker, as the press of business has been so great with him this fall that sufficient time could not be spared to give the subject named by the Committee the thought necessary, or the few thoughts he had, the proper expression. I dislike to offer the Association an apology after promising to write, but it has been impossible to prepare a paper worthy of the subject or the occasion.

The notice which I received from our Secretary stated that I had been appointed to prepare a paper on the "Utilization of of Residual Products" to cover the probable return, not only in my own immediate neighborhood, but from other sections as well.

While thanking the Committee for the compliment implied by the appointment, yet it has seemed to me that they laid out a very large subject for one person to write about—so large that the time at my disposal did not warrant the undertaking, and in consequence I have ventured to change the subject somewhat, and shall treat simply of the " Residuals of a Coal Gas Works."

What I desire to call your attention to is not so much the value of residuals in themselves—with that you are all familiar—but to the probable revenue that can be derived from them; to the necessity of paying a large amount of attention to their sale, and to point out some methods followed successfully by some companies with which the speaker is familiar, in disposing of these bye products. In the first place, what can be derived from the sale of residuals in a coal gas works? It is a fact that in a large European works the entire cost of manufacture is paid for by profits derived from the sale of coke, tar, and ammonia water, and their products, so that the gas in the holder costs absolutely nothing.

At the other extreme is the small works, poorly managed, where the tar runs into a convenient sewer or river, where nearly all the coke is used in heating the retorts, and where at the end of a year the total returns from residuals amount to fifty cents per ton of coal carbonized, or less. Between these extremes there is a wide margin. Few of us, perhaps none, can ever expect to reach the high results of the foreign company referred to, but all of us, it is to be hoped, make a better return than the last named.

How shall the sale of residuals be expressed? If in so many hundreds or thousands of dollars, it means nothing unless the size of the company be known. If in so many cents per thousand feet, the statement is misleading, for the reason that the price received for coke, which is by far the largest item, must depend entirely on the local price of fuel. For illustration : Suppose A is the manager of gas works in a city where the cost of the coal for domestic purposes is $6.50 or $7.50 per ton—he may be able to obtain 11 cents per bushel for his coke, and if he sells fifteen bushels per ton of coal carbonized, the receipts would be

$1.65. B, on the other hand, manages a works where good coal for domestic purposes is sold at $2. He sells, let us say twenty-five bushels per ton of coal carbonized, but can receive at most but five cents per bushel, or $1.25. If expressed in thousand feet sold, and each sells 10,000 feet per ton, A would receive 16½ cents per M. and B but 12½ cents, and yet B manages to sell sixty-seven per cent. more coke per ton than A.

It seems to the speaker that the proper way to express sales of residuals is in percentage of cost of coal carbonized. This gives an intelligent statement at once of the results reached, and enables us to compare results with others in the fewest words, and in the most comprehensive manner possible. The coal has cost one hundred per cent., the returns from residuals are fifty, sixty or seventy per cent.

In the case of A and B referred to before, A would probably pay $5.50 per ton for his caking coal, for with high prices for domestic coal, gas coal is almost invariably correspondingly high, and vice versa, and his receipts for coke being $1.65 per ton would be thirty per cent. of cost of coal carbonized. B, on the other hand, would undoubtedly purchase his coal for $2 or less— and his receipts being $1.25 per ton, would be sixty-two per cent. I submit to your judgment if these percentages, thirty and sixty-two, do not more nearly represent the comparative working of the two managers, so far as relates to coke, than can be expressed in any other way.

Let me say frankly that I started in the preparation of this paper with the hope of proving that in most works well managed, the residuals could be made to pay ninety per cent. of the cost of the coal; but here on the seaboard and through New England, with good caking coal costing from four to five dollars per ton, I have very reluctantly come to the conclusion that most of us must content ourselves with 70 to 80 per cent.

But what does this mean in this part of the country? Let us assume that the cost of coal, including cannel or other enriching material is $4.30 per ton in the coal shed. Seventy per cent. of this will bring an income of $3 from each ton carbonized, and if the capital be no larger than $60 per ton of coal used or $6 per thousand feet sold, the income from residuals will pay 5 per cent. on the capital.

Can this standard be reached under ordinary conditions? I believe it can, and the fact that better results than 70 per cent. are obtained at one works on the seaboard here, and results reaching closely to 100 per cent. in a Western city, where cheaper coal is obtained, ought to be all the proof needed that my statement is not exaggerated.

In the order of value the residuals can be named coke, tar and ammonia.

First—Coke, and how much can be obtained from it? The answer to this depends upon the quantity saved, the rapidity with which it is sold after being made, and the price received.

First—The quantity saved. This, in turn, depends on the settings for the retorts, and whether regenerative furnaces are employed. All will agree, I think, that no gas manager can afford to use a poor setting or a poor stack; the waste of heat, and consequent waste of money, are too great; but all may not agree with the desirability of using regenerative furnaces. After an experience of seven years, I unhesitatingly say that I am strongly in favor of these furnaces, and one of the principal reasons is the larger amount of coke left for sale than with the ordinary setting. It is well known that certain gas works using furnaces are selling 30 bushels of coke per ton of coal carbonized. The day when a gas manager can rest content in selling 15 or 18 bushels of coke per ton has passed, and 25 to 28 bushels, or higher, must be the standard.

Second—The rapidity with which coke can be disposed of affects to a large degree, the quantity, provided, of course, it is sold by measure and not by weight. If a pile is allowed to accumulate and the coke handled over a number of times, the consequent shrinkage in bulk is very great, reaching, so I am told, to as much as 30 per cent. Coke should be sold, if possible, as fast as made. If customers do not come and leave their orders, then seek the customers; devote time and energy to its sale. Push it with the same enterprise that we use in selling our gas, and the results sought for are sure to follow. I have in my office a large poster which has been used very successfully by a New England gas company. With an accumulation of coke in their yards, the bill-boards, dead walls, and fences in the city where that company is located are covered with that poster, with coke and its virtues printed in glowing colors, so that he who runs not only may but must read. The result, I am told, is invariably the same, the demand increases and the surplus disappears, and that, too, without lowering the price.

Third—The price at which coke is sold. It is the fixed belief of the speaker that the same price per pound or per ton ought to be obtained for this product in every place as is paid in that place on an average for a good quality of steam and house coal. I believe this because some careful experiments at the gas works in my charge convinced me that a pound of coke would evaporate a trifle more water than a pound of coal, and because (and this, perhaps, is the most convincing proof) I obtain that price and have done so for years, almost without exception.

The experiments referred to were made in an upright tubular boiler: 7.36 pounds of water were evaporated with a pound of good anthracite coal, and in the same boiler, under the same conditions, 7.55 pounds of water were evaporated per pound of coke. Or expressed in dollars—if the coal were worth $5.00 per ton of two thousand pounds, coke would be worth $5.13 for the same quantity.

The price at which coal has been retailed in the town in which the speaker lives has varied from $5.00 to $6.00 per net ton for a number of years. And the price of coke has been fixed at nine cents per bushel in the yard or ten cents delivered within a mile of the works for the past six years, and has not been deviated from except on rare occasions. As a Winchester bushel of dry coke weighs about 37.5 pounds, there are 53.3 bushels in a ton of 2,000 pounds, and at 10 cents per bushel, the price received for coke must have been $5.33 per net ton. As the cargo prices, or those at which the manufacturers buy their coal, are much lower than the retail prices, I think that the statement made above is fairly proved that the company with which the speaker is connected has received for its coke the full average price at which coal is sold in its neighborhood.

I have been told that the company is very fortunate to be able to obtain such a price for coke, and probably that is a fact; but back of the good fortune lies a great deal of labor, and the price is as much the result of hard work as any other successful enterprise is the result of well-directed thought and effort.

Besides, other companies in New England receive the same or higher prices. Our Secretary can, if he will, tell you of one which receives on an average ten cents per bushel for broken coke; a neighbor of his receives about the same price; another, exceptionally situated, receives 12½ cents per bushel, and so on.

In selling coke there are a few essentials which to the writer seem quite important. Have a fixed price, "like the law of the Medes and Persians which altereth not." Make it as high as you think the market will bear, and then adhere to it. Nothing will destroy a good coke trade so quickly as a rise in price. Seek a house trade; it is the most reliable in many ways, and can be depended on to last better than almost any other; and one great point in its favor is the fact that it varies in its demand almost directly as our production of coke—being heaviest in the winter, and lightest in summer. To secure this trade it is a matter of necessity to break the coke—without that, the attempt will be a failure, for nothing but a coal famine will force any large number of people to try to use the large lumps of fuel, in their cooking stoves, which we haul out of our retorts.

The breaking of coke seems to be quite a bugbear to some of our ablest members—and yet in small works with hand hammers or in large works with machines, the breaking can be done at a very slight expense.

These gentlemen claim that between the labor, the shrinkage and the breeze produced, it would be as well to sell the coke for a very small sum. The answer to this is, to charge a sufficiently higher price for the broken coke to cover these items. The speaker has sold broken coke at eleven cents per bushel in yard, or twelve cents delivered, for a number of years; and from some careful experiments the following results are arrived at:

One hundred bushels of large coke is worth at 9 cts., $9.00; when broken it makes 85 bushels small coke worth at 11 cts., $9.35; and 7 bushels breeze worth for steam, at 6 cts., 42; total, $9.77—leaving an excess of 77 cts. to pay for labor in breaking, which more than covers the cost.

In this connection it may be of interest to relate a personal experience which happened this past year. From some changes in the retort house, a larger quantity of coke was saved last year than ever before, and during the present year a still larger quantity was expected. The question naturally came up, how can a market be found for this surplus coke ? The factories were tried without success, and finally it was decided to work up a house trade if possible. Various means were resorted to, posters, advertisements in papers, circulars, etc., till finally a card was sent out out in February last, which on one side read as follows :

At the following prices, small coke will be delivered and binned on any floor of any building within one mile of Gas Works.

2 bushels		$0.36	14 bushels		$1.79
3	"	51	15	"	1.90
4	"	66	16	"	2.01
5	"	80	17	"	2.12
6	"	91	18	"	2.23
7	"	1.02	19	"	2.34
8	"	1.13	20	"	2.45
9	"	1.24	21	"	2.56
10	"	1.35	22	"	2.67
11	"	1.46	23	"	2.78
12	"	1.57	24	"	2.89
13	"	1.68	25	"	3.00

The results can be stated in a few words. From March to September inclusive, of 1886, 74 coke orders were received at the office, representing 2,930 bushels, and in the same months of 1887, 448 orders were received, representing 9,293 bushels, and besides a larger quantity has been sold from the yard. So large has been the increase that it has been necessary to purchase some coke from a neighboring gas works in order to keep up with the demand. In this connection it can be stated that a careful account has been kept of the cartage. The excess on the prices quoted, above 11 cents per bushel have been credited to the carting, and it can be stated positively that no money is lost on that account.

TAR.—The question of how to dispose of tar to any profit is a very difficult one for many companies to answer satisfactorily. It is well understood that to put up a tar distillery, and run it successfully, needs a product of such an amount that few works in this country can undertake it. The tar can be sold to the tar distillers, who, of course, have to make a profit, and in consequence can offer only a small sum, small compared to what we would like to obtain; or it can be sold to rubber factories to be made into "pure gum" shoes; or to the electric light carbon factories to stick the particles of carbon together; or it can be sold to the tar-walk man. But all of these, except the last named, involve transportation charges, which must in the long run be deducted from the price received for tar. It is desirable to have a home market for everything pertaining to a gas works, and that is especially the case with coal tar; without it a small amount only will be received for this product—with it a price can be obtained which will net the company from 50 to 75 cents per ton of coal carbonized. All through the western part of Connecticut tar sidewalks are very popular, and in some towns stone or brick are the rare exceptions. As this makes the most desirable market that I ever heard of, a description of the method followed in laying the walks may not be out of place, and may be of some assistance to the gas manager who has no market for his tar.

The space to be covered is leveled off about 3½ or 4 inches below the grade of the walk and rolled, and if bordered by grass or desired to be confined, a board ½ inch thick and 6 inches wide, is set upon edge along the sides. If the ground is of a sandy or gravely nature, this is all the preparation needed; but if of loam, the soil must be excavated to the depth of two feet, and the space filled in with stone, gravel, cinders or sand. If this is not done, the walk when laid will be sure to crack, and heave when the frost comes out in the spring. The material is prepared as follows:

If a gravel bank be convenient, stones from 1 inch to 2½ inches in diameter are carefully screened out, tar thrown over them and the pile turned over, so that each separate stone shall receive its coating of tar. These are laid on the space which is already prepared for the walk, to the depth of three inches. They are then rolled with rollers weighing three hundred pounds and upward. Care should be taken that sufficient tar be used to cause the stones to stick well together, or otherwise the walk will disintegrate. The speaker has never seen it tried, but is of the opinion that broken stone would make a better walk than the round cobble stones which are generally used in Connecticut, as the rough surface of the broken stone would make a better surface for the tar to adhere to than the smooth surface of the round stones.

The "top dressing" is prepared as follows: Coarse, sharp sand and fine coal ashes are mixed carefully together, "dry," in the proportion of one part of ashes and two parts of sand. The tar is then added, the pile turned over a number of times, each time being carefully raked, so that the tar shall thoroughly permeate the entire mass. Care must be taken not to use too much tar, as in that case the walk will be too soft; and on the other hand, if too little be used, the particles of sand will not adhere to each other. When thoroughly mixed the pile should have a dry, spongy appearance. This is now laid evenly on top of the first course to the depth of an inch and a half. It is then carefully rolled, and the pressure of the rollers will reduce it to one inch in thicknes or a trifle less. The walk is allowed to stand for twenty-four hours without being used, and is then ready for public travel. The prices asked by the tar-walk men vary from fifty to ninety cents per square yard, but it can be truly said of the quality that the walk is very apt to vary with the money. If the former price be paid, a walk will be laid that will last for a few years only, for the latter a walk *can* be laid that will last fifteen or twenty years, with ordinary use; and then for repairs, need only have a renewal of the top course.

The speaker has found it necessary, in order to sell tar for this purpose, to divide that produced at his works into two qualities. All condensing in the hydraulic main and hot tar scrubber is sent into one well, all beyond that point, in the exhauster, condensers and standard scrubber, into a separate well. For the first he has had no difficulty in obtaining $3.00 per barrel; for the second, $1.50 per barrel, averaging $2.50 per barrel, each holding fifty gallons.

If my company had no demand for tar, and could not develop one which would bring a fair price, I should certainly burn it. Tar is worth to burn under the retorts one-half the price of a bushel of coke, and that fixes the price under which I will not sell it, so long as the matter is left in my hands. If all the gas companies in the country could be induced to act on this idea, and one-third or one-half of the tar produced were consumed under the retorts, there would be little difficulty in obtaining a reasonable price for the balance.   As you know, this course is recommended and practiced by one of the leading gas engineers in England, Mr. George Livesey, and I would commend it to the careful consideration of every gas manager who fails to obtain a good, round price for his tar product.

Ammonia.——Until very recently most of those present allowed their ammonia water to run to waste, but thanks to some of our friends in the ammonia business, a plant has been developed in the past two years for concentrating ammonia water with very little trouble, and at slight expense, from 7 or 8 ounce liquor to 60 and 70 ounce strength.   By this means a great weight of water is gotten rid of, and it is now possible to ship the concentrated at a profit, where before the freight charges would have left the balance on the wrong side.   By this apparatus, companies carbonizing 1,500 tons annually, or even less, can obtain a return from this residual.   The cost of operating the concentrating apparatus belonging to my company is:

For labor per day, not over	$1.00
For additional coke used in boiler, 5 bushels at 9 cts.,	45
	$1.45

In addition to this some additional breeze is used to make the steam required, but it has not been included.   There are besides the items of interest, depreciation and repairs.   A run of eight hours will work off 600 gallons of 8 oz. liquor, and will produce about 75 gallons of 60 oz. liquor.   This will weigh about 650 pounds, and can be sold at prices which will vary with the location of each place.   From what I hear there is no difficulty in a contract being made that will net 18 cents per ton of coal carbonized.

It is proper to state, however, that the concentrator will not work well with less than 5 oz. liquor, and a higher strength gives better results.

And now, gentlemen, I have nearly done.   I am afraid some of you will think I have been indulging in the possible, and not the probable, return from residuals, and some replies received from inquirers, which are tabulated below, tend to confirm that idea.

	Bush. of Coke sold per ton.	Per cent. of cost of coal, cannel and oil rec'd from coke.	Price per bush. in yard.	Average retail price of coal.
1	—	16.78	.07 X	5.75
2	.73 of coke made	50	.05	2.50
3	—	25	.05	5.75
4	22	33	10 for broken	6.25
5	22.63	42	8.77	5.50

As these figures, with two exceptions, do not bear out the optimistic views presented in this paper, and as the weight of evidence is against me, I submit the following table to show the facts on which my faith in this matter is founded.

The sale of residual products at the works in my charge have produced the following percentages of cost of coal and cannel (no oil is used) for the past five years. In all cases the cost of delivering the coke is deducted. The labor of breaking coke is deducted only in part, but at most this item is small during these years. The labor of pumping tar is not deducted, but the labor and all charges connected with ammonia are.

For year ending April 1st, 1883, 47.8 per cent.

1884, 46 "

1885, 57.5 "

1886, 54 "

1887, 57.6 "

As the company is now selling six bushels of coke more per ton than last year, and as this additional sale will add more than 10 per cent. to the figures of 1886, it is safe to claim that the residuals are now paying nearly 70 per cent. of the cost of coal carbonized.

I trust you will pardon the length of this paper. It has grown much larger than I had wished or expected—as you probably have discovered, it is a subject in which I take great interest, and it is not impossible that I exaggerate its importance; but I feel confident that if the dollar problem which our Mr. Greenough gave us years ago as being the great problem of the day among gas men—if this problem be ever solved in this part of the country, it must be done by working up the receipts from the residuals to the highest possible point. With success there the problem may be solved successfully—without success it never can be.

MR. PEARSON—Mr. Nettleton spoke very favorably of the results obtained from the regenerative furnace, with reference to the quantity of coke obtained from a ton of coal. I would like to ask him if he obtains as much tar, and if the tar is of as good a quality as that obtained by him previous to using the regenerative system?

MR. NETTLETON—I am unable to answer that question positively. For years I have been figuring that a ton of coal yields 14 gallons of tar, because my sales bore out those figures. That allows 3½ tons to each barrel of tar of 50 gallons. I think, however, that with higher heats a somewhat smaller quantity of tar would be made. I did not notice any difference in the quality of the tar in the matter of its use for tar-walk purposes. The hydraulic main tar is somewhat thicker, and the tar-walk makers think it is somewhat better for their purposes. Certainly they do not complain of it, and it is being used very generally in my neighborhood.

MR. PEARSON—You do not speak positively as to how much less you obtain; but you think you get nearly as much?

MR. NETTLETON—I think that I get nearly as much, but I cannot speak with positiveness.

MR. PEARSON—Do your tar-walk makers heat the tar before using it?

MR. NETTLETON—In cold weather, when the tar does not run readily and they cannot work it as they need to do in connection with the other materials employed, they heat the tar, but in the summer they do not.

MR. A. C. HUMPHREYS—Do they dry the ashes and sand which they use?

MR. NETTLETON—In wet weather they dry the sand, and, I think, dry the ashes; but, as they ordinarily work on bright days, they use the sand just as it comes out of the pit, and the ashes as they come from the cellars, screening out the coarse particles. When they lay pavements over which horses and wagons are to be driven, they put in a lower course of coarse stones, and in the top course use some soft pitch. What percentage of that is used I do not know. For ordinary pavements they do not use the pitch. They merely use the tar, and, without heating, except in cold weather.

Mr. Clark—Does not that soften in warm weather?

Mr. Nettleton—If the pavement is laid in the spring it will be somewhat soft the following summer, but by the following year it will be very hard.

Mr. Lowe—Did I understand you to say that a ton of coke is worth 13 cents per ton more than a ton of coal for the purpose of generating steam in boilers?

Mr. Nettleton—Yes; in my opinion.

Mr. Lowe—It seems to me that that touches somewhat the point which the Secretary has been so anxious to hear something about—the generation of steam from coke. Can you give us some idea of that?

Mr. Nettleton—I have given you the results concisely.

Mr. Lowe—Were the price of coal to go down then the results would be in favor of coal, rather than in favor of coke, as I understand your paper.

Mr. Nettleton—If the prices of coal go down, then the price of coke must drop correspondingly; but the coke is worth a little more than coal.

Mr. Lowe—You stated that the price generally received for this hard pavement was from 50 to 90 cents per square yard. I have just paid 30 cents for a lot of this work.

Mr. Nettleton—I doubt if that work will last.

Mr. Page—In an address by Dr. Siemens, delivered before the British Association some six years ago, he stated, what was then a fact in the case of one coal gas company in England, that the receipts for residuals—coke, tar, ammonia and sulphur—paid the cost of putting the gas in the holder. Five years ago, when ammonia and ammoniacal liquor of 8 ounces sold in England at an average price of 60 cents per ton of coal carbonized, coal tar was selling at 65 cents per ton of coal carbonized. Therefore, and in the case of many companies, more than the cost of the coal was obtained from the residuals. Why has there been such a change in the value of the two residuals? In the first instance, the vast increase in the production of anthracene and benzole from coal tar, by which the value of the benzole and the anthracene was diminished, and the vast increase in color manufactures in Germany, Switzerland, Belgium and in England, caused so great a reduction in the value of the coal tar dyes that the market price of coal tar fell from 65 cents to the present price in England of about 25 cents per ton of coal carbonized. In this country, singular to state, a larger average price is being obtained for coal tar than in England, because of the wider uses of the products. Pitch is being used so much more largely here for roofing and for paving, and creosote oil for wood preservation. The light products, to some extent, are increasing in value; but, as the values on the other side are so low that it does not pay to export the benzole and anthracene, our manufacturers receive nothing for the latter once very valuable product, the base of artificial madder. Yet, with the advance in chemical industry applied to the use of coal tar products, and to the manufacture of new products on the other side, in Germany especially, where technical schools have been educating their young men in this line for 25 or 30 years, to-day not less than 2,500 bright and intelligent men are employed exclusively upon some one or more of the local tar products.

Professor Baeyer has produced artificial indigo, synthetically, which is being imported, sold and used in this country to-day at $20 per pound, when the price of vegetable indigo is $1.50 and $1.60 per pound. Why? Because it gives a brighter and more distinct color, and, therefore, can be used for certain purposes where the vegetable indigo cannot be used so advantageously. By cheapening the modes of producing it, which will doubtless be accomplished in due time, competition with indigo for all its varied uses will be possible. Then the fifteen or twenty million dollars per annum now paid for indigo will be paid for this product from coal tar, just as to-day the artificial madder has displaced every acre of natural madder grown in the world.

A most interesting discovery has been made in our country, and mainly by a distinguished American chemist. I hold in my hand a sample of saccharin. A letter just received by me from

Dr. Ira Remsen, of the Johns Hopkins University, of Baltimore, gives its history as follows :

" The facts in regard to the substance commonly called saccharin are simply these : During the year 1879 a Russian, by the name of C. Fahlberg, was working in the laboratory of the Johns Hopkins University under my guidance. At his request I suggested to him a line of original investigation, which was a continuation of some work I had previously done, the result of which had been published. He undertook the work, and was constantly under my guidance. When the work was completed I wrote and published an article giving an account of the results, and describing the sweet substance under the name of benzoic sulphinide. As is the custom in all scientific laboratories of the world, I placed Fahlberg's name with my own at the head of the article. This kind of partnership is perfectly understood by scientific men. The article to which I refer was published in the *Berichte der Deutschen Chemischen Gesellschaft*, XII., 469 (1879). Afterward, in January, 1880, I wrote a second and more detailed article on the subject, and this was published under my own and Fahlberg's names in the *American Chemical Journal*, in April, 1880, Vol. I., page 426. Since that time I have, with the aid of advanced students, continued my investigations of the substance, and have published other articles on the subject. In the meantime it appears that Fahlberg has occupied himself with devising methods for preparing the substance, and has patented it without consulting me. This I object to ; and all who are familiar with the facts recognize that Fahlberg is entirely unjustified in appropriating the results of our joint labors. My opinion is that he has acted dishonestly in the matter."

The famous chemist, Sir Henry Roscoe, President of the British Association, pronounced saccharin 220 times sweeter than sugar. While we cannot say that that is going to displace the cultivation of the sugar cane, yet it is claimed that in medicine the product is invaluable. Saccharin does not assimilate and therefore can be used where sugar cannot be. The manuture of it, which ought to have been begun here, and which rightly belonged here, is conducted in Germany. The Russian went to Germany, obtained a patent for the invention, is manufacturing the product there and sending it back to this country. It sells at retail for $2 per ounce. I also exhibit another product, antipyrine. Some of the best scientific authorities in the world say that this is a more powerful febrifuge than quinine. It has no bitter taste, and it works more quickly. It is now being made and sold largely. Another product, salol, is used in medicine in increasing volume as a remedy for rheumatism. But one of the latest and most interesting discoveries is thalleine, which has been used successfully in fevers, and is a curative of yellow fever. Oil of myrbane, having the odor of the oil of bitter almonds, is made in this country. I have here cumarin, identical with the extract obtained from distillation of the sweet-scented grasses, known in perfumery as "new mown hay." It is made from coal tar. Let me impress upon you that while we have not these industries now, they are coming; because the introduction of skilled talent in the gas industry and other manufactures will enable us by and by, to establish here that enormous color industry, and other chemical industries, which are now held firmly in the grasp of Germany. Let me say a word on the subject of ammonia. That is increasing in use very largely, especially for artificial refrigeration. There are to-day in this country not less than 1,500 artificial ice-making machines. The number is increasing at the rate of 200 a year. Cities, towns, and even villages in the South, United States forts and naval vessels and ocean steamships, are introducing that mode of producing ice and cooling, because it is cheaper and better, and gives a purer product than ice obtained from the North River or from any of the northern lakes. The residual from gas-making furnishes the cheapest and best source of obtaining the ammonia which is used, not only for this, but for so many other purposes. There will be a steadily increasing value for that product. Therefore, there is certainly encouragement in knowing that in the near future the coal in the coal sheds will be paid for by the products obtained therefrom.

On motion of Mr. Clark, a vote of thanks was tendered to Mr. Nettleton for his interesting paper. The Convention then adjourned to reconvene on Thursday, October 20, 1887, at 10 A.M.

Second Day—Thursday, October 20—Morning Session.

The Association met pursuant to adjournment.

PLACE OF NEXT MEETING.

Mr. Clark—The Committee appointed to select the place for holding the next meeting of the Association, recommend Toronto, Canada. They originally desired to go South, to Atlanta, Nashville or Louisville, but as they received a very cordial invitation from Toronto, they decided to accept it. I will read the letter of invitation :

"Consumers' Gas Company, }
Toronto, Ont., Oct. 15, 1887. }

" C. J. R. Humphreys, Esq.,
" *Secretary American Gas Light Association,*
" *Sturtevant House, New York :*

" My Dear Sir : As it is possible that I shall not be able to attend the meeting of the Association until the afternoon of Wednesday, the 19th inst., and fearing that some decision may be arrived at before then, regarding the place of meeting next year, I write to say that our President, Vice-President and Directors have unanimously and cordially authorized me on behalf of the Company, to extend to the Association a hearty invitation to hold their next meeting in the city of Toronto.

" We trust that as the Association has never met in Canada, and as we hope to have finished by that time a works that will not be unworthy of inspection, and as our city possesses many objects of interest, that this invitation will be favorably entertained.

" I assure you that we shall do our best to entertain the members of the Association, and to make their sojourn as pleasant as possible.

" As the weather here is somewhat colder toward the end of October than in the latitude of New York, I would suggest that, if practicable, the meeting take place in the first week of October, when it will be pleasanter weather for driving.

" Sincerely yours,　　　　　W. H. Pearson."

The President—Does the Committee make any recommendation with regard to the time of holding the meeting ?

Mr. Clark—The Committee recommend that the meeting be held, as Mr. Pearson suggests, in the first week of October.

The Secretary—The Constitution provides that the meeting shall be held on the third Wednesday ; and we cannot amend the Constitution except in the regular form, or by unanimous consent. This has been done once before—at the time of the Chicago meeting—when it was found desirable, by reason of a political convention being held in Chicago, to have our meeting on the second Wednesday instead of the third.

The report of the Committee was accepted, and it was voted that the Association hold its sixteenth annual meeting in the city of Toronto, on the date determined by the Constitution, and it was voted that a vote of thanks be extended to the Consumers' Gas Company of Toronto, for their cordial invitation.

REPORT OF COMMITTEE ON PRESIDENT'S ADDRESS.

Mr. Taber—The Committee to whom was referred the President's Address make the following report with reference to the suggestion of the President as to the formation of a Committee of Investigation, so to speak. The idea of the Committee was to undertake it at this meeting, if possible, as a tentative plan, and to appoint a Committee which shall make a report upon its work, and advise next year as to a permanent organization. They make this report :

" A Committee should be appointed sufficiently large to have one member, at least, in each of the larger geographical divisions of our field of work. Each member should then be called upon for advice by those in his vicinity ; and any question arising which he cannot decide, or is not willing to take the responsibility of so doing, can be submitted to the entire Committee, and they in turn, if desirable, can submit it to the entire Association. Let us start at once, and, by the time when we shall meet again, this Committee can report upon its work and advise as to its permanent organization. We would recommend that the President appoint a small Committee to select proper names for the members of this Investigating Committee—one each from Canada, the Eastern States, the Middle States, the Southern

States, the Western States east of the Mississippi River, the Western States between that river and the mountains, and the Pacific slope. This Investigating Committee to serve one year, and be allowed to draw, through its Secretary, upon the treasury of this Association for its necessary expenses, not exceeding $300, and report at the next meeting its work and a plan for permanent organization."

With reference, also, to the subject of badges, which the President suggested, we recommend :

" That a committee of three be appointed by the President to invite designs for a permanent badge for the Association, to select from these designs the most suitable, ascertain its cost, and report to the next meeting."

They also recommend that a reprint of 800 copies of the President's Address be made and distributed among the members of the Association.

Mr. Clark—Do I understand that the Committee recommend the formation of a Committee by this Association to pass judgment upon all gas questions which may be submitted to them, for the benefit of local managers ?

The President—Substantially that.

Mr. Clark—I am opposed to it, and for this reason : There are men in this country who make a living out of gas engineering by giving advice, and this plan, if adopted and carried out, would effectually put an end to that living. It would put it in the power of any gas manager to call upon the best talent in the business, and, without recompense, get from him, as a matter of right, the best advice that he can give ; and not only call upon him, but also compel him to call upon others to assist him in giving advice. I think that will be a very bad principle to establish, and would effectually put a stop to all individual efforts to make money out of gas engineering in this country.

Dr. Amory—I move the adoption of the plan recommended by the Committee. In making this motion I have no desire to trench upon the question which Mr. Clark has raised. I doubt very much whether the investigation proposed, being a local affair, would interfere in the way he suggests. Of course, the Committee is appointed to investigate certain matters relating to the production of gas, and to report upon the plans which are known uncommercially. No gas manager would feel that he had a right to obtain, at very low cost, the advice of such Committee, and he would undoubtedly employ such experts as are known in the business. I think, therefore, that the fear which Mr. Clark expresses would not be realized. I certainly hope that this Association will take some such course as is suggested. We, who are business men, and connected with gas works, would very much like to take some such concert of action. If there is any scientific investigation of value in the production of gas, or which will cheapen or improve the production, I think that the expert will come in for his share in the investigation, and will receive his proper fee.

THE PRESIDENT—I would remind Mr. Clark of the fact that this is a proposition upon my part to do what there seems to be a large demand for among gas companies. I understand that Mr. Egner received something like 100 letters from gas companies, agreeing to pay something toward the expense of a scheme such as he proposed. It seems to me this could be done, and, without subjecting those gas companies to that expense, produce the same desirable results. Concert of action by the gas companies seems to be demanded. This is an attempt to do what he proposes, but to do it somewhat better, and also to benefit the whole profession by giving us at our meetings the results of the investigations, whatever they may amount to. I may say I agree with Dr. Amory, for I do not think the business of the expert is going to be done away with in this country, even if there is sufficient business to be done in that direction to keep an investigating committee busy.

MR. CLARK—I wish to call attention to the difference between the Egner plan and the plan suggested by this report. Mr. Egner proposes the employment of an engineer, and the use of an experimental station. He proposes to try, practically, all the patents that are issued for the manufacture of gas. In this report the Committee propose the appointment of a Committee who shall give their advice as to the practicability of plans, but shall do so without trying them. There is a decided difference in the two methods. Mr. Egner would have an actual trial of a plan, but this Committee would simply give advice with reference to it. As I have said, men are making their living by giving such advice, and it seems to me a pity to take that method of making a living out of their hands. It places before every gas manager the temptation to obtain, at very little trouble and expense, whatever information he may desire to secure with regard to the conduct of his gas works.

MR. A. C. HUMPHREYS—I am disposed to think, after some consideration, that the plan of Mr. Egner is quite impracticable; and it also seems to me that the method now suggested is rather cumbersome, although there are certainly some excellent ideas in it; but why would not the whole subject be covered by the more efficient organization of this Association ? We, as the representatives of a great many companies, meet from year to year, and are doing more or less all the time in the way of investigation. If we could so organize and arrange that work as to have individual members devote time enough, year after year, to thoroughly digest the results of investigations made by the members of the Association, I think it would afford a much better prospect of advantage than the method suggested. For myself, I can safely say that I would have no time to serve on such a committee, and I do not see how any busy gas man could. He would be called upon to investigate in respect to subjects that did not interest him at that particular moment; consequently he would not work so thoroughly, nor produce results as valuable as he otherwise would. We all know that a man is better able to do effective work on any line of thought if he is forced to it by some necessity or consideration at that particular moment. Such is' human nature. But by this plan you may be called upon to make an investigation into something which, up to that moment, has been entirely thrown out of sight by reason of other considerations. I think the whole subject resolves itself just into this —if we determine to make this Association more efficient in investigating these subjects, and in keeping track of what our members are doing, there will be no necessity for anything of this kind. I recognize the value of one argument, and a strong one, which can be brought against that plan—it does not give a member the opportunity of finding out anything until the next meeting; but I do not think that there are any of us who would not feel entirely at liberty to call upon any member of the Association whom we thought particularly qualified to give an opinion upon any particular subject.

MR. BOARDMAN—In support of the recommendation of the Committee, let me say I think we are striving, by this very means, to reach what Mr. Humphreys has suggested as being so desirable—we are attempting to organize our experience. Individually, we are all making experiments, and individually we are all willing to give our experience to our brother members. This Committee will simply be organizing this experience, and bringing it properly before the Association in a digested form, and in which it can be better assimilated by the individual members. I would ask, if any subject comes up which this Association wishes to decide upon, does it not appoint a committee to investigate it? Is this committee composed only of men who are at the moment engaged in considering that particular subject? I think that that Investigating Committee would be capable of taking up any question which might be brought to them.

The recommendation of the Committee was adopted.

THE PRESIDENT—I await a motion as to the appointment of such a committee. It seems to me the best way to secure an effective committee is to recommit this matter to same committee, with a request to report this afternoon the names of an Investigating Committee, who shall enter upon this investigation.

On motion of Dr. Amory the suggestion of the President was was adopted.

ELECTION OF OFFICERS.

MR. SHERMAN—The Committee appointed to nominate officers for the ensuing year, recommend that the following named gentlemen be elected:

President—Thomas Turner, Charleston, S. C.

Vice-Presidents—A. B. Slater, Providence, R. I.; Emerson McMillin, Columbus, O.; J. P. Harbison, Hartford, Conn.

Secretary and Treasurer—C. J. R. Humphreys, Lawrence, Mass.

Finance Committee—C. H. Nettleton, Birmingham, Conn.; A. E. Boardman, Macon, Ga.; W. H. Pearson, Toronto, Ont.

Executive Committee—William Henry White, New York City; G. G. Ramsdell, Vincennes, Ind.; H. B. Leach, Taunton, Mass.; D. H. Geggie, Quebec, Canada; T. G. Lansden, Washington, D. C.; F. S. Benson, Brooklyn, N. Y.

On motion of Dr. Amory, the Secretary cast the ballot of the Association for the list of officers recommended by the Committee, whereupon the President announced that they were duly elected officers for the ensuing year.

Mr. Harbison and Mr. Clark were appointed a Committee to conduct the President-elect to the platform.

THE PRESIDENT—Allow me to present to the Association Mr. Thomas Turner, the incoming President.

MR. TURNER—Gentlemen of the Association, I suppose that our worthy President expected a few remarks from me; but I have no remarks to make this morning, except to thank you most heartily for the honor you have done me in electing me to the Presidency of this Association. [Applause.]

Mr. Emerson McMillin, of Columbus, Ohio, then read the following paper on

FUEL GAS.

Some years ago one could seldom glance over the pages of any journal, and especially of those devoted to gas interests, without his eye falling upon the words " water gas." From about 1883 until recently, "natural gas " were the magnetic words. Now the absorbing theme seems to be " fuel gas." While water gas and natural gas are both " fuel gases," still neither seems to be the ideal gas in demand.

Water gas probably fails to meet the conception in the minds of the public of what a fuel gas should be : (1) because it has not yet been offered to would-be consumers at prices that tend to bring it into general use; (2) because water gas, pure and simple, possesses elements of danger, at least greater than those of illuminating gas, made by any of the processes now in vogue; and (3) because of a strong prejudice, partly warranted by facts, and partly cultivated (involuntarily in many instances) by many of us who are prone to belittle the merits and magnify the evils of things that we prefer should not succeed.

Natural gas fails to satisfy our wants as a fuel gas, simply because where we look for it we generally fail to find it. We know that it can be had only in limited portions of our great country, and believe that it will be obtainable in these few favored localities for but a limited time.

If natural gas cannot be had, and water gas is considered in any sense undesirable, why not resort to illuminating gas for fuel?

Too expensive, must be the answer. If anthracite coal or coke could be had in the Lima, (O.) oil-field, at about $1 per ton, and used in connection with the crude oil at present prices, a cheap and excellent illuminating fuel gas could be made. Pittsburg, located on the margin of the Youghiogheny coal basin, should be able to make a good and very cheap fuel gas. Whether fuel gas can be made cheaply in any particular locality, will depend largely upon the quantities in which it shall be produced. If all our consumers would, with one accord, agree to use illuminating gas to the exclusion of all other kinds of fuel, I think most of us could reduce our prices twenty-five to fifty per cent. from those now prevailing.

But the consumers will not all agree, nor any great number of them, to do this, and therefore the gas companies are unable to make such startling reductions as above suggested. When the writer first embarked in the gas business, his employers were selling gas at $4 per 1,000 feet and were unable to make a greater profit than was then considered a fair return on the investment.

The consumers, of course, thought the price too high (as they always do), but we said to them that if more people would burn gas, and all who did burn it would do so to the exclusion of other modes of lighting, we would sell the gas cheaper.

Most of you have probably used the same argument, and also received about the same answer, viz: " If the gas company would reduce its price, we would burn more gas and many more would use it." In this the consumers were right (as they sometimes are). Twenty years later we find ourselves using the same argument and receiving the same answer respecting the sale and use of fuel gas. But the gas fraternity will profit by the twenty years and more of experience, and you will, if I mistake not, soon find gas companies launching out into the business of manufacturing fuel gas that will be sold at prices ranging from twenty-five to forty cents per 1,000 feet.

Do not understand that I believe that illuminating gas can soon be sold even at the maximum price named; but a gas that will meet the requirements of a fuel gas will be sold much below the maximum figure.

Good illuminating gas has been sold on some streets in a neighboring city, at so low a figure as thirty-five cents per 1,000 feet, and I believe the gas has not been extensively used for fuel, other than for culinary purposes; but this fact is doubtless due to a conviction in the minds of the people that the low prices were but temporary, and liable to be terminated any day.

Good illuminating gas, of whatever make, would be as cheap a fuel at $1 per 1,000 feet as would uncarburretted water gas at fifty cents per 1,000 feet. Yet, it is quite probable that if the public could have immunity from danger, real or fancied, they would take much more readily to the use of the latter than to that of the former; such would be the magic effect of a low price.

The relative calorific value of the various gases now in use for heating and for illumination have been frequently published, yet, in the discussion of this subject we cannot well avoid a reproduction of some of the figures.

Notwithstanding the fact that tables of this character have been so often published, we are all more or less confused occasionally by seeing statements made that make the comparison totally different from our preconceived ideas as to their relative calorific values.

This confusion occurs from the fact at one time we see the comparison of the gases made by weight, and at another time the comparison is made by volume. We present here the comparison made both by weight and by volume, and shall use natural gas as the unit of value in both comparisons:

TABLE I.—RELATIVE VALUES.

	By Weight.	By Volume.
Natural gas	1000	1000
Coal gas	949	666
Water gas	292	292
Producer gas	76.5	130

The water gas rated in the above table—as you will understand—is the gas obtained in the decomposition of steam by incandescent carbon, and does not attempt to fix the calorific value of illuminating water gas, which may be carburetted so as to exceed, when compared by volume, the value of coal gas.

You will observe in the table of values given above that one pound of coal gas is almost equal to a pound of natural gas, while 1,000 feet of coal gas has but two-thirds the value of a like quantity of natural gas. The relative values of water gas and natural gas are the same, whether compared by weight or volume. This is due to the fact that they possess the same specific gravity.

TABLE II.—COMPOSITION OF GASES.

VOLUME.

	Natural Gas.	Coal Gas.	Water Gas.	Producer Gas.
Hydrogen...............	2.18	46 00	45.00	6.00
Marsh gas...........	92 60	40.00	2.00	3.00
Carbonic oxide..........	0.50	6.00	45.00	23.50
Olefiant gas.............	0.31	4.00	0.00	0.00
Carbonic acid...........	0.26	0.50	4.00	1.50
Nitrogen.	3.61	1.50	2.00	65.00
Oxygen..................	0.34	0.50	0.50	0.00
Water vapor..............	0.00	1.50	1.50	1.00
Sulphydric acid..........	0.20	—	—	—
	100.00	100.00	100.00	100.00

TABLE III.—COMPOSITION OF GASES.

WEIGHT.

	Natural Gas.	Coal Gas.	Water Gas.	Producer Gas.
Hydrogen...............	0.268	8.21	5.431	0.458
Marsh gas...............	90.383	57.20	1.931	1.831
Carbonic oxide...........	0.857	15.02	76.041	25.095
Olefiant gas.............	0.531	10.01	0.000	0.000
Carbonic acid............	0.700	1.97	10.622	2.517
Nitrogen................	6.178	3.75	3.380	69.413
Oxygen..................	0.666	1.43	0.965	0.000
Water vapor.............	0.000	2.41	1.630	0.686
Sulphydric acid..........	0.417	—	—	—
	100.000	100.00	100.000	100.000

Some explanations of these analyses are necessary. The natural gas is that of Findlay, O. The coal gas is probably an average sample of coal gas, purified for use as an illuminant. The water gas is that of a sample of gas made for heating, and consequently not purified, hence the larger per cent. of CO_2 that it contains.

Since calculating the tables used in this paper, I am satisfied that the sample of water gas is not an average one. The CO is too high and H is too low. Were proper corrections made in this respect, it would increase the value in heat units of a pound, but not materially change the value when volume is considered, and as that is the way in which gases are sold, the tables will not be recalculated.

The producer gas is that of an average sample of the Pennsylvania Steel Works, made from anthracite, and is not of so high grade as would be that made from soft coal.

The natural gas excels, as shown in Table I, because of the large per cent. of marsh gas. In no other form, in the gases mentioned, do we get so much hydrogen in a given volume of gas.

It is the large per cent. of hydrogen in the coal gas that makes it so nearly equivalent to the natural gas in a given weight, but much of the hydrogen in coal gas, being free, makes it fall short of natural gas in calorific value per unit of volume.

Water gas is composed, as you know, chiefly of carbonic oxide and hydrogen, both good heating gases, but nearly all the hydrogen being free, makes the actual weight of hydrogen in a given volume, far below that of natural gas, and again you will notice by the analyses given, that three-quarters of the weight of water gas is CO, and of this compound four-sevenths is oxygen, which possesses no calorific value; in other words, more than forty per cent. of the weight of uncarburetted water gas, even when free from CO_2, and nitrogen fails to add anything to the value of the gas as a heat producer.

The producer gas, of which an analysis is given above, does not possess as high calorific value as it would if made from soft coal, but a greater volume can be made from a ton of anthracite or hard coke than can be made from a like quantity of bituminous coal.

A further comparison of the value of the several gases named may be made by showing the quantity of water that would be evaporated by 1,000 feet of each kind of gas, allowing an excess of twenty per cent. of air, and permitting the resultant gases to escape at a temperature of 500°. This sort of comparison, probably, has more practical value than either of the others that have been previously given. We will assume that the air for combustion is entering at a temperature of 60°.

TABLE IV.—WATER EVAPORATION.

	Natural Gas.	Coal Gas.	Water Gas.	Producer Gas.
Cubic feet gas...............	1,000	1,000	1,000	1,000
Pounds water..............	893	591	262	115

The theoretical temperature that may be produced by these several gases does not differ greatly as between the first three named. The producer gas falls about twenty-five per cent. below the others, giving a temperature of only 3,441° F.

Water gas leads in this respect, with a temperature of 4,850°. A formula for calculating the temperature theoretically obtained may be as follows:

$$T = \frac{U+H}{W\,S} \text{ where}$$

$T=$ Temperature obtained.
$U=$ Units of heat from combustion.
$H=$ Heat units carried in by air.
$W=$ Weight of resultant gases.
$S=$ Specific heat of resultant gases.

A comparison of the resultant products of combustion also shows water gas to possess merit over either natural or coal gas, when the combustion of equal quantities—say 1,000 feet—is considered. An excess of twenty per cent. of air is calculated in the following table:

TABLE V.—Resultant Gases of Combustion.

Quantity—1,000 feet.	Natural Gas.	Coal Gas.	Water Gas.	Producer Gas.
Weight of gas before combustion, lbs	45.60	32.00	45.60	77.50
Steam	94.25	69.718	25.104	6.921
Carbonic acid	119.59	68.586	61.754	36.456
Sulphuric acid	00.36	—	—	—
Nitrogen	664.96	427.222	170.958	126.568
Total weight after combustion	879.16	565.526	257.816	169.945
Pounds oxygen for combination	167.462	107.961	43.149	19.677

While the combustion of 1,000 feet of natural gas vitiates the atmosphere when consumed under the conditions named, more than five times as much as does the combustion of 1,000 feet of producer gas, yet for the work performed the former vitiates the atmosphere less than does the latter gas.

You will observe, by the following table, that, with the exception of producer gas, each kind gives off nearly one pound of waste gases for each pound of water evaporated. This quantity includes twenty per cent. excess of air.

TABLE VI.—Weights of Water Evaporated and of Resultant Gases.

	Natural Gas.	Coal Gas.	Water Gas.	Producer Gas.
Weight of water evaporated	893.25	591.	262.	115.1
Weight of gases after combustion	879.16	565.526	257.816	169.945

The vitiation of the atmosphere per unit of value in water evaporation is practically the same in water gas as in natural gas.

Coal gas shows about three per cent. better than either of the two gases named, in this respect, and about fifty per cent. better than producer gas.

In the above comparisons, all of the resulting products of combustion, including excess of oxygen, are regarded as being of a deleterious character, tending to vitiate the atmosphere.

However, the excess of oxygen does no harm, and the steam and nitrogen cannot be regarded as very objectionable products. The gas that robs the air permanently of the most oxygen, and produces the greatest quantity of carbonic acid per unit of work, must be classed as the most objectionable from a sanitary standpoint.

TABLE VII.—Oxygen Absorbed and Carbonic Acid Produced.

In Combustion.	Natural Gas.	Coal Gas.	Water Gas.	Producer Gas.
Pounds of oxygen absorbed per 100 lbs. water evaporated	18.75	18.27	16.47	17.96
Pounds of CO_2 produced per 100 lbs. water evaporated	13.40	11.60	23.57	31.70
Oxygen absorbed plus CO_2 produced	32.15	29.87	40.04	49.66

Here, then, it is shown that if pollution by carbonic acid and impoverishment by the absorption of oxygen are equally deleterious to the atmosphere, coal gas stands at the head as being the least objectionable.

It will be conceded that the gas that gives the greatest number of heat units for a given volume, with the least weight of resultant gases of combustion, must possess the greatest value for all ordinary purposes of heating. Notwithstanding this fact, there are purposes for which gas is used where this rule would not apply. For instance : Natural gas is not so desirable for gas engines as is coal gas, chiefly because the flame that lights the explosive mixture is too easily extinguished ; again, the explosive mixture will not ignite so readily when natural gas is used as it will when coal gas or water gas is used.

For metallurgical purposes, the producer gas has one advantage over all other gases in this—that it contains less hydrogen in any and every form than either of the others, and where metal, and especially iron or steel, is to be heated to very high temperatures by direct contact, it is questionable if anything like the full value of the hydrogen is utilized, unless it be combined with oxygen in recuperators and the heat returned in the air used for secondary combustion. While this advantage does not bring producer gas nearly up to the value of any of the other gases, yet it does bring its value nearer to the others than appears from a theoretical calculation.

The producer gas, on the other hand, possesses a disadvantage in connection with metallurgical work, in this, that the resultant gases having to pass off at high temperatures, and the weight of these per unit of work being so much greater than that of the other gases, more heat units will thus be wasted.

This disadvantage, however, will not be very great where recuperators are employed, nor will it be great when the gas is used for raising steam, or for culinary purposes, or for any purpose which permits the waste gas to finally escape at a low degree of temperature.

In the utilization of coal gas for fuel we do not obtain, even theoretically, but little more than twenty-five per cent. of the energy of the coal from which the gas was made; but this is not a fair way to put it, because we have in the coal gas manufacture the valuable residuals, coke, tar and ammonia.

It will only be convenient to compare the processes for the manufacture of two of the gases, water gas and producer gas, and ascertain in which the greater loss of energy is sustained.

In making these comparisons, we must accept data obtained from practice rather than what might be deduced by theoretical calculation. It would be difficult to calculate what quantity of energy would be wasted in blowing up a heat in a water-gas apparatus.

We might tell how much heat would be lost in the generation of the steam required, if we knew exactly how much of the steam was decomposed. But upon this point there is a great diversity of opinion, some claiming that ninety per cent. is decomposed, while others claim that not more than twenty-five to forty per cent. is utilized in the cupolas.

The net results obtained from fuel by the many different works using water-gas apparatus vary greatly, doubtless because of the varied conditions under which they are operated. In some works the cupola may run almost constantly, and there the minimum quantity of hard fuel will be required. In smaller works the cupolas will be idle half the time, and there the maximum quantity will be used.

After consultation with a number of the best authorities, and with those of the largest experience, I conclude that about thirty-five pounds of hard coal or coke is required in the generation of 1,000 feet of water gas for illumination purposes.

But only about two-thirds, or 667 feet, of this is made from the coal and steam, the other third coming from the oil used for enriching. If this be true, then, on that basis, it would require fifty-two pounds of coke or hard coal to produce 1,000 feet of water gas without the aid of oil.

That, however, is an unfair way to rate it. A large quantity of fuel must be used to vaporize and fix the oil gas, and where oil is not used, this fuel may be converted into gas. Here, then, I think we may cut down the fuel required per 1,000 feet from fifty-two to forty-two pounds.

The most accurate trial of which I have obtained a record shows on a month's run an average of about 8.75 pounds coke required for the generation of steam for each 1,000 feet of gas made, and this when using oil. It will, of course, take more steam when oil is not used. We will increase the steam fuel then from 8.75 to ten pounds, giving total required fifty-two pounds. But if gas is being made for fuel purposes, it is probable that the apparatus would be operated more nearly continuously than it would be in making illuminating gas, and this would tend to a reduction of fuel requirements. We may safely say, then, that not more than fifty pounds of coal or coke would be required in the production of 1,000 feet of fuel water gas. The energy of one pound of hard coal or coke ought to equal 13,000 heat units, but we will rate it at 12,500 units; then 12,500 multiplied by fifty pounds equal 625,000 units, which represents the energy expended in the production of 1,000 feet of water gas; we obtain from, or by the combustion of the gas, but 322,346 units.

In the production of producer gas, we need not be at a loss as to the energy required to be expended, as it is represented simply by the difference between the energy of the coal used and of the gas produced, the coal in the producer furnishing its own heat.

There will be about 5.85 pounds of gas made for each pound of hard coal or coke charged if no steam is used, which is seldom the case, the weight decreasing with the increased use of steam.

If 5.85 pounds of gas are made for each pound of fuel charged, then there will be 13.25 pounds fuel used for each 1,000 feet of gas made. This is equal to about 150,000 feet per ton of 2,000 pounds.

The heat generated in the manufacture of this producer gas would much more than be sufficient to generate the steam that could be advantageously used in blowing air into the producers, so that no fuel is lost there.

Then we have the quantity of gas made in each instance from a ton of coal as follows:

TABLE VIII.—FROM 2,000 POUNDS COAL.

	Water Gas, feet.	Producer Gas, feet.
Quantity	40,000	150,000
Heat units	12,893,840	17,468,975
Per cent. of the total value of coal,	51.9	68.8

In determining the quantity and value of producer gas, I have assumed that in a ton, or 2,000 pounds, of hard coal there are 1,750 pounds carbon, the calorific value of which would be 25,375,000 units. Now, if we convert this carbon to CO, there must be a loss of $1,750 \times 4,325$, or 7,568,750 units, and this deducted from 25,375,000, leaves 17,806,250 units, instead of 17,468,975 units, as given in table above. This difference is due to using 4,325 as the figures that represent the units of heat produced by burning one pound of carbon to CO, and also for representing the heat units generated in burning a pound of CO to carbonic acid.

In calculating the energy derived from the coal used in the producer furnace, we have assumed that the carbon consumed was converted to CO by oxygen from air, and that there was no hydrogen present. This is never the case, however, as there is always some hydrogen in the coal, and some moisture both in the coal and in the air admitted. The hydrogen thus admitted from these sources, as well as that blown in if a steam jet is used, tends to decrease the quantity of gas produced, and to increase the calorific value of a unit of weight, but does not materially change the theoretic value of the total product.

The quantity is decreased in the use of steam by diminishing the quantity of nitrogen that would otherwise be admitted with the oxygen of the air.

If the producer gas is made without the introduction of steam or hydrogen in any form, it will have a value of but 117,315 units per 1,000 feet, instead of 143,375, the value given to the gas of which the composition is shown in Tables II. and III.

Natural gas cannot be had for general use; coal gas is too expensive; uncarburetted water gas is expensive, and a prejudice exists against its use; producer gas, while it can be very cheaply made, is bulky, and requires a high temperature for ignition. None of these several gases, taken alone, seem to meet the requirements of a good and cheap fuel gas.

That a cheap fuel gas is in demand, is a fact that will not be questioned, and that this demand can and must be met, we all believe.

How, then, shall the gas be supplied so as to make its use the most effective, the safest and the most popular, and at the same time with the least expenditure of capital on the part of the existing gas companies is, to my mind, the problem to be solved.

In order to use plants now erected, and to give heating power as well as to impart odor to the product, I would make part coal gas; in order to work up the coke from coal gas benches, and greatly cheapen the final product, I would make part producer gas; and in order to keep up the calorific value of the gas, which would be too low if all the coke from coal gas was converted into producer gas, I would make part water gas.

I would so proportion these several kinds of manufactured gas that the final product would have about the calorific value of water gas. I would do this, not specially because it would be more advantageous to the consumer to pay forty cents for gas that contains 350,000 units of heat, than it would to pay eighty cents for gas that contains 700,000 units. Neither would I supply that character of gas wholly because it would cost less per unit of heat to the manufacturer of the gas — but chiefly because the less the price is per 1,000 feet — *the price per unit of heat being the same in each instance*—the more gas will be sold.

If it be a fact that fuel gas must be sold at a low price to induce the public to generally adopt gas for heating and cooking, in lieu of solid fuel—without much reference to comparative values, then it appears to me that uncarburetted water gas is about the only product now being offered to the public with any reasonable prospects of being received with favor.

Now, if we can by a mixture of these several gases, obtain a product of equal value with water gas as a heat producer, at a less cost, we will be taking a step forward. Let us, then, base our estimates on what may be obtained from one ton (2,000 pounds) of bituminous coal, equal in quality to that obtained in the Youghiogheny coal field of Pennsylvania, one pound of which has a calorific value of, say, 13,500 units.

This ton of coal would produce 10,000 feet of gas, 1,300 pounds of coke, 120 pounds of tar, 120 pounds ammoniacal liquor, leaving 110 pounds to cover loss of manipulation. The tar may be converted into 500 feet of gas, leaving 100 pounds residual (of which no further notice is taken), making the total quantity 10,500 feet. The tar at present could be sold with greater profit as tar, but should the manufacture of gas fuel become general, the market for tar would soon become over-supplied. Of the 1,300 pounds coke, about 300 pounds would be used in heating coal-gas retorts. It can easily be shown that the waste heat of the gases from the coal-gas furnaces, together with the heat of the gas from the producer, will be much more than sufficient to raise the steam required for the production of the proportion of water gas that is to be made, and still let the furnace gases escape to tall stacks at a temperature in excess of 500°.

The water gas and producer cupolas should be so located that the hot coke could be dumped (if not drawn) into them from the retorts. In this way, we would introduce heat with the coke from each ton of coal more than equal to that required for the production of 1,000 feet of water gas.

There can be no reasonable doubt, I think, of the possibility of making water gas in this way with very much less expenditure of fuel than is now required. But to be safe, we shall only estimate the production at the rate of 50,000 feet from 2,000 pounds of fuel.

We will introduce 500 pounds of the coke into the water gas cupola and the remaining 500 pounds into the producer furnace.

From the water gas apparatus we will obtain 12,500 feet of gas, and from the producer 36,800 feet. These quantities added to the 10,500 feet of coal gas, makes a total of 59,800 feet, with a calorific value of 17,160,258 units, which equal 63.5 per cent. of the energy of the coal. Considering the character of the gas, the quantity produced by 2,000 pounds of fuel seems small.

It may be well to notice how the quantities of water gas and producer gas were or could be obtained.

In putting 500 pounds of coke hot from gas retorts into cupolas, we will introduce about 220,000 heat units; thus: 500 × 2,000 × .22 = 220,000. Having the benefit of this heat and not requiring any of the solid fuel to be used in the generation of steam for water gas, our estimate of 25 feet to the pound will not be excessive; 25 × 500 = 12,500 feet water gas.

We will go more into detail respecting the production of producer gas, as, perhaps, all of you are not so familiar with its manufacture.

In the 500 pounds of coke to be used, we will have 440 pounds of carbon. By reason of imperfect working of the furnace, we must assume that we will get some carbonic acid.

This gas is generally made in the producer when there is an excess of steam, low heats, or by the gases escaping through channels in the fuel. We will assume, therefore, that forty pounds of the carbon is converted to carbonic acid. This gives a little larger per cent. than is previously shown by analysis.

This leaves 400 pounds carbon of the 500 pounds coke introduced. Of this quantity we will use 133.3 pounds in the decomposition of 200 pounds of steam into H and CO, and the remaining 266.7 pounds carbon will be converted to CO by oxygen from the air. In this manipulation we have a heat production as follows:

From hot coke 500 pounds×2,000×.22   220,000
  "   40 pounds carbon (to CO_2) ×14,500   580,000
  "   400 "   "   (to CO) ×4,325 1,730,000
                                                              ─── ───
       Total heat units. 2,530,000

This takes no note of heat carried in by steam.
Heat expenditure will be about as follows:

By radiation and convection.............   253,000
In the decomposition of 200 pounds
of steam (=22.22 pounds hydrogen
×62,000 =)   1,377,640
Absorbed by heating from 250°, to 1,250°,
50 pounds steam that will probably escape decomposition 50×1,000×.475=   23,750

Total heat units expended.........   1,654,390

Units of heat remaining............   875,610

With this quantity of heat will we have sufficient intensity for
the decomposition of steam? Experience says yes, but to
determine this theoretically, we must first ascertain the composition and the specific heat of the mixture.

TABLE IX.—Specific Heat of Gases.

Carbonic acid................ ....   146.67 × .2164= 37.74
Carbonic oxide. ....   933.34 × .248 = 231.47
Nitrogen..........................   1,525.35 × .244 = 372.18
Hydrogen ....   22.22 × 3.400 = 75.55

2,627.58   716.94

$$\frac{716.94}{2,627.58} = .273, \text{ or the average specific heat.}$$

Then, $$\frac{8,756.10}{2,627.58} \times .273 = 1,221° \text{ of temperature.}$$

With free escape from the producer it is not probable that the
gases would take up the temperature of the fuel. Experience
has shown that the gases escape at a temperature of 750° to
900°. If the gases shall escape at a temperature of 1,000°, then
an equal weight of the fuel would be increased, thus:

$$\frac{221 \times .273}{.220} = 274°,$$

and this, added to the 1,221°, would give the temperature
of 1,495°.

The gas made in the producer would be about as follows:

TABLE X.—COMPOSITION, QUANTITY AND VALUE OF PRO-
DUCER GAS.

Gas.	Weight.	Cubic Feet.	Units.
CO	933.34	12,000	4,036,695
H	22.22	4,000	1,377,640
CO$_2$	146.67	1,200	—
N	1,525.35	19,600	—
	2,627.58	36,800	5,414,335

Then we have the mixture of the three products in the proportions given below:

TABLE XI.—COMPOSITION, QUANTITY AND VALUE OF
MIXED GAS.

Product.	Quantity, feet.		Value per 1,000 feet.		Total Units.
Coal Gas	10,500	×	734,976	=	7,717,248
Water Gas	12,500	×	322,346	=	4,029,325
Producer Gas	36,800	×	147,175	=	5,416,027
	59,800	×	287,000	=	17,162,600

It thus appears, then, that 1,000 feet of this mixture has but eighty-nine per cent. of the value of water gas, thus:

$$\frac{287,000}{322,346} = .89.$$

The heat units per 1,000 feet can only be increased at the expense of reduction in total quantity. The results obtained are not so good as we ought to have. What part of the process has failed to do good work? Let us see.

With 16.8 per cent. of the weight of coal in the coal gas, it gives 28.58 per cent. of the total heat units possible from the coal; with twenty-five per cent. of the weight of coal used in the production of the producer gas, it gives twenty per cent. of the energy of the coal; with twenty-five per cent of the weight of the coal used in the production of the water gas, it gives but 14.92 per cent. of the energy of the coal in heat units. Here, then, it is clearly shown that the fault lies in the low results, obtained from the fuel converted into water gas.

I believe that 25 feet is about all that will, in practice, be obtained from a pound of coke or hard coal, with generators as now constructed, but we ought to get better results. Notwithstanding the fact that the water gas gives us poorer net results than either of the other processes, if we are to increase the calorific value of the mixed gas, it must be done by decreasing the producer and increasing the proportion of the water gas product.

We will note what the result would have been had the ton of coal been differently treated.

Had all the carbon of the surplus coke from the ton of coal been treated in water-gas apparatus, the quantity would then have been 10,500 feet coal gas plus 20,000 feet water gas, or a total of 30,500 feet, with a total calorific value of 14,164,168 units, which would equal but 52.46 per cent. of the energy of the coal.

In practice, then, the results obtained are about as follows :

From a ton of hard coal in water-gas apparatus, we get 40,000 feet and 51.9 per cent. of energy.

From same quantity of hard coal in producer furnace, we get 150,000 feet and 68.8 per cent. of energy.

From ton of gas coal, when all the surplus coke is treated in water gas apparatus, we get 30,500 feet and 52.46 per cent. of energy.

From same quantity of soft coal, with half of surplus coke converted to water gas and half to producer gas, we obtain 59,800 feet of gas and 63.5 per cent.

From a ton of gas coal converting all the surplus coke to producer gas, we will obtain 84,500 feet of gas, and 64.98 per cent. of the energy of the coal. Producer gas alone cannot be used for domestic purposes, nor do I think it would be safe to use so large a per cent. of producer gas as can be made from the surplus coke of a ton of gas coal. It would not easily ignite, and, under certain conditions, might become extinguished without having the supply cut off, and it would therefore be dangerous to use so large a per cent. of it.

Now, had the ton of soft coal been converted directly into water gas, making permanent gas out of the volatile hydrocarbons, we possibly would have obtained as large a per cent. of the value of the coal as would be obtained by first retorting the coal, though this may be questioned; but in passing the volatile hydrocarbons down through incandescent coke in the presence of steam, we would in a large measure, if not entirely, break up the compounds of the olefiant gas series, to which the odor of coal gas is so largely due, and would also form compounds of less calorific intensity; that is, the carbon would be largely taken from the hydrocarbon compounds and converted into carbonic oxide.

To give the mixed product as high value in heat units per 1,000 feet as water gas contains, we must change the proportions somewhat, and use 667 pounds of the coke in water-gas apparatus, and but 333 pounds of the coke in the producer furnace.

Then we will have the proportions and values shown in following table:

TABLE XII.—Mixed Gas.

Product.	Quantity, feet.	Value per 1,000 feet.	Total Units.
Coal Gas	10,500	734,976	7,717,248
Water Gas	16,600	322,346	5,350,944
Producer Gas	24,500	147,084	3,603,558
	51,600	323,096	16,671,750

The flame temperature of the mixed gas will equal about 4,000° F., and in percentages the mixture will contain coal gas 20.35, water gas 32.17, and producer gas 47.48 per cent.

By thus changing the proportions, we reduce the total quantity in feet by 8,200, and total heat units by 490,850, but the mixture has been increased in value from 287,000 to 323,096 units per 1,000 feet, or to a value that is a fraction better than water gas, while the quantity of gas is twenty-nine per cent. more than we have estimated that 2,000 pounds hard coal or coke would produce of water gas alone.

Having now ascertained the quantity of gas that can be produced from a ton of gas coal, and of a quality that we believe will be desirable, it is necessary to know the cost of the same:

TABLE XIII.—Estimated Cost in Holder.

	Coal Gas. Cents.	Water Gas. Cents.	Producer Gas. Cents.
Labor............................	12	5.5	1.
Repairs and Incidentals........	3	1.5	.25
	15	7.	1.25

Coal Gas....................	10,500 × 15. cents =	$1.57.5
Water Gas...................	16,600 × 7. " =	1.16.2
Producer Gas................	24,500 × 1.25 " =	30.6
	51,600	$3.04.3

$$\frac{3.04.3}{51,600} = 5.897,$$ or about six cents per 1,000 feet. If the coal costs $2 per net ton, this item of fuel will add 3.88 cents, and if it costs $3 it will add 5.81 cents, and if coal costs $4 per net ton, it will add 7.71 cents, making gas cost per 1,000 feet in holder, 9.78 cents, 11.71 cents and 13.61 cents, respectively.

Do these prices appear very low? They are not only obtainable, but I believe even better results may be had. I may add that the wages item is intended to cover superintendence.

Here we may note some features that to my mind are interesting: That is, the cost of various gases per 1,000,000 units of heat of which they are theoretically capable of producing.

In working out these figures, I put wages, repairs and incidentals as given in last table, and the cost of a ton of good gas coal at $3, and a ton of hard coal or coke at same price, and the quantities of production as follows: Coal gas from soft coal, 10,000 feet; water gas from hard coal, 40,000 feet, and producer gas, 150,000 feet.

TABLE XIV.—Cost per 1,000,000 Units of Heat.

Coal Gas..........	734,976 units, at 27.5 cents =	37.42 cents.
Water Gas.........	322,346 "	14.5 "	= 44.95 "
Producer Gas......	117,000 "	3.25 "	= 27.78 "
Our mixture	323,096 "	11.71 "	= 36.24 "

Thus will it be seen that after all coal gas costs but 3.26 per cent. more per unit of heat than the mixture that we have worked out, while water gas, per unit of heat, costs 24 per cent. more than the mixed product.

In arriving at these ratios of cost, I speak from knowledge respecting cost of coal gas, and from the testimony of the producers of water gas respecting that product.

If 2,000 pounds good hard coal or coke can be made to generate the necessary steam and produce 50,000 feet of gas, then upon that basis, the cost per 1,000,000 units will be 40.33 cents, or 11.3 per cent. more than that from the mixture.*

The mixed gases would have the following composition :

TABLE XV.—ANALYSIS FOR FUEL GAS.

	Per cent.
Hydrogen	29.00
Marsh gas	8.78
Carbonic oxide	31.18
Olefiant gas	0.81
Carbonic acid	2.94
Nitrogen	26.24
Oxygen	0.26
Water vapor	0.79
	100.00

The specific gravity is .683, and 1,000 feet will weigh about 54.6.

Gas of this gravity will require greater pressure to force it through pipes of given diameter than would be required for either coal gas or water gas.

If 2 inches water column pressure is required for the delivery of a definite quantity of coal gas, then 2.4 inches would be required for water gas, and 2.6 inches would be required with the fuel gas for the delivery of equal quantities through same length and diameter of pipe.

Having decided on the kind of gas that will be the most satis-

---

* In the paper as originally read, there were two errors made. The first was in the cost of the mixed gas per 1,000 cubic feet, and the second was in the cost of water gas per 1,000,000 heat units. In this corrected copy I have worked out the comparative values from the *average* price of coal ($3), instead of from the *lowest* price ($2). With the addition of $1 per ton to the cost of coal we add 10 cents to cost of coal gas, as the same *quantity* of residuals will be sold in each instance; but, assuming that the residuals will be worth more where the coal sells for $3 than where the coal sells for $2, I have added but 7.5 cents, instead of 10 cents, to the estimated cost of coal gas.

factory, all things considered, and also determined the cost per 1,000 feet for manufacture, it remains now for us to find a market.

In a city of 100,000 inhabitants, there will be used for fuel, other than for manufacturing, not less than 200,000 tons of coal per year.

Gas mains will ordinarily pass the localities where three-fourths of the total quantity of coal would be consumed; but to be within bounds, we will assume that we can, without more miles of mains than are now in use, substitute with gas fuel one-half, or 100,000 tons of the coal. What quantity of gas will be required to make this substitution? It will require 80,000 feet of our gas to equal in theoretical value one ton (2,000 pounds) of coal. But it is well known to all that not ten per cent., if indeed five per cent. of the theoretical value of coal is utilized in domestic heating.

We will be very liberal, and base our calculations on the larger utilization. This, then, brings the coal down to the value of 8,000 feet of gas, provided the full value of the gas can be obtained in practice. But this cannot be done.

With proper facilities, seventy-five per cent. of its value might be utilized, but we will put it at only fifty per cent. Then we have 16,000 feet of gas as the equivalent in practice to 2,000 pounds of coal.

We will assume the price of coal at $3. This price, divided by 16, gives a value to the gas of 18.75 cents per 1,000 feet.

We may, I think, safely add 6.25 cents to that price for the saving in kindling, handling of ashes and general cleanliness, making value of gas twenty-five cents per 1,000 feet.

If it requires 16,000 feet of gas to substitute one ton of coal, it will require 1,600,000,000 feet to substitute 100,000 tons of coal. This will require a daily production of about 4,400,000 feet, varying in quantity probably from 3,000,000 feet minimum in summer to 7,000,000 maximum in winter. The capital required would be very much less per 1,000 feet output than is required in the manufacture of illuminating gas. The distributing portion of the plant would not cost more than one-third, and the manufacturing part not more than one-fourth that required for a coal gas illuminating plant.

Upon this basis an investment of $2,000,000 should be sufficient. If the gas costs, including repairs, twelve cents in holder, it will cost when sold and collections made, seventeen cents per 1,000 feet. Then selling 1,600,000,000 feet at a profit of eight cents, net $128,000.

Six per cent. on estimated investment equals $120,000. Thus it will be seen that if you want ten per cent. on your investment, you will have to sell gas at about thirty cents per 1,000 feet.*

You will observe that in the estimate of cost of coal, that each dollar of the price per ton equals two cents per 1,000 feet on the cost of gas. Therefore, to arrive at the cost of gas in localities where coal is above or below $3 per net ton, additions or subtractions will be made to the estimated cost of ten cents per 1,000 feet, of one cent for each fifty cents variation in price of coal.

The margin for profit deducted is not large. However, it will be borne in mind that I gave a value to coal very much above actual results obtained, and placed the value of the gas below where all authorities put it.

By a proper adjustment of the values of the two fuels and by a close estimate on cost of plant a fair profit may be figured out.

How this gas shall be consumed is an important problem.

Of course the best way would be to use all the gas in stoves, the way in which that applied to cooking will be used. It will, however, not be possible to induce all the public to substitute stoves for grates. But grates can be filled with refractory material of good radiating power, and the flues above the grates can be closed so as to leave but a very small opening, say that of one or two inches area, which will be sufficient to carry off the products of combustion, and at the same time, confining, as it were, the hot gases, until the heat shall be imparted to the air and walls of the room.

The total quantity of heat required to be generated for heating a room in this manner will be almost insignificant, compared with that required to be generated when the flues have to be open to produce draft, and under which condition there is probably forty to fifty tons of heated air carried up the chimney for

* In the paper as originally read and printed the cost of gas was put lower, the coal being estimated at $2 per ton. It is now put at $3. The plant was then estimated at what now seems too high a figure.

every ton of coal consumed. The expense that would be incurred in preparing an ordinary grate for the economical use of gas would be very small.

Fewer hot-air furnaces and fewer steam and hot water radiators would be used were gaseous firing in general use. But the gas could be adapted to these systems very readily, by reducing the exit flues and filling furnace boxes with refractory material.

If we are to use our present plants for the manufacture and distribution of fuel gas, then what is to become of the present lighting system?

There are two substitutes. First there are two or three devices for incandescent gas lighting now struggling for recognition. It has not been the good fortune of the writer to see but one of these in use, and it did not impress him favorably, still, it certainly gives more promise of future usefulness than did the incandescent electric light ten years ago. Should there be an incandescent gas burner invented, or improved, and made a success, then, of course, the problem would be solved.

Again, it is proposed to substitute incandescent electric lights for the gas. There is nothing impracticable in this, if you can satisfy the consumer that it is to his interest to make the change.

During the period of transition from gas to electric lighting, one holder may be used for fuel gas; the gas from this to be led to a square or block already provided with incandescent lights.

Here the gas main can be cut off from illuminating gas mains and attached to the fuel gas supply. Then the next square can be treated in the same way, until the entire system is changed without inconvenience to consumers. If it shall be found that there are districts supplied with gas, which from any cause it would not pay to supply with electric lights, those districts could still be supplied with illuminating gas with but slight changes in the distributing lines.

Whether electric lighting has made such advancements as to warrant such substitution, is a question that must be decided by others. However, from the hundreds of thousands of incandescent burners that we now know are in use, we may be justified in asserting that the change is not impracticable.

But that either the incandescent gas burner or the incandescent electric burner should be substituted for gas light, is not absolutely essential to the manufacture, sale and use of fuel gas.

Gas companies can and ought to manufacture fuel gas, even if, in doing so, it becomes necessary to duplicate their present lines.

The demand for fuel gas, like the demand for electric light, has come to stay. It will not down. Scientific investigators, as well as the public, insist that there ought to be, and must be, a change in the mode of domestic and industrial heating. Our present systems are not in keeping with the progress of the nineteenth century.

In consideration of the powers, rights and franchises conferred on corporate gas companies by the public, these companies should endeavor, even at some financial risk, to solve the problem.

But, aside from any moral obligation, as a matter of policy, the gas companies should lead off in these investigations. If they do not do it, we will, before long, find other companies asking for franchises and the right to tear up the streets. These companies will lack the experience now possessed by the old gas companies, and must work with less probability that success will crown their efforts.

Let the policy and practice of gas companies be such as shall discourage the duplication of capital. Where one capital can do the business, it is almost criminal to permit two to be invested.

DISCUSSION.

Mr. A. C. HUMPHREYS—Quite likely it is apparent to all of us that it is almost impossible to discuss such a paper as this without having the paper before us. I think that fact alone should force upon us at this meeting the necessity of having the papers recommended by the Executive Committee printed at least two weeks ahead of the meeting of the Association, so they may be sent in advance to the members for their study, to the end that we may be prepared to discuss them properly. Such is the practice in some of the engineering societies in this country, and I do not think we should be behind. I think every member of the Association who listened to this paper will feel that a vote of thanks will not repay Mr. McMillin's efforts. We ought individually to feel grateful to him for such a presentment of the subject, for I think it is the most important subject we have before us at this meeting. The questions of fuel gas and incandescent lighting run right together. We have heard in the address by the President, as well as in some references by Mr. McMillin, something on the subject of incandescent lighting. Now, it is not my purpose to drag in any discussion on that point—in fact, as far as I am concerned, I would not be dragged into it; but, since the subject did come up, it is perhaps incumbent on me to say I know positively that the experiments given do not cover all the ground. In fact, referring to the most prominent burner before you—the Welsbach—I will say we at least are perfectly willing to leave that without discussion, for we know what will be the result. There are one or two questions I would like to ask, for the better clearing up of the subject. In the figures given as to the relative evaporative powers of the gases, were there any experiments made, or was the result simply determined from calculation?

Mr. McMillin—The figures are the result of both. I think recorded experiments, generally speaking, will verify the data upon all such questions. These theoretical values are obtained from experiments in the first place; and any experiments that I have ever known to be made have usually verified those as closely as it would be possible for crude apparatus to so do.

Mr. A. C. Humphreys—Of course I make that inquiry, as Mr. McMillin knows, because (especially in the case of water gas) the statement has been made by metallurgical men that the theoretical value could not be arrived at. Does or does not Mr. McMillin think that the 20 per cent. air dilution could be greatly improved upon by the aid of improved devices?

Mr. McMillin—It would not materially change it. I put it at figures which should not be excelled in any event. Certainly one ought not to use more than 20 per cent. I will say, however, that in the neighborhood of Pittsburg, although they use a great deal more than that, there is no necessity for it. But there is no object in economizing there, as they buy the gas for so much per ton of iron or steel.

Mr. A. C. Humphreys—You believe the methods now pursued in the consumption of natural gas are extremely crude?

Mr. McMillin—Yes.

Mr. A. C. Humphreys—In burning off the C after the CO—do you call that an entire loss? In other words, is there a partial combustion of coal in the generator?

Mr. McMillin—In calculating the value of it I take the gas after it leaves there, whatever that may be. If you were using that gas where you could utilize the heat generated at the time, you could then doubtless utilize a great deal of it, because you might get it in there at 500° or 600° of temperature. But if it must be cooled and put into holders, of course it would only have the value of CO afterward.

Mr. A. C. Humphreys—Then it is taken in the account that that partial combustion can be recovered to a greater or less extent?

Mr. McMillin—Yes.

Mr. A. C. Humphreys—With regard to the mixture of gas, I believe the final outcome will be that a mixture of coal gas with water gas will be made directly. In other words, we will be able to make water gas from soft coal. That there is a necessity for a gas other than what we now call non-luminous water gas, is very apparent. It would not be safe, in my opinion; and I would be unwilling to recommend the distribution of uncarburetted water gas, simply because we are unable to detect its presence. But I do not regard that as being at all out of the way. I do not think we should be discouraged in that direction, as we can easily impart an odor to the gas. I think it will be done by making water gas from soft coal—in other words, that there will be a union, finally, of the water and the coal gas men-

Mr. McMillin—I want to add I heartily agree with Mr. Humphreys upon that point. Notwithstanding the fact that, if done at all, certainly not until recently has water gas been successfully manufactured from soft coal, I feel sure that eventually not only the coal gas but water gas and producer gas will all be made in the same vessel. There, to my mind, would be the greatest economy in the manufacture of producer gas, because you can decompose enough steam by the heat which would otherwise be wasted in the production of producer gas to a very considerable extent. I believe I showed in my paper, by the burning of 133 pounds you can decompose 200 pounds of steam, and it is possible you might go still further. Certainly there is no other way in which you can so economically utilize the heat that is made in the producer, in the burning of air and carbon to CO, as in converting steam into water gas. The three gas mixtures will, I think, eventually be made in that way. I think that is what we will all have to come to. It is a little hard for us coal gas fellows to feel that after a while we will be making our coal gas in a water-gas apparatus; but still I think we will have to come to it.

Mr. Graeff—Do I understand you to say that water gas would be made from bituminous coal, or that it was being so made?

Mr. McMillin—I said it had not been successfully made—certainly not until recently. We hardly have time to investigate all the things as we go along. I believe Mr. Loomis has a process in use in Philadelphia, where he is using bituminous slack; and I have seen a notice to the effect that Prof. Lowe is lighting up Los Angeles, Cal., under a somewhat similar plan. These systems, of course, may not prove to be all that is desired; but it will come eventually, even if we have not got it now. There are several generators on the market, or struggling for recognition at the present time, with which it is proposed to use soft coal, right in the cupola. I can only wish them a hearty success.

The President—I entirely agree with Mr. Humphreys as to the value of the paper we have just had read. Certainly all these papers which carry statistics ought to be printed before the meetings of the Association, and I think it is well worthy the attention of the Executive Committee to see that hereafter this shall be done; but it would be pretty hard to require that they shall be sent two weeks in advance of the meeting of the Association, as most men who write papers find it impossible to prepare them until the last moment—or at any rate, which amounts to the same thing, they are apt to postpone their preparation until that time. I would like to say something in reply to what Mr. Humphreys said in regard to the suggestion of Mr. McMillin, as well as that made by myself, in the matter of incandescent gas burners. You will find, in reading what I have said, that I carefully qualified my remarks; and so has Mr. McMillin. I suggested that, in my opinion, incandescent gas burners, although not in every way desirable at the present time, still are shown to be much further advanced than were the electricians 15 years ago. As to the incandescent burners heretofore put upon the market in Europe, I will stand by my statement that they have not been the success which has been desired.

MR. KING—I would like to understand the basis of the heat units in the calculations made by Mr. McMillin.

MR. McMILLIN—I used the English unit, because I supposed most of our members were more familiar with it.

MR. LOWE—I had no intention of speaking of the Los Angeles matter. In fact, I do not think anything that has been in operation only a short time, like our method there, or that of the Loomis people, in Philadelphia, is worthy of discussion here, because these things are foreign to our subject. I want to ask Mr. McMillin as to the cost of gas in the holder, based on coal at $5 per ton. I have been unable to follow the tables given.

MR. McMILLIN—The tables show the cost, practically, to be ten cents with coal at $3. If you add one cent for each fifty cents increase in the cost of coal per ton, you can make the calculation.

MR. LOWE—That would make the cost of your gas 14 cents in the holder, as I understand you. This gas has a calorific value, then, of about what ordinary crude water gas has?

MR. McMILLIN—Yes.

MR. LOWE—Quite flattering to the water gas, at any rate. Then your gas consists of about one-fourth nitrogen. I think you stated it at 26 per cent.

MR. McMILLIN—Yes.

MR. LOWE—As matter of fact, then, your gas is considerably poorer than water gas, and lower in calorific value, inasmuch as you must heat up that nitrogen at the cost of combustion of your gas before you have the value of your combustion of gas.

MR. McMILLIN—You speak of calorific value ; I supposed you referred to the theoretic value. The available value is a matter that I called attention to in my paper.

MR. LOWE—That would be greater where your gases escape at a high temperature; and it would be smaller where they escape at a low temperature.

MR. McMILLIN—Yes.

MR. LOWE—But, as a matter of fact, you use more nitrogen to heat up that gas.

MR. McMILLIN—Yes.

MR. LOWE—Then your gas would not be as good as water gas. How could you——

MR. McMILLIN—Make your speech and then I will make mine.

MR. LOWE—You gave us 40,000 feet of gas per ton of coal as the fair output of water gas. Have you ever made fuel water gas ?

MR. McMILLIN—Not very extensively.

MR. LOWE—In Lynn, on the very small daily quantity of gas now being made there we get 60,000 feet of gas out of 2,240 pounds of coal. I am sure I can get as high as 80,000 feet from one ton of coal on a production of 500,000 feet of gas per day. Of course the cost of the gas depends to a great extent on the amount made. I do not know that your paper stated anything about the amounts of gas made in proportion to the cost of the gas ; but that has a great deal to do with the matter. I think, in the case of water gas, it has considerable more to do with it than in the case of the gas you mentioned, because we can, by increasing the size of our apparatus, get considerably more gas from it for the same labor than you can by increasing your retort system, inasmuch as when you increase your retort system you increase your labor account, which we do not do at all. I do not think, on the whole, that the gas is as good in any respect as uncarburetted water gas. You could not use your gas in a gas engine, as made to-day, nearly so well as we can, for the reason that one-quarter of the gas in the cylinder of the engine would be an incombustible mass. Therefore I doubt whether your gas would have much value for driving a gas engine.

Mr. McMILLIN—But it is driving more engines now than water gas is.

Mr. LOWE—We are only driving five in Lynn, but we are doing so quite satisfactorily. I think this gas you speak of is made by the proceess advocated by the Westinghouse people, of Pittsburg; is it not ?

Mr. McMILLIN—Not that I am aware of.

Mr. LOWE—I think I saw something of that kind stated in a paper which you had read before a geological society in Ohio, mentioned recently in a Philadelphia paper.

Mr. McMILLIN—That had a different composition.

Mr. LOWE—So far as I can judge, I do not see you have shown us, that your gas, taking water gas as a standard, is as good as our crude water gas; that you have shown that it costs more than I can put gas into the holder for; and that you have not allowed a fair amount of gas per ton of coal. I do not know but what that would be in your favor in your case, because we can make more than you could.

Mr. McMILLIN—I am glad you noticed that.

Mr. LOWE—I think the point that I called your attention to before is one generally overlooked by gas men when they speak of the difference of thermal units in the gas. They do not take into consideration the amount of heat which they carry away from the gas when they mix it with air. As matter of fact, I have taken a quart of water and boiled it with less water gas than I could with coal gas diluted with air. By differing the amounts I have reversed that. In fact, I do not know but I can show, in favor of almost any system, very satisfactory results in theory. I do not think you have shown that your gas is any better than the crude water gas. I am a strong adherent of crude water gas. I would like to have you show us just where the gases are of equal theoretical value, as far as heat is concerned, and where your gas is as good as water gas.

The President—If any one else desires to question Mr.

McMillin I hope he will do so promptly. We are pressed for time, and must soon draw this discussion to a close.

MR. LOOMIS—I am very much pleased with Mr. McMillin's paper. I think he has given us a very fair account, and that the paper is well worthy our consideration. With regard to this mixture of gases, I may say I have an apparatus at work at Turner's Falls, Mass., and hope in a few days to be able to give the results. I am arranging to have these gases mixed, or so that we can use pure water gas, and any quantity of coal gas, having them mixed in one holder or the other. Meters will be supplied and the gas will be put on to the forges, to be used in crucible steel melting, iron melting, and all that class of work. I will make this gas, as well as pure water gas, in the same generator, and carry it into the different holders, in the same operation—only at different times; and then I will invite this Investigating Committee which you propose to appoint, to come there and investigate it, and they will be able to report just what can be done. We shall have an analysis of the gas made in each case.

THE PRESIDENT—I think that will be beyond the scope of that Committee.

MR. LOOMIS—Or any other committee you may appoint. Any who wish to come there will be able to see what is done.

MR. A. C. WOOD—I have listened with a great deal of pleasure to the paper read by Mr. McMillin, and if I understand the case aright, his presentation of it is altogether theoretical or speculative. I am quite surprised at the results he arrived at in the volumes of gases required for the work, for we have the testimony of our own members here, who tell us their actual experience of the volume of natural gas required to do the work of a ton of coal. If I remember rightly it varies in different localities, from 22,000 to 30,000 feet to do the work of a ton of coal of 2,000 pounds. Further than that, we have the written testimony of the projector of a water gas system, claimed to be far superior to all others, that from actual test (nothing speculative about this), and from his own knowledge, 1,000 feet of fuel water gas, is equal in value to 40 pounds of coal, or, 50,000 feet to 2,000 pounds of coal, consequently I am quite surprised at the volume that Mr. McMillin arrives at in producing equal value to a ton of coal.

MR. McMillin—Out of 16,000, do you mean?

MR. A. C. Wood—Yes.

MR. Lowe—I would like to ask another question   Will you kindly tell me the ignition temperature of this mixture which you speak of?

MR. McMillin—I do not believe I figured that out.   I should judge it was about 4,000.   I will say, in figuring these values of the gases, I was aware that, in water evaporation of a 1,000 pounds of each, the extra nitrogen or the extra quantity of air that may be in any of them, is taken into consideration— that is, of all the gases escaping at 500°. First we have to compare the specific heats of the gases, working upon that basis. That is already accounted for in any statement I have made.   I do not think I worked out the flame temperature of the gas, but judged it to be about 4,000—quite high enough.   The producer gas makes a temperature quite high enough for all metallurgical purposes.   Mr. Wood speaks of 20,000 or 25,000 feet of natural gas being equal to a ton of coal.   That is a theoretical value and not a practical one.   Just so it is with your water gas.   I cannot help what men may have said; I speak of what the fact is.   In respect to water gas the theoretical value is given.   I give the theoretical value of this as requiring 80,000 feet to a ton of coal; yet I say 16,000 feet, would in practice, be equal to a ton of coal.   As to the nitrogen in the mixture, I would prefer to have that mixture without the nitrogen.   Not being an expert in the manufacture of that gas, of course I could not get it done as cheaply as Mr. Lowe makes water gas at Lynn.   In figuring the cost of water gas I did not take my own ideas about it at all, I took those of large water gas producers, such as the firms in Chicago, Philadelphia, and other places—and, among others, Professor Lowe.   I have taken all the testimony that I could get as to the cost of the gas.   I do say we ought to get better results; but I question whether it is a physical possibility to get 80,000 feet of gas and generate your steam and decompose it. I question very seriously whether there is heat enough there to get 80,000 feet of water gas per ton of coal.

Mr. Lowe—Theoretically you can get 120,000 feet of water gas.

Mr. McMillin—I beg your pardon ; you cannot do it theoretically.

Mr. Lowe—You can, providing the coal is pure carbon.

Mr. Clark.—Recognizing the importance and value of Mr. McMillin's paper, I move a hearty vote of thanks be extended him, and that printed copies of his paper be distributed among the members at as early a day as possible. Seconded by Mr. Lowe.

Mr. McMillin—I have always opposed the distribution of printed copies of papers, and I must oppose this motion now. When I was President of the Ohio Association I broke through the rule with respect to having the President's address printed. This will all come out in due time through the regular journals, so do not let us make any exception in respect to the printing of papers, or distributing them, unless the party does it himself before the meeting. You will get the paper in a few weeks anyhow, and it will keep.

The President—I think Mr. McMillin's suggestion is a good one.

Mr. Clark's motion was passed.

Report of Special Committee on a Uniform Standard of Meter Connections.

Mr. Goodwin—If it is the pleasure of the Association the Special Committee appointed yesterday morning to consider the subject of a uniform standard of meter connections beg leave to make a report. I will say also that the meter manufacturers named on the Committee were all present, with the exception of Mr. Tufts, who was not able to arrange for leaving his city at such short notice. This is their verdict:

The Committee to whom was referred the question of uniformity of meter couplings, beg leave to submit the following report : That it is the sense of the meter manufacturers that there should be a uniform standard of couplings, but the subject is of such importance that the time at their command will not admit of its proper consideration at this date. They therefore ask that they be continued until the next annual meeting, at which time they will be prepared to report.

In the meantime your Committee ask that the Association express its opinion on the desirability of adopting a uniform standard. Your Committee further request, if it is the sense of the Association to adopt a standard, that the Secretary of the Association be instructed to forward a certified copy of such action to the New England, Western and Ohio Associations, and solicit similar action on their part.

MR. HARBISON—I move the report of the Committee be accepted, and that the matter be recommitted to them, to report definitely at the next annual meeting. Also, that it is the sense of this Association that a standard coupling is desirable. Adopted.

Mr. E. J. King, of Jacksonville, Ills., then read the following paper on—

THE ADVANTAGES OF GAS COMPANIES ENGAGING IN THE ELECTRIC LIGHT BUSINESS.

That the electric light must either be looked upon as a rival interest and an active competitor, or a part of the gas undertakings of this country, can no longer be doubted. I take it that your Committee, in assigning me this subject, had in mind the discussion of the question whether or not the advantages that gas companies may have over all others are such as to warrant them in the necessary outlay for the installation of a plant, with not only the possibility but probability of competition.

From the number of companies " joining the ranks " I think it has been decided that it may be considered a legitimate part of our business. That, with a properly constructed plant conducted on business principles, it can be made a profitable investment, I no longer doubt.

In a reported interview the manager of a large electric lighting system is quoted as saying he did not advocate the policy of selling to gas companies, as they would not endeavor to push the light as others would who depended solely on this light for their business. It seems to me he could not have looked very far ahead; for when gas companies shall have taken hold and made it a part of their business, he who has courted their trade will certainly come out in the lead.

I do not believe that electricity is to drive gas for illumination out of the field, and that we can be comforted by knowing that our existing plant is to be devoted exclusively to "sending out" fuel. I do believe there is a place for electricity, that we as gas men are the proper ones to supply it, and that the time is coming when it will be so considered by all.

There was a good deal of philosophy in the reply of a certain gas man, who, when asked if it were true that his company was going to enter the electrical field, replied: "Yes; and I should not be surprised if we were selling coal oil before long. We are in the light business."

So far the competition of electric light has not seemed to diminish the use of gas to any extent; in fact, most gas companies report not only the average but even a larger increase than usual in their "sendout." But if the use of electricity continues to increase as it has in the last few years, will this always be true?

In our section of the country the arc light has almost superseded gas for street illumination. All buildings in course of construction, of any size or importance, in the various cities of the country, are being wired for incandescent lighting. The report comes that all manufacturing establishments supplying electric lighting material are far behind their orders. Does all this mean that after 6 or 7 years' use it has been found unprofitable to engage in electric lighting? or that the demand is growing less?

Undoubtedly there have been failures and unprofitable investments in this field; but has failure been the rule? I certainly have not heard of a gas company that tried the experiment and failed. Now, let us see what advantages the average gas company may have:

First—I would say, in saving on cost of installation, the probability is that all companies can find the small piece of ground necessary on the property they own, and, maybe, sufficient room in present buildings, by rearranging and economizing in space. For necessary foundations, a grout made of old retorts, firebricks and refuse of various kinds, broken to the proper size, can be utilized with spent lime, which is almost as good as cement for this purpose.

Second——The saving in expense of management cannot be questioned. That, with the force necessarily a part of the gas plant, fewer men will be needed, must be apparent.

Third—Gas companies have a certain amount of refuse that otherwise would be waste, which can be used for fuel. For instance, coal dust, coke breeze, and more or less coke that can be secured by screening their cinders. All these we use on ordinary grate bars, with the help of a Parson's blower. If a furnace adapted more especially for this kind of fuel, say, something on the plan of our regenerative or recuperative furnaces, made to supply a battery of boilers, were used, the expense might be reduced to a minimum. Many are using the "Jarvis setting" to good advantage. Burners for using oil and tar are also being perfected. Possibly, when prices for tar are such as have obtained during the last few years in many parts of the country, it might be found profitable to make light of it.

Lastly—Fuel gas. Who can realize the possibilities and advantages that gas companies may have over all competitors when they shall be able to use for fuel, or directly in the engine, a gas that costs them but from two to three cents per 1,000 cubic feet ? This, you know, we are promised.

In several discussions in our Western Association it has been argued that interest on the proportion of value absorbed from the existing gas plant in construction, and its proportion of the expense of managing, etc., should properly be charged up to electric light, which would decrease the reported per cent. of profit. Grant this be true ; but would you not then have another advantage to gas companies, in that their expenses would be decreased just so much——the result to the stockholder, however, being just the same in dollars and cents ?

Now, may it not also be an advantage to the consumer? It has been the history of gas companies that they have endeavored to furnish gas at as low a price as possible, in justice to themselves—the "dollar mark" being the dream. May we not expect them to carry the same policy into any new departures ? I know this to be the feeling of the Directors of the Company I have the honor to serve. Taking hold of the electric light when a local company made a failure of it, they have reduced the price from $12 and $15, for an 11-o'clock circuit, to from $6.25 to $8 for a 12-o'clock circuit. What company in the country, without competition, is supplying arc lighting at the price noted ? What company can do so, and pay satisfactory dividends, with only a 63-light plant, unless it be a gas company ? Is it not true, also, that men educated to the business of furnishing light will understand the necessities and wants of their patrons better than men who have suddenly entered a new field ?

The tendency of the day is to trusts and combinations generally, with the understanding that a great saving may be expected. How truly this may be applied to the question we have now under consideration. I have corresponded with and talked to quite a number of the members of gas companies who have made such a combination, and in no case have I heard them complain they made a mistake. There are, no doubt, many other advantages that might be claimed which have not occurred to me ; but I believe those I have enumerated are sufficient to make an electric light plant a profitable investment to gas companies, when to others not so favored, it would prove an absolute loss—at least this is true in small and medium-sized cities.

DISCUSSION.

MR. PEARSON—I belong to a company (Toronto, Can.) which has not yet seen its way clear to adopt the electric light. My opinion is that it depends a great deal upon the ability of the company to sell cheap gas as to whether or not it would be advisable to adopt the electric light. So far as Toronto is concerned, we have been enabled successfully to compete with the electric light. The fact of the matter is that the use of the electric light in our city has not advanced at all since they commenced it some three years ago, excepting as to the number of lights which the city leases. As a matter of fact I think I am within truth in stating that scores of people that tried the arc electric light, after a time gave it up, because the expense was greater than that of gas, and also because of its inconvenience. The introduction by our company of gas lamps of high illuminating power, has enabled us not only to successfully compete with the electric light for inside illumination, but also to have these lanterns substituted for electric lights on the outside of buildings. The lamps that I refer to (of course there are many others probably equally good) are what are called the "Lambeth Lanterns," made in England. These consume about 25 feet of gas per hour, and supposing they are lighted, say for 5 hours (which is really as long a time as they are required to be lighted for advertising purposes), then the amount of gas consumed would be only 125 feet, which, at our lowest gas rate, would only amount for the whole night to about 13 or 14 cents, as against from 30 to 50 cents charged by the electric light company for their lights. Therefore, you see that with this lantern—which is quite as effective for their purposes, and sometimes more so than the electric light, for a little more than one-fourth of the price—they have an excellent service. The Gas Company's business in Toronto has increased, as we reduced the price of gas, very largely, far more than the increase in population of the city, which also is large. The electric light, as I have just said, has not increased. We have in our city, with a population of over 140,000 people, but 66 private arc lights, and, I think, 100 public lights, while we have 9,065 gas consumers, and 3,020 ordinary gas lamps. We have introduced for the city 63 of these Lambeth lanterns, and we supply 83 of them to private consumers. The price charged (of course, this is an important factor) by the electric light company to the city was 55 cents, but it has been recently reduced to 50 cents per night. The price charged for the gas lanterns and for ordinary gas lamps—the Company putting in the pipes, attending to the lamps, and doing everything connected with them—is, for a burner, 3½ feet per hour, $20.50. The price for gas charged by the Company to ordinary consumers is now $1.25; to consumers of over 200,000 feet, $1.15; over 500,000 feet, $1; to gas stoves and engines, $1. The actual increase in the business of the Company during the past year has been nearly 17 per cent., whereas the actual increase in the population has been about 8 per cent. I do not say that it may not be well for gas companies in some places to use the electric light, but I cannot see that it would be well for us in Toronto. Why should we, even if we could supply electric light cheaper than other people, thus bring it into the market?

Why should we do that, and make a smaller profit out of that light than we make out of our gas, and thereby hurt our business by so doing? Again, what guarantee have we, should we adopt any one system, that somebody else would not come in to oppose us, and, perhaps, do so without a profit to themselves for a considerable time.

THE PRESIDENT—I think the Association would like to hear from some gentlemen who are doing this thing. Perhaps Mr. Stiness will be willing to say something upon the subject.

MR. STINESS—I suppose that for many years I have been regarded as somewhat of a crank for favoring the adoption of the electric light by the gas companies of this country. That a very large number of them have now come into line is a matter of satisfaction to me. As our friend from Toronto says, perhaps individual cases exist where it may not be for the best interests, financially, of the gas company to adopt the electric light system; but, sir, as sure as the sun shines to-day, the electric light has come to stay, and to exist as an active competitor of gas. I am not one of those who believe or maintain that the gas works of the United States are to be annihilated, or are to be entirely turned into mediums for furnishing heating gas. The electric light has its field and will maintain it, and so has the illuminating gas of the present day. The policy of furnishing electric light to their consumers when they demanded it has been pursued by many gas companies throughout the United States. I have always maintained that the term " gas company " was, and is at the present time especially, a misnomer. We should be called " artificial light companies;" and, even if our consumers demanded us to supply oil, I do not know why we should not do so, if the operation be a profitable one. Apart from other considerations, I believe there are so many advantages in the use of electricity at the present day that the people will have it. I have no knowledge of any lamp, at the present time, that can be used successfully in the lighting of streets, that can be compared with the arc light of to-day, although I believe there are many gas lamps which will more than successfully compete and compare with the incandescent. When we pass through the streets and see, as we can in almost any city in our country to-day, the arc illumination that is being carried on, I contend that it is a benefit to mankind.   The statement was once made, and I repeated it in our New England Association, that the Mayor of the city of Providence once said, " A city well lighted is more than half policed."   I believe that statement; I know that it is strictly true.   A few years ago, in your own good city, Mr. President, where (accidentally) I was thrown into the company of the Chief of Police, he stated to me, in speaking of this matter of electric lighting, that it was of vast benefit to the city of Boston; and that while he complimented—a compliment which I know was well deserved—the Company with which our worthy President is connected upon the pure quality of the light furnished by the Boston Company, yet he said that the public demanded the arc light for the purpose of lighting the crooked streets of that well-conducted city of Boston.   I believe no gas company exists that cannot make use of the electric light, and successfully carry it forward.   There is one matter which has been suggested to my mind in regard to gas companies. Undoubtedly many of you, gentlemen, have seen in the papers the account of a gas and electric light company in the little town of Spencer, Mass.   Two weeks ago to-night I visited that town ; and, gentlemen, I say to you it will well pay you to also visit it. Situated upon the hills, in the centre of the State, it is one of the most beautiful places I ever visited, and I was well repaid for the hours I spent there.   There they have three 15-horse power Otto gas engines driving 63 arc lights.   I remained in the dynamo room for 25 minutes, and there was never a " wink " of an arc light.   I started last night from the Hoffman House, marching up Broadway, and there beheld those waves of light which Prof. Morton spoke to us about yesterday.   They were more than waves ; they were pronounced undulations.   But that was not the fact with regard to the effect of the gas engines in the dynamo room in the town of Spencer.   I must say I was more than surprised at the regularity and efficiency of these engines to run the dynamos.   They claimed, I think, that there was economy in the use of gas at $2 per thousand.   In my investigation I did not take any man's statement, except in one particular—with regard to the consumption of gas per hour for running the dynamos I did take the statement of the gentleman in charge; but there were three large 50-light dry meters, one attached to each engine, and the three engines were directly connected with one line of shafting, and over that shafting was a belt to the dynamo. The consumption of gas would equal about 1,000 cubic feet per hour for the three engines. At a meeting of our New England Association, a short time since, one of our engineers questioned the accuracy of the statement as to the consumption of gas. I believe that is pretty nearly what they claimed is the consumption of gas by a 15-horse power engine. I did not verify the statement by an inspection of the meter, because what I did see was so fully verified by what I had seen in the papers that I accepted their statement. My own experience, covering a period of three years, in running Otto engines of similar horse power, driving an exhauster to exhaust gas five miles from my works, has convinced me that their statement with regard to the consumption of gas was absolutely within the line. Now, if a 15-horse power gas engine can be run on 300 cubic feet, the possibility of the electric light lies in the possibility of gas companies to furnish the electric light at a a very much reduced cost.

THE PRESIDENT—I think the Association would like to hear from Mr. Nettleton on this subject, as he has also had some practical experience.

MR. NETTLETON—The Company with which I am connected went into the electric light business in November, 1885. We were one of the first companies, if not the first, in New England to take hold of it; and I said then, as I say now, if we had not made any money, but had merely covered expenses, I would still be glad that we entered the field. It seemed to me, in a town as small as ours, where the field for lighting was so narrow, that two companies could not live and do business. It ought to be done by one company. Since that time a town in Connecticut selling one-third the quantity of gas that we do, has had a competing electric company. The men who owned the electric light plant have pushed the business so strong that the Gas Company has felt very much like going out of business. That may be an exceptional case; but although they have never sold more than one-third the gas sold by our Company, they have a good many more electric lights than we have. It simply shows the difference between an electric light plant in a small place, operated by the electric company, pushed by consumers, and pushed by people who feel that their existence depends upon pushing the business to the utmost possible limits, and an electric light plant operated by a gas company who simply run it to supply the demand which everywhere exists for electric lights. Now, as to the results. We run by water power, and for that power we have as yet paid only $1,000 per year. The actual running expenses have been charged up to the account, also the small repairs which have been made so far, and nothing else. In starting, through the month of September, we had only 3 lamps, but shortly afterward (in January) we secured a small street lamp contract. Up to the 1st of April following we had 33 or 34 lights; and we had lost, up to that time, $275. For the following year, ending April, 1887, we ran from 33 lamps up to 64. We had at that time an investment of $15,000, all told ; and we had made on that investment only $500—which is not very much. For the year ending April 1st, 1887, we only did a business of $3,300. We have gained now so that we have to-day the equivalent, turning incandescent into arc lamps, of 90 arc lamps. We are doing business at the rate of over $6,000 per year. The account at the present time stands on our side by considerably more than the whole of last year. Unless we meet with some accident or something which causes a large expenditure, we shall make on an investment which now stands at about $20,000, not less than $2,000 ; and it may run higher. The profits would increase proportionately as the business expanded, and be considerably larger than they are now. It is very much like the gas business. If you do but a small trade your income is eaten up by the expenses ; if you do a somewhat larger business you make a little money ; if you do a still larger business, then you make considerable money. That is very true of the electric light business. I shall not feel satisfied—shall not feel that the Company is whole, is being paid directly in money, until we shall have made 16 per cent. upon the capital actually invested. I do not think we have earned it at the present time. That 16 per cent. I would divide as follows : 6 per cent. for interest ; 8 per cent. for depreciation ; 2 per cent. for office expenses. When we reach that point I think I can safely say the Company is whole. But indirectly I feel that it has been one of the best investments the Company has ever made.

MR. HELME—How much do you get for gas ?

MR. NETTLETON—Last year $1.71 was the average.

MR. NEAL—I will not enter into details, as there is not time ; but I will state that the Charlestown Gas Company, which I represent, entered into the supply of electric lighting on the 15th of September, 1886, and the business has been carried on, financially and practically, with great success. We furnish the arc light and also the incandescent. The incandescent is not the Edison, nor the alternating current, but the "individual cut-offs," as it is called. Each lamp has a regulator by itself. We have but one price for each arc light for commercial lighting, and one price for 8 incandescent lights for commercial lighting. We have a contract with the city for three years at a different price. We have no reason to regret having taken this step. I cannot give the figures that I would like to give, but the results are very satisfactory.

MR. LANSDEN—I would like to ask Mr. Nettleton whether or not the introduction, and what he has done with his electric light, has had any effect upon gas consumption ? Whether his gas consumption has increased or decreased ; and what amount in his profits he has charged up to the superintendent of the works ? Also, whether he has put it all on the gas company, or divided up the expense with the electric light company.

MR. NETTLETON—In answer, I will say that the consumption of gas is increasing slowly—not so rapidly as it did four or five years ago ; but I think this is due largely to the fact that the town is not growing so rapidly as it did then. As I stated in my remarks, the expenses given were about the actual operating expenses. Nothing is charged off for my salary, or for office expenses ; and nothing is charged for superintendence or collections as yet.

MR. MONKS—I would like to ask Mr. Nettleton whether he can do a larger electric light business without further expenditure ; and how far he can go in that direction?

MR. NETTLETON—The plant consists of two 45-light and one 50-light dynamos, making a total of 140 lights.

MR. KING—I desire to say a word or two in answer to Mr. Pearson. His experience with high-power burners has been entirely different from ours. I have put the electric light in stores and rooms which I tried to light by high-power burners, and the result has been eminently satisfactory to the parties using the electric light. The argument in favor of the electric light is this: When I used the high-power burners, I had it on my mind all the time, if there was not a customer in the store, that I had the gas to attend to, and that I must shut up early and save gas, if there was no business. I had that on my mind all the time—the care of the burners. But since I have had the electric light I know that when I shut up and go home my store is illuminated brilliantly, my windows are nicely illuminated, and I have an advertisement there until 12 o'clock at night. I have to pay no attention to lighting or putting it out, and have no care whatever on my mind. The increase in the sales of gas has not only kept up with the average, but is about 2 per cent. more than the average. So far as the profits are concerned, we have reached what we hoped for, and 1 per cent. more, for the last year's business. As far as competition is concerned, I may say I care not who comes; for I claim that my advantages are such, as a gas man, that, with the advantages which I have enumerated in my paper, I certainly can compete and hold my own against any one. As to depreciation, of course, with only something over two years' experience, we cannot judge what will be the proper charge to make; but I think that probably what Mr. Nettleton states (8 per cent.) would be fair. Our plant shows very little depreciation at this time, but, of course, we cannot tell what is in the future. It is high-speed machinery, and there must be more or less charged over to depreciation.

MR. C. NETTLETON—What price does Mr. King get for arc lights burning until 12 o'clock?

MR. KING—Eight dollars where there is one light, $6.25 for others.

MR. PEARSON—What is the price of gas?

MR. KING—Our price is from $1.50 to $2 per thousand, according to the amount of consumption.

MR. PEARSON—When you speak of $6.25, it is for how long ?

MR. KING—Until 12 o'clock at night ; $6.25 per month.

MR. C. NETTLETON -- What price does Mr. Neal get, and how many hours does the light burn ?

MR. NEAL—What we call commercial lights are now lighted at dark and turned off at 11 o'clock. We stop the current then. We charge 50 cents per night—that is, for the arc. If we give them 8 incandescent lights, we charge 50 cents for those. We have in some cases put in incandescent lights in stores, or business places, where they never used any gas, but have always used kerosene oil.

MR. PEARSON—If the same energy had been put forth in introducing these high-power burners in opposition to the electric light as the electric light people put forth in introducing their burners in opposition to the gas companies, in many places the gas companies would succeed in defeating competition. I believe that, comparatively, a small cost and little effort would succeed in having them put in. Our experience, as I have stated, has been exactly the reverse of that of Mr. King.

THE PRESIDENT—Mr. Pearson's situation is somewhat different from that of smaller companies. Most large companies can afford to wholly ignore the question of introducing arc lights, but the question of incandescent lighting is a very different matter.

MR. LOWE—Does Mr. Neal use the incandescent on the arc light line ?

MR. NEAL—I do.

MR. LOWE—What system do you use ?

MR. NEAL—The Brush.

On motion of Mr. Pearson, a vote of thanks was tendered to Mr. King for his paper.

COMMITTEE ON BADGES.

THE PRESIDENT—The Chair will appoint as the Committee on Badges, according to the resolution, C. H. Nettleton, G. B. Neal, and S. G. Stiness. The Chair appoints those three gentlemen from the same locality, in order that they may confer together. I think it would be more convenient than to have them scattered about the country.

Committee of Arrangements for Toronto Meeting.

The President appointed as the Committee of Arrangements for the next meeting, at Toronto, Messrs. W. H. Pearson, of Toronto; J. S. Scriver, of Montreal; F. W. Gates, of Hamilton; G. A. Hyde, of Cleveland, O., and M. Cartwright, of Rochester, N. Y.

Mr. C. W. Blodget, of Brooklyn, N. Y., here read his paper on—

THE COMPARATIVE ILLUMINATING POWER OF GAS PURIFIED WITH LIME *VS.* OXIDE OF IRON.

Something over a year ago the Company with which I am connected commenced to use Connelly & Co.'s iron sponge for purification. Being fully impressed with the fact, as laid down in all the text-books, that carbonic acid was highly detrimental to the illuminating power of gas, and knowing that oxide of iron had no affinity for CO_2, it was deemed essential to bring the gas in contact with lime in order that the CO_2 might be eliminated; otherwise the benefits it was expected we would derive from the use of sponge would be more than lost through the depreciation of the illuminating power of the gas due to its presence.

To avoid such a contingency a layer of lime, 4½ inches deep, was spread on trays resting on the lowest offset in the purifying boxes, with the object of not only extracting the CO_2, but, in addition, to serve the purpose of arresting any particles of tarry nature which occasionally come over with the gas from the scrubbers, and preventing same from permeating the sponge, which rested on trays placed immediately over the lime.

With this arrangement of materials matters ran smoothly for about a month, when we commenced to find carbonic acid in the gas long before it would be necessary to change the purifiers on

account of the oxide being fouled, although the latter was purifying but little more per bushel than formerly.

In accordance with the precepts this condition of affairs was
not allowable, and consequently we adopted the (to us) novel
programme of endeavoring to change the purifiers whenever
CO_2 was shown to be present in the gas, without waiting for
the sponge to show indications of being fouled with sulphur
compounds; but this plan proved a flat failure, for we would
find carbonic acid in the gas within two hours after changing.

Finding it impossible, by means of the plan adopted, to get
rid of the objectionable visitor, and being loath to abandon the
use of sponge, it was determined to discard the lime entirely, to
substitute sawdust for the purpose of arresting any substances
deleterious to the sponge from passing to it, and to ascertain from
personal experience what would be the effect upon the illuminating power of the gas of allowing the carbonic acid, still present after leaving the scrubbers, to remain. As soon as this
change was inaugurated the candle power was most carefully
noted, and to our astonishment the quality of the gas was found
to be fully equal to that which it was our custom to make.

In order to corroborate the candle power of the gas as determined by the bar photometer, we caused to be made and placed
in the photometer room two small purifying boxes (20 in. by 20
in.), through which gas from the outlet of the scrubbers was
passed to the bar to be tested. In these boxes was placed,
respectively, lime and iron sponge to the depth of 12 inches,
each containing the same amount of moisture they ordinarily
had in our practical operations. We were then (supposedly) in
a position to make a comparison of the candle power of gas
with and without carbonic acid.

One important factor, however, had been overlooked, viz., the
constantly varying character of the gas being made; and as
some little time necessarily elapsed between the readings, the
obtainment of accurate results was impossible.

Two governor burners, which upon test were proven to consume equal quantities of gas under varying pressures, were then
placed on either end of the bar, and the luminosity of the two
flames compared—the piping having been previously so arranged
that the gas from each purifier could be passed to either burner

at will ; but as, for some unaccountable reason, the height of the two flames constantly varied, no dependence could be placed upon the observations. Further experiments were (owing to press of business) abandoned until last month, when the matter was again taken up.

A second experimental meter was procured, each purifier connected with one, a " Bray Special, No. 7 " burner put on each end of the bar, and pressure gauges placed before the inlet of the meters.

The separately purified gas was passed to each meter at one inch pressure, when it was found that each burner consumed exactly six cubic feet per hour.

A comparison of the illumination of the two lights, one against the other, showed them to be equal ; for although each gas was repeatedly switched from one end of the bar to the other, the disc remained in the center. This would seem to verify beyond the shadow of a doubt that the illuminating power of gas, purified with oxide of iron, was as great as that purified with lime, and to fully substantiate the correctness of the candle power of the commercial gas, as observed daily.

The average results obtained during eight months' practical operations, with lime as against iron sponge, are as follows :

	Make, per pound.	Candle power.	Candle feet.	Per cent. of cannel used.	Candle feet for each per cent. of cannel used.
Lime gas (CO_2 not present..........	4.94	18.6	91.9	9.64	9.53
Sponge gas CO_2 present..	4.9	19.	93.1	9.64	9.65

Admittedly, carbonic acid is detrimental to the illuminating power of gas in which it is present. How, then, are we to account for the fact, demonstrated day after day for months, and verified by the experiment above mentioned, that gas (made in both instances from the same coals) containing an average of two per cent. CO_2 is equal to that from which this deleterient has been eliminated ?

It was suggested to me that the cause for this apparent paradox might be found to be due to the fact that the lime robbed the gas of some of the hydrocarbons which the oxide of iron allowed to remain, and that the increased percentage of illuminants contained in gas purified with the latter material equalized the baneful effects of the CO_2.

To determine whether this .was a fact, I arranged to have thorough analyses made of the lime and sponge gas, so to speak, by the Bunsen method, the results of which are here given :

	Lime.	Sponge.
Hydrogen	48.92	47.33
Carbonic oxide	6.02	5.84
Carbonic acid	.00	2.19
Marsh gas	36.86	36.05
Illuminants	5.65	6.14
Oxygen	.12	.09
Nitrogen	2.43	2.36
Total	100.00	100.00

It will be observed that while the sponge gas contains 2.19 per cent. of the CO_2, it has also .49 per cent. more illuminants than was found in the gas purified with lime, which fully accounts, I believe, for the fact that the illuminating power of gas thus separately treated as to purification was found to be equal.

DISCUSSION.

Mr. McMillin—It gives me much pleasure to listen to papers of this character, for two reasons; first, because of its eminently practical nature, and, secondly, from its substantiation of views advocated by me at some risk to my reputation as an engineer. For many years I have contended that gas, purified by oxide of iron, was as good as that purified with lime alone. I had supposed that gas, purified with a little lime and a great deal of oxide of iron, would be better. That point, however, I never determined. All the analyses I ever made demonstrated that there was a higher per cent. of illuminants in gas purified with oxide of iron alone. I have made no analyses recently, and cannot give results. While Mr. Blodget's paper only shows one-half of one per cent. of illuminants, it is nearly equal to an

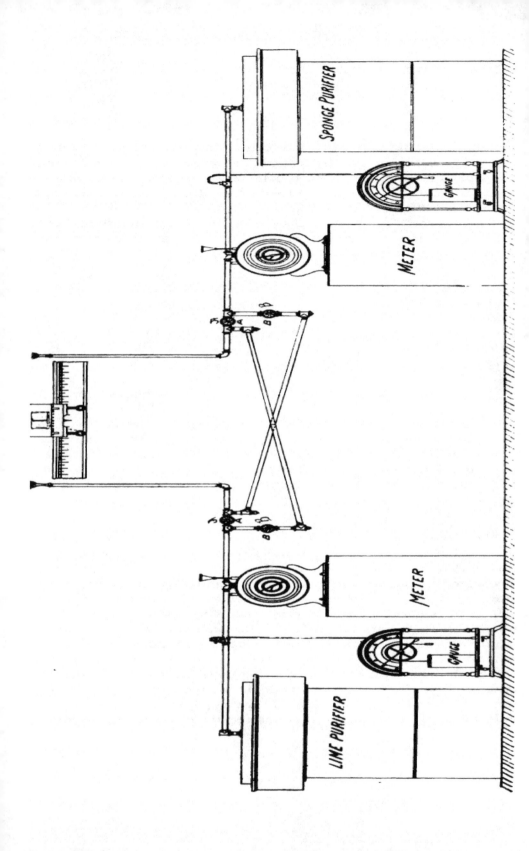

increase of 10 per cent., there being but little more than 5 per cent. of illuminants in the lime gas, and a little more than 6 in the other. Really, it shows about 10 per cent. of increase of illuminants. Some years ago I made an experiment in retorting my lime—the lime had been used for some time—to determine whether there was anything absorbed by the lime that would make light. It was mixed with coke screenings, which would probably make a difference in the quantity of gas to be made—not because there was gas in the coke, but because from the moisture present in it we might get a little water gas. I made from lime taken from the bottom of the purifier, which had been in use ten days, 1.85 feet per pound of 13-candle gas. Necessarily some illuminants must have been taken from the gas before you could get any such result as that. I would not advise you to use it as a regular provender for making gas; but, unquestionably, the lime does absorb a great deal of illuminants.

THE PRESIDENT—Was there any tar in that lime?

MR. McMILLIN—Not noticeably. I will say that, before the gas reached the lime, and in addition to the ordinary scrubbing it had received, it went through three feet of coke screenings, used in the old purifiers that were to be abandoned, but that were still in position; hence it would have been impossible for much tar to have accumulated. I would have supposed that the quantity came rather from the coke moisture. The illuminants came, of course, from the illuminants absorbed by the lime.

THE PRESIDENT—We have another paper on a kindred subject to be read, and I think it would be better to read it at this time, and have the two papers discussed together.

No objection being offered, Mr. Thos. Turner, of Charleston, S. C., read his paper on

PURIFICATION PUZZLES.

Mr. President and Gentlemen of the Association: Our worthy Secretary, who is indefatigable in his pursuit of literary matter for our meetings, requested me to prepare a paper on " Purification with Iron Sponge," forgetting, I suppose, that I have been fully occupied in recovering and repairing damages from a bad attack of the " shakes." In consequence I feared I would not be able to do justice to the subject. However, I therefore submit the following on " Three Purification Puzzles," hence the title.

I do not know that there is anything unique about them, as some of you may have had similar experiences; but still I think they will promote discussion, and probably develop some information which may be of benefit to all of us.

A description of our condensing, scrubbing and purifying arrangements is as follows : A Pelouze & Audouin condenser, 27 feet from take-off of the hydraulic main; 300 feet of 12-inch main, partly under floor of retort-house, an 8-inch air condenser, in 4 rows, 18 feet high, about 1,000 feet of 8-inch pipe; a scrubber 19 ins. by 5 ft. 6 ins., filled with wooden trays; a second scrubber, 15 ins. by 4 ft. 4 ins., filled with wooden laths set on edge; and 4 purifiers 12 ft. by 8 ft., by 2 ft. 6 ins., with dry center-valve and 12-inch connections. The purifying surface is, quite evidently, too limited for a manufacture of 200,000 or 300,000 cubic feet per diem.

For years we worked with dry lime, in the usual manner, that is, 4 or 5 trays with lime about $2\frac{1}{2}$ inches in depth and mixed so as to ball in the hand without staining. As our manufacture increased we found the increase of pressure so great that, at times, it was sufficient to unseal the inlet to dry center-valve and blow out the water lute to boxes. In addition to this we were frequently compelled to change two and three purifiers per day. It had been recommended to our Board that we should increase the capacity of our purifiers; but before acting on the matter we received a welcome boon, in the shape of Mr. Theobald Forstall's paper* on " Lime Purification," read at our meeting in Washington, in May, 1875.

This mode of preparing lime was immediately put into effect, proceeding cautiously in the use of water. This did very well, purifying from five to six thousand cubic feet per bushel of hydrate of lime, and even as high as 8,000 cubic feet, whereupon we were tempted to cry " Eureka "—when the process suddenly collapsed, and gave us Puzzle No. 1.

Box after box was changed, but the gas seemed to run right through the lime without its scarcely taking effect; in fact, we

---

* See Vol. 2, Page 22, of Proceedings.

were purifying not more than 1,200 cubic feet per bushel. The lime came out of purifiers almost unstained, and, after a few days' exposure to the atmosphere, seemed to regain its original purity. For a week we were compelled to change box after box—sometimes two, and even three, in a day. There seemed to be no remedy for this state of things, but when we tried the experiment of putting in a dryer charge of lime the evil ceased at once.

From this time we worked along very comfortably, purifying between six and seven thousand cubic feet per bushel of hydrate of lime, when we were suddenly confronted with what I call Puzzle No. 2.

At home one evening I took a match to light the gas, and, as sometimes happens, the match went out before the gas was ignited. The tap meanwhile being open, my attention was attracted by the peculiar smell of the gas, and, on applying the nitrate of silver test, I discovered a considerable trace of H_2S. A hurried visit to the works and a test of the purifiers showed everything to be correct, but the gas coming from the station meter showed a strong trace of H_2S. The center-seal and connections were next examined, and all seemed to be in perfect order. On the next change of purifiers the trouble disappeared, only to return again in a few days; and so it continued, on and off, for weeks, much to my annoyance, during which time every conceivable thing was tried to find out the difficulty.

The disease, after all, was very simple, and the remedy applied was equally simple though effective. It appeared that the water used to seal the bottom of the center-seal had become supersaturated with H_2S, and as the clean gas passed out over the surface of this water, it took H_2S in sufficient quantities to produce a very decided stain, when the usual test was applied. The remedy was a simple washing out of bottom of center-seal once or twice a week, and we had no further trouble. And here, let me say, I think it is a wise precaution to occasionally test the gas at the station meter.

In October, 1884, after various vicissitudes with dry lime, owing to the large manufacture on the limited surface for purification, we decided to try the experiment of using iron sponge with the hope of reducing the resistance in the purifiers. We were somewhat disappointed for several weeks, but eventually succeeded in working satisfactorily, or, with a manufacture of 280,000 cubic feet per diem passing through our small boxes, and with about 3 inches back pressure, we were purifying 9,000 cubic feet per bushel of sponge. From some unaccountable reason we afterward began to have trouble from sudden increases of pressure in purifiers, and from the rapid changes to reduce the pressure, out results fell off 50 per cent., and, eventually, 66 per cent. This was simply from increased pressure—the sponge not being fouled in the least; and yet we would make a complete round of changes in 24 hours.

From the prevailing state of things we got the impression that the material was in too finely a divided condition, and so absorbed moisture from the gas and clogged the screens, as it seemed to form into a pasty mass right at the screen. With this idea, earthenware pans, containing SHO, were placed in bottom of boxes to absorb moisture, and shavings, sawdust, gunny-bags and breeze were placed on an extra screen; but all to no good result. As a last resort a letter was sent on to the Messrs. Connelly—for of course (?) the fault could lie nowhere else than in the material—whereupon they suggested the addition of saw-dust to the material. However, in the interval of receiving their reply, Puzzle No. 3 had been solved. The remedy applied was simply by passing the Pelouze & Audouin condenser for a few hours, and keeping the purifiers at a slightly higher temperature. It was the same old bugbear of the gas manager, viz., naphthaline, although it was not readily perceptible among the sponge.

Now, the query is, "Was this over-condensation?" Does the P. & A. condenser, under certain conditions, when removing the tar, carry along with it too many of the light hydro-carbons, rendering the gas more liable to deposit naphthaline on any sudden change of temperature?

Notwithstanding an occasional drawback from the causes above mentioned, we are still using iron sponge; and, under these very disadvantageous circumstances, our present lot has purified about 122,000 M. cubic feet.

If the above will aid some brother gas manager in avoiding such annoyances—which, at the time of their occurrence, were serious matters to us—the purpose of this paper will have been fully answered.

The

was then proceeded with.

MR. GRAEFF—I would like to ask Mr. Blodget what kind of photometer he used in making those tests?

MR. BLODGET—I stated that I used a bar photometer.

MR. McMILLIN—I have had similar experience to two of the "puzzles" of Mr. Turner—that of foul gas getting into the holder, although pure in the purifying house. We have had it so on several occasions. I heard of his success in cleaning out his center-seal, still, I could hardly believe that that was the difficulty, without any increase of temperature, or that the sulphuretted hydrogen would pass off in such a quantity as to make the gas foul; yet I naturally tried it, knowing that it had succeeded with him. I derived no benefit from it. I could never get the same results. After some time I discovered that one chamber of the center-seal would occasionally leak, and it would continue to leak. When I changed off from it the trouble ceased, but when I next got round to it the same difficulty would appear. We would be obliged, while on that section, to run the gas into the holder by itself, and let that be used in the day-time for cooking, or for leaking in the streets, and turn the other on at night during the burning hours. Of course we ground our center-seal all we could. After a while it stopped. We have been troubled for two or three weeks at a time, once or twice a year, for two or more years. With "Puzzle No. 3" we had difficulties last winter. From October, 1885, to March, 1886, we never changed the purifier because the oxide was foul, but always on account of the pressure. I am almost afraid to tell you that I have measured the naphthaline on the top of the outlet pipe of the box, five and a half inches deep; and, for weeks at a time, when I would lift the lid, the entire surface of the oxide would be covered so that you could not see any of it. It was not surprising we had back pressure with that much naphthaline. It was better, however, to have it through the works than to have it in the services about the city. We were having no trouble there. But, in March, 1886, I put in a lower layer, a tray of all coke, then another tray of half coke and half oxide of iron, and then a couple of feet of pure oxide of iron on top of that, but received no relief. I have recommended that medicine to all my friends who have been afflicted, and am prepared to take it myself. Two months ago, after we had been running along for some time, changing the box once a week or ten days, our pressure suddenly began to run up. We naturally concluded that it was the old trouble, but when we changed the boxes we saw no sign of naphthaline on top of them—not a particle. We examined all the boxes, took out the coke, put in fresh material, fixed everything in good shape, and ran 24 hours, and then changed again. Then we mixed in new sawdust. We had been running on that oxide for some time. We made the oxide nearly one-half sawdust, but without helping it one iota. It was a box which we changed every day, because of the pressure. We had continued that up to the time I left home. I left home with some misgivings. We started in just before I left home, to put on three inches of coke screenings in the second tray, and oxide on top of that. I have had two or three telegrams from home since my arrival here, and the pressure has not increased any. The surprising thing was that no naphthaline passed out; although the pressure would go from three-fourths of an inch on each of the second and third boxes, and an inch or an inch and a half on the first, up to 10, 12, or 14 inches, sometimes in an hour. Very seldom it happened that more than three hours from the time the pressure began to show an abnormal condition of affairs, we did not have to change. There was no naphthaline in sight, yet we were satisfied that naphthaline was what was the matter. My friend, Turner, remedied his difficulty by cutting out the P. & A. condenser. I have sufficient condensing and scrubbing capacity; and we cooled our gases down as low as 58° and 60° during the cool weather that we had, and we ran it as high as 125. We by-passed the half of our scrubber in the condensation; then we by-passed all of it, and ran the gases into the boxes hot, without being either washed or scrubbed. I ran steam, at a pressure of 60 pounds, through a ¾-inch pipe, for four hours, when the pipe became so hot that you could not bear your hand upon it, but not an iota of relief was granted.

THE PRESIDENT—I think a French philosopher has said there was something in the misfortunes of our friends that always caused us pleasure. I think if we once begin to take the experience of the members of this Association we shall have business enough to occupy us for the whole of our session, without doing anything else. I think Mr. McMillin, when he sat down, meant to move a vote of thanks to both of these gentlemen, and I take great pleasure in putting the motion—which was carried.

Mr. Richard J. Monks, of Boston, Mass., read a paper entitled,

DISADVANTAGES OCCASIONED BY FLUCTUATIONS OF CANDLE POWER IN GAS FURNISHED TO CONSUMERS.

The practical and scientific advance made in the manufacture of illuminating gas since its first introduction, has resulted in a double advantage to the consumer—while he pays a less price he gets a much better light. That the light averages much better than of old is easily demonstrated; and while the average of your candle power is an important point, the uniformity is an essential one.

It is certainly true that so delicate and sensitive an organ as the eye acquires a strong habit in favor of uniformity in the volume of artificial light. Now, if your eyes find the volume of light uniform, the satisfaction this affords you reduces your disposition to complain of the light furnished.

In glancing over the history of our industry, the standard of illuminating power adopted a quarter of a century ago seems absurdly low; and this fact illustrates how comparison so often becomes the basis of our judgment, and how necessary it is that unfavorable comparisons as to the article we furnish should not prevail among our consumers.

Step by step we have advanced from being content to produce a twelve or fourteen candle gas, and while we have been educating ourselves to produce a superior light, we have been educating the community to call for and require it. The older members of this Association can recall how, step by step, this process went on. Your modern consumer knows nothing about all this, and he cares less, but argues thus : Your gas is poor to-day, because it is not so good as it was yesterday.

Suppose you assert that to-morrow you will please him, and, if your gas was "off" two candles, you put it up four. You are then like the milkman giving an unusual amount of cream to his customer; you must keep right on, for the moment you return to your normal standard you are denounced ; and, should you happen to again get below it, you add to the general dissatisfaction.

It may be argued that such fluctuations as this are extreme, and unusual ; and certainly the truer this argument is in any case the better for the company, although it may be said that occasionally men are put in charge of gas works whose frequent experiments amount to a tinkering with the quality of gas sent out.

Gas carefully made by any of the leading processes, when consumed, will produce a light which, for uniformity in candle power, will take front rank and can be kept within a very close range.

It will not be so brilliant as an electric arc, but it will not indulge in those light-giving gymnastics, which are sometimes observed in arc lighting. It will also surpass the incandescent light, not in steadiness of flame, but in uniform intensity.

This is a strong hold we still have over our modern competitor—electricity ; and we ought to work it for all it is worth.

In the matter of how much light can be got out of a given quantity of gas, due allowance being made for the material and the process used, many gas men are now agreed, and endeavor to live up to the modern standard and keep close to it at all times.

Let us briefly consider some of the causes which tend to interfere with this.

Defective construction in some part or parts of our machinery; lack of vigilance in frequent examinations of the photometer; dead ends on mains where little gas is used; experiments carelessly carried on ; and the mingling of different gases at irregular times and in irregular quantities. During the year, since we last met, a case was brought to my attention where a new process had been introduced. The superintendent told me that the gas had produced varied from 6 to 30 candles, and had made lots of trouble among consumers.

In another case the gas furnished at times was all coal gas, at other times all water gas, and sometimes was part one kind and part another. It seemed to me that the trouble this latter company experienced with its consumers was largely owing to this cause.

The rustic who comes to the city for the first time, born and bred far from the "maddening crowd," and accustomed to a tallow candle or a cheap kerosene lamp, is dazzled and almost blinded by the brilliancy of a modern lighted city. The quantity of light is so unusual that he makes no account of any lack of uniformity.

Your city man, on the contrary, is a critic, and a severe one when he deals with gas matters.

He will give you a rap whenever he can through your collectors or the daily press. Praise he will never bestow upon you; but good gas, of uniform quality, will be least liable to his censure.

Having finished reading his paper, the author thus continued :

My time was limited for preparing this paper, and I would like to explain at greater length the comparison I made with regard to gas and electric light. It seems to me to be a fact that we are able to keep our gas within closer range of candle power than any other known substance used for lighting. The gentlemen present who attended a lecture* given by President Morton at the Stevens Institute, Hoboken, N. J., before this Association some years ago, will remember the beautiful illustration he gave us by throwing the arc light upon the stereopticon, which made it very apparent why this unsteadiness of the arc light exists, and I do not know if it has been entirely remedied. The defects that an electric engineer must overcome in order to keep his candle power steady, as I understand them, are not only the volume of electricity, but the intensity that is furnished to any given lamp. It is also a fact that the particles of carbon, as they are burned, are torn off irregularly from the carbon

---

* See Vol. 3, Page 299 of Proceedings.

pencil. In the illustration given by President Morton, the ends of those carbons were extremely beautiful. They had the appearance of the top of a mountain covered with snow. As the light played from side to side, it would appear like a mountain on one side, all shaded, but the shadow would pass to the other side, showing that these particles of carbon were being torn off at frequent intervals. In the incandescent light the trouble seems to be of a different character. Of course, the question still arises as to the quantity of electricity required to produce the light, and the intensity. The trouble that I have observed in all companies that I am connected with (notably at Woburn, Mass.) is that the lamp itself degenerates. We do not observe this in a great city like New York; and there are two or three reasons why we do not observe it here. One reason is that all the apparatus used for the purpose of producing incandescent light is new, and the various manufacturers are naturally very ambitious and anxious that their light shall make a good show here so that they may introduce it elsewhere. There is another reason—they can employ special electrical talent here ; and it does not so much matter to them here what the light costs. In order to get at what the incandescent light will do on the average, you must go to some small place, like Woburn, for instance, which is still a town, although it aspires to be a city. There we find in practice that the electric light company, which is competing with the gas company, is offering to supply electric light to any store at the price of gas. The first lamps they put in give a 20-candle light, which is better than our gas light, the latter averaging from 16½ to 17 candles. But the character of that electric light gradually degenerates, until it gets down to 8 or 10 candles ; and there it stays. That amounts to a serious fluctuation in the long run, and is a matter which, in the hands of outside companies (not gas companies, who have studied this subject in the way of looking after their consumers and rectifying evils), amounts to an evil sure in the long run to be very vexatious. If you will take the readings of your photometer often enough, after your gas is ready to go into the holder, and see to it that your consumers are not using worn-out and wasteful burners—a matter that every company ought to look after— then I make the claim that, month after month, and year after year, we have, in gas, a more uniform lighting value than can be shown in any other known method of artificial illumination.

On motion of Mr. King, a vote of thanks was tendered Mr. Monks.

THE PRESIDENT—As the next two papers to be read are on kindred subjects, we will hear them both read before we discuss them.

Mr. O. B. Weber, of New York city, read his paper, entitled:

DEVELOPMENT OF THE HALF-DEPTH REGENERATIVE FURNACE, AND SOME OF THE RESULTS.

Firing retort benches with gaseous fuel has occupied the attention of the gas world for the past 25 years. As practical results of these labors, the various regenerative systems show how much ingenuity and scientific learning has been expended. The first attempt to fire with a regenerative adjustment in this country was made at the 42d Street Station of the Consolidated Gas Company, New York city (known then as the Metropolitan Gas Works), and was due to the progressive and enthusiastic ideas of the President, Mr. O. Zollikoffer. The form of furnace used was the Liegel, or Slit, which enjoyed at that time the privilege of being the first regenerative furnace tried in this country. This system, through the untiring and zealous devotion of the late Mr. Herzog, the engineer of the works, after several alterations, made necessary by the difference in the fluxing quality of European and American coke, has maintained itself at these works with great success. The next departure was the substitution of a grate furnace for the slot, suggested by Mr. Alexander Strecker, engineer of the works at that time. This change showed conclusively that, as far as this country was concerned, the most successful furnace would be one with a grate. This was the turning-point in the use of this system. It became apparent now, through the successful operation of these furnaces, that, if not too costly in construction and elaborate, nor requiring any more than ordinary care to run them, they would become valuable adjuncts to small gas works. It seemed a comparatively easy matter to translate a Liegel furnace to any gas works in the country. In one's mind, perhaps, this was so; but, practically, alas! What insurmountable and fearful obsstacle

were in the way! My friend, Mr. Baxter, had low retort houses
and chimneys; Mr. Sherman was not able to excavate any distance below, owing to attraction of the waters of the Sound;
another well-known gentleman discovered an iron spring bub-
bling forth in one of his arches, after digging down a few inches
below the floor-line, and so I might multiply the cases, almost
ad infinitum. It was all very well to speak of raised iron floors
and charging platforms; but fate, in the shape of a stern Board
of Directors, often withheld its sanction, scared by the increased
cost of building. It was necessary in order to obtain the advantage of regenerative firing, to construct a furnace possessing all
the cardinal features of the large one, without its elaboration or
depth. Opportunity soon offered itself, through Mr. A. C.
Wood, of Syracuse, N. Y. The half-depth furnace placed in his
works was the first trial of this system. It possessed all the
features of a large furnace together with its weak points. The
air for primary combustion was taken in directly under the grate
bars, without previous warming. The height of the combustion
chamber was very small, so that scarcely any very important
results could have been looked for from it. Still, it served as a
guide; and subsequent trials show that the lines of construction
as laid down in that furnace were correct and permanent. The
practical application, now, of this system on a larger scale—*i. e.,*
under many benches in one stack—was made at the works of
the Williamsburgh Gas Light Company, Williamsburgh, N. Y.
The enterprise of Mr. C. W. Blodget made this trial possible. A
stack containing 20 benches of six retorts each was erected.
The details of this plant may interest the gentlemen of the Association. To begin with: The depth below the floor-line is 30
inches. The arches are 7′ 6″ wide, and 10′ long, accommodat-
ing retorts 14″x28″x10′. The benches are built back to back,
and the draught for them is furnished by one main flue running
below the entire length of the stack to a chimney 75 feet in
height. This does away altogether with the chimneys on each
bench, affording a steady and uniform pressure on each bench.
It will be assumed, naturally, in working regenerative furnaces,
all that is to be done is to fill and light the furnace, then charge
the retorts and expect 9,000 to 10,000 cubic feet yield. This is
all very nice; but it takes a little persuasion to secure this.

Before getting there, however, make up your mind that it will not all be easy work. The presence of clinker, hard enough to build houses on, soon manifests itself. An increased consumption of coke surprises and alarms you. To make matters worse, the heats, of whose uniformity and regularity you have been led to expect so much, go down, so that hardly 200 pounds of coal can be carbonized. Speculations as to the probable cause are numerous, and pet theories are manufactured to suit the case.

Experience similar to this has been frequent, but the causes producing such effects have been discovered, as well as the way to avoid them. In the first place, the passage of the products of combustion through the parallel flues to the chimney is at times interrupted by a hard metallic clinker depositing itself in the last flue. Why it should remain there is obvious : carried around in a highly heated condition, the infusible particles of the coke are in suspension until the vertical or chimney-flue is reached. Then their specific gravity prevents them from ascending ; and, gathering additional volume, soon the most beautiful and exasperating clinker ever seen is formed. To obviate this becomes, then, a prime necessity. This is partially accomplished by heating the primary air supply, as well as permitting it to come to the grate-bars at ordinary pressure. An important feature, also, is the draught on the bench. There must be no rush of air, either primary or secondary ; but all of it must go in easily and naturally. In fact, the damper on the bench chimney should not be opened any wider than to insure an easy but constant draught. Since the time this fact was established clinker has troubled us but little. The relation of the supplementary air supply to the primary oftentimes is a perplexing factor to the men in the retort house, or until they have become accustomed to the working of the furnace. It is a safe rule when employing an ordinary bench chimney furnishing through draught, to open the primary air supplies all the way and the secondaries about half. The area of each slide is 25 square inches. When the furnace is once in working order the men in the retort house find no difficulty in running it successfully. At first they generally express some doubt as to the ability of the furnace, but when they see that it lessens their labor, besides doing away in a great measure with stopped standpipes, there is a rush for the position of fireman.

In small works, with an output of only 20,000 cubic feet per day, the saving of labor to the man in charge is quite a factor. The uniformity of the heats carried, and the comparative ease with which the furnace can be run, invite inspection. The percentage of the saving in coke is much higher than expected, and the average yield per mouthpiece compares favorably with the average results of the deep furnaces. I am indebted to Mr. Blodget of the Williamsburgh Gas Light Company for some of his results obtained during this season's run. In retorts, 14″x28″x10′, charges averaging from 280 to 300 pounds have been burned off every four hours, with an expenditure of about 25 per cent. of the coke made, figuring 40 bushels to a ton. The general averages of the various ″furnaces in other cities show, besides the marked saving in coke, an increased output per mouthpiece, as well as a decrease in the wear and tear of the furnace and retorts. If, perhaps, the half-depth furnace as at present built does not pave the way to " Dollar Gas," it is not the fault of its economizing qualities.

Mr. Fred Bredel, of New York city, then followed with a paper on

THE ADVANTAGES OF REGENERATIVE FURNACES FOR LARGE AND SMALL GAS WORKS.

Gentlemen of the Association : Every gas engineer will admit, in a general way, the advantages of regenerative furnaces, but my present purpose is to show to you in a specific way the financial advantages secured by their use. Take, for example, the case of a large gas works, in which the retort-house is fired under the old system, and that the plant is still in good or perfect working order. To replace it with the improved style of furnace would cause, say, a total loss of that which it succeeded. Assuming that to be so, and the maximum production to be estimated at 1,300,000 per diem, with the total annual output fixed at 300,000,000 cubic feet, such a condition of things would call for a retort-house containing fourteen benches of 9's, the cost of which would be about $84,000. At the start, then, we are obliged to charge $5,040—$84,000, at 6 per cent. per annum — to interest account. Now, we could carbonize 60,000,000 pounds (30,000 net tons) of coal per annum, and have left for sale, at the rate of 1,080 pounds coke per ton of coal carbonized, 32,400,000 pounds, or (at 40 pounds per bushel) 810,000 bushels of coke. Under the old system we would not be able to sell more than 700 pounds, or about 17½ bushels, of coke per ton of coal carbonized, or a total of 525,000 bushels. This shows a gain in available coke production of 285,000 bushels. Assuming that the coke is worth only 4½ cents per bushel, the net gain in money is shown to be $12,825.

When using regenerative furnaces one man can make from 30,000 to 32,000 cubic feet of gas per day, besides bringing in the coal, charging the retorts, attending to the fires, and removing and quenching the coke. This man's services would cost you upon an average say, $2.75 per day, hence the retort-house labor would figure out at about 8.6 cents per 1,000 cubic feet. On the other hand, in the retort-house fitted with benches of 5 or 6 retorts, fired under the old plan, one man generally makes from 18,000 to 20,000 cubic feet of gas per day, and also attends to the other duties above-mentioned. At the same rate of wages, therefore, the charge for labor would be about 13.75 cents per 1,000 cubic feet, which shows a gain secured in this item for the improved plan of 5.15 cents per 1,000, equivalent (on the total make of 300,000,000) to the sum of $15,450. Add to the latter the gain of $12,825 from coke sales and we have a total of $28,275, from which we must deduct the interest charge to arrive at the net profit, which figures out at $23,235 per year. In reality, when a new improved retort-house is to be constructed with a view to increasing the capacity of the plant, or for an entirely new works also, necessarily the cost would be $84,000, *minus* the cost of a similar house fitted with 30 free-fired benches of 6's, which latter cost would amount to about $60,000, thus showing that actually interest ought only to be charged on the difference, or but $24,000.

Now, as to the other advantages, prominent among which is the greater regularity which can be maintained in the working of regenerative benches. You can at all times adjust them to the required make of gas, and you are independent of skilled firemen. The capacity can be increased at will, in about 2 hours, from say 9 to 10 thousand cubic feet of gas per retort per diem; or, on the contrary, can be diminished from 9 to 8 thousand cubic feet in the same space of time. A greater yield per pound of coal is secured; the life of the retorts is lengthened, and the cost of their replacement is about 20 per cent. less than in that of ordinary benches—capacity, of course, being duly considered. A pronounced advantage, especially in large cities where ground is expensive, is the gain in increased producing capacity per square foot, which may be stated at from 35 to 50 per cent. over the old style.

Let us next take the case of a small gas works having, say, a maximum capacity of from 60 to 70 thousand cubic feet per day, with a minimum of about 30,000, and a total capacity of 15 millions cubic feet per year, the coal carbonized amounting to about 1,500 tons per annum. In such works a regenerative bench of 8's, with a reserve bench of 5's, would be ample for the purpose. These could be put in at a cost of about $6,000, entailing an interest charge of $360. Assuming that 26 bushels of coke (40 pounds to bushel) were left for sale from each ton of coal carbonized, a total of 39,000 bushels could be disposed of. Under the old firing system the coke available for sale would not exceed 24,000 bushels. We thus secure a net gain of 15,000 bushels, which, at 6 cents per bushel, shows a profit in money of $900 per annum. The savings in labor would approximate to the services of one man for 365 days, plus the services of one day and one night man, each on 200 days of the year, or a total of 765 days. This, at $2 per diem, means a saving of $1,530 per year. Add thereto the money gain in value of coke sold ($900), subtract therefrom the interest charge ($360), and we have a net gain of $2,075 per annum.

The benches could be worked in the following manner: Use a bench of 8's all the year round. In the winter season charge 300 pounds per retort every 4 hours, or 1,800 pounds per retort, or 14,400 pounds per bench in the 24 hours, giving a yield of, say, 70,000 cubic feet. When the consumption is about 60,000 cubic feet, charge the same quantity 5 times in the 24 hours. That can be done by simply shutting off the dampers and keeping the heats down. The yield per pound of coal will be exactly the same, and the consumption of fuel proportionately less.

When sending out only 30,000 cubic feet per 24 hours but

one day and one night man would be required. The retorts
having been charged, at 6 P. M., with 290 pounds of coal, that
charge could be drawn at midnight, and the retorts again
refilled, the operation being repeated at 5:30 A. M. At that hour
the night man, having filled the generator and closed the
dampers, can go to his home. He is followed by the day man,
who tends to the necessary work around the purifying house and
the yard, sells the coke, and draws the last charge, the latter
will be burned off by, say, 5 P. M., and opens the dampers. At
6 o'clock the bench will again be ready for firing. The consumption of fuel during this time ought never to exceed from 3
to 4 bushels.

JOINT DISCUSSION.

THE PRESIDENT—We have been interested in this matter now
for a considerable length of time, and are beginning to get some
results which are reliable. The Association would like to hear
from Mr. A. C. Wood, as to whether his furnaces have worked
as well during the past year as they did before.

MR. A. C. WOOD—I believe I have nothing to add to, or to
take from, the previous statement made to the Association with
regard to the working at Syracuse of the Stedman-Stanley furnace. It has continued to give us satisfaction, and perhaps we
may report an improvement on the reports previously given.
As to labor, our experience therewith holds good as to any
previous statements. We have improved somewhat in the item
of fuel. The ease with which the production can be increased
and diminished is a very great advantage. At times of unusually
dark weather, contrariwise, in bright weather, we can vary the
production of those benches of 6's from 40 to 60 thousand feet
(perhaps more than that if we desire) with very great ease, by
increasing the draught, increasing the amount of coke in the furnace, and the charges in the retorts.

MR. SHERMAN—We would like to have the experience of our
President in the use of the regenerative furnace.   .

THE PRESIDENT—My experience was given you, to some
extent, in the address read yesterday. My feeling is that if a
man gets a first-rate improved furnace working right, he ought to
be extremely thankful, for he has been exceptionally fortunate.

Every additional flue put in for the purpose of saving waste heat is put in at your own risk; and there is nothing more embarrassing than to have one of those things crack at an unfortunate moment, and so render your bench almost inoperative. We are at this time putting in a most elaborate setting in our double retort house, and our benches are doing so well that my impression is there is more going to be done in that way than in any other. There are gentlemen here who have had more experience with thoroughly constructed regenerative settings than I have. We would like to hear what Mr. Nettleton has been doing with his improved setting.

MR. NETTLETON—I hardly want to express an opinion. The furnaces are not working as well as we would like to have them; but yet I cannot doubt that this is partly my own fault. The heats do not seem to be under my control in the way that they have been in all the other furnaces that I have ever tried. I think, however, and of course hope, that with more experience I will be able to manage them as easily as I have the others. There can be no question about the economy in coke. They have been in operation now for something over four weeks. Just before I came here I had the coke that had been sold from our yard tallied up, and, for 20 days, commencing September 28th—I take those dates simply because on the morning of each day there was about 300 bushels of coke in the yard—176 tons of coal were used, and nearly 28 bushels of coke to the ton of coal carbonized had been sold. This is with benches of sixes. If I can in the future say as much for the heat as I can for the economy of the furnace, it will be eminently satisfactory.

THE PRESIDENT—Mr. Harbison has been doing a good deal in getting ready to construct a new retort house. The Association would like to hear from him as to the result of his investigations in the matter of furnaces.

MR. HARBISON—The time has been devoted to getting ready, and we have not as yet put any retorts into the arches. We are building a stack of five benches on the Stedman-Stanley plan. The President alluded awhile ago to some of the older members of the Association. I may say that some of the older members may remember that a certain New York State gentleman some time ago referred to his retort house or works as being a model. We went to look at his works and tried to copy the model and to improve upon it. We hope a year from this time to have had some experience in working the benches that we are now building. We will then be able to give you, I trust, some satisfactory results. If we have any success you will hear from us then. I have nothing in connection with it that I could state, except the manner of construction, which would not, of course, be of any interest.

MR. NETTLETON—Our Secretary has had some experience in the matter, and we would like to hear from him.

MR. C. J. R. HUMPHREYS—The very little that we have done at Lawrence has been in the direction of a furnace in front of the bench. A couple of years ago we felt that we ought to put in improved furnaces on account of the value to us of the coke. Every year we had to bring coke from Boston. We wanted to save coke, but at the same time did not care to go to the expense of putting in a full regenerative furnace, because our stacks were comparatively new, and to tear them all down to put in full regenerative furnaces seemed too expensive. So we had to find some furnace that we could use without tearing down the stacks. It may be that there are one or two furnaces which could be used in that way, but they were not altogether satisfactory to us. So we worked up something of our own. I think I may say that there are only two peculiarities in those furnaces. With regard to the furnace itself, it stands out in front of the bench, thus avoiding the necessity of pulling down the arches ; and, instead of being square or rectangular, it is made in an oval form. My idea in thus designing it was that I felt that in an ordinary rectangular furnace the coke did not get down into and fill up the corners, leaving a chance for the air to get in, or causing air-holes, so to speak, and thus burning the carbonic oxide in the furnace itself. That was the reason why I made the furnace on this oval plan. The other peculiarity is about the flues. I can best describe them as being a pipe inside of a box. The pipe is the smoke flue, and the space between the outside of the pipe and the inside of the box would be the air flue. It is just like a fire clay pipe in a fire clay box. My idea was that the smoke coming down, as it goes over the side, and then comes down into the flue—the flue being round—would cause the gases to travel more greatly in a whirling motion than would be the case in an ordinary straight flue. Whether it is so or not I do not know. Those are the only peculiarities of the furnace. As to our working with it I must say it has done better than we expected. We have had no trouble from clinkering, and, from the first, the furnace has worked very easily indeed. I expect to put in some more next year. I hardly know of any change that I want to make. As we only have two of the furnaces in our retort house of twelve benches, of course I cannot give you any complete results stretching over any period of time; but I did collect the figures for a week lately, keeping an account of the amount of coal burned in those benches, and of the amount of coke used. The amount of coke used was obtained simply by keeping an account of the number of retorts of coke used, so as to avoid any conflict in items with regard to the measurement of the coke. On the first day our weight of coal per retort charge was only 254 pounds; on the next day, 292 pounds; and on the third, 304 pounds. The percentage of coke used varied, but averaged at about 20 per cent. During the last two days it ran along at 20 per cent. I should say that the retorts, instead of being a full nine feet, only measure about 8 ft. 4 in. on the outside. Of course, 8 inches of very valuable space is lost, otherwise we might possibly do a little better.

MR. C. NETTLETON—Can Mr. Humphreys give us the diameter and height of the chamber?

MR. HUMPHREYS—The short diameter is 1 ft. 11 ins., the large diameter being 3 ft. The height is about 5½ or 6 ft. I have here a detailed statement of the workings from October 1st to October 6th:

RESULTS FROM TWO OF HUMPHREYS' FURNACES—LAWRENCE GAS WORKS.

Date.	Coke used, bench No. 7.	Coke used, bench No. 8.	Lbs. coal carbonized, benches Nos. 7 & 8.	Wt. coal per retort per charge.	Per cent. coke, bench No. 7.	Per cent. coke, bench No. 8.
Oct. 1	$8\frac{4}{5}$ retorts	8 retorts	18,300	254	24.4	22
" 2	$8\frac{2}{5}$ "	$8\frac{2}{5}$ "	21,000	292	23.3	23.3
" 3	$8\frac{2}{5}$ "	8 "	21,900	304	23.3	22.6
" 4	$8\frac{3}{5}$ "	$7\frac{4}{5}$ "	21,900	304	24	21.7
" 5	$8\frac{2}{5}$ "	$7\frac{2}{5}$ "	21,900	304	23.3	20
" 6	$8\frac{2}{5}$ "	$7\frac{2}{5}$ "	21,900	304	23.3	20

N. B.—Percentage of coke is in volume. Retorts, 14" x 22" x 8' 4".

On motion of Mr. Wood, a vote of thanks was tendered to Messrs. Weber and Bredel.

Mr. J. L. Hallett, Springfield, Mass., read a paper on

THE USE AND VALUE OF COKE FOR GENERATING STEAM.

Gentlemen: The Springfield Gas Light Company have used their surplus coke for steam heating since 1878. At that time, 1,792 feet of three-inch pipe was laid as an experimental line, connecting the boiler with the company's office, also several stores, offices and dwellings, the space heated aggregating 145,000 cubic feet.

Steam was generated in a 4 x 16 tubular boiler, with 60 three-inch tubes. There were 12,526 bushels of coke used, being 2,840 bushels in excess of the previous year, when steam was made exclusively to run the exhauster and for general use about the works. The results were satisfactory financially, and especially in providing a medium for the dispensing of a large accumulation of coke. Since 1878 extensions have been made to the steam heating plant and additional boilers erected. Last winter 5,358 gross tons of fuel were consumed, which is equivalent to 294,000 bushels of coke. That is two-thirds more than our surplus coke, and having used bituminous and anthracite coal of different grade and size, both separately and mixed, it has given opportunity for comparative tests, and we unhesitatingly affirm that coke is the best fuel for producing steam—unless it be crude oil, with which we have not had any experience.

To obtain a given result, we found that coke is superior to anthracite (egg size) coal by 10.8 per cent. Compared with buckwheat and pea coal, mixed with bituminous slack, coke will evaporate the same quantity of water with 26.9 per cent. less fuel. Our records show conclusively the superiority of coke over coal for making steam. Without advocating the erecting of a steam plant, as that must depend largely on the location of the gas works and cost of reaching the consumer, it may be of interest to know that 250 horse-power could consume the surplus coke of a 5,000 ton gas plant.

Under ordinary conditions, a gross ton of coke would evaporate 15,680 pounds of water, which is equal to 10,453 meter units of heat (evaporating 1,500 pounds of water to 1,000 meter units).

Reduced to dollars and cents, on the basis of seventy-seven cents per 1,000 units, a ton of coke would produce $8.04 worth of steam, less 10 per cent. loss in distribution—net, $7.24, or 13.1 cents per bushel used under the boilers.

By utilizing the waste heat of the retort benches to heat the feed water, we have a saving of 100 tons of coal for each bench.

A prejudice exists among some against the use of coke on account of a *supposed* damaging effect on the grate bars and tubes of the boiler. That is not true, in our experience. We have used coke exclusively under one boiler since 1870. Continuous use, day and night for eight months in the year, and careful inspection find it in as good condition as other boilers fired with coal. The grate bars have not been renewed and are apparently in as good condition as when they were set.

Bearing on the subject of the value of coke for making steam, I submit the following answers from persons that have given the subject their attention :

No. 1.—" A factory tried coke under one of their boilers, and found that it took an equal weight of coke or coal to do the work ; but as coal cost $6.25 per gross ton, and coke at 8 cents per bushel, but $4.96, they saved 20 per cent. and continued the use of coke."

No. 2.—" When it has been used it has been invariably estimated as the cheapest fuel. It has been difficult to supply the demand for such use."

No. 3.—"A company used six tons of hard coal under their boilers in one week. The next week they used coke against the protest of the fireman, and burnt just seven tons."

No. 4.—" Likes it better than anything he ever used; prefers it to any other fuel, as it makes steam faster, and is cheaper than any kind of coal."

No. 5.—" Number 5 says that coke at 10 cents per bushel is cheaper to him than coal at \$7.00 per ton."

No. 6.—" A prejudice formerly existed in this place against coke for firing boilers. It was claimed that coke injured the boiler and setting; but such prejudice, born of indolence, has long since passed away. Can sell all the coke made to users of steam."

No. 7.—" Our experience has been that the use of coke does not damage the iron of the boiler."

No. 8.—" Have used coke 25 years under a boiler at gas works. It has been in constant action, and apparently is in good condition."

No. 9.—" Nothing used but coke, eight to nine years, and boiler now in perfect condition."

No. 10.—" Over 15 years continuously, night and day."

No. 11.—" Used coke under boiler for 10 years, the boiler being in use 24 hours each day."

DISCUSSION.

MR. BREDEL—Did the gentleman find any difference between the use of hard and soft coke—that is to say, coke produced by high and low heats?

MR. HALLETT—No difference at all. We have been supplying steam now since 1878, and one 45-horse power boiler consumed 50 tons the first year. Our business has grown to 1,000-horse power, with the consumption last year of 5,200 tons. We have used all kinds of fuel, and in all ways. Considering that the Lehigh egg coal was the best we could obtain, we tried 100 tons of the same, compared it with coke, and found the result to be in favor of the latter, on what we supposed was the best coal that we could possibly use. We also used soft coal and the small sizes of Lehigh coal, but every test made showed that we could make more steam with coke than with coal. We run our retorts at high heats, and our yield of gas per lb. of coal carbonized will average, throughout the year, 5 ft.

THE SECRETARY—The following tables, handed to me by Mr. A. E. Boardman, contain a report of the results at the pumping-station of the Macon (Ga.) water works:

TABLE NO. 1, showing comparison of coal (bituminous) and coke as fuel consumed in the Waterville pumping station of the Macon (Ga.) Water Works. Average steam pressure, 70 lbs.; average water pressure, 100 lbs. Pump, a Worthington Compound Duplex, 12 in. by 20 in.. by 10 in. by 15 in.

Date, 1885.	Water pumped, gallons.	Fuel used, lbs.		Waste per cent.	Duration of test.	Gallons pumped per lb. fuel.	
		Coal.	Coke.				
April	14,728,000	68,974	......	7-79	30 days		
May	17,102,000	74,448	......	6.35	31 "		
June	19,084,000	71,628	......	7.62	30 "	Av'age 270.68	
July	21,746,000	75,012	......	7.52	31 "		
Aug.	21.875,000	75,858	......	7-43	31 "		Av'ge duty 41,699,000
Sept.	21,049,000	78,481	......	7-34	30 "		
Oct.	21,715,000	72,870	......	7-65	31 "		
Nov.	20,282,000	......	93,060		30 "		
Dec.	17,273,000	......	67,330	Av'ge 12.7	31 "	Av'ge 235.74	
1886							
Jan.	19.192,000	......	87,580		31 "		
Feb.	16,780,000	......	67,640		28 "		Av'ge duty 37,036,000
Mar.	15,719,000	......	63,050		31 "		

Taking the value of coal to be 100, the above shows coke to be 87.

TABLE No. 2, showing further tests with the same pump. Steam pressure, 60 lbs.; water pressure, 68 lbs.; duty, 32,148,000 gals.

Date. 1886.	Water pumped, gallons.	Fuel used, lbs.		Duration of test.	Gallons pumped per lb. coal.	Gallons pumped per lb. coke.	Waste per cent.
		Coal.	Coke.				
May	3,038,080	......	15,625	94½ hrs	......	194.45	.....
"	4,207,280	Mixed	18,421	133 "	228.40		.....
"	12,911,940	41,800	......	415 "	309.73	......	8.91
July	5,605,740	19,200	......	9 days	291.92	......	...
"	12,842,700	......	51,640	18 "	......	248.70	12.56
"	3,359,900	Mixed	12,400	4 "	270.72		.....
Aug.	7,922,820	......	36,780	11 "	......	215.41	.....
"	10,167,040	39,200	......	12 "	259.62	......	.....
"	6,245,760	......	30,580	7 "	......	204.24	.....
1887 Jan.	18,055,620	61,200	......	19 "	295.02	......	.....
"	9,729,900	......	41,120	12 "	......	236.62	.....

By these tests we find the value of coke to be 77, taking coal as 100; and a mixture of about equal quantities to be 82½. A fair estimate would be, coal, 100; coke, 80.

Mr. C. Nettleton—What sort of coal is that from which Mr. Boardman obtained his coke? Of course some coals contain more ash than others, and that might make a difference. The South Alabama coal might give different results from Pittsburg coal.

The Secretary—The document does not show that. It simply shows that the coal against which the coke is compared was bituminous coal.

Mr. Helme—I know that Mr. Boardman gets his coal from Tennessee, near Chattanooga.

On motion of Mr. Sherman a vote of thanks was tendered to Mr. Hallett for his paper.

The President—Is Mr. Taber ready to report the names of the proposed Committee of Investigation?

Mr. Taber—At the request of the members of the Committee appointed for that purpose, I report the following names: Frederick S. Benson, Brooklyn, N. Y.; Charles F. Prichard, Lynn, Mass.; T. Littlehales, Hamilton, Ontario; James Somerville, Indianapolis, Ind.; A. E. Boardman, Macon, Ga.; Wm. J. Fay, Denver, Col.; and J. B. Crockett, San Francisco, Cal.

THE PRESIDENT—The Chair awaits a motion.

MR. HARBISON—I move that the report of the Committee be accepted, and that these gentlemen be declared the Investigating Committee, in the expectation that every man will perform his duty.   Adopted.

THE PRESIDENT—Mr. McMillin wishes to present reports on two additional matters referred to the Executive Committee. The members of the Association may remember that last spring a donation of 5 pounds sterling was sent by a Scottish gentleman to the proprietors of the AMERICAN GAS LIGHT JOURNAL, to be devoted in such way as they thought best for the interest of the fraternity on our side of the Atlantic.   The JOURNAL folks turned the money over to this Association, and the Association turned it over to its Executive Committee, who are now ready to report, through Mr. McMillin, a recommendation in regard to the disposition of the sum named.

MR. McMILLIN—I think we have had no question harder to wrestle with than this.   We finally determined on our report only within the last few minutes, which is as follows:

" The undersigned were appointed by the Executive Committee to take into consideration a communication received by the AMERICAN GAS LIGHT JOURNAL from a resident of Scotland, who desires that his identity be concealed under the title of ' An Old Scottish Subscriber.'   In this communication the donor desired to convey to the American gas fraternity a slight token of his esteem in the shape of a draft for five pounds sterling, to be used or disposed of in such manner with any of the gas associations in this country as the editor of the JOURNAL might suggest.   The JOURNAL people have kindly suggested that the Association offer this money (about $25) to the best paper on some subject to be selected.   Your Committee suggest that the Association offer this as a premium for the best paper on the subject of ' Naphthaline,' the paper to be read at the next meeting of this Association.

" They further suggest that the Secretary convey to the donor the thanks of the Association for his generous offering.

E. McMILLIN,
W. H. WHITE, } Committee."
J. P. HARBISON,

On motion of Mr. Sherman, the report of the Committee was accepted, and the disposition of the money recommended by the Committee approved.

THE PRESIDENT—Does the Executive Committee couple with that any suggestion as to who shall be the judges?

MR. McMILLIN—No ; they leave them to be appointed at the next meeting.

MR. McMILLIN—The same Committee had another question before it—that of the publication of our proceedings—a subject which has become something of a chestnut. The Executive Committee feel that the question must be met at this meeting, in deference to the parties who are interested in the matter. We have made our decision and I will announce it, but I will have to reduce the report to writing after I have made it orally :

It is the sense of the Committee that, in the future, the Association should employ its own stenographer, make its own report, and furnish copies of that report to all of the gas journals willing to pay their pro rata share of the expense. In short, that is the substance of their recommendation.

MR. CLARK—I move that the report of the Committee be accepted and adopted.

THE PRESIDENT—You have heard the report of the Committee, recommending that for future meetings of this Association the stenographer be employed by the Association instead of by the AMERICAN GAS LIGHT JOURNAL, and that the report of the proceedings of the Association be then furnished by him to : the journals that are willing to pay their proportionate part of the expense of his employment.

The motion of Mr. Clark was adopted.

MR. PEARSON—As I was not here when it was decided to accept the invitation (tendered by the Toronto Gas Light Company), to the Association, to hold its next meeting in that city, I wish to take this opportunity of expressing my gratification with your action, and my appreciation of the honor you do us by meeting there. I hope that at the conclusion of the next meeting of the Association no member will have reason to regret the acceptance of the invitation.

MR. A. C. HUMPHREYS—I move that at the future meetings of this Association the five papers to be read, as designed in advance by the Executive Committee, be printed by the Secretary in time for distribution among the members at the opening of the session; and that the Executive Committee take the proper action to insure the completion of those papers long enough in advance of the meeting to permit them to be printed. In making that motion, I would say I do not believe this will make it any harder for any member to prepare his paper. Although I put off preparing my paper until last Friday, I could have written it just as well a month ago—perhaps a little better —if I had been compelled to do it at that time. The motion was adopted.

MR. NETTLETON—If there is no other business now before the Association, I, for one, would be very glad to hear from Mr. Spice as to how gas matters are in England.

MR. SPICE—Mr. President and gentlemen: If I had received notice that such a question would be asked me, I would have prepared myself to answer it in a proper manner; but in default of such intimation you will have to take whatever may happen to come into my mind. I may say that the English gas industry is in a prosperous condition, notwithstanding all the efforts of the electricians of the world, who find their way to London as well as to the United States. It is an axiom that it is safer not to prophesy until you know what is before you; but about eight years ago, when a bombastic message from America arrived in England to the effect that the gas industry was doomed, that the gas works of the world were to be covered with a pall such as that which descended many centuries ago upon the old city of Pompeii, that they were to be covered up and never more seen, that the place that knew them then should know them no more, I ventured, at that desperate epoch in our business, when the holders of gas stocks were frightened almost out of their senses, to prophesy that the advocates of electric lighting would prove to be blessings in disguise. And so it has turned out. The rate of progress, of development—or call it what you will—the rate of the growth of the consumption of gas in England has been about nine per cent. per annum. I understand that greater things are done in America, in the way of progress, than in England. In America, a city beginning with but a thousand people, will, before you really know where they are, become a city of 50,000 inhabitants. If you make allowance for that very rapid growth of population (of which we know comparatively nothing in England), you will see that gas matters in England and in America have gone hand in hand, from prosperity to prosperity.

In one way or another, by cheapening the production, by increasing the purity, by applying that stimulus to every department of gas production and delivery, and by disseminating information of all kinds for the benefit of that great public who are our customers, we have thriven, and are going on to thrive, and have had no check to that development of growth by which we are becoming greater and greater. One thing has tended to maintain the position of the gas companies, and that has been the application of gas as a motive power for the production of electricity. We have had, in the last year, in London, a notable example of that, where a very large hotel, built after the model of your large American hotels, really pay more for gas (after the whole house had been lit with electricity) than they ever did before. There is no economy in electric lighting, so far as they are concerned; but they want it. I have said that electric light is, and always must be, a luxury. It is not the poor man's light; it is the light for those who can afford to pay for it. And that is one of the assurances which we as gas men have that we shall always be able to hold our own. I thank you, gentlemen, for your kindness and attention.

MR. McMILLIN—Having to make two reports a while ago, it seems that I did not do all that was expected of me. My attention has been called to the fact that I did not make one as full as was intended. I still think that I did, but will state what the Committee wish me to, and then leave the matter for the Association to settle. The Committee instruct me to report the recommendation that the resolution (passed some years ago) making the AMERICAN GAS LIGHT JOURNAL the official organ of this Association be rescinded, and that the proceedings be hereafter reported and furnished as I suggested. The Association will employ the stenographer, and furnish copies of the reports to such gas journals as will pay their pro rata share of the expense. Before we could properly act upon the resolution already adopted, the Committee thought it was necessary that the resolution formerly passed, making the AMERICAN GAS LIGHT JOURNAL the organ of the Association, should be rescinded.

THE PRESIDENT—As that is a somewhat different motion from the one already put, I will have to put the question to the Association again.

MR. NETTLETON—I sincerely hope the amendment now offered by Mr. McMillin will not pass, and I say so from motives of personal kindness toward Mr. Thomas, who is now so sick that he is confined to his bed. Personally, although I was sorry to see it adopted, I was content to have the previous resolution decided without protesting against it. I would, however, be very sorry to have this action added to that.

MR. WOOD—I quite agree with the remarks made by Mr. Nettleton. I believe it would be a very unjust and ungenerous act on the part of this Association to pass a resolution of the kind proposed. If not directly, it is certainly indirectly, reflecting upon the conduct of Mr. Thomas, an old and honored member of our Association. I sincerely hope the recommendation of the Executive Committee will not be approved.

MR. GRAEFF—As one who is, perhaps, as much interested in this matter as any one else, I wish to say I trust the matter will be allowed to remain as it is. If Mr. Thomas were present, I might not take this position ; and I confess the fact of his absence did not occur to me when I asked Mr. McMillin whether the Committee's report, as made, covered all the matter of their recommendation. I, therefore, if it is proper to do so, ask the Committee to reconsider its report, and to limit it to the recommendation already made and acted upon.

MR. A. C. HUMPHREYS—I ask if the passage of the first resolution is not, in effect, the same as if we passed the resolution now suggested.

THE PRESIDENT—Not exactly.

MR. BROWN—I wish to say I heartily agree with what Mr. Graeff has stated.

THE PRESIDENT—We have now heard from the editors of the other papers having an interest in this matter. I hope the resolution which constituted the AMERICAN GAS LIGHT JOURNAL the official organ of this Association, will not be rescinded. Under the circumstances, will the Committee withdraw the resolution, or shall we vote it down ?

MR. MCMILLIN—As chairman of the Committee, of course, I have no authority to withdraw the resolution which they instructed me to report. I thought the first resolution virtually covered it ; but some of the gentlemen of the Committee insist that it did not. I cannot withdraw the resolution, for I have not the authority to do so—whatever my personal feeling may be upon the subject.

MR. A. C. HUMPHREYS—I would like to ask how the AMERICAN GAS LIGHT JOURNAL can remain the organ of this Association if the original motion is passed.

THE PRESIDENT—The question has been raised as to whether this covers the question of the notices which are sent by the Secretary of the Association to the JOURNAL, and which are published in it. I would ask the chairman of the Committee whether, in his judgment, the notices are hereafter to be sent to the other journals, or are only to be sent to the paper which has heretofore published them.

MR. MCMILLIN—I have only made the report as I was instructed to make it by the Committee. If you want to know any further as to what that report means, I shall have to ask you to take the understanding of the Committee with regard to it.

MR. CLARK—But the Committee were discharged, by vote of the Association, after having made their first report.

MR. A. C. WOOD—As I understand the matter, the AMERICAN GAS LIGHT JOURNAL, as the official organ of the Association, has heretofore had its stenographer here to report the proceedings of the Association, and has done so without any expense to the Association ?

THE PRESIDENT—Yes.

MR. WOOD—And the recommendation of the Committee is that hereafter the Association employ its own stenographer, and publish the proceedings in such papers as may desire to print them.

THE PRESIDENT—Copies of the report are to be furnished by the stenographer to such papers as are willing to bear their proportion of the expense.

MR. WOOD—The effect of that would be to take the entire matter out of the hands of Mr. Thomas, our old friend and honored associate. I appeal to the leniency of the Association, and to the forbearance of the Committee. I move that the motion to accept the recommendation of the Executive Committee be rescinded.

MR. HELME—I second that. I do not think that an old member of this Association, one who has been with it from the beginning, can fail to recollect how the AMERICAN GAS LIGHT JOURNAL has always stood by us, and rendered all the aid possible in the promotion of the interests of the Society, and in the protection of the gas business generally. I have, on one or two occasions, made a movement toward having the JOURNAL paid for the great expense they were at in publishing the proceedings, but the publishers of the JOURNAL have refused payment every time. Now, if that conduct on their part—if that treatment of our Association, is not worthy some consideration at our hands, especially from the older members, then I must say that good treatment goes for nothing. I, for one, as a member, shall be very sorry indeed to see the thing changed from the course which has been followed for some time past—from a time, in fact, when it was very doubtful whether this Association could be made a success. I can recollect very well, when, in this city, Mr. Steel, of Buffalo, moved that this Society take steps toward its dissolution. But that resolution did not pass— thank heaven !—and we are here to-day under prosperous circumstances. I do not know from what source we got more or better aid in attaining our present prosperous condition than we got from the AMERICAN GAS LIGHT JOURNAL, and I do think something is due to them in consideration for the great help they then gave us. They at least deserve good treatment at our hands. Let us not cast them aside as we would an old horse for which we have no further use.

MR. FLOYD—As one of the old members of this Association I can second everything that Mr. Helme said. I think we ought now to stand by the AMERICAN GAS LIGHT JOURNAL, for it stood by us in our adversity. It deserves our assistance now.

THE PRESIDENT—A motion is made by Mr. Wood that we reconsider the vote by which we resolved hereafter to employ our own stenographer.

MR. McMILLIN—I do not know whether the other two members of the Committee are in the hall or not to speak upon this motion—

MR. WHITE—I am right here with you, McMillin.

MR. McMILLIN—There has been a good deal of dissatisfaction expressed that the Association should father one journal to the exclusion of all others; and the Committee has endeavored to consider this question from all its various standpoints. I do not believe that any of the gentlemen who have spoken upon the other side of the question, and against this report, entertain any higher opinion, personally, of Mr. Thomas, or of the managers of that paper, than do the members of this Committee. (Applause.) They have received favors from him; they are all under obligations to him; they are all his personal friends. But I think it would be in just as good taste for an old gas engineer of twenty or thirty years' experience to come into this Association and ask us to protect him against the rising young fellows who are coming up every day, as it is for the AMERICAN GAS LIGHT JOURNAL to be always asking the support of this Association, as against its competitors. Certainly, there is no feeling on the part of the Association against the JOURNAL—it has been the friend of us all, at all times; but other papers are now struggling for existence, and they are doing their duty and are doing it well. I see no reason why we should deny them what we give to the secular press. Other associations permit the publishers of the daily papers to attend their meetings, take notes of the proceedings and publish them. If they send a shorthand reporter he can take down the papers which are read, and they can be published also. That course has not been followed in this Association. We have given to one journal the exclusive privilege. I am opposed to rescinding what we have already done in this matter. We certainly have not done anything more than is fair, and I think Mr. Thomas would admit that if he were here with us.

MR. HARBISON—As a member of the Committee that made this report to the Association, I wish to say I am not willing to stand second to any member of this Association in the expression of high esteem in which I hold Mr. Thomas and the gentlemen who are connected with him in the management of the AMERICAN GAS LIGHT JOURNAL. I have never received from them anything but the most courteous attention. I have always entertained for them, and still do, the kindest of feelings, and the most hearty wishes for their prosperity and success. My desire as a member of the Committee (and I know that the same feeling existed with each of the other gentlemen,) was simply to perform our duty with reference to the welfare of the Association. We could not permit our personal preferences to influence our action. We could not allow our kind feeling toward the gentlemen connected with the JOURNAL to influence our report. We could not, as a Committee of this Association, make a report which simply expressed our personal wishes with regard to the matter; otherwise our report might have been very different from what it was. As Mr. McMillin has said, there has been for years the growing feeling that the proceedings of this Association should be published in more than one journal. It was only the deference due to that largely expressed wish on behalf of many members of the Association which induced me to give my vote for the action which has been recommended by the Committee. As I have said, I could not in justice to the members of this Association, who have honored me with a position on the Executive Committee, do otherwise than I have done, by agreeing to the report which has been presented by Mr. McMillin on behalf of the Committee. The reason leading to the recommendation by the Committee that the resolution, passed years ago, making the AMERICAN GAS LIGHT JOURNAL the organ of the Association, be rescinded, was because we did not see, with that vote standing on the records of the Association, how any different action from that provided for by that resolution could be taken by the Association. As long as that vote stood no other action could consistently be taken. The first thing to be done, therefore, was to repeal that vote. If Mr. McMillin had not added that recommendation to his report, the balance of the report would be of no effect. You cannot, in my opinion, pass a vote giving to this Association the right to employ its own stenographer, and call on the various papers that choose to publish this report for their proportion of the cost of furnishing it, so long as that vote stands on record which makes the AMERICAN GAS LIGHT JOURNAL the official organ. It is stultifying yourself to attempt to do it. I want the Association to understand that fact. We must, in my opinion, reconsider that vote before any other action can be taken which will be of any effect or avail.

MR. SHERMAN—Is there any objection to permitting other papers to send their own reporters here to take a record of our proceedings?

THE PRESIDENT—Yes. The objection is made by the AMERICAN GAS LIGHT JOURNAL that they, being the official organ of the Association, alone have a right to publish a stenographic report.

MR. SHERMAN—Have the other papers no right to send a reporter here?

THE PRESIDENT—They have no right to send a reporter to take a stenographic report. Reporters may come in here and take brief notes, but they cannot furnish stenographic reports to other journals. Nor can the papers which are read here be printed in any other journal until after they have been printed in the AMERICAN GAS LIGHT JOURNAL. The members of the Association know that sometimes in the stress of business it has been a long while before the papers have appeared in the AMERICAN GAS LIGHT JOURNAL.

MR. SHERMAN—I supposed any paper had a right to send a reporter in here to make a report of our proceedings.

THE PRESIDENT—No; that has not been permitted.

MR. WOOD—But has there been any vote or resolution against permitting other journals to do that?

THE PRESIDENT—The Executive Committee have always understood that it would not be allowed. In fact, my attention has been called, during this meeting of the Association, by the Manager of the AMERICAN GAS LIGHT JOURNAL to the fact that other reporters were here, and I have stopped them from taking notes. That is just what is the matter.

MR. A. C. HUMPHREYS—Then it is evident that Mr. Wood, and some of the other gentlemen, have made their remarks under a misapprehension.

MR. WOOD—I think I fully understand the situation ; and, with due respect to the report of this special Committee, I still insist upon my motion. I must say I think the thing is altogether wrong, and must have been misconstrued by them. The resolution heretofore passed by the Association makes the AMERICAN GAS LIGHT JOURNAL our official organ. I do not understand that any action of this Association has ever restricted any other newspaper from sending a reporter here to take down the proceedings of the Association. If there is any such resolution I would like to have the Secretary call attention to it. If this special Committee now propose to divide the reports of our proceedings with the AMERICAN GAS LIGHT JOURNAL, and with the other two now existing journals, as suggested by Mr. Harbison, what shall be done with the next, and with the next and so on with all the other journals devoted to our industry which may come up hereafter?

MR. MCMILLIN—Whatever journal is willing to pay for the report will get it.

MR. WOOD—So long as we have an official organ of the Association I do not see the necessity of giving that preference to any more journals. But I would grant the privilege to other journals of reporting and publishing the proceedings, if they desire to do so.

THE PRESIDENT—How about the papers which are read ?

MR. WOOD—Let them repo.t those also, if they wish to.

THE PRESIDENT—Would you let them have copies of the papers ?

MR. WOOD—If they send a stenographer here he may take

down the papers as they are read; or, if the writer of the paper desires, he may furnish copies of his paper to the other publishers.

Mr. McMillin—That is just what this Committee proposes to do.

Mr. Wood—It seems to me you proposed to make all the journals "official organs." That is the effect of it.

Mr. McMillin—No; the Committee propose to put them all on the same footing, so far the publication of the reports is concerned. While the resolution stands as it is, it is not the proper thing for parties reading papers to give copies to other journals than the American Gas Light Journal, our official organ. At least, I have always been governed by that understanding.

Mr. Wood—It seems to me that, as we long ago proclaimed the American Gas Light Journal to be our official organ, it should continue so—at least for the present.

Mr. Sherman—What does the Committee propose to do with the papers which are read? Will copies be sent around to the different offices?

The President—I understand Mr. McMillin proposes that, in the future, the publisher of any journal who wishes to do so, shall have a chance to publish any of our papers as early as the American Gas Light Journal does; and that they shall also have a chance to report stenographically the debates, or to have a copy of the report made by the Association's stenographer, upon paying their proportion of the expense. All the gas light journals of the country, if they like, can hereafter report the proceedings of our Association.

Mr. Sherman—But they cannot all have the papers at the same time.

The President—Certainly they can, if they are printed before hand.

Mr. McMillin—That will be their business. If they can get the copies, they can publish them.

Mr. Wood—I think this Association, representing the vast amount of capital engaged in the gas business, should have an official organ. I still insist upon my motion to rescind the previous action of the Association in adopting the report of this special Committee.

MR. LOWE—As I understand it the AMERICAN GAS LIGHT JOURNAL is still our official organ; and I do not think we want more than one. I do not think the last resolution contemplates that we shall have more than one. If Mr. Wood is willing to permit each journal to send a stenographer to take minutes of the proceedings of this Association, and publish them, then I do not see why we would be any better off by rescinding the motion already passed. It would involve merely the question of letting them contribute to the expense of furnishing the report, and I am quite sure that each one of the existing journals would be happy to pay one-third of the expense, and would prefer to do so, rather than pay the entire cost of procuring a report. So far as the papers read are concerned, they can have those at any rate, inasmuch as they are to be printed.

MR. GRAEFF—My opinion of this official organ business is that a report of the proceedings can be furnished by the Association to any paper that wishes it, without at all disturbing the relation which the present JOURNAL sustains to the Association as its official organ. My idea in asking the question I did was to ascertain whether the motion carried with it the publication of the official notices of the President and Secretary. I understood the President to rule that it did not. I consider that so long as the AMERICAN GAS LIGHT JOURNAL is the sole recipient of the official notices which come from the President and Secretary, it continues to be the official organ. I consider that the placing of the report of the proceedings of this Convention within the reach of other journals does not disturb the official organ at all. I understand that to be the President's ruling.

THE PRESIDENT—That is my opinion.

MR. GRAEFF—I do not understand that any member of this Association is better posted on parliamentary law than is our worthy President; and I am quite content to accept his understanding of the effect of the motion which we have adopted. Speaking as the editor of one of the journals, I wish to say I do not care to disturb the position of the official organ. I would not have the official organship transferred from the old journal to my own, for I have no desire for it. But speaking now as a member of the Association, I believe that we ought to publish our proceedings as widely as possible, so that they may be read by members of all the industries that we represent. I have in mind the case of the Western Architects' Association, which had been confining its reports to one journal. Finally they got tired of that, because, while the journal had a good representative circulation, there were other journals coming up which went into quarters where that journal did not necessarily go, and so they departed from the old custom. Now, instead of having one report published, they permit nine journals to have a report, and any architect who does not get a copy of the proceedings of the convention must be a very sorry sort of chap—if he does not take one paper of the nine. As a member of the Association, I believe we should place the proceedings of this convention and of all our conventions, within the hands of every gas man who reads. On that ground I ask for the support of this report made by the special Committee, if you rule that such further support be necessary.

THE PRESIDENT—The motion now before the house is that the action just taken by the Association, in accepting the report of the sub-Committee of the Executive Committee, be reconsidered.

THE PRESIDENT—Those in favor of reconsidering the acceptance of the report of the Executive Committee will say " Aye ; " those opposed to reconsidering it will say " No." The Chair rules that it is not a vote. Therefore, the report of the Committee stands accepted.

MR. NETTLETON—I wish that the Chair would state just what that report is, so that there may be no misunderstanding.

MR. MCMILLIN—The report, as voted upon, was that the proceedings be furnished to those journals paying their proportionate share of the cost of making the report.

THE PRESIDENT—But it does not affect the official standing of the AMERICAN GAS LIGHT JOURNAL, as being the organ of this Association. (Applause.)

MR. HELME—Will the papers which are read be handed as usual to the AMERICAN GAS LIGHT JOURNAL ?

The President—I would say they would be entitled to the first copy; and if anybody else wants a copy he can get it.

Mr. Helme—It seems to me that by this resolution that matter is left open. You had better decide that question here and now.

The President—I think that that will arrange itself, because we are to have the papers printed hereafter before they are read.

Mr. Harbison—Do I understand that the report of the Committee, which we have acted upon and accepted, is to the effect that hereafter the Association shall employ its own stenographer?

The President—Yes.

Mr. Harbison—And that the papers paying their pro rata of the cost shall have a copy of the proceedings, and of the papers read?

The President—Yes.

Mr. Harbison—We did not provide that any one journal should have all the papers handed over to it.

The President—I understood Mr. Helme's question to be, not with regard to the report of the stenographer, but with regard to the papers which were read. The stenographer, as I understand it, will furnish a copy of his report to each of the journals, but the papers read will not be reported.

Mr. Harbison—It is well to understand that right here. Are not the papers read considered as being part of the stenographer's report?

The President—They have not been reported by the stenographer heretofore.

Mr. Harbison—But they might be, hereafter, if the Association employs a stenographer. It is simply a question whether he shall make a stenographic report of the papers, or whether the original paper shall be furnished to him.

The President—The Chair is open to instruction on this matter. I suppose if a journal wants a copy of a paper it will be able to get it.

Mr. Harbison—I would like to know, for my own guidance, what the proper action will be.

MR. GILBERT—As I understand it, the papers which are hereafter to be read are to be printed and ready for distribution at
the meeting of the Association.

THE PRESIDENT—Some will be printed; all may not be.

MR. GILBERT—Those which are accepted to the number of
five, are to be printed.   As to those papers, of course, the journals wishing to publish them will have copies furnished to them
simultaneously.

THE PRESIDENT—Certainly.

MR. GILBERT—This year, as I understand it, the papers must
follow the ordinary course, and go to the paper which we recognize as our official organ.

THE PRESIDENT—But, if the other journals wish to take copies
of those papers after they were printed, they are now at liberty
to do so.

MR. GILBERT—But they may not care to do that after they
have been published by the AMERICAN GAS LIGHT JOURNAL.

THE PRESIDENT—If I have not correctly stated the views of
the Association, or if there is any doubt as to just what is intended by the action we have taken, it would be well to have it
stated more explicitly.

MR. A. C. HUMPHREYS—Then, I move that it is the sense
of this Association that the stenographic report referred to by
the special Committee is understood to be the report of the entire proceedings of the meeting.

THE PRESIDENT—Mr. Humphreys offers a resolution explan-
atory of the vote previously passed, to the effect that the words
" stenographic report," which has already been ordered to be
given to all the journals willing to pay their share of the expense,
shall be understood to mean a report of all proceedings of the
Convention, including the papers which are read.   So that any
journal may publish all the proceedings, including the papers.
There is to be no preference given to any journal as to any of
the papers.

MR. MCMILLIN—Our report is to the effect that we furnish
a copy of the proceedings, inclusive of the papers, to all journals

willing to pay their part of the cost of making the stenographic report. That was the idea of the Committee.

MR. HELME—It may take some time to make two or three copies of the papers. In the meantime, is each of the journals to remain out of possession of the papers until these copies have been made and handed to the other journals? Let us see how that thing will work.

THE PRESIDENT—You will have to ask the Executive Committee as to that.

MR. HELME—What I want know relates to the five papers which are to be printed. I understand that copies are to be furnished to the journals, when they are distributed to the members. How will it be as to the others?

THE PRESIDENT—At the next meeting of the Association the papers (five in number) designated by the Executive Committee will be printed before the meeting of the Association, and hundreds of copies distributed. A copy will be given to each journal that wants it.

MR. HELME—That is all well enough as to those five papers. How will it be as to the others?

THE PRESIDENT—The resolution adopted to-day provides only for the printing of the five regular papers. If more than five papers are presented, I would ask Mr. Harbison what he wants to have done with them. My ruling did not apply to those. I do not understand what disposition the Executive Committee wish to make of those other papers.

MR. HELME—Suppose two or more papers are read after the five regular ones are disposed of. Will the AMERICAN GAS LIGHT JOURNAL have those; or must duplicate copies be made for every other journal?

THE PRESIDENT—I will leave that for Mr. McMillin to answer.

MR. McMILLIN—The stenographer can make type-written copies of those, and they will then form a part of his report.

[The motion of Mr. A. C. Humphreys that " It is the sense of this Association that the stenographer's report, referred to by the

Special Committee, is understood to be the report of the entire proceedings of the meeting," was then agreed to.]

Votes of Thanks.

THE PRESIDENT—Is there any other business to come before this meeting of the Association ?

MR. LOWE—Before bringing this very interesting and valuable meeting to a close, I think we ought, in justice to our worthy President—Malcolm S. Greenough—tender him a hearty vote of thanks for his very able and interesting address—the best that we have had, according to my notion, at any meeting of the Association.   I think we also owe him a cordial vote of thanks for the very masterly and forbearing manner with which he has conducted the proceedings of this Association.   I, therefore, move that such action be taken, and that we spread it in full upon the records of our Association.   The motion was put by the Secretary, and unanimously adopted.

THE PRESIDENT—Gentlemen, I am obliged to you all.   At times, I feared that I hurried up your proceedings with rather more alacrity than civility ; but if I have given satisfaction as your presiding officer it is a matter of great gratification to me to have done so.

MR. HARBISON—As a member of the Executive Committee it has fallen under my notice, during the past as well as in former years (particularly so during the past year) that the Secretary of this Association has a large amount of work to perform.   There are very few of the members of this Association who fully appreciate that fact, owing to their lack of knowledge of the extent of it.   They may come in contact with him a number of times, in a very pleasant manner, during the year ; but it has come to my knowledge that he performs a very large amount of work in the interest of this Association, of which the members generally have no knowledge.   I am thoroughly aware of the very able, earnest and painstaking way in which the duties of his office have been performed.   His report to this Association of the management of our finances would do credit to an able New York banker.   He has taken care of them in a remarkably able and successful manner.   He has performed all his duties equally well. He is ever obliging, ever good-natured and never gets out of patience. I move a vote of thanks to Secretary Humphreys for the exceedingly able and efficient manner in which he has performed the duties of Secretary during the past year.

THE PRESIDENT—I think the entire Association is ready to second the motion made by Mr. Harbison, and it gives me very great pleasure to put it before you. Those in favor will say " Aye." I will not put the negative question, simply because it has no negative side. Adopted.

THE SECRETARY—I am exceedingly obliged to all the members of the Association for this very kind expression of their approval ; and I am particularly obliged to my friend Mr. Harbison for his kind remarks in moving the question.

VOTE OF SYMPATHY.

MR. VANDERPOOL—Mr. Thomas, one of our friends, and an honored member, has been sick in bed for some weeks. I think it would be an appropriate token of our respect for him if this Association were to pass a resolution of sympathy with him in his illness. I make that motion. Seconded by several.

THE PRESIDENT—It is moved that the sympathy of this Association be tendered to Mr. Jos. R. Thomas in his affliction, and that the Secretary be requested to communicate to him that fact. Adopted.

MR. HARBISON—Let me suggest that a hearty vote of thanks is due to the Committee of Arrangements who superintended our entertainment at this meeting. Therefore, I move the thanks of the Association to the members of that Committee for the able and efficient manner in which they provided for our welfare. Adopted.

The Association then adjourned.

SIXTEENTH ANNUAL MEETING

OF THE

AMERICAN GAS LIGHT ASSOCIATION,

HELD AT

TEMPERANCE HALL, TORONTO, CANADA,

OCTOBER 17, 18 AND 19, 1888.

FIRST DAY, MORNING SESSION—WEDNESDAY, OCTOBER 17.

The Convention was called to order by the President, Thomas Turner, Esq., of Charleston, S. C., at 10.30 A.M.

On motion of Mr. Slater, the reading of the minutes of the last annual meeting was dispensed with, the same having been published in the AMERICAN GAS LIGHT JOURNAL.

ROLL CALL.

The following members were present:

Adams, H. C.,	Philadelphia, Pa.
Atwood, H. A.,	Plymouth, Mass.
Bates, J. W.,	Hoboken, N. J.
Baxter, Robert,	Halifax, N. S.
Benson, F. S.,	Brooklyn, N. Y.
Blodget, C. W.,	Brooklyn, N. Y.
Borgner, C.,	Philadelphia, Pa.
Bredel, F.,	New York City.
Capelle, G. S.,	Wilmington, Del.
Clark, W.,	Philadelphia, Pa.
Cartwright, W.,	Oswego, N. Y.
Cartwright, M.,	Rochester, N. Y.
Coffin, J. A.,	Gloucester, Mass.
Collins, A. P.,	New Britain, Conn.
Cole, T. W.,	Altoona, Pa.
Coggshall, H. F.,	Fitchburg, Mass.
Connelly, J. S.,	New York City.

Connelly, T. E.,	- -	New York City.
Corbett, C. H.,	- -	New York City.
Cornell, T. C.,	- -	Yonkers, N. Y.
Cowing, J. H.,	- -	Buffalo, N. Y.
Cressler, A. D.,	- -	Fort Wayne, Ind.
Cushing, O. E.,	- -	Lowell, Mass.
Daly, D. R.,	- -	Jersey City, N. J.
Davis, F. J.,	- -	Waltham, Mass.
Dell, J.,	- -	St. Louis, Mo.
Denniston, W. H.,	-	Pittsburgh, Pa.
Diall, M. N.,	- -	Terre Haute, Ind.
Dickey, C. H.,	- .	Baltimore, Md.
Dickey, R. R.,	- -	Dayton, O.
Down, W. H.,	- -	New York City.
Findlay, J. H.,	-	Ogdensburg, N. Y.
Flemming, D. D.,	-	Jersey City, N. J.
Floyd, F. W.,	-	New York City.
Fodell, W. P.,	- -	Philadelphia, Pa.
Gates, F. W.,	-	Hamilton, Ont.
Geggie, D. H.,	- -	Quebec, Can.
Goodwin, W. W.,	- -	Philadelphia, Pa.
Graeff, G. W., Jr.,	-	Philadelphia, Pa.
Green, J.,	- -	St. Louis, Mo.
Gribbel, John,	- -	New York City.
Griffin, J. J.,	- -	Philadelphia, Pa.
Harbison, J. P.,	- -	Hartford, Conn.
Hanford, L. C.,	- -	Norwalk, Conn.
Hookey, G. S.,	- -	Augusta, Ga.
Humphreys, A. C.,	- -	Philadelphia, Pa.
Humphreys, C. J. R.,	-	Lawrence, Mass.
Isbell, C. W.,	- -	New York City.
King, E. J.,	- -	Jacksonville, Ills.
Krumholz, J.,	- -	Buffalo, N. Y.
Keuhn, J. L.,	- -	York, Pa.
Leach, H. B.,	- -	Taunton, Mass.
Learned, E. C.,	- -	New Britain, Conn.
Lenz, E.,	- -	New York City.
Lindsley, E.,	- -	Cleveland, O.
Littlehales, T.,	- -	Hamilton, Ont.

Ludlam, E.,	Brooklyn, N. Y.
Mayer, F.,	Baltimore, Md.
McDonald, W.,	Albany, N. Y.
McIlhenny, J.,	Philadelphia, Pa.
McElroy, J. H.,	Pittsburgh, Pa.
McMillin, E.,	Columbus, O.
Mooney, W.,	New York City.
Nettleton, C. H.,	Birmingham, Conn.
O'Brien, W. J.,	Philadelphia, Pa.
Odiorne, F. H.,	Boston, Mass.
Page, G. S.,	New York City.
Park, W. K.,	Philadelphia, Pa.
Pearson, W. H.,	Toronto, Ont.
Perkins, J. D.,	New York City.
Pratt, E. G.,	Des Moines, Ia.
Prichard, C. F.,	Lynn, Mass.
Quinn, A. K.,	Newport, R. I.
Ramsdell, G. G.,	Vincennes, Ind.
Richardson, F. S.,	N. Adams, Mass.
Rogers, J. F.,	Jamaica Plain, Mass.
Roots, D. T.,	Connersville, Ind.
Ross, A. Q.,	Cincinnati, O.
Russell, D. R.,	St. Louis, Mo.
Scriver, J. F.,	Montreal, Can.
Sisson, F. N.,	Albany, N. Y.
Slater, A. B.,	Providence, R. I.
Smedberg, J. R.,	Baltimore, Md.
Smith, M.,	Wilkesbarre, Pa.
Snow, W. H.,	Holyoke, Mass.
Somerville, J.,	Indianapolis, Ind.
Starr, J. M.,	Richmond, Ind.
Stedman, W. A.,	Newport, R. I.
Stein, E.,	Philadelphia, Pa.
Stiness, S. G.,	Pawtucket, R. I.
Stanley, I. N.,	Brooklyn, N. Y.
Stacey, W.,	Cincinnati, O.
Thompson, J. D.,	St. Louis, Mo.
Thomas, J. R.,	New York City.
Tufts, N.,	Boston, Mass.

Turner, T., -	-	Charleston, S. C.
Warmington, G. H.,	-	Cleveland, O.
Watson, C., -	-	Camden, N. J
Weber, O. B.,	-	New York City.
White, W. H.,	-	New York City.
Wood, A. C.,	-	Syracuse, N. Y.
Young, J., -	-	Allegheny City, Pa
Young, R.,	-	Allegheny City, Pa.

The following gentlemen, subsequently elected members, were also present :

Active Members.

Bell, H. J., -	-	Camden, N. J.
Betts, E.,	-	Wilmington, Del.
Boardman, H.,	-	Bangor, Me.
Chadwick, H. J.,	-	Lockport, N. Y.
Chollar, B. E.,	-	Topeka, Kan.
Clark, G. S.,	-	Kansas City, Mo.
Douglas, David,	-	Savannah, Ga.
Forstall, A. E., -	-	Chicago, Ill.
Higby, W. R.,	-	Bridgeport, Conn.
McCleary, A. J.,	-	Philadelphia, Pa.
Nute, J. E.,	-	Jersey City, N. J.
Pearson, W. H., Jr.,	-	Toronto, Ont.
Read, J., -	-	Stratford, Ont.
Rowland, C. L.,	-	Brooklyn, N. Y.
Rusby, J. M.,	-	Jersey City, N. J.
Shelton, F. H.,	-	Philadelphia, Pa.
Stoddard, C. H., -	-	Brooklyn, N. Y.
Thomas, M. B.,	-	Dundas, Ont.

Associate Members.

Norton, H. A., -	-	Boston, Mass.
Persons, F. R.,	-	Chicago, Ill.
Van Wie, P. J.,	-	Cleveland, O.
Wilson, W. J.,	-	New York City.
Wright, W. S.,	-	Chicago, Ill.

The Secretary read a communication from the Consumers Gas Company, of Toronto, inviting the members of the Association to attend a banquet, to be given by the company, in honor of the Association, at the Rossin House, on Thursday evening, October 18.

On motion of Mr. Somerville the invitation was accepted, with the thanks of the Association.

The Secretary read the following applications for membership:

Betts, E., - -	Wilmington, Del.
Boardman, H., - -	Bangor, Me.
Bigelow, H. N., - - -	Clinton, Mass.
Chollar, B. E., - -	Topeka, Kan.
Clark, G. S., - -	Kansas City, Mo.
Douglas, D., - -	Savannah, Ga.
Forstall, A. E., - -	Chicago, Ill.
Hambleton, F. H , - -	Baltimore, Md.
McCleary, A. J., -	Philadelphia, Pa.
Nute, J. E., - - -	Jersey City, N. J.
Persons, F. R., -	Chicago, Ill.
Rusby, J. M., -	Jersey City, N. J.
Rowland, C. L., -	Brooklyn, N. Y.
Read, J., - - -	Stratford, Ont.
Shelton, F. H., -	Philadelphia, Pa.
Williams, C. H., - -	Waterbury, Conn.
Wilson, W. J., - -	New York City.

On motion of Mr. Ramsdell all applications for membership were referred to a committee of three, to be appointed by the chair.

The President appointed as such committee Messrs. G. G. Ramsdell, Walton Clark and E. McMillen.

Mr. W. H. White, Chairman of the Executive Committee, then read the report of that Committee as follows :

REPORT OF EXECUTIVE COMMITTEE.

At the last meeting of the Association it was ordered that the papers to be read at this meeting should be printed, in order that while papers were being read from the platform the members might more readily follow the reading, and be better prepared to take part in the discussions following the presentation of papers. This has been done, under the direction of the Executive Committee, and the Secretary will place before you printed copies of all the papers that are to be read at the meeting, with the exception of the paper written by Captain Ross, which was unfortunately not presented to us in time to be printed. The several papers presented have been considered by the Executive Committee, and the following have been approved by them, and will be read in due course.

1. Daily Experience and Observations of a Gas Manager, by James Somerville.

2. Construction of Gasholders with Wrought Iron or Steel Tanks Above Ground, Frederick Mayer.

3. Experience in Distributing Gas under Extremely Low Temperatures, by D. H. Geggie.

4. Gas Coals, with Especial Reference to Provincial Coals, by James D. Perkins.

5. Observations During Many Years' Experience in the Gas Business, by James R. Smedberg.

6. The Ross Steam Stoker and Improved Charger, by A. Q. Ross.

The Committee have adopted a programme for the meetings, printed copies of which have been placed in the hands of the members. It will be as closely adhered to as possible during the sessions of the Association.

The sum of $25, which was some time ago placed in the treasury of this Association by a Scotch gas engineer, to be given as a prize to the writer of the best paper upon any subject which the Association might designate, has been offered by your Committee to the writer of the best paper upon " Naphthaline," which may be read at this meeting. All of the members of this Association have been notified of this fact, and have been invited to compete. It is to be hoped that a number of papers may be presented, and a decision reached, as this money has been in the treasury for some time awaiting distribution.

The subject of a permanent badge for members of the Association has been talked up at several sessions, and at the meeting in New York a committee appointed was charged with the duty of procuring designs for such a badge. The committee have been in correspondence and consultation with jewelers in New York and elsewhere, and have received from them several designs; but fearing they might be deemed too expensive, that committee have come to the Executive Committee and asked for their instructions in the matter. Your committee recommend that the committee on badges be instructed to proceed with their labors, to the extent of getting a badge of suitable design, which shall not exceed in price $4. They have several designs, but, at present prices, somewhat in excess of this figure. It is supposed that if an order for 200 was given the badges could be obtained for $3.50 or not to exceed $4. The Executive Committee recommend that these badges be purchased by the Association from its own treasury and presented to the members, and that hereafter new members, in paying their initiation fee of $10, shall be entitled to receive a badge from the Association. We make this recommendation because we feel that even a $4 badge may possibly not be purchased with any great degree of unanimity by the members, and that while some might have them others might not. If we desire to have a distinctive badge the committee believe that it is best for the Association itself to purchase the badges and present them to the members. We now have a surplus of nearly $3,000 in our treasury—a sum of money for which we have really only little use, as our current expenses are more than met by the current income of the Association. The committee feel that this money belongs to its members, and can be disposed of in no better way than by returning a portion of it to the members in the shape of a neat badge. It is, therefore, for you to approve our action, so that the committee on badges may be authorized to secure the badges, or else be instructed to drop the matter entirely.

The annually recurring question of proper compensation to the Secretary for his labors in our behalf has been considered by the Executive Committee, and we recommend that the salary to be paid to the Secretary for the ensuing year be fixed at $600. I presume there is not a gentleman in the room having any acquaintance with the duties of that office who will hesitate to agree with us that even this salary is, perhaps, less than we ought to pay. His work is not only great and pressing, but it is increasing all the time. The matter of printing these papers has thrown an unusual amount of work upon your Secretary. The fact that, by resolution passed at the last session, we have dispensed with the services of the various papers in obtaining reports of our proccedings, and now employ our own stenographer and place upon the Secretary the duty of revision of the reports of our discussions, throws upon him an additional and onerous duty.

The Executive Committee, in carrying out your instructions on the subject of reporting the proceedings, have employed a stenographer, and the report will be made under the direction of the Association, and not under the direction of any gas journal; and any one of the journals paying its proportionate share of the cost of reporting the proceedings will be entitled to a copy for publication.

I believe, Mr. President, the Committee have no further recommendations to make at present.

THE PRESIDENT—You have heard the report of the Executive Committee, and the various recommendations they have made. What action will the Association take upon it ?

On motion of Mr. Harbison the report of the Committee was accepted and its recommendations adopted.

The Secretary read the following reports, which were, on motion of Mr. Stiness, received and placed on file :

REPORT OF FINANCE COMMITTEE.

The undersigned members of the Finance Committee have examined the books and accounts of C. J. R. Humphreys, Treasurer, for the year ending September 30, 1888, and find the same to be correct.

CHAS. S. NETTLETON,   Finance
W. H. PEARSON.   Committee.

REPORT OF TREASURER AND SECRETARY.

Receipts.

Initiation fees..........................	$	300.00
Dues for year 1885...............		10.00
" " 1886....................		50.00
" " 1887...................		110.00
" " 1888.....................		1,115.00
" " 1889, in advance.........		10.00
Interest......		95.42
Contribution for prize................		25.00
		$1,715.42
Cash brought forward from last year		2,437.72
Total amount to debit.........		$4,153.14

Expenditures.

Expenses of New York meeting........ ..	$297.38	
Salary of Secretary and Treasurer.......	500.00	
Printing and Stationery................	134.25	
Expenses of meeting of Executive Committee at New York, April 20, 1888 ..	186.25	
Postage, stamped envelopes and sundries.	172.31	
	$1,290.19	
Cash carried forward to next year	2,862.95	
		$4,153.14

Memo. of cash on hand—

Deposit in South Brooklyn Savings Inst........		$1,240.87
" Williamsburgh Savings Bank......		838.12
" Lawrence Saving Bank		634.82
" National Pemberton Bank, of Lawrence.......................		113.40
Cash in Treasurer's hands		35.74
		$2,862.95

Due from members, including year 1889...... $2,270.00

Roll call of the American Gas Light Association for the year ending September 30, 1888 :

Honorary Members.

Number on the roll, Sept. 30, 1887	7
Number on the roll, Sept. 30, 1888	7

Active Members.

Number on the roll, Oct. 1, 1887	310	
Admitted Oct., 1887	30	
		340
Resigned during the year	2	
Died during the year	5	
Number on the roll, Oct. 1, 1888	333	
		340

Deceased Members.

J. H. Collins, Phila., Pa.; Wm. Helme, Phila., Pa. ; J. M. Murphy, Chicago, Ill.; J. C. Pratt, Jamaica Plain, Mass.; T. F. White, Houston, Texas.

C. J. R. HUMPHREYS, Sec. and Treas.

On motion of Mr. White, the Secretary was instructed to make the proper entry upon the minutes of this meeting of the deaths of the following members of the Association during the past year :

Joseph H. Collins, Jr., Assistant General Superintendent, United Gas Improvement Company, Phila., Pa.; William Helme, Engineer Atlanta Gas Company, Phila., Pa. ; J. M. Murphy, with Maryland Meter Company, Chicago, Ills. ; John C. Pratt, Prest. Jamaica Plain Gas Company, Boston, Mass.; T. F. White, Treasurer and Superintendent Houston Gas Light Company, Houston, Texas.

MR. NETTLETON—I desire to say, on behalf of the Committee on Badges, that our report has practically been made already by the Chairman of the Executive Committee. As he has stated, the Committee have procured designs from some jewelers in New York and Boston, and a majority of the Committee reported unanimously in favor of one of the designs. I have the designs with me, and will be glad to show them to the members at any time during the meeting. The design selected will make, we think, a very handsome badge, and one that will please most of the members. The price asked for it ($6) is, however, somewhat higher than we think the Association ought to pay; but we believe that by ordering the large number which you have now authorized to be purchased (about 300), the badges can be obtained for $4 or less.

Mr. Harbison—I suppose there is no doubt the Chairman of the Committee can assure us that by the next annual meeting this badge will be ready for distribution among the members.

Mr. Nettleton—I have no doubt that the badges will be sent to the members some time during the coming winter.

The President—The next business is the address of the President. I am sorry to say that I met with a very severe accident about five weeks ago, and that although I had my address then blocked out, I have not been able to devote as much care to its preparation as I would have liked, and it will necessarily be somewhat brief. I do not feel that I am in a condition to read it, and, with the permission of the Association, I will ask Vice-President Slater to read it for me.

PRESIDENT'S ADDRESS.

Gentlemen of the American Gas Light Association :—As we meet but once a year, and representing as we do such a vast extent of territory, many of the members traveling more than a thousand miles to attend the meeting, we are justified in expecting in the address of the President not only a general resume of the condition and progress of the business during the previous year, but reference to matters of importance as affecting the vast industry which has been committed to our care and management, and also such suggestions as in his judgment seemed to be worthy of occupying the attention of the Association. The consideration and discussion of technical details more properly receives attention in the various papers which are read before the Association, and in the general discussions which occur upon special points and matters which they bring to our notice. In the present instance, perhaps I should apologize to the Association for attempting to say anything under the circumstances, but knowing the feelings of indulgence which I am sure the members of the Association will extend to me, I will proceed with the consideration of such matters as have occurred to me.

First.—I desire to congratulate the members of the Association upon the general and almost unprecedented prosperity of the business during the past year. I believe there has never been greater activity made necessary in the extension of manufacturing plant than during the past one or two years. The increase in the quantity of gas distributed over that of the previous year has been from 5 or 10 to more than 30 per cent. This fact has developed the feeling among engineers, especially where the land area is limited, that we must have greater carbonizing capacity upon a given area of retort house. This is seen in the larger size of retorts used, and a greater number set in a single bench; and again in the larger gasholders constructed. The largest gasholder in America is now in process of construction in the city of New York.

Can we suggest any explanation of this large increase in the quantity of gas called for by our consumers, particularly when we know that the electric light is not an inconsiderable portion of the light now used in our large cities? I think there are several reasons which may help to explain it.

1st. The natural tendency with all consumers is toward the use of more light. This is noticeable in our own individual cases. As we grow older we require more light. As the eye becomes accustomed to a strong light it produces conditions whereby a still stronger light is necessary.

2d. The low price at which gas is sold, in the large cities especially, allows of more freedom and more extended use of gas. It is an acknowledged fact that the cheaper any of the necessaries of life are, and even what are called luxuries, too, the more will be used, and less pains will be taken to curtail their use.

3d. The use of gas for cooking and heating is constantly increasing, and will go on increasing in a greater ratio than heretofore. As our consumers come to realize the comfort, convenience, economy and utility of a good gas stove or range, and which are now attainable in all our large cities, they will wonder how they ever lived without it.

4th. The application and use of electric light has really had the effect of almost compelling people to have more light ; and for this reason we can afford to be generous and give electric light credit for its assistance in increasing our sales of gas. In fact, I think I am not magnifying the conditions when I say that, had the people of all our cities required and demanded the quantity of artificial illumination, together with the quantity of gas now used for other purposes than illumination, and the electric light unknown, the gas companies—with the aid of all the present gas works construction companies, and individuals pursuing that line of business, doing their utmost— would be severely taxed to keep the gas plants of the country in a condition to supply it. Even now some of the larger companies have been forced to make strenuous efforts to keep their works in the necessary condition to get through the winter. I am aware the market price of gas stocks has at times suffered from the progress electric light has made and is making ; but the business as a whole has not suffered, but rather increased.

Some gas companies and gas engineers have pursued the policy of, as they say, " fighting " the electric lights. This I regard as a mistaken policy. No gas company or gas manager can afford to stand in the way of the development and march of improvements of any kind. Development and improvement is the order of the day in this age. The world must go forward, onward and upward toward perfection ; and the man or men who would endeavor to stop the wheel of progress, in any direction, does or do not comprehend the tendency or drift of things in the age in which we live. The electric light has its advantages. Let us acknowledge them. It also has its defects, which are ample enough to interfere with its progress to that extent which will drive gas from its full share in the business of artificial illumination, to say nothing of its use for heating, which has even now hardly begun.

Our true policy, then, is rather to lend our energies to the development of the possibilities in our own business which are still greater, I believe, than most of us are aware of to-day ; and you may be sure that in the future we shall hear from the young men who have chosen our profession for their life-work, and are being educated especially for the work, rather than to drift into the business from accident, as many of us did years ago when the business was comparatively new in this country.

It may not be improper to remark that when we stop to consider the consistent experiments and research made, particularly during the last ten years, by men of eminent ability and special education and training for the work, and the amount of money expended in the development of the science of electricity as applied to the production of artificial light since its first introduction, the wonder is that the gas industry is in existence to-day. This fact alone would seem to be sufficient evidence that illuminating gas has qualities inherent in itself, and that when the same energy and scientific ability, together with the experience of the past, are applied to its further development, it must still remain, as it has been in the past, the light best adapted, all things considered, for universal artificial illumination and heating. As a rule, the gas business has not been managed by men who have had special education and training for the work before engaging in it; but I am glad to know that a gradual but sure change is already upon us; and I am certain that the business of gas manufacture will receive a fresh impetus when the young men who are now coming up, with especially trained minds and hands, bend their energies to the work of developing the science of manufacture of illuminating, and, I may add, heating gas.

There are many gas engineers and managers who warmly advocate the policy of amalgamating the business of electric lighting with the gas light business. I must say I am not entirely of that opinion. I cannot see why gas companies should engage in the electric lighting business any more than they do in the kerosene oil and candle business, simply because kerosene oil and candles furnish light. There is ample room for us all. I do not think any man can manage two different kinds of business, entirely dissimilar in many respects, as he can one; especially when we consider that with the one he is entirely familiar and the other is entirely new to him. One or the other must, in some degree, be neglected; perhaps both. At the same time, I am willing to acknowledge that, in some instances, advantages would accrue to both interests if consolidated. Local circumstances and conditions will generally settle the policy of consolidating the two interests, and wise managers will be governed by the circumstances rather than by the questionable policy of endeavoring to monopolize the entire business of supplying artificial light.

With the progress of the business during the past year, then, we may be fairly satisfied and take encouragement for the future. At the same time we must be diligent and work with renewed energy and spirit; for it is to the intelligent worker, rather than the talker, that success is most likely to come.

No. radical changes as especially marked improvements in manufacture have been brought out during the past year; but there has been a general improvement, particularly in the older works where old apparatus has been replaced with new and improved sorts; the construction of new benches, with larger and increased number of retorts in a bench, and also adopting some form or kind of generator or regenerator furnace, all of which tend to largely increase the product of the retort house with marked economy in the consumption of fuel.

With the best known apparatus of the present day, and the handling of coal, coke, etc., by machinery, as is now done in some of the large modern works, the day of dollar gas is not far distant; and is even now reached in some cities where conditions are favorable. As I have already said, we may expect marked improvement in working results and utilization of residual products to be derived from more accurate information which will be brought to bear by the young men who are being thoroughly educated and trained for the work. If the business has prospered during the past thirty or forty years and in the hands of men who, as a rule, had no special training or technical education necessary for it, but who were brought into it more by accident or circumstances than knowledge of the business, what may we expect when the conditions are changed and the carbonization of coal and the treatment of the resultant gases are more thoroughly understood and more definite and positive results assured?

Much has been written and said upon the subject of naphthaline; and yet, where is the man to-day who can accurately foretell all the conditions which conduce to its appearance, or its remedy when present? It is true that many remedies have been suggested, and in some cases, where certain conditions have been observed, it has not appeared in its crystallized form; and yet, in other places, where the same conditions have apparently been maintained, it has been deposited in increased quantities. One is troubled with naphthaline when he uses certain kinds of coal, another uses the same kind of coal and is never troubled with it; but when he uses some other kind of coal it always puts in an appearance. We all know very well that, as a scientific principle, like causes always produce like results, consequently such arguments go for nothing, because there must of necessity be some cause or conditions in one case that do not obtain in the other.

Much is yet to be learned in the retort house. The almost universal rule seems to be now to produce high heat in the retorts and charge them with all the coal they will burn off, without any special care as to the character of the coal or the length of time it remains in the retort. If six-hour charges are run, the coal must remain in the retorts just six hours, even if the gas is all worked off in three or four hours. From one kind of coal the gas may be worked off in three hours, another will require four or five hours under the same heat, so that we have the problem before us still, of being able to produce certain results from certain kinds of coal—not only the certain results, but the best possible results which can be theoretically obtained from the coal. Whether the present form of retorts and the present method of carbonizing the coal are the best are questions which still remain unanswered. Although many attempts have been made and much experimenting has been done without successful results, yet the continuous carbonization of the coal is a thing still to be hoped for. Whether this and other radically new ideas are to be practically developed by the theorist, or by the practical man, is a question; but probably through the aid of both.

The engineer in charge of large works has little time at his disposal for experimenting, and he who has only the chemical laboratory for his work has not the advantage of working out his ideas practically and on a large scale; but the engineer who is to be the most successful in the future is he who has taken the advantage of a thorough technical education coupled with actual practical ability and application. It is one fault of our system of education that the young man who is kept at school until he is prepared for the university or technical school often grows up without the advantage of the experience which comes only from actual work with his own hands, and so never acquires that practical judgment which must needs accompany a theoretical education in order to place him in the best possible position as a manager of any great industrial establishment.

This is one pre-eminent reason, why, in the past, the man who has had practical experience, learned a trade and worked with his own hands has been, as a rule, more successful than the one who has acquired a theoretical education and has never had the advantage of practical experience in the work, and so never had his judgment and practical ability developed as does the man who has, perhaps, been compelled to work with his own hands. Theory and practical judgment and ability must go together, if we would secure the best results.

Without doubt the English, French and German engineers in the past have had the advantage of a more thorough technical education and training than have the majority of American engineers; but the standard of comparison in this country is being rapidly reached through the various institutions which are fitting the young men for the active duties of engineer or manager of our special industry.

There are many matters which I might refer to, some of which will be brought before you in the several papers which have been prepared for this meeting by gentlemen of experience and ability, and which will be presented in a more acceptable form than I could hope to do; but I have already taken too much of the time of the Association. Yet I cannot conclude without referring to the great work which has been accomplished by this Association, the proceedings of which have been published and are preserved in a permanent form, the reading of which is of absorbing interest even to the members who have attended all the meetings. But all the results of our meetings have not been published, and never can be. The acquaintances made, the enduring friendships formed, the little private interviews and conversations which have taken place upon all the multitudinous matters that a gas engineer has to deal with, all go to make up the sum total of the benefits which have been derived from attending our meetings, and have served to largely increase the prosperity of the companies we represent.

Many members have grown old in the service of their company, some have dropped from the roll by death, some have been disabled by accident, while others have reached an age which disqualifies them from active participation in the management of the business, and their familiar forms and faces are missed in our gatherings. New members are constantly being admitted to the duties and privileges of membership in our Association, and those now present will, one by one, pass over and "join the silent majority." During the past year several of our members have gone from us, due notice of which will be taken by the Association, and a proper minute will be placed on our records.

Let us strive to do our work well ; and when we are obliged to step out of the scenes of active work and duty, which others will take up and go forward with, let it be said of us that our record and work is worthy of emulation.

MR. McMILLIN—I am sure we all sympathize with our President in his recent affliction, and sincerely trust that he may never meet with such another accident. I move the address be referred to a special committee, with instructions to report thereon during this session of the convention.

The motion prevailed, and the Chair appointed as such committee, E. McMillin, A. C. Wood and James Somerville. The committee subsequently submitted the following report, which was accepted and ordered placed on file.

REPORT OF COMMITTEE ON PRESIDENT'S ADDRESS.

To the Members of the American Gas Light Association : Gentlemen : Your Committee, to whom was referred the President's address, submit the following report :

We find that the subjects mentioned in the address were exhaustively treated, and nothing that we could say would add either to the force of the President's suggestions or to their elucidation.

We recommend that the Secretary make a proper record in his journal of the deaths that have occurred, and that he prepare and publish, with the proceedings in the bound volume, a memorial for each of the members who died during the past year. Respectfully submitted.

E. McMILLIN, ⎫
A. C. WOOD, ⎬ Committee.
JAS. SOMERVILLE, ⎭

The President appointed the following committees :

On Nomination of Officers.—S. G. Stiness. Pawtucket, R. I. ; E. J. King, Jacksonville, Ill. ; G. S. Hookey, Augusta, Ga. ; Marcus Smith, Wilkesbarre, Pa. ; Jos. Krumholz, Buffalo, N. Y.

On Place of Meeting.—Frederick Mayer, Baltimore, Md. ; Robert Baxter, Halifax, N. S. ; John P. Harbison, Hartford, Conn. ; Robert Young, Allegheny, Pa. ; James Somerville, Indianapolis, Ind.

THE PRESIDENT—We will now hear the report of the Executive Committee on proposed amendments to the Constitution.

MR. WHITE—I have the pleasure of reporting, in behalf of the Executive Committee, a new Constitution, which is submitted in print for your examination and approval. The Executive Committee, having had this matter placed in their charge by the Association, have held several meetings for the consideration of the subject, and the Secretary has been more than energetic in procuring from various sources matter that might be of use to the Committee in preparing this form of Constitution. It has seemed desirable to the Committee that such a form of Constitution should be secured for this body as would not have to be hauled up for amendment and worked at, to the exclusion of other and more important business, at every meeting of the Association. In offering this the Committee assure the Association that they have worked very diligently in the effort to obtain something whicn seemed to them to cover all requirements of the Association. We trust that no more time will be occupied this morning than is necessary in settling this matter once for all.

THE PRESIDENT—What action will the Association take on the report of the Committee ?

MR. KING—I suggest that the Chairman read simply the changes which have been made in the Constitution.

MR. WHITE—That would be almost impossible, there are so many.

MR. HARBISON—I move that the chairman of the Executive Committee read the Constitution recommended by the Committee for our consideration and adoption.

The motion prevailed, and Mr. White read the proposed Constitution as follows:

Constitution of the American Gas Light Association, as Reported by the Executive Committee, October 17, 1888.

I.—*Name.*

1. The name of this Association shall be the American Gas Light Association.

II.—*Objects.*

2. The object of this Association shall be the promotion and advancement of knowledge, scientific and practical, in all matters relating to the construction and management of gas works, and the manufacture, distribution and consumption of gas.

3. The establishment and maintenance of a spirit of fraternity between the members of the Association by social intercourse and by friendly exchange of information and ideas on the before-mentioned subject matters.

4. The inducement and extension of more cordial and friendly relations between the manufacturers of gas and their patrons, based upon the mutuality of interests.

III.—*Members.*

5. The members of this Association shall consist of three classes—Active, Honorary and Associate members.

6. To be eligible as an Active Member, a person must be a president, secretary, treasurer, engineer, consulting engineer, or superintendent of a gas company, or a manager of a gas works.

7. Associates shall be persons holding a responsible position in a gas works, or persons whose pursuits constitute branches of gas engineering, or who are otherwise qualified to assist in promoting the objects of the Association.

8. Honorary Members shall be gentlemen whose scientific or practical knowledge in matters relating to the gas industry, and

whose efforts and interest in that behalf shall recommend them to the Association.

IV.—*Election of New Members.*

9. Every application for membership shall be made in writing to the Secretary, endorsed by two Active Members, and must be accompanied by a statement in writing of the grounds of the application, and an agreement that he will conform to the requirements of membership if elected. Application shall be made upon a printed form supplied by the Association, and shown in Schedule A, appended to these rules.

10. The preceding rule shall apply equally to any person soliciting admission as an Associate Member, application to be made upon a form, as shown in Schedule B, appended to these rules.

11. It shall be competent for any Associate Member to apply to the Secretary to be transferred from the class of Associate Members to that of Active Members. Such application shall be submitted to the Council, who may, if the applicant is eligible to active membership, recommend the transfer for approval at the next meeting of the Association, the application to be made on a form to be supplied by the Association, as shown in Schedule C.

12. Application for Active Membership, or for Associate Membership, or for transfer from Associate to Active Membership, must be received by the Secretary at least ten days prior to the meeting at which the application is acted upon.

13. Honorary Members shall be proposed by the Council, at a general meeting of the Association.

14. An applicant for admission to any class of membership, or for transfer from one class to another, must receive the votes of two-thirds of the members present, to be elected.

15. If any person, proposed for admission to the Association, or for transference from the class of Associate to that of an Active Member be rejected, no notice shall be taken of the proposal in the minutes.

16. Any person elected to the Association, excepting Honorary Members, must subscribe to the rules and pay to the Treas-

urer the initiation fee, before he can receive a certificate of membership. If this is not done within six months of notification of election, the election shall be void.

V.—*Management.*

17. The affairs of the Association shall be managed by the Council, subject to the control of the general meeting.

18. The Council shall consist of the President, three Vice-Presidents, eight Active members and the President or Acting President of the preceding year. The Secretary shall also be, *ex-officio*, a member of the Council. Five members shall constitute a quorum.

19. The Council shall appoint from their own number, immediately after the meeting at which they are elected, a Finance Committee of three members.

VI.—*Election of Officers.*

20. The President, Vice-Presidents, Secretary and Treasurer shall be elected annually.

21. Four Active Members of the Council shall retire each year.

22. All elections shall be by ballot.

23. The President and the four retiring Active Members of the Council shall not be eligible for election the following year.

24. Previous to each annual meeting it shall be the duty of the Council to appoint a Nominating Committee of five members. It will be the duty of the Nominating Committee to present at the annual meeting a list of Active Members, whom they recommend as officers for the ensuing year.

25. No member of the Council shall be eligible as a member of the Nominating Committee.

26. The Council shall have power to fill vacancies in its own body.

VII.—*Duties of Officers.*

27. The officers-elect shall assume office immediately after the meeting at which they have been elected.

28. The President shall take the chair at all meetings of the Association or committees at which he is present.

29. In the absence of the President one of the Vice-Presidents shall take the chair, and in the absence of the President and Vice-Presidents a Chairman shall be appointed by the Council from the members of the Council.

30. The duties of the Secretary shall be to take minutes of all proceedings of the Association and of the Council, and enter them in proper books for the purpose. He shall conduct the correspondence of the Association, read minutes and notices of all the meetings, and also papers and communications, if the authors wish it, and perform whatever duties may be required in the Constitution and By-Laws, appertaining to this department.

31. The duties of the Treasurer shall be to receive and keep all annual dues, and funds of the Association, to keep correct accounts of the same, and pay all bills approved by the President or a member of the Finance Committee, and he shall make an annual report to be submitted to the Association.

32. The duties of the Finance Committee shall be to audit the books, accounts, and statements of the Treasurer; to invest the funds of the Association, and to care generally for the finances of the Association, subject to the control of the Council.

33. The duties of the Council shall be to have the general management of the affairs of the Association, to designate the writers of papers at each meeting, and the subjects to be discussed, and to prepare for the meetings of the Association The Council shall have the power to appoint, from time to time, a Committee of Arrangements from among the members, to assist the Council in arranging for the meetings of the Association.

VIII.—*Meetings and Proceedings.*

34. The annual meeting of the Association shall be held on the third Wednesday of October of each year, at 10 o'clock A.M., at such place as shall be designated by the Association at the previous meeting.

35. At the annual meeting of the Association the order of business shall be: (1) The reading of the minutes of the last meeting; (2) the report of the Council on the applications for membership, and for transfer of membership; (3) the election and introduction of new members; (4) the report of the Council

on the management of the Association during the previous year; (5) the report of the Treasurer and of the Secretary; (6) reports of Special Committees; (7) election of officers; (8) the address of the President; (9) reading of papers, and discussion on the same; (10) general business.

36. At other general meetings of the Association the order of business shall be the same, except as to the 4th, 5th and 7th clauses.

37. The Secretary shall send notices to all members of the Association at least 14 days before each general meeting, mentioning the papers to be read, and any special business to be brought before the meeting.

38. Special meetings may be called at the option of the Council, and the Secretary shall call a special meeting on the written request of 20 members. The notices for special meetings shall state the business to be transacted, and no other shall be entertained.

39. Thirteen members shall constitute a quorum.

40. All questions shall be decided by any convenient system of open voting, the presiding officer to have a second or casting vote when necessary.

41. Questions of a personal nature shall be decided by ballot.

42. Any member, with the concurrence of the presiding officer, may admit a friend to each meeting of the Association, but such person shall not take part in any of the discussions unless permission to do so be given by the meeting.

43. All papers read at the meetings of the Association must relate to matters either directly or indirectly connected with the objects of the Association, and must be approved by the Council before being read.

44. All papers, drawings or models submitted to the meetings of the Associations, shall be and remain the property of the authors.

45. The Council shall meet before each general meeting of the Association, and on other occasions, when the President shall deem it necessary. Of such special meetings reasonable notice shall be given by special call, in print or writing, specify-

ing the business to be attended to. The President shall be required to call the Council together on the written request of five members of the same.

IX.—*Privileges and Duties of Members.*

46. Every person elected as an Active Member shall pay an initiation fee of $10, which shall include the dues for the current year.

47. Every person elected as an Associate Member shall pay an initiation fee of $10, which shall include the dues for the current year.

48. Every Active Member shall pay annually, in advance, the sum of $5.

49. Every Associate Member shall pay annually, in advance, the sum of $5.

50. Honorary Members shall not be required to pay an initiation fee, nor annual dues.

51. No member who owes for two years' dues shall be entitled to vote, or to participate in the deliberations of the Association or to receive a copy of the proceedings.

52. Any member may retire from the membership by giving written notice to that effect to the Secretary, and the payment of all annual dues to date, unless released from said payment by a vote of the Council.

Any member whose dues shall remain unpaid for a term of three years, may be dropped from the roll of membership by a vote of the Council.

53. A member dropped from the roll for non-payment of dues, may, upon paying the amount he owes the Association, be reinstated at the option of the Council.

54. Any member may compound for his annual payments by paying $50 in one sum.

55. Each member of the Association shall be furnished, by the Secretary, with a copy of the proceedings of the Association for the current year, and the Constitution, and also a list of the names and address of the members.

56. A member may be expelled from the Association by a

recommendation to that effect made by the Council at any general meeting of the Association.

The vote shall be by ballot, and shall require two-thirds of the votes cast for its adoption.

57. An Associate Member will be entitled to all the privileges of the Association, except voting and holding office.

58. An Honorary Member will be entitled to all the privileges of the Association, except voting and holding office.

Amendments.

59. All propositions for adding to or altering any of the provisions of the foregoing Constitution shall be laid before the Council, who may bring it before the next general meeting of the Association, if they see fit, and the Council shall be bound to do so on the requisition, in writing, of any five members of the Association. All propositions to amend this Constitution shall be decided by ballot, and shall require two-thirds of the votes cast for their adoption.

Discussion.

MR. WHITE—We submit this Constitution as our report, and as the result of our deliberation. I move its adoption as a whole.

MR. STINESS—I second the motion.

MR. HARBISON—Before that motion is put I beg to suggest that the Committee on applications for membership present their report, because if this Constitution is adopted now, some of the names that have been presented to the Committee may be reported upon as not entitled to come in now. I, therefore, move that this proposed Constitution be laid upon the table in order that we may hear the report of the Committee on new members.

THE PRESIDENT—Is the Committee on applications for membership ready to report ?

MR. RAMSDELL—At the meeting held in New York one year ago it was understood that we were to receive no further associate members, except under the provisions of this new Constitution. In the list of applications handed in this morning there are but two that come under that head, and those are the applications of Mr. William J. Wilson and F. R. Persons. The other applicants are entitled to come in as active members under either the old or the new Constitution.

Your committee, therefore, approve all the applications for membership except that of Mr. Wilson and Mr. Persons, and suggest that their applications be laid over until final action is had on the adoption of the new Constitution.

MR. HARBISON—Does the committee recommend that these applications come in under the new Constitution, and be acted upon at this meeting.

MR. RAMSDELL—Yes.

MR. HARBISON—I would like to have that understood so that they will not be left until next year.

MR. RAMSDELL—Another application has just been handed me, that of W. H. Pearson, Jr., of Toronto. He would come in as an active member.

MR. HARBISON—I move that the report of the Committee on new members be accepted, and that the Secretary cast the ballot of the Association for the names of the gentlemen recommended by the committee.

The motion was passed. The Secretary cast the ballot of the Association accordingly. And the following were declared duly elected active members of the Association :

Betts, E.,	Wilmington, Del.
Boardman, H.,	Bangor, Maine.
Bigelow, Henry N.,	Clinton, Mass.
Chollar, B. E.,	Topeka, Kan.
Clark, G. S.,	Kansas City, Mo.
Douglas, D.,	Savannah, Ga.
Forstall, A. E.,	Chicago, Ill.
Hambleton, F. H.,	Baltimore, Md.
McCleary, A. J.,	Philadelphia, Pa.
Nute, J. E.,	Jersey City, N. J.
Rusby, J. M.,	Jersey City, N. J.
Rowland, C. L.,	Brooklyn, N. Y.
Read, J.,	Stratford, Ont.
Shelton, F. H.,	Philadelphia, Pa.
Williams, C. H.,	Waterbury, Conn.

Mr. Harbison—Now I move that we take from the table the proposed Constitution, and I second the motion for the adoption of the Constitution as read.

Mr. McIlhenny—This is too important a document to be adopted without any discussion ; and I think the proper way would be to receive it and then proceed to discuss it, either in parts or as a whole.

Mr. McMillin—I raise the point of order that, as the present motion is to take it from the table, it is not now open to discussion. We must take it from the table before we can discuss it.

The motion to take from the table prevailed.

The President—The proposed Constitution is now before us for our consideration.

Mr. White—There seems to be a lack of understanding as to the status, under this new Constitution, if adopted, of some of our members, who are not actually engaged in the gas business, and who would, if proposed for membership under the new Constitution, come in as associates, and not as active members. Nothing that this Association can adopt in the way of a Constitution will affect the standing of any present member. He is still an active member. The idea is to divide all future applicants for membership into two classes—active and associate. All of the present members, no matter in what way they are connected with the gas industry, remain as active members, and there is nothing in the Constitution which can in any way affect their present standing.

Mr. McIlhenny—Is the Constitution now before the Association ?

The President—It is now before the Association for adoption as a whole, as I understand the motion.

Mr. McIlhenny—There is one clause in it to which I wish to call attention, and it is not in regard to the status of existing members, because, of course, their rights cannot be taken away from them by any action we may now take with reference to this Constitution. I wish to call attention to this particular clause :

" It will be the duty of the nominating committee to present at the annual meeting a list of active members, whom they recommend as officers for the ensuing year."

If I recollect rightly it has been the practice of this Association to appoint a committee for the purpose of nominating the officers. If I am not correct in this I wish to be corrected. The object of appointing this committee to name the officers has been to save the time of the Association. But now it is proposed to make this method of selecting officers a part of the fundamental law; and it takes away from individual members the right of nomination. I believe it is the practice in all legislative bodies to accord to every member the right to make nominations. Will not the adoption of this Constitution take away from us that right ?

MR. WHITE—No, sir.

MR. HARBISON—If the gentleman will notice the provisions of the Constitution he will see that the Council appoint the nominating committee—the President presiding at the meetings of the Council. The custom now is for a motion to be made that the President appoint a committee on nominations, and the President thereupon appoints such committee, as has been done this morning. The new Constitution provides that the Council (the President being in the chair) shall name a nominating committee—no member of which committee shall be a member of the Council. So that the Council must go outside of their own members in selecting the committee on nominations.

MR. MCILHENNY—I understand that, but that does not meet my objection.

MR. HARBISON—This method saves the time and the necessity of a motion that the President appoint such a committee.

MR. MCILHENNY—But my point is that this clause of the Constitution gives to this committee the right to nominate officers, and takes from individual members the right of nomination.

MR. HARBISON—This will not take from the Association the right of substituting on the nominating committee other members than those named by the Council ; and it does not prevent any member of the Association from making any addition to the number of nominees made to the Council by the nominating committee. The object is simply to facilitate business, and it is not the intention to take away any right from any member.

MR. MCILHENNY—I understood from the reading of this that when this committee comes in with its nominations the Association only has a veto power. It requires a vote of two-thirds of the members present to sanction the nominations made by the committee; but there is nothing said about the right of members to make nominations. I think it would be better to have that right of nomination stated in express terms.

MR. A. C. HUMPHREYS—I think if the gentleman will read the paragraph again he will see that his point is covered, for this committee are simply to present " a list of active members, whom they *recommend* as officers for the ensuing year."

MR. THOMAS—I think it would be a good idea to have this matter lie over until to-morrow morning, so as to give all the members an opportunity to read the proposed Constitution, and understand what they are going to adopt. There seems to be a difference of opinion in relation to it, and a good many do not understand it. I do not know why the President is not just as competent as the Council to appoint a nominating committee, or why the members themselves are not entirely competent to name their officers. If action on the Constitution is postponed until to-morrow morning, all of the members will be afforded an opportunity of reading and understanding it, and will then be prepared to vote intelligently upon it.

MR. KING—It seems to me that in reading this Constitution one cannot fail to be impressed with the idea that the Committee have done their work very thoroughly. They seem to have considered every point; and I, for one, am willing to take the result of their deliberations just as they have presented it to us—although I think I can see several points that may give us trouble in the future. But they have certainly discussed those points among themselves, and have arrived at their conclusions, and I, for one. am willing to accept their view of the case. If we enter upon the discussion of the Constitution, and take up all the debatable points, it will occupy all the time of this meeting. It therefore seems to me it will be better to adopt it as it stands; and hereafter, if we find it does not work just as we had hoped, it can be amended.

THE PRESIDENT—The pending motion is on the adoption of the Constitution as reported by the Executive Committee. Are you ready for the question ?

The motion prevailed, and the Constitution was declared adopted.

THE SECRETARY—I have another application for associate membership—that of Mr. H. A. Norton, of Boston, Mass.

THE PRESIDENT—Let it be referred to the same committee.

MR. RAMSDELL—The committee make the same report as to this application.

MR. HARRISON—I move that the recommendation of the committee on membership on the applications of Messrs. Persons, Wilson, Pearson and Norton be adopted, and that the Secretary be instructed to cast the ballot of the Association for the election of Messrs. Wilson, Persons and Norton as associate members, and Mr. Pearson as an active member, so that they may come in with the rest under the present Constitution.

The motion prevailed, and the three applicants named were declared duly elected.

THE PRESIDENT—Mr. Pearson, of the Committee of Arrangements, has something to say to the Association.

MR. PEARSON—Gentlemen, I welcome you to the good city of Toronto, personally, and also on behalf of the Company which I represent. I trust that your stay may be pleasant, and that none of you will regret coming. My object in addressing you now is to ask that all the members of the Association who intend to be present at the banquet to be tendered by the Consumers' Gas Company, on Thursday evening, will be kind enough to give their names to Mr. Cartwright, who will be on the platform at the close of this meeting. We ask you will do this promptly, as the hotel-keeper desires to know as nearly as possible how many will be present. I trust that every member of the Ass ciation will accept the invitation. Those who give in their names this morning will receive their tickets at the close of this afternoon's session.

Mr. Mayer—The Committee appointed to recommend the place for holding the next meeting of the Association instruct me to say that we unanimously recommend that the next annual meeting be held in the city of Baltimore.

On motion of Mr. White, the Association concurred in the recommendation of the Committee.

On motion of Mr. Harbison, the President appointed as a Committee of Arrangements for the next meeting the following:

Frederick Mayer, Baltimore, Md.; F. H. Hambleton, Baltimore, Md.; Charles H. Dickey, Baltimore, Md.; John P. Harbison, Hartford, Conn.; Wm. Henry White, New York, N. Y.

Mr. Pearson—The Government Gas Inspector of Toronto has requested me, on his behalf, to invite the members of the Association to visit his office, where he will be most happy to show the various apparatus used in testing gas. His office is at No. 10 and 12 Toronto street, and I think you will be interested in visiting him.

The Convention then took a recess to 2.30 P. M.

First Day—Afternoon Session.

The Association met at 2.30 P. M.

The President—The first business this afternoon will be the reading, by Mr. Pearson, of a description of the Lux Gas Balance.

Mr. W. H. Pearson, of Toronto, then read the following description of the latest improved form of

THE LUX GAS BALANCE:

The ordinary methods hitherto employed for determining the specific gravity of gas, are the "Direct Method" of weighing, in which process, as you are aware, a hollow vessel is weighed by means of a very sensitive scale, first in the exhausted state, afterward when filled with air, and lastly, when containing the gas to be examined—the specific gravity of the gas is then ascertained by dividing the weight of the gas by that of the air; and the "Effusion Test" of Bunsen, based upon the fact that if gases are expelled under the same pressure, through a small aperture made in walls of minute thickness, the squares of the velocity of the expulsion are in inverse ratio to the specific gravity of the gases.

Recognizing that these, and other methods, all have the serious drawback that they require so much time to make them, as well as skill on the part of the operator, Mr. Lux set about devising an apparatus by the aid of which the specific gravity of gas might be ascertained in the same automatic way in which it is possible to ascertain temperature and pressure by means of the thermometer and the barometer, and the specific weight of liquids by the hydrometer. He first constructed what he called the " bareometer," based upon the Archimedean principle, a description of which is given in his pamphlet, which, though he found on the whole to satisfactorily answer the purpose, he delayed presenting to the public, from fear that it might be too fragile for ordinary use—the globe being of glass; and because, under certain conditions, water or any other liquid would be unavailable for the test. He then directed his efforts toward the solution of the problem by means of the principle upon which the common lever balance is constructed, and claims that in devising the " Gas Balance " he has accomplished the task to his entire satisfaction.

Mr. Lux claims that, with the aid of this balance, the specific gravity of any gas can be determined to within .001.

The apparatus, which is a beautiful construction, consists of a pillar or stand, divided at its upper extremity into two branches, forming a kind of fork. Fixed in the top of these branches, on either side, is an agate plane, upon which the beam of the balance is made to rest, upon a knife edge. The beam consists of a central body, to one end of which is fixed a hollow globe of metal, containing about one liter ($\frac{1}{28}$th of a cubic foot), while at the other end is a scale divided into 120 parts, provided with a rider or counter weight. From the upper extremity of the central body two narrow tubes issue, at right angles, to the plane of oscillation, one of which enters the tube, which practically constitutes the continuation of the beam of the balance, inside of the globe, while the other enters the globe directly through the annular orifice in the central body. These two tubes are bent, at their outer ends, at right angles, in a downward direction, and terminate in small saucers, which, being filled with mercury, constitute an effectual hermetic seal. In order that any solvent action which the mercury might have upon the metal may be evaded, the ends of the tubes, and also the saucers, are made of ivory. Through the mercury a small tube enters from below into each of the saucers, and terminates in a joint piece. It will thus be seen that the gas introduced enters through one of the tubes, one of the saucers and one of the annular tubes, into the globe, thence passing through it continuously, leaving the globe through the annular tube at the other end, and finally passing through the second annular tube, mercury saucer and outlet tube.

There are two adjusting screws fixed in the center of the beam, one horizontal and the other vertical, which constitute the pivots of the whole system. By turning the vertical screw up or down, the center of gravity of the balance can be fixed at a longer or shorter distance from the center of motion, thus lessening or increasing the sensitiveness of the instrument. By turning the horizontal screw the balance is so adjusted that the weights on either side of the central fulcrum are identical.

There is an arched scale, fixed at the base of the standard of the balance, with forty divisions (twenty on the plus side, and twenty on the minus) in front of which is a steel pointer. The divisions on this scale are equivalent to those on the beam, and are positive on the right and negative on the left.

A thermometer is fixed to one of the arms of the pillar, and a pressure gauge, partially filled with glycerine, on the other. Underneath the case are adjusting screws, to enable the operator to fix it in a perfectly horizontal position. The apparatus is placed in a case to prevent the action of the air affecting the balance, which is extremely sensitive, and also to keep it clean.

To prevent any moisture or tarry matter from entering the globe, a gas filter, containing cotton wadding, is provided, through which the gas passes before entering the balance.

The working of the apparatus is very simple and easily understood. In making a test, the beam being arrested (by means of a button in front of the case) before filling the globe with gas, the sliding weight is put upon point 1, on the beam scale. The arrestation is then raised, and the balance adjusted by means of the screws on the top of the beam already referred to, until the motion of oscillation of the steel pointer to the ivory scale is o. After being properly adjusted, the beam is again arrested and the sliding weight placed, for example, upon .8. As the divisions on the ivory scale should be of the same value as those on the beam, the steel pointer ought to go to plus .2, because $.8 + .2 = 1$, as above. If this is not found to be the case, the balance is again adjusted, by means of the screws, until properly regulated.

If it is intended to test coal gas, its specific gravity ranging from, say, .350 to .500, the sliding weight may be removed from .1 to .4, and to ascertain the specific gravity, the arithmetical mean of the oscillation of the pointer upon the front of the ivory scale is to be taken, which, if on the plus side, is added to, and if on the minus side deducted from, the indication of the sliding scale. This will give the exact specific gravity of the gas. For instance, if after raising the arrestation the steel pointer oscillates between $+ .8$ and $+ .12$ the arithmetical mean being .10 (which represents .1) specific gravity is found to be $.4 + .1 = .5$. If the steel pointer should oscillate, say between $+ .5$ and $+ .10$, the specific gravity would be $+ .4 + .075 = .475$. In the case of an examination of gas of a higher specific gravity, say, between .500, .600, or .700, the slide may be placed upon .5, .6, or .7 as the case may be. Heavy gases can be tested by putting two sliding weights on the beam scale.

Once properly regulated, the apparatus can be ready for use at any time without further re-adjustment, and, if desired, the gas, under a low pressure, can be allowed to pass through it continuously and the specific gravity can at any time be ascertained in a minute or two. This obviously is a very great advantage. Whenever necessary the balance can be readily re-adjusted in from ten to fifteen minutes.

This balance was exhibited at the last meeting of the English Gas Institute, where it was favorably received, and Mr. Lux has written informing me that he has just obtained the highest distinction (the gold medal) at the Brussels International Exhibition for his collection of gas balances.

Discussion.

MR. GEGGIE—Does Mr. Lux say whether it can be used for

testing for sulphuretted hydrogen and carbonic acid, as well as for ascertaining the specific gravity ?

MR. PEARSON—No.

MR. GEGGIE—I think it can be used for that purpose also.

MR. PEARSON—I think not for testing for sulphuretted hydrogen. It will be useful in determining whether there would be carbonic acid in the gas, because the extra weight of gas, as shown by the test, would indicate its presence ; but I have not heard that he has used it for the purpose of testing for sulphuretted hydrogen. He uses another apparatus for that purpose.

MR. SOMERVILLE—It seems to me the accuracy of the test depends upon the friction of the movement. If it should be a a little stiff it would not be accurate.

MR. PEARSON—The construction of it is such that it seems almost impossible for it to get stiff.

MR. SOMERVILLE—I suppose it should be kept in a dry room.

MR. PEARSON—It is intended that the filter shall remove almost all of the moisture. Of course the presence of moisture would affect it. Mr. Lux states, from a number of tests made, he has ascertained that the very small quantity of moisture present is of very little account, and does not interfere with the accuracy of the balance. I think this is the fourth balance that Mr. Lux has made. He has made quite a number, and he claims that this is practically perfect.

MR. SOMERVILLE—Does it keep an automatic record of the specific gravity ?

MR. PEARSON—He has another apparatus arranged in such a way as to keep a record, but this one is not of that type.

MR. DIALL—What is the price of it ?

MR. PEARSON—I do not know. Mr. Lux claims that it will be especially useful in testing the gravity of furnace gases. Probably it will be more useful for that than for testing ordinary gas. You see that his claim is a very strong one. He claims that with this particular apparatus he can ascertain the specific gravity of gas within .001 part, which is near enough for anything we might need.

MR. McMILLIN—I probably owe the Association an apology for asking the question, but I did not pay very close attention to the reading of the paper. May I ask if the object of the balance is chiefly to determine the quantity of carbonic acid.

MR. PEARSON—It is chiefly to determine the weight of the gas.

MR. McMILLIN—Of what advantage would that be to us ?

MR. PEARSON—Probably you can tell that as well as anybody else.

MR. McMILLIN—I do not see that it makes much difference whether a given quantity of gas weighs a pound or an ounce. I might care to know what it was composed of, but be indifferent as to its weight. That question, however, was with the view of leading to another, and that is—to determine the quantity of carbonic acid by testing the specific gravity, what would be the effect of running extremely high heats and decomposing a good deal of the marsh gas—thus removing a large per cent. of hydrogen, but leaving carbonic acid in it ? Would it not have about the weight of a good gas, and still be of very poor quality ? If that be so it would not be an absolute test as to whether there is a large per cent. of carbonic acid or not. This is certainly a very pretty piece of apparatus to look at, and my object is to ascertain whether it has any inherent utility.

On motion of Mr. Slater the thanks of the Association were voted to Mr. Pearson for his paper.

THE PRESIDENT—We will now listen to the reading of Mr. Somerville's paper.

DAILY EXPERIENCE AND OBSERVATIONS OF A GAS MANAGER.

By JAMES SOMERVILLE.

In complying with the request of the Committee to read a paper before you on the above subject, I am well aware that I can find nothing that will be new to the majority of you. For my experience, from the nature of things, will be very similar to yours. Therefore, I will only be telling you something which you already know. But, no doubt, the Committee, in asking for such a paper, had in view the younger members of our Association, and that our experience might be of some value to them. I will, therefore, ask that class among us to accompany me on one of my daily walks through the works, and we will relate our experience and make observations as we proceed.

The first place we will visit is the retort house, which is built on the stage principle, and although the plan is more expensive to build and maintain, yet it has so many advantages, that in the end I consider it to be the best and cheapest; and, no matter how small the works, I would advocate the adoption of this plan. One of its chief benefits is that you have ample space for the large modern gaseous furnace, which, in my opinion, is indispensable to the production of cheap gas; and if, as some of our sanguine friends predict, in a few years we will all be making fuel gas, then, with the two-story retort house the change to the new order of things can be more easily and cheaply made. You will perceive that the settings are very open, only braced in front and rear, which I have found quite sufficient. This allows ample space and time for the proper combustion of the furnace gases. I should like just here to lay some stress on this element of time in all our operations. My daily observation is that time is an important consideration in the condensing and purification of the gas. Nothing is more injurious to the gas than to suddenly rush it into a lower temperature. It requires time to cool slowly, time to get rid of its tar, time to purify.

You will observe that the heats are good, but not high. I find that there is no advantage in running high heats, that is, heats approaching a white. The gas from such heats is entirely denuded of its light naphthas, and is in a poor condition to stand any change of temperature, but deposits the crystals of naphthaline the first opportunity, which occurs generally before or in the purifiers. I judge of a good heat when the lid is taken off and the retort presents a bright red, sparkling appearance, without a trace of smoke. The coke is curled up at the sides, and comes easily out when the rake is applied to it. I have observed that, when the heats are low from any cause, there is a corresponding decrease of ammonia; when the heats are good, the strength of the liquor increases. I am not prepared to say just why this should be, but the fact is well established in my mind that the higher the heats the greater is the production of ammonia. It is possible that a greater amount of nitrogen may be taken from the coke during high heats and so cause the increase.

These self-sealing lids are only so in name. They do fairly well for the first year or so. But my experience is that beyond that period they are unable to stand the wear and tear of the retort house. The parts begin to wear out, perfect contact cannot be obtained, their efficiency is ended, and we have to fall back to the old lute. I confess I have given the subject of self-sealing lids much thought, but the difficulties appear to be insurmountable. They must be able to stand all changes of extreme temperature. Their efficiency must not be impaired by the wear and tear of the parts, and they must be able to make a perfectly air-tight joint every time they are shut, notwithstanding that they have to be handled by men who believe only in the existence of muscle.

We now come to what I call the hot scrubber. It is so hot you cannot keep your hand upon it. Here the gas takes a rest, as it were, and gets rid of all its heavy tar. You can hear it trickling down between the plates; but the light tars or oily naphthas still flow on with the gas which is gradually cooled. What tar is left is taken out by the Pelouze & Audouin condenser, which stands next to the ammoniacal liquor scrubber. I am aware that some object to placing the Pelouze at this point in the works, preferring to put it before the exhauster, where I have my hot scrubber. I think they are wrong; for it acts at that point too efficiently, if I may say so. It not only takes out the heavy tar, but the light naphthas also, and puts the gas in the same condition as if the naphthas had been burned up in the retort through extra high heats; and, moreover, the specific gravity of the tar at that point is so high that some will get through the Pelouze, not enough to help the gas any, but enough in the course of time to find its way to the liquor scrubber to seriously impede its efficiency and make it necessary to clean it out once or twice a year. This I never have to do; for no tar finds its way to the liquor scrubber nor into the liquor. This is important when making your own sulphate; for when tar gets into the scrubber it seems to neutralize in some way the action of the water on the gas. I do

not use fresh water in the scrubber. I have found it more effectual to use a mild liquor of about two or three-ounce strength.
Gas has an aversion to cold water.

My experience with purifying material is that, when we used
all oxide, it not only absorbed all the impurities, but a large
proportion of the hydrocarbons also. I also attributed to its
use an increase in the number of meters brought in for repairs.
I had, therefore, to discontinue partially its use, and fall back
on lime. I find that the center-seal, to perform its work properly, requires to be thoroughly scraped and cleaned once a
year. I prefer the open drip, because it can be kept clean, and
easily supplied with fresh water. I do not think it is right to
pass the purified gas over foul water in the seal.

My observation of the daily working of the holders leads me
to this conclusion. Whenever trouble has occurred it can
invariably be traced to one source, viz., the weakness of the
bottom curb. Let the bottom rollers get out of place, then the
stability and safe working of the holder is destroyed. I have
had a curious illustration of this fact. We have a holder 130
feet in diameter and only 16 feet in height. Why it was built
with these dimensions I cannot tell. It is strongly trussed. The
centre of gravity is nearer the top than the bottom, so that a
little gale of wind invariably tipped it over. Indeed, I have
seen it at right angles ; one side jammed into the tank, the
other high in the air. This occurred shortly after I took charge
of the works. But the workmen were so used to it that it
excited in them little surprise. But, as the cost of broken
wheels and carriages was excessive, I resolved to see what
could be done to make it work more steadily. As soon as we
got into it I found, as you anticipate, that every roller was out
of place, and the bottom curb badly bent in. I substituted
wrought iron for cast wherever it could be done with the rollers,
and put a heavy log chain or brace against them on the inside,
fastened to the curb, and jammed the rollers tight against the
guides. I filled it up again, and no one was more surprised
than myself to see how steady the holder has worked ever
since, now nearly ten years ago. It has given no trouble and
is working every day. There are twelve columns to the holder ;
but, as for keeping it steady, it might as well be without them.

So I think we may conclude from this instance that the safe working of the holders is dependent entirely on the strength of the bottom curb and rollers, constantly tight against the guides,

In my daily photometrical tests I find very little variation. If the specific gravity increases without a corresponding increase in candle power, then it is time to examine the exhauster governor or the self-sealing lids. Much has been said and written lately against the candle as a standard of light. Its imperfections have been dwelt upon with great minuteness. But my experience is that, when the candle is burned under proper conditions, and due corrections made, it does for all practical purposes fairly test the illuminating power of the gas.

I have had some new experience in main laying lately, which may be of some benefit to you should you be fortunate (?) enough to find a supply of natural gas near you. We had ten miles of eight and six inch mains, which were laid by an opposition company, and which we did not need. We agreed to turn them over to a natural gas company for the distribution of their gas. The city ordinance required that they should be laid three feet under the surface, and that they should stand a pressure for one hour of fifteen pounds to the square inch. We had about 1,100 services on these mains, 300 of them only in use. These all had to be cut off, and carefully plugged, for none of them were large enough for natural gas. For the purpose of testing, I cut the main into sections of about 2,000 feet each, and exposed and set up every joint. I then screwed a sensitive diaphragm spring gauge into both ends, and, with a portable steam-boiler, having a Westinghouse air-pump attached to it, pumped the main full of air, until the gauges showed seventeen or eighteen pounds to the square inch. Then the inspector, appointed by the city, went over every joint with soap bubbles, and, with such a pressure on, the smallest leak was easily detected and made sound. If the gauges stood perfectly during the hour at that pressure, the section was accepted. If they showed the slightest drop, it was rejected. But I had very little trouble to get them to stand the test; indeed, many of the joints under the street car tracks, which it was almost impossible to reach, I had to risk, and, without any setting up, they stood the test. It would happen sometimes during the test that the sun would be clouded, or a shower of rain would come on, which cooled the air in the pipe, and of course contracted it. The gauge would immediately show it, and the inspector would reject the test. It was of no avail that I should try to instill into that functionary's mind something of the science of pneumatics. His orders were that the gauge should stand. If it went up, as would sometimes happen, by the expansion of the air, he would make no objection. I observed during the progress of this work, that where the mains had not been properly laid in line, these were the joints that were the most liable to leak.

My experience is that every meter ought to be brought in, examined, repaired (if needful), and tested every five years. All our new meters are tested and stamped with the date of test before sending them out. The following table will show you the result of our testing for one year. All the new meters (419) were correct, 56 per cent. of the consumers' meters brought in for testing were correct, 25 per cent. slow and 19 per cent. fast. The two last columns give the average per cent. of error—8.6 per cent slow, and 7.3 per cent. fast :

List of Meters Tested by the Indianapolis Gas Company During the Year.

CONSUMERS' METERS.

Months.	No Tested.	No. Slow.	No. Fast.	No. Correct	% Slow	% Fast.
January	18	1	1	16	5	5.5
February	29	4	10	15	9	6.95
March	21	3	5	13	7.33	8.5
April	19	5	4	10	8.6	6.37
May	15	4	5	6	8.12	6.2
June	16	6	3	7	6.33	4.5
July	11	3	1	7	16	17.5
August.	10	3	0	7	8	0
September	10	3	1	6	7.66	5
October	19	8	2	9	5.42	9.5
November	19	4	4	11	4.8	3.97
December	22	9	4	9	13.55	12.25
Totals	209	53	40	116	ave. % 8.6	ave. % 7.3

NEW METERS.

Months.	No. Tested.	No. Slow.	No. Fast.	No. Correct	% Slow.	% Fast.
January	0	0	0	0	0	0
February	50	0	0	50	0	0
March	0	0	0	0	0	0
April	25	0	0	25	0	0
May	48	0	0	48	0	0
June	51	0	0	51	0	0
July	0	0	0	0	0	0
August	0	0	0	0	0	0
September	85	0	0	85	0	0
October	42	0	0	42	0	0
November	62	0	0	62	0	0
December	56	0	0	56	0	0
Totals	419	0	0	419	0	0

Consumers' Meters.
$\begin{cases} \text{\% Correct} \dots 56 \\ \text{\% Slow} \dots 25 \\ \text{\% Fast} \dots 19 \end{cases}$

" If you wish a thing well done, you must do it yourself," is an old remark, which applies with much force to the supply of gas for cooking and heating purposes. It was not until we took this business into our own hands that we had any success. We have now over 2,000 stoves out and giving great satisfaction, and, strange to say, even with the introduction of natural gas into our city, the sale of stoves has not ceased. I can only understand this from the fact that there is some uncertainty just how long the supply of natural gas will last, and our housekeepers desire to have at least two strings to their bow. I have observed that the main point in fitting up a gas stove is to give it an abundant supply. The pipes should be large, and should come direct from the meter.

We have 600 consumers who pay weekly, most of them at their own desire. Of course this short reckoning entails some extra work; but our aim is, if possible, to meet the wishes of all our customers.   I have found it beneficial to both company and consumers to conduct our business as though we had constant, active opposition to contend with.

There are several matters connected with this subject to which I have not alluded.   Such as, what my daily experience would lead me to expect and receive from a ton of coal in gas, coke, tar, and sulphate of ammonia; also in the management of men, and the maintenance of works, but I am sure the length of this, of necessity, rambling paper has already exhausted your patience.

Discussion.

MR. KING—I confess when I was told the subject assigned to my friend Somerville, I wondered how he was going to take it up, and I now wish to congratulate him on the entire success of his paper.   It seems rather difficult, with so much to discuss, to decide just what to take up.   There is enough food in the paper to feed us for a long while.   It is a good deal like the report of the Executive Committee on the Constitution—it will take a long while to take up each of the questions raised.   I started out by marking various passages that interested me, as he was reading; and I find the longest mark made is where he touches on the subject of the holder.   It is so much in line with the discussions now going on abroad (brought forward, I believe by Mr. Gadd), on the construction of holders, that it may be interesting to refer to it.   It would seem that Mr. Somerville's conclusions are entirely in line with those of Mr. Gadd.   He says, for instance, in regard to the construction of the holder, and his means for strengthening it:

"There are twelve columns to the holder; but, as for keeping it steady, it might as well be without them.   So I think we may conclude from this instance that the safe working of the holder is dependent entirely on the strength of the bottom curb and rollers, held constantly tight against the guides."

That is a very interesting point to me, and I am glad to hear that the experience of Mr. Somerville confirms what is claimed by Mr. Livesey, Mr. Gadd and others in England.   I would like to hear some discussion of that topic.

MR. CLARK—There are some points touched upon by Mr.

Somerville in which my experience does not lead me to agree with him. For instance, referring to self-sealing lids, I will say that I have used them year after year without the trouble which he has experienced, and the only care taken with them was to see that they were carefully scraped. I do not mean that they were taken off to be scraped, but scraped in position, with a chisel. This is all that was ever done to them, and they have worked year after year and gave perfect satisfaction.

Another point is in relation to the position of the hot scrubber. He says that he prefers to put it before the exhauster. Where there is no local obstacle in the way, it seems to me that the position of the exhauster should be as close to the hydraulic main as it can be got, and that the exhauster should take the gas before the condenser.

The advantages of this arrangement are that the exhauster needs no lubrication and that there is then no vacuum between the exhauster and the hydraulic main. If you put the P. & A. condenser between the exhauster and the hydraulic main, to make the condenser efficient you must have about twelve-tenths of an inch vacuum behind your exhauster, which, of course, puts a considerable portion of the apparatus in a vacuum, and, in case of a leak, draws air into the gas. I have never built a hot scrubber, although I have used them, and I think they are excellent indeed. I have in mind one works where they are suffering severely from napthaline where there was at one time a hot scrubber, afterward removed. The trouble with napthaline dates from the removal of the hot scrubber. I have an idea that this vessel will go back again before long.

My idea is that if you can put an exhauster close to the hydraulic main after the gas passes through the hot scrubber it should then go to the P. & A. condenser. I do not think the tar that the P. & A. condenser takes out will have any bad effect on the gas at the temperature at which it will be taken out, if it is placed near the hydraulic main. At one works I changed the position of the P. & A. condenser, and put the exhauster, which had previously been after a considerable portion of the condensing apparatus, between the hydraulic main and the P. & A. condenser. The effect was at once an increase in the illuminating power of the gas.

I have remarked Mr. Somerville's experience with oxides, and it was so different from the experience of others, who have spoken of it before this Association, that I was rather struck by it. He says that when he used all oxide, it not only absorbed all the impurities, but a large proportion of the hydro-carbons also. Last year Mr. Blodget read a paper before the Association in which he took directly the opposite position. He claimed that lime purification had a bad effect upon the illuminating power of gas as compared with oxide purification. Mr. McMillin, in the course of the discussion on that paper, stated he had obtained considerable illuminating gas from foul lime. Until now I supposed the statements of Mr. Blodget and Mr. McMillin settled that question, but it would seem that it is still open to experiment and discussion. I believe that those are all the points upon which I differ with Mr. Somerville. The points on which I agree with him are very numerous.

MR. MOONEY—Mr. Somerville says the difficulties attending the use of self-sealing lids appear to be insurmountable. That is a pretty big word. Self-sealing lids are in use in many places, and there are some who scrape the lid every time it is shut— even if there is a pinhole in it it is easier to have luting put on it than to have the men wheeling the lids around and luting them every time they are taken off.

MR. SCRIVER—This question of the use of self-sealing lids is a very serious and important one to me at the present time, and I am glad to get all the information on that point that it is possible to obtain. I am very much surprised indeed at the experience of Mr. Somerville. We are putting in at our works at the present time no less that 288 mouthpieces on the regenerative principle, and we are putting in self-sealing lids. I have come to the conclusion that they are the very best lids that can be adopted—after having made a pretty extended tour to England and Scotland last winter I came to that conclusion. They were almost universally used in every gas works that I visited, and were giving first-class satisfaction. I therefore concluded they were the best thing that we could adopt. I am inclined to think Mr. Somerville's retort lids must be of a very inferior kind, because on the other side they were experiencing no trouble at all, and in many cases the lids had been in operation for years. I see that Mr. Somerville is a very progressive man, and that he has gone in for the extensive introduction of gas stoves. He states he has over 2,000 gas stoves out, and that they are giving great satisfaction. His experience is very similar to ours. We went in for gas stoves about 6 years ago, and now have about 2,500 in use. I would like to ask Mr. Somerville if he sells gas for stoves at the same rate as for illuminating purposes.

MR. SOMERVILLE—Yes.

MR. SCRIVER—We have adopted another plan—I do not say it is the best one; but I believe it is. We have reduced the price of gas to $1 per thousand for gas stoves, and have found by so doing that we have increased our output of gas very materially during the day time, when our retorts would have been comparatively idle. I would also wish to state here, while speaking about gas stoves, we are quite progressive in this line, as we make our own gas stoves, and sell them to the consumers as cheaply as possible and clear ourselves. We give them the advantage of cheap manufacture, and I believe that we have benefited our company very materially by doing so. I do not know whether Mr. Somerville manufacturers his own stoves or not, but we think that it is a good thing for us to do so. Whether other gas men think it would be a good thing for them or not, they must decide for themselves.

MR. HARBISON—I have been exceedingly interested in following Mr. Somerville in the reading of his valuable paper.

Eternal vigilance is the price of a high illuminating power and a low price for gas to the consumer, on behalf of gas managers. Our friend Somerville has just led in the front ranks in that behalf. He is the leader; and like faithful followers we will follow right along, trusting to be able to keep him in sight. I quite agree with him in every conclusion he stated. What little experience I have had has led me right along in the same path. I do not see how my friend on my right could have been so misled in his journeyings abroad as to come to the conclusion he has with regard to the use of the self-sealing lids. Luting is good enough for me. And yet he may be right, and I may be wrong. I do not see how on that point we can come to a unanimous verdict. Some have had a very satisfactory experience with self-sealing lids, and some quite the reverse. In making some investigations during the past two or three years on this subject, while considering the question of erecting a new retort house, the item of lids has been a very important one with me. In starting up a new stack of benches ten days ago, to make gas with them for the first time, I used the luted and not the self-sealing lid, because I was not entirely satisfied that there was any one made which would continue to do the work it was intended to do and would be satisfactory to me. I do not agree with my friend from Montreal that he is doing the right thing in selling gas for cooking purposes at a reduced rate. He was not quite sure about it himself, although it was satisfactory to them, of making a distinction as to the price of gas to his consumers. If we can afford to reduce our gas to $1 per thousand for domestic purposes, in the shape of fuel, why can we not afford to do it for illumination? The results to him were entirely satisfactory, because he has put out 2,000 stoves, selling gas at $1 per thousand for that specific purpose; but he did not say to us that his company must necessarily have made quite a large investment in order to supply the meters for those 2,000 stoves with which to measure the gas used at $1 per thousand—because the same meter will not measure gas for fuel and for illumination at the same time; therefore, he must duplicate his meters, and that adds largely to the investment. There is no reason why John Smith, who is burning gas at No. 19, should get his gas for $1 per thousand because he is burning it in a stove, while John Jones, at No. 21, shall be required to pay $1.25 because he is using it for light, or for manufacturing purposes. I believe in a uniformity of price, and I believe in having that price so low that everybody can afford to use it for every purpose, and thus largely increase the consumption. Neither do we follow his plan of manufacturing the stoves. But we buy them as low as we can, and we sell them to the consumer at what they cost us, stating frankly to the consumer that we furnish the best stove we can obtain, at the lowest price for which we can purchase it, and sell it to them at just what it costs us. By doing this they are perfectly satisfied and we are happy. I believe it is a good way to serve the public. We do not all agree in all these details. One system may work well in one place and another in another, and it is by stating our experiences in these meetings and comparing them that we get at satisfactory results.

MR. McMILLIN—I want to enter a little protest against the abuse of self-sealing lids. I would not think of using any other kind. One-half of the lids in use at our works are self-sealing. The other half is the old lid, that has to be luted each time. While I recognize the fact that the self-sealing lid does wear out, I really do not think it takes half the money to keep them in order that it does to furnish new lids of the luting type. They break and they wear out, and they are taken off by men who burn their fingers, and throw them down, and break them ; and they warp, and get out of shape ; but I have never yet found any serious objection to the self-sealing lids. The self-sealing lid will leak a little, perhaps ; but what if it does ? Probably \$10 per year would cover the cost of the gas which is lost in that way. I think when we have deep furnaces, and can draw out hot coke directly from the retorts into the furnace, and have self-sealing lids, we have divided into about equal parts the labor of the stokers. They do not have to shovel in any coke or to seal any lids, and so their work is cut down to about one-half what it was in the old way of doing it. I speak on this subject, because the inference might be drawn that our friend Somerville had bad luck because he probably bought his lids from the only establishment manufacturing self-sealing lids in his State— at Fort Wayne. I want to say also that the self-sealing lids which I have had good success with also came from Fort Wayne. I speak of this for fear that some one may draw an incorrect inference.

MR. HARBISON—Will my friend state why, when he is so much in favor of self-sealing lids, one-half of the lids in his retort house are luted ?

MR. McMILLIN—It is for the reason that they were there when I took charge of the works, and the benches were a little too good to throw away, and the mouthpieces would run a few years longer ; but whenever they have had to be renewed, or whenever they will have to be renewed, there will be some other kind of lid put in.

MR. SOMERVILLE—I would like to reply to some of the questions put to me now, first, as to the P. & A. condenser that Mr. Clark spoke about. The reason I came to the conclusion stated was this: I visited a works a few years ago, where the engineer said that they were having trouble with the condenser. I said I thought the condenser was one of the grandest inventions of the age; that is was a splendid thing. He replied: "If you think so much of it you can have it. I do not want it." I inquired in what part of the works he had set it. He told me it was put just before the gas got to the exhauster—between the hydraulic main and the exhauster; that it did not work, did not give any satisfaction, and that he had to take it out. I was just then putting one in at the place where my gas is cooled; and I could not concieve of any nicer machine than a P. & A. condenser for taking out—not exactly the tar, but the oily matter that is left at the condenser, and does not have to be scrubbed at all. I do not think of cleaning out my scrubber. It does not require it. There is no tar in it. No tar gets into the liquor at all. The tar being a little cold at the P. & A. condenser, it requires cleaning oftener than if at the scrubber. I went to another place where the engineer was troubled a good deal with naphthaline in his works; and the P. & A. condenser was in that same position again— between the exhauster and the hydraulic. He was very much troubled with naphthaline, and his candle power was not as good as it should have been. The light naphtha seemed to be taken out and there was trouble in the scrubber and from naphthaline. I told him I believed if he changed its position and put the hot scrubber there it would be better. He came to the same conclusion. As to the use of oxide for purification, I have stated my own experience—that the candle power went right down and then went back again. As to the lids, I can only congratulate my friend McMillin that he finds the self-sealing lid works satisfactorily. It is a very serious matter with me. I run a little vacuum on the exhauster all the time, and do not like the candle power to get down for any cause—and I have suffered severely from just that thing—from trying to keep the lids tight. He speaks about the old country. I will say that if I had the machine which most gas works in England have, where they can take the lid off, put it on the scraper, turn it around and smooth it off again, then it would be all right. As we have not got such a machine here, I, therefore, cannot get similar results from the lid. I would like to say that it was not at all the fault of the maker of the lids.

As to gas stoves. At first we made them ourselves, but afterward we purchased them from manufacturers, who made them better and cheaper than we could.

Mr. McMillin—What is the temperature of the gas in the P. & A.

Mr. Somerville—I cannot answer that question. The condenser is so hot that you cannot keep your hand upon it. I think it must be about 120°.

Mr. Harbison—I will say in this connection, that in adding to our works, as I have been doing in the last two or three years, I have not got any hot scrubber; and the exhauster is as near the hydraulic main as I can conveniently place it. It did not work satisfactorily; and recently I have put in a Walker tar extractor, which thus far has done its work admirably. It is placed just ahead of the Standard scrubber. Of course I have not been working it very long, and do not know just what the result will be, but I find it is doing very nicely now. I might say in this connection that in Hartford, where we charge the same price for gas, whether consumed as fuel or for illumination, we have a little over 1,400 stoves in use, and are selling every one.

Mr. Nettleton—I am sorry to hear Mr. Somerville thinks the difficulties with the self-sealing lid are insurmountable. I have been working at that matter, and trying to get something satisfactory, for a number of years; but so far my experience has been unsatisfactory. Some years ago I saw a lid in one of the large works in New York that seemed to be perfectly tight. I made a trial of them. They leaked badly, and it was only a few months before they were given up. It turned out that the trouble lay in the difference in size of the mouthpieces—those of New York being 12x20, while mine were 14x25. It is an easy matter to obtain a self-sealing lid which will work well on small mouthpieces, but a difficult matter on large ones—that is, to have the lids as tight as when they are luted.   Perhaps I may say, in this connection, that I have tried three kinds of lids, and am now trying the fourth.   On the other hand, I agree with Mr. McMillin that it is very desirable, if possible, to get rid of the labor of luting lids.   I think with him, that by putting the hot coke directly into the furnace, when drawn from the retorts, and also by doing away with the luting of the lids, we can decrease the labor of the stoker nearly one-half.   Consequently we can, without calling on him for an unreasonable amount of work, increase our yield of gas per man to twice what it was before. There is no reason why we should not increase from the old standard of 12,000 or 15,000 feet to 25,000 or 30,000 feet, and a good many works are doing it.

MR. STARR—I did use self-sealing lids, but finally abandoned them.   I found that without a great deal of care I would draw in air through the mouthpieces, and so bring down the general average of the gas to about 12 candles.   When I went back to the luted lid I had better gas.

MR. FLOYD—I object to any general condemnation of self-sealing lids, and also to the statement that they cannot be made tight for large as well as small retorts.   In fact I know that the results obtained from self-sealing lids, in three or four of the larger cities, where very large retorts and large mouthpieces are used, give fully average results.   My observation has shown me that the principal difficulty lies in the treatment of the lids.   It is necessary that a lid which has been turned out in a machine shop should have different treatment from the ordinary luted lid It should have a mechanic to look after it.   It must be made smooth, and the mouthpiece itself must be straight.

MR. RAMSDELL—We have used self-sealing lids, of two different patents, for the past eight or ten years, and have not experienced any of the difficulties mentioned here.   One kind of lid fits into the mouthpiece with V shape, and the other is one of the kind that is supposed to clean itself.   Once in a while a little hardened matter will accumulate on its surface, but it is very easily taken off.   It can be easily scraped off with the shovel.   Even if there was (as has been suggested here) a slight escape from some part of the lid, it would be a very easy matter to put a little luting on that spot. I think, remembering the cost of maintaining the luting and the labor necessary to keep them, there is no comparison between the two kinds of lids.

Mr. Harbison—I quite agree with the last speaker. If you will only lute the self-sealing lids you will make them tight.

On motion of Mr. Thompson, a vote of thanks was tendered to Mr. Somerville.

The President—We will now hear the report of the Committee on Standard Meter Unions.

Mr. Goodwin—In behalf of the Committee I make the following report :

Gentlemen :—Your Committee, appointed at the last meeting of the American Gas Light Association (held in New York), to consider the question of Standard Meter Unions, and to report to the Association at its next meeting, would state that they held several meetings and carefully considered the question submitted for their consideration. Your Committee find that the subject has required more than ordinary consideration and care, owing to the differences that have been found to exist between the sizes of unions of the several manufacturers, and their desire to prevent any difficulty in the adoption of such standard as might be presented for the Association's consideration. They would report that, to prevent any serious expense or difficulty to the various gas companies in making any changes, that they have agreed upon the following sizes for adoption, viz., 3, 5 and 10 lights, and that this Association be requested to submit the same to its sister Associations for their approval and adoption, and that, should the Association desire that the changes be made in all sizes, the Committeee be and is hereby authorized to continue its labors and report fully at the next meeting.

The following are the sizes as recommended :

Size.	Standard Thread.	Diameter.	Tail of Swivel.	Nose of Swivel.
3 lights.	18	$\frac{63}{64}$ in.	$\frac{44}{64}$ in.	$\frac{42}{64}$ in.
5 "	12	$1\frac{8}{64}$ in.	$\frac{84}{64}$ in.	$\frac{48}{64}$ in.
10 "	$11\frac{1}{2}$	$1\frac{28}{64}$ in.	$1\frac{6}{64}$ in.	1 in.

Respectfully submitted,

W. H. Down, Chairman.

W. W. Goodwin, Secretary.

MR. WHITE—I move that the report of the Committee be accepted, and that the Committee remain in charge of this matter in order to complete their labors by reporting standard unions for meters of other sizes.

MR. McMILLIN—I second that motion.

MR. HARBISON—Before the vote is taken I would like to ask the Chairman of the Committee to kindly state, for the benefit and information of the members of the Association, in what respect, if any, the proposed schedule differs from those now in use, in order that we may understand the report more fully. I do not know that half a dozen men in the room can tell how near the dimensions given for these three sizes agree with those now in use. I, therefore, ask him to state what changes have been made. I am entirely in favor of adopting the report as to the sizes recommended, but I would like to have the Chairman state, for my own advantage as well as that of other members of the Association, what changes have been made from the unions now in use, in the standard adopted.

MR. DOWN—I will state, in answer to Mr. Harbison, that in measuring the different screws we found quite a difference in their diameters, in the number of threads to the inch, and also in the shape and depth of the thread. We endeavored to reconcile these differences by adopting a standard which should come nearest to the unions most generally in use, and in that way save as much expense as possible to the gas companies, and make the change more easily effected. The threads will be of a standard size and of the same shape. The changes can be made gradually and without anybody feeling the expense. Should these sizes be adopted, and gas companies state what sizes they want, so that the meter-makers will know exactly what to give them, there will be no trouble. I think the greatest change which will be necessary is about 3-64 of an inch. That would be, more particularly, on 3-light meters. We found some threads were 18, 18½, 19 and, in one instance, 20. In adopting the thread at 18 for 3-lights the change can be made more readily than in any other way, and thus bring about a standard size. Some of the makers will have to go up a trifle, while others will have to come down a trifle, in order to make them more readily interchangeable.

Mr. Harbison—I desire to express my gratification at the unanimity of feeling that exists in this matter between the manufacturers of meters. This committee was composed of gentlemen who represented various meter manufacturers and interests in the country; and it is personally gratifying to me—having been somewhat active in the formation of this committee, and the introduction of this matter—to know they have fallen in so heartily with the wishes of the members of this Association, and of the other Associations of the country. Their action will enable us to have a uniform standard meter coupling, so that whether we do business in the West or in the East, whether we buy from one manufacturer or another, the meters we buy will fit our unions, and we will not have as much trouble as there has been in some cities in the attempt to have a meter made by one manufacturer fit a coupling made by another. I think the gentlemen engaged in this industry deserve our sincere thanks for their efforts, and for so readily acting in conformity to the wishes of the Association. Their interests are ours and ours are theirs. I like to see this friendly feeling existing among them, and to know that they have come up so promptly in response to the wishes of the Association in respect to adopting standard unions, and have agreed among themselves to make such changes as are necessary, and to go to such expense as is required, and to so manage their business as to best suit the wishes of their customers. I hope the report of the Committee will be accepted and adopted, and that the committee by another year will have completed their labors, and given uniform standards with reference to all sizes.

Mr. Goodwin—While there seems to be a very considerable difference in sizes, as you hear them mentioned, still, when you come to deal with the figures that we are dealing with there is not so much difference as there would seem to be. For instance, four of the manufacturers make the diameter of the thread $\frac{4}{4}$, and two of them $\frac{6}{4}$; and the recommendation is that the standard thread shall be $\frac{5}{4}$. So you see that there is not so much difference after all. What the committee propose to do, if we are continued, is to get up a set of steel standards, at our own expense, to present to the Association, and these will thereafter be known as the standards of all meter manufacturers.

Mr. Down—Gentlemen probably do not recognize what difference the sixty-fourth of an inch will make in the diameter of a screw. It is enough of a difference to bother anybody in attempting to make the coupling. It is a much greater difference than we want. As Mr. Goodwin says it is the desire of the committee, if these standards are adopted, to make steel standards and place them in charge of the American Gas Light Association, to be known as standard gauges for all unions, to which all meter makers will have access at any time they require to test the gauges in order to keep them in proper condition.

Mr. McDonald—I feel that this matter has been very carefully handled by the committee. The greatest difficulty we anticipated was that the gas companies would be put to trouble if these changes were made, and, therefore, it was desirous that we should know whether the gas companies, and those representing them, would accept these standards. It is easy for any meter manufacturer to make standard sizes, if we know what the sizes are. The changes are not wholly on the thread, or the size of the thread, but on the size of the tail piece. There has been more change in that than in the actual size of the screw. Considerable complaint is sometimes made because one manufacturer's tail piece or lining will not go into the ring of another. We had to make material changes in those respects; and we will have to ask from the people who are using the unions some consideration in this respect. I say this the more freely because I do not think it bears on one manufacturer more than it does on another, as no two of them were exactly alike; but the manufacturers have tried to arrange sizes of standards in such a way that the changes will be as slight as possible. Still there will be changes which will make difficulties, if those standard sizes are used with some of the old ones.

Mr. Young—I think it is very important they should be so made as to go into the couplings of the old meters.

Mr. McDonald—There will be no trouble about that point. That will be taken care of.

Mr. A. C. Humphreys—If this motion to recommit should pass, will the standards as adopted go into use at once, or will the whole subject wait until next year? Furthermore, I would like to ask if the committee have made provision for stamping or designating their standard unions, so that we will know just what we are getting. There should be something to designate that it is the new union. That would be a great convenience to the men who are actually handling the work.

Mr. Down—That can be done so that there should be no mistake made. It can be designated in several ways. It can be done by making a difference in the shape of the union, or by simply stamping with an " S."

Mr. Harbison—I would suggest to the manufacturers who are present, and who have spoken, that they designate their standard union with the letter " S," and that this be done uniformly, so that all the makers and gas men will understand it. My understanding of this report, and of the motion to adopt it, and to continue the committee, is that the union recommended for three, five and ten lights, shall go into use at once. That is my understanding of it, and I wish that the Chair in stating the question would be kind enough to so state it. Let it be the understanding of the Association that the agreement of the meter manufacturers, through their committee, is that the standard sizes for three, five and ten lights are now to be made, and stamped with the letter "S," so that we may all know them.

Mr. Down—In answer to Mr. Harbison I would say that it is impossible to do this immediately, as it will take some little time to make the necessary changes ; but the meter men are a very liberal sort of people, and although they do not care to make changes if it is possible to avoid doing so, still they are quite willing to meet the wishes of the Association in this regard, and to do so as promptly as possible. I will say, for my confreres and for myself, that the standards will be put in such a shape, or so designated, that there need be no mistake made in taking them. Perhaps soon after the first of January we can get the thing in working shape.

Mr. Griffin—This report asks you to submit the matter to the other gas Associations for their approval and adoption, and if they adopt it, then we can all go into it. In the meantime we will all get down as close as we can, so that by the time it is adopted by the other Associations we will all be ready to adopt the standard.

MR. MCMILLIN—I think the suggestion of Mr. Harbison is in the right line, that if this is a good thing it should be adopted at once, and without waiting for another year. All the sister Associations are represented here—I believe I belong to all of them myself; and there are many others here who belong to the other Associations. There is, therefore, no necessity for awaiting their endorsement of what we do, because they will have to indorse it any way. I congratulate myself and the Association that the meter men have been so unanimous in working this standard union up. My friend Harbison takes great pleasure to himself in having been a sort of instigator of this matter; but I think he has really planned better than he knew.

MR. GOODWIN—The committee thought they had better not proceed further than those first three sizes until they obtained the sense of the Association; but as it appears to be the sense of the Association that we shall proceed at once with the manufacture of those three sizes, as suggested, I would ask, in behalf of the parties in interest, that you name a period of three or four months from the present time, for the reason that we have to make some material changes, and it would take some time to do it. If you name three or four months hence, we will be able to comply with your wishes, say, by the first of January or February, 1889. I ask you to say that on and after the first of March all unions shall be stamped in that way. It will put us to considerable expense to get these standards up, and we want everything done to the satisfaction of the Association; and as each meter establishment will require a set of the standards, it will be no small job to make them all and be sure of their accuracy.

MR. HARBISON—I move that the recommendation of the committee with regard to the size of standard thread for three, five and ten lights, be accepted, to take effect the first of March; and that the committee be continued and requested to designate other standard sizes. (Carried.)

The motion prevailed.

Mr. Frederick Mayer, of Baltimore, Md., then read the following paper, entitled

CONSTRUCTION OF GASHOLDERS WITH WROUGHT IRON OR STEEL TANKS ABOVE GROUND.

It has been the desire and aim of gas engineers in all modern constructions of magnitude and importance to provide an easy access to all parts of an apparatus, even to the gas main and its drips, as far as they are located in the works. The advantages of this system are apparent.

In a works where all the apparatus are constructed above ground, surrounded by plenty of air and light, it is an easy matter for the engineer to control the condition of the apparatus and maintain it in a proper state.

Little or no attention in this direction has been paid in this country to the construction of gasholder tanks, although they form a part of the most expensive apparatus which enter into the construction of a gas works.

It has been the custom to repeat the old and well-known con-struction of brick tanks in almost every instance where a new gasholder was erected, although it is well known that the guar-antees for perfectness of construction and proper results are exceedingly doubtful, even in good building ground. Numer-ous instances of defective brick tanks prove the correctness of this assertion. For this reason it seems to me very necessary to look forward to a construction of gasholder tanks which will overcome the above objections.

With this view I have proposed and advocated during the last three years the construction of wrought-iron or steel tanks built above ground; and have designed and erected several holder tanks from which I have obtained results that appear to me to give the advantages which I hereafter enumerate and present for your consideration, and trust that they may prove of some assist-ance in enabling you to determine whether or not the adaptability of iron or steel gas-holder tanks, constructed above ground, is advantageous.

The advantages of wrought-iron or steel tanks as compared with brick tanks are :—

(1), Reduced cost of construction ; (2), less time required in their construction ; (3), positive assurance of perfect construction ; (4), accessibility to all parts of the tank and inlet and outlet pipes ; (5), no deterioration of ground.

It is very difficult to estimate the probable cost of a brick tank previous to its construction, when the same is to be executed in treacherous ground ; whereas the cost of a proper foundation to support the iron tank is comparatively easily determined and provided for, as even in iron tanks of 35 feet in depth the load per square foot only amounts to 2,200 pounds, which is not an unusual pressure upon foundations.

In very bad ground piling becomes necessary, and, according to its formation, either wood, sand or concrete piles must be applied.

The character of such piling is readily determined if an iron construction is to be used ; but proper tests to determine what is required for a brick construction can only with difficulty be obtained, owing to the increased depth.   In consequence of the unreliability of these tests, it frequently becomes necessary to resort to piling after the excavations for tank have been made ; and in such cases where piling was not contemplated, as well as in others where water and quicksand become factors to be dealt with, large expense is incurred in providing steam boilers and pumps, and keeping them in operation during the progress of construction.   This expense is not infrequently supplemented by the necessity of sheet piling ; with the added expense is coupled the delay of completion ; and many engineers who have been confronted with these obstacles have been compelled to spend double the time originally counted upon in the construction of the gasholder tank, and during this time could not avail themselves of the probably much-needed additional storage capacity.

The time of completion for the construction of an iron tank of average dimensions can, with certainty, be established to within a week or two, and in large tanks to within two or three weeks ; and when compared with the time required to construct a brick tank, under the most favorable conditions, in good building ground, can be accomplished in from 20 to 30 per cent. less time than that required for the brick tank.

It is the opinion of many engineers that a brick tank of large dimensions should be constructed the year previous to the holder.

This has, no doubt, many advantages, but again adds to the cost of construction, on account of the necessary protection against frost and deterioration during the winter months ; the ordinary protection during this time being the filling of the tank with water, which of course has to be pumped out previous to the construction of the holder.

When properly constructed and carefully executed, it is reasonably to be expected that iron tanks will have the desired results as to perfectness ; but this cannot be asserted of the brick tank, as often its defects are not developed until the same is being filled with water, when, in many instances, apparently good and sound tanks show a large amount of leakage.

There are many causes which may render a brick tank defective before the holder is completed. Where much water is encountered and pumping has to be continued after the tank is completed, to admit of the erection of the iron-work, it is possible that the back-filling on the exterior of the tank wall near its base is undermined, thus forming a receptacle for the water that penetrates the brickwork at this point, and is, no doubt, in many instances, the cause of leaks that appear to be unaccountable. As the exterior of the tank is not accessible, the most careful examination of the interior of same would not detect the defect. These conditions do not exist in the construction of iron tanks ; and should any defects be developed in the latter, they are at once observable and easily remedied.

The claim that the erection of an iron tank does not deteriorate the ground is, of course, only of importance under peculiar conditions. In our large and rapidly growing citities, where ground in favorable locations increases in value with the growth of the population, a lot of ground occupied by a brick gasholder tank remains comparatively valueless, as it is not applicable for anything else but a gasholder ; but iron tanks are susceptible of being taken apart and reconstructed in different locations, thus admitting of the disposal of the original site upon advantageous conditions.

The gradual development and progress in the construction of wrought-iron tanks is clearly shown by the exhibited plans and photographs. The appearance of the guide-frame shown upon these drawings, especially for three-lift holders, will probably raise the question, at the first sight, if the latter is sufficiently strong in all its parts.

Fortunately, the engineer is not forced to construct from personal perception, but from measure of numerical values; which are applicable, with entire safety, for the resisting capacity of the materials that enter into the construction of the guide-framing.

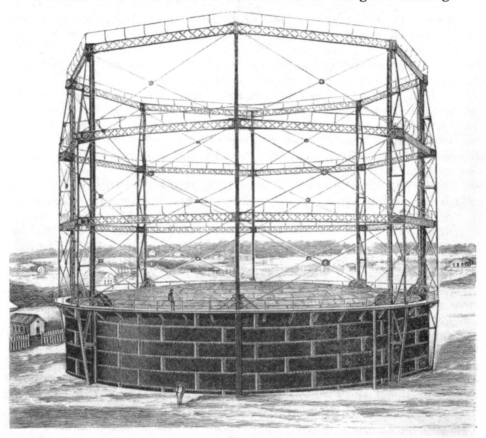

My first construction was a tank 22 ft. 6 in. in diameter by 11 ft. 0 in. deep, erected in 1885 for the Equitable Gas Light Company, of New York city. The standards of the guide-frame were supported directly upon the concrete foundations below tank. This idea was abandoned in the construction of the second tank at Lynn, Mass., in 1886, where the entire weight of guide-framing is supported by the side plating of tank. In all later constructions the idea of supporting the entire weight of guide-framing upon side plating of tank was maintained.

The bottoms of tanks are all perfectly horizontal, and must be solidly embedded upon the foundations with cement grouting. The latter is poured under the bottom, after the same is in position, through hand-holes constructed for this purpose on the inner surface of bottom.

The strains imposed upon the iron work of tank by internal pressure, are, for the shell, directly proportional to the diameter of same, and in the construction shown do not exceed in any part of the riveted joints 10,700 lbs. per square inch, and the strength of riveting, as compared with the plating, is, for the lower vertical triple riveted seams, 81 per cent., for the upper double riveted seams, 76 per cent. of the plating.

The required strength at the upper edge of tank is obtained through a horizontal continuous circular girder of plate iron.

The supports for standards of guide-frame consist of large brackets extending through the entire depth of tank, constructed of angle and bar iron of suitable dimensions.

After the standards have been attached to the brackets they form a part of them, and through them the entire weight of guide-frame is uniformly distributed through the side plating of tank and its foundation. By these means the pressure from the weight of guide-framing upon the foundation is not only uniformly distributed, but is also reduced to the minimum per unit of surface.

The overflow near the upper edge of tank is provided with two outlets at different levels, so that the water-line can be lowered when necessary to admit painting the inner and upper surfaces of tank to prevent oxidation at this point. In large tanks it is very necessary to make provision for expansion and contraction.

The guide-framing consists of wrought iron trussed standards composed of shape and bar iron, solidly riveted together, and are connected at each other and to the tank by wrought iron latticed girders provided with polygonal braces of plate iron, and diagonal braces of bar iron. Through the polygonal and diagonal bracing the entire structure is so secured that the strains imposed upon the same by wind pressure are transferred to the continuous circular girder surrounding the upper edge of tank and to the side plating of same.

A careful static calculation of the strains in the guide-framing has resulted in a construction light in appearance as compared with the usual arrangement of guide-framing, and yet one possessing greater resistance to the heaviest wind pressures than the ordinary construction, especially where the columns are connected to the masonry of brick tanks.

I received a practical proof of the correctness of this construction from a test of a triple-lift holder and iron tank recently erected in Memphis, dimensions 100 ft. 0 in. in diameter by 100 ft. 0 in. high. When the holder was being tested and was inflated to its full height, it was caught in a tornado, in which the wind reached a velocity of seventy miles per hour, passing through the ordeal without the slightest damage, although buildings in the immediate neighborhood were demolished, trees uprooted, etc.

With the construction of iron tanks it becomes an important question how to prevent the formation of ice. If sufficient steam can be spared from an already existing boiler, this system of heating the water should be applied; but where an additional apparatus is required for this purpose, the system of heating by hot water has the preference.

I have no practical data at present as to the heating surface required in proportion to the volume of tank, but shall be glad to lay before you during our next meeting the results of my experience in this direction during the coming season.

A system of heating the tank water by hot water circulation deserves probably the preference, on account of the little attention necessary, as only the fuel supply to the boiler demands the latter. With either the low pressure steam or hot water systems it is required that the heating surface is uniformly distributed around the inner circumference of tank. A circulating pipe near the inner circumference of tank, entering the same immediately above the bottom and leaving the same at an adjacent point, is all that is required for tanks of ordinary dimensions. For larger tanks, two or three circulating coils must be applied;

and if each of them is provided with proper valves, the amount of heating surface and consumption of fuel can be proportioned to the temperature of the atmosphere.

There have been erected under my supervision single, double and triple-lift gasholders with wrought-iron tanks above ground, varying in capacity from 3,000 to 500,000 cubic feet.

The two triple-lift holders constructed at Memphis and New York are probably of special interest on account of their large dimensions, which are as follows:

Memphis—Erected in 1887; inner section 93 ft. 6 in. diameter by 24 ft. 4 in. high; middle section, 95 ft. 0 in. in diameter by 24 ft. 4 in. high; outer section, 96 ft. 6 in. in diameter by 23 ft. 4 in. high; tank, 99 ft. 0 in. in diameter by 25 ft. 4 in. deep. (See illustration.)

New York—Erected during the present season and about to be completed; inner section, 85 ft. 9 in. in diameter by 28 ft. 4 in. high; middle section, 87 ft. 3 in. in diameter by 28 ft. 4 in. high; outer section, 88 ft. 9 in. in diameter by 27 ft. 4 in. high; tank, 91 ft. 6 in. in diameter by 29 ft. 4 in. deep.

In the construction of these holders particular attention was paid to the arrangement of guide rollers and carriages. For the rollers the combined systems of radial and tangential rollers were applied. All the carriages are constructed entirely of wrought-iron under recently obtained patents. The carriages are so arranged that by their application all strains imposed upon the channel bars of the cups by the weight of the different sections are eliminated and transferred directly to the vertical stiffeners of the same.

The numerous recent executions of gasholders with wrought-iron tanks above ground apparently prove the correctness of the often heard assertion, " that the majority of brick tanks are defective."

During the present year the excavation for a brick gasholder tank in the city of New York, for the Standard Gas Light Company, had progressed to nearly one-third of its intended depth, when it became exceedingly doubtful if the continuation of the excavation and erection of the brick tank would warrant the desired results.

After carefully considering the condition, the Gas Company

decided to abandon the construction of the brick and substitute the iron tank.

It is apparent that if the iron tank is suitable to replace a brick tank under extremely unfavorable conditions, it is much more able to do so under favorable conditions, when the cost of the foundations for the same is reduced to the minimum.

Discussion.

Mr. Smedberg—In 1868 I had a tank split through about one-third of its outer length, and up the sides to the top. We repaired it by cutting out and repatching with brick and Portland cement. If we had had an iron tank there I am certain that it would not have happened; for I think that an iron tank, constructed according to Mr. Mayer's ideas, would have stood the strain of the shock. I have no doubt President Turner will agree with me in regard to that point.

Mr. Harbison—I doubt whether there are many men in this room who have not had more or less experience with leaky tanks. There may occasionally be a man who has had the good fortune to build his tanks on such ground or rock that the foundation has not given away; but I think not many of us can make that boast. If we can have tanks constructed in a manner somewhat after Mr. Mayer's description and plan, I think it will be a great step in advance of our experience up to this time. I know that it would be a very great advantage to me if my tanks were all as tight as I think that these iron or steel tanks can be made. I am unfortunately (or otherwise) located where there is a rise and fall of 27 feet in the water level and hence the ground is made ground, so-called. I have had a good deal of difficulty with tanks. I have 4 tanks—one 60 feet in diameter, one 75 feet, and two are 90 feet or more. In two of those tanks I have already put in a lining of four-inch brick wall on the inside, and, of course, have lessened the space that it is desirable to have between the inside of the tank wall and the holder. One tank that is now leaking (it is 94 feet in diameter and 24 feet deep) has caused me to consider the question of putting in an iron or steel lining instead of a brick one; it is split from top to bottom, having been built on made ground, and up to this time I have not been able to make it tight. I think if I were going to build a new one I would be very strongly disposed to try this innovation, as we may call it, which has been recommended. I think it is a practical solution of the difficulty, which is encountered in the construction of brick tanks, in the effort to make our tanks perfectly tight. I do not apprehend that the difficulty of keeping it free from ice would be much greater than the brick tank, according to the plans suggested by Mr. Mayer. I suppose it would not be a practical difficulty to house the holder and tank together, when the difficulty from frost would either be practically obviated or greatly reduced. It would not be a particularly expensive matter to cover the whole tank, in addition to covering the holder built in a brick tank. I think that this is a step in the right direction.

MR. SOMERVILLE—As Mr. Harbison says, that is something quite new—at any rate it is new to me; for I had no idea that they were making gasholder tanks of wrought iron. It puts me in mind of the old days when we used cast iron tanks. Our cast iron tanks I can understand; but I do not think we would have ever thought of putting wrought iron tanks upon the ground. It does not hurt a cast iron tank to rust; there is no oxidation at all—you can put a piece of cast iron in the ground and it is as good as ever when taken out, no matter how long it has been there; but we know that that is not the case with wrought iron, for oxidation commences immediately if the air gets to it. I would like to ask Mr. Mayer what is to prevent the bottom of the tank from rusting, and how does he know when it is rusting? I think, too, there would be some difficulty in keeping such a tank from freezing. Another question I would like to ask him is, what pressure would be upon that holder, 100 feet in diameter and 100 feet high?

MR. A. C. HUMPHREYS—I am glad to hear a paper read on this subject, and especially glad to hear it presented by a gentleman so well able to do it justice. There is no question in my mind but there is something in the construction of wrought iron tanks. I fully agree with everything that Mr. Mayer said with regard to the trouble that we have with broken tanks; and I do not think that any of us are warranted in putting a dollar in a brick tank if we have even a doubt about the foundation. We put up a couple of small wrought iron tanks three years ago, and they have never given us a day's trouble since. As to the advantages claimed for wrought iron or steel tanks, as compared with brick tanks, as stated by Mr. Mayer, I think I can personally agree with three of them. It certainly reduces the cost of construction ; less time is required in construction, and there is positive assurance of perfect construction, or, at least, there is every chance of getting what we call perfect construction. We also have accessibility to all parts of the tank. Of course it does not give us accessibility to the bottom of the tank; but I think that that can be perfectly provided for by the first setting of the tank. The method that Mr. Mayer has suggested is new to me ; but I think that it would fully cover the difficulty. Of course, setting in concrete is not new ; but the method of getting at every part through a small hand-hole, which can afterward be made good, seems to be satisfactory. I think there will be no difficulty in 50 years from rust, under that construction. We have seen what can be done in this way by oil tank constructors. They throw it right down on the ground ; practically, right in the mud ; but I think if you will take up those tanks and examine them, as long as they are painted where they are exposed, you will find no trouble with them from year to year. I have suggested to some of the oil men the possibility of rusting of the bottoms of oil tanks and they have been surprised at the suggestion. There is one point in regard to starting brick construction a year ahead which is important. I do not think that Mr. Mayer put that as strongly as he might. In such a case we have to add interest on the cost of the ground and of the tank, which, of course, we do not have to do in the case of the wrought iron tank. The greatest trouble that I anticipate from the use of these tanks is from the frost. As Mr. Mayer has pointed out, we may provide for it in many ways; the trouble is with the cost of doing it. There will be that standing objection to it as compared with a brick tank. It will radiate more rapidly than a brick tank will do.

MR. MAYER—Mr. Humphreys has answered Mr. Somerville's first question. As to the oxidation on the under side, I do not think it is of any consequence. I believe that the oxidation on the inside of the tank, where it is covered with water, will only penetrate to a certain thickness; and the outside can be made perfectly free from oxidation by painting it. The outside is exposed to examination at all times.

Mr. Page—It was my pleasure to inspect the largest of these holders, and I was certainly impressed with the great importance of this marked improvement in the construction of gasholders. It is doubtless known to most of the Association that this mode of construction has already been adopted to a considerable extent in England; and at the recent meeting of the Gas Institute it was believed it would gradually supersede the previous manner of building gasholder tanks. It was not adopted, however, in the construction of that marvelous gasholder at East Greenwich, which is 280 feet in diameter, nearly 200 feet high. and holding 8¼ millions cubic feet. Neither has it been adopted in the construction of the two next largest holders—at Birmingham—which were erected at the same time, and which hold 6½ millions cubic feet each. The suggestion as to these increased sizes and dimensions of gasholders is important, because it is doubtless the tendency here (as shown in the great holder just completed in Chicago, holding 3¼ millions cubic feet, and the one built in New York, of about the same capacity), to believe that the greater the size of the holder the less is the percentage of cost. The point made that the ground taken by holders is most often taken at points where the land is expensive, has an important bearing. Another interesting point in the discussion which may be alluded to is as to the cost of this improved mode of building holders. The general impression, so far as I had opportunity of speaking with English engineers, was that the cheaper method, the stronger method and the far less expensive method (dispensing with columns) would speedily prevail; and, as has been stated, this is one of the largest and most extensive expenditures of a gas company. That fact is of deep interest, in view of the largely increased capital account rendered necessary by improvements of this nature.

Mr. Somerville —Of what thicknesses are the plates?

Mr. Mayer—In the Memphis holder the bottom plates are, I think, 11-16ths or ¾ of an inch; in the New York example the bottom plates are ⅞ of an inch.

Mr. Somerville—What is the size?

Mr. Mayer—Practically about four feet wide by 16 feet in length. Of course they are reduced in size as they grow up. As the pressure is reduced the thickness of the plates is reduced proportionately. They are triply riveted for the bottom and doubly riveted for the upper seams.

The President—I think Mr. Corbett might give us some interesting information on this subject.

Mr. Corbett—I believe Mr. Mayer has filled the bill pretty well. I do not know that I have anything to add, excepting that the wrought iron tanks have been built for quite a number of years—even longer than he states.

Mr. Nettleton—I would like to ask Mr. Mayer whether it is a well understood fact that iron under water is merely covered with oxide, and then stops rusting. Is that so beyond all question?

Mr. Mayer—Yes.

On motion of Mr. Corbett, the thanks of the Association were voted to Mr. Mayer.

Mr. D. H. Geggie, of Quebec, read the following paper, entitled :

EXPERIENCE IN DISTRIBUTING GAS UNDER EXTREMELY LOW TEMPERATURES.

Mr. President and Gentlemen : In presenting to the Association the paper which the Executive Committee allotted me, I have no expectation that you will hear anything new or novel ; so I will not encroach much upon your time, as there are papers of more importance to be read by other gentlemen.

The title of my paper I think should have been the " Difficulties of Distributing Gas Under Low Temperatures," as the situation of Quebec is so far north, and the winters so long and severe. The temperature from the first of November to the first of April averages 15° F., and for at least two months of that time it is below zero, and frequently reaches 36° below.

Before proceeding with the subject under review, a short description of a portion of our apparatus may not be out of place.

After the gas passes through the air condenser, it enters into a St. John & Rockwell scrubber condenser, where it is washed by the liquor from the hydraulic main, and the volume of gas is divided many hundred times by mesh-work, and all traces of tar completely arrested. The gas then enters a series of upright pipes, which are provided with a lattice-work of corrugated plates, and then makes its exit to the Standard washer.

I find this apparatus not only eliminates the tar, but will never permit naphthaline to be deposited about the works, inlets to the gasholders, or carried to the street mains and services. In fact, I have never experienced the trouble naphthaline gives so many gas engineers when there is a sudden change in the temperature.

The candle power of the gas in winter, tested by our Government Inspector, at his office about half a mile from the works, averages 17½ to 18 candles, using Newcastle and Provincial coals, with 4 per cent. of cannel ; and I attribute the small percentage of enricher required to the effective manner in which the St. John & Rockwell apparatus breaks up and adds the vapors of benzole to the gas.

The gasholders are all in brick and stone buildings heated by steam, entailing a heavy cost on capital ; but owing to the severe frost and snow storms it would be impossible to work them if they were not protected from the weather.

The distributing plant of the works which I manage consists of three leading mains from the holder houses to the three principal districts of the city and each of these mains, with their valves and governors, being subdivided into several smaller districts by valves. This has been carried out so that, in case of a break in the mains or a fire, the district in which it occurs can be shut off without interfering with any other portion of the distributing system. Gas engineers generally are well aware of the importance of districting mains ; and I would urge every one present who has not done so to try it, as it is an easy method of locating leakage on the mains and services.

As it is a well-known law that for every 5° of cold gas decreases in volume about 1 per cent. and *vice versa*, the gas which leaves our holder in winter at an average temperature of 55°, having to pass through the mains to a great extent embedded in frost, reduces the quantity about 5 per cent., thus increasing the unaccounted for gas.

Our street mains are all laid from four to six feet deep on one or both sides of the street, near the curb line; and in wet ground in the lower portions of the city, and also in the upper part where there is a great deal of rock which conveys frost readily, we have placed many of our mains and service pipes in wooden boxes with tar and sawdust.

A diversity of opinion exists as to the best form of joint to adopt; but in my experience, although we have both the lead and turned and bored, I prefer the former, as it is more elastic and is less liable to fracture by frost, contraction or subsidence of the ground. I now use lead joints altogether, as I find when the frost penetrates below the pipes, it is invariably the body of a turned and bored pipe that breaks, owing to the rigid nature of the joint, and we have several broken every winter, causing a heavy leakage and expense digging through the frozen ground to make repairs.

As in many other cities, the water and drainage pipes were laid subsequent to the gas pipes; the city authorities, taking advantage of cheap labor in winter, frequently open streets to lay their pipes and services, and as these pipes are all laid about eight feet deep, our mains and services are often uncovered, exposing them to frost, and entailing the use of large quantities of spirits to thaw them.

During the severe weather last winter, about 1,000 water mains and services were frozen and burst in the city, and at least 200 trenches were made in the streets to repair them. As the earth is all frozen when these trenches are filled, the greatest trouble occurs in the spring, when our pipes bag, fill with water, and often break, owing to the subsidence of the ground.

In extremely cold weather the service pipes easily deliver the necessary quantity of gas; but whenever the temperature gets warmer, frost forms rapidly in many of them, close to the walls of the houses, and shuts off the supply. For these stoppages, I place on the leading pipe from the services a funnel and cock, into which spirits are poured to cut the frost.

It is unnecessary for me to say anything about the difficulties experienced in keeping the lamp services clear of frost, as our streets at present are all lighted by the arc light, and the details would probably be a repetition of the experience of the majority of the members present.

Discussion.

MR. ROBERT BAXTER—This is a subject which of course does not directly interest a majority of the members ; but as I happen to be a native of the frigid zone, though my city is not quite so cold as Mr. Geggie's place, I think a word or two on this subject may not be unacceptable. In Halifax the temperature does not fall so low as it does in Quebec—we may have it down once or twice during the winter to 16 degrees below zero, but it is only for a day or so, although the frost there will sometimes reach a depth of eight feet. Our experience generally has been pretty much the same as his at Quebec. I think that Quebec, from what I know of the place, is peculiarly well adapted for districting, while Halifax is not so well adapted for districting ; but I presume it is, in this respect, on a par with many other towns in Canada and the United States. Our streets run the whole length of the town, and are cross cut, and it would be an extremely difficult matter to district it, however advantageous it might be to do so. Our street mains are laid from four to five feet deep, but sometimes we find that the frost gets down under them. We do not often find that the turned and bored joints break. We use them altogether, and rarely have a broken joint. The trouble with the breakages in our mains, and especially with the service pipes, is caused by the people laying drains and not filling the ground up properly underneath. As a rule we pack the pipes underneath with stone on the ground, so that the downward pressure is equalized as much as possible. We have a large number of pipes broken in winter from that cause, and we find what, of course, is a natural result, that the breakage of the pipe is wider at the bottom than at the top, showing that the action of the frost is a downward pressure. Of course you know when anything freezes it expands ; and after the surface of the ground is frozen, and the frost gradually descends, it cannot raise the cake of frost above it, and, therefore, the pressure is downward. We often find the upper part of the pipe perfectly closed while it is open underneath. As the ground is removed for some little distance in order to make the repairs, it generally springs up again to its proper position and straightens itself out. We have another difficulty in distributing the gas in those temperatures, and that is with regard to meters. We use wet meters almost entirely, and set them in a place where they will not freeze. We use methylated spirits in the proportion of two to one. While that is a little troublesome because of the evaporation of the liquid, we find it very useful. We did use glycerine, and are about to try it again. As a correct measuring instrument, we consider the wet meters better than the dry, taken as a whole. The registration is more to be depended upon. We have this advantage over the ordinary cold wet meter in that we have them all fitted with a reserve fountain. In a three-light meter we have a reserve supply of 3½ to 4½ pints of water, and in a ten-light the reserve supply is 16 pints of water. That gives us an excellent meter of unvarying correctness.

With regard to the stoppage of pipes. We supplied the railway department with a three-inch service pipe. They built a grain-elevator right over the pipe, and changed the position of the pipe in the basement of the elevator so as to pass one of the bins—it was in the winter time, and we had a stoppage of the gas supply. We cut the pipe just after it came through the wall, or at least where the bend came to one side, and changed its direction, and we found that was packed full of hoar frost. We could push in our finger and pull it out. That never occurred there before, and it proved to us, what we had a faint idea of before, that there was a deposition of hoar frost in parts where a constant change of temperature comes, as from a comparatively warm ground to a cold ground, or where a cold draught is passing through. It gave us a good deal of trouble until the building was thoroughly finished, and then the trouble ceased.

MR. SCRIVER—I happen to be one of the unfortunate fellows who live in a cold country. Coming from Montreal, I am not very much farther south than our friend Mr. Geggie, and yet I am far enough south to experience a little milder weather. I do not know that we get down to 36 degrees below zero there, but we very often have it at zero, which is quite cold enough to be comfortable. We have a great deal of trouble, as you have heard, from the extremely cold weather of our northern climate; but the greatest trouble which we experience is the trouble with capital. We require at least double the capital to construct gas works in Montreal, Quebec, or Halifax that you need in New York, Brooklyn, Washington or any point about there. We have to put our pipes down to a very great depth in the ground. We lay our pipes with a covering of at least five feet, and find it is not safe to have them any nearer the surface than that. We have to construct over all our machinery very expensive buildings. I wish we could run our gasholders in the open air, as they are represented in the pictures which are exhibited here; but we cannot do so, and we have to put up very expensive buildings, with costly iron roofs over them. We have to cover in our purifiers and condensers—in fact, all the machinery has to be thoroughly housed. We have not only to keep them covered with buildings, but we have also the additional expense of keeping them warm, to prevent them from freezing. It would not do for us to allow the gasholder to freeze; and, therefore, we have to keep an immense space heated. With regard to the freezing of pipes I may state that in Montreal we have on more than one occasion found our pipes frozen solid for at least 100 feet. Then, with the temperature below zero, we have to open the ground, expose the pipes, and thraw them out. The only way to get the frost out of the pipes under such circumstances is to build coke fires upon them; and it is rather a strange sight in the middle of winter to see about 100 feet of ground open, filled with hot coke, burning away night and day for three or four days, until the frost is removed. Another difficulty with which we have to contend is that bugbear naphthaline. The cold weather makes naphthaline very readily. Our greatest difficulty, however, is not in the extremely cold weather, but when the winter sets in. We are not troubled with it very much about our works, but outside of the works for a distance of half a mile is where we get the most. We do manage to keep the naphthaline out of our works, but when it travels from cold pipes to pipes that, perhaps, lay in low, damp ground, the naphthaline accumulates to a large extent, although I am happy to say it has not troubled us to the extent that it seems to trouble people in Hamilton at the present time. Another additional expense (I refer to it because it requires additional capital) is the furnishing of buildings for the storage of our coals. Our American brethren get their supply of coals in daily I presume, as they want them; but in Montreal we have to store 35,000 or 40,000 tons of coal for our winter's supply. Therefore, we have to purchase a great deal of ground on which to erect our shed. We do not pile our coals high in Montreal. We find we cannot pile our coals more than six or seven feet high. We build our sheds with open sides, with the roof sustained by iron columns, to allow a free circulation of air; and you can readily understand that it requires a great deal of ground to pile up, to a height of six or seven feet, 40,000 tons of coals. This is absolutely necessary with us, because we have not railroad communication with the mines, and have to lay in a sufficient supply in the summer season.

MR. SHELTON—The reference by Mr. Scriver to the cold weather recalls an experience that I had last winter, in which I used a substitute for coke to enable us to get at the pipe beneath the ground, at a low temperature, where the street was very badly frozen. I used slacked lime. I had read of this remedy, I think in the AMERICAN GAS LIGHT JOURNAL, and finding a pipe stopped about four o'clock one afternoon (it was too late to clear it that night) this idea occurred to me. I therefore took off from over the pipe some four or five inches—just a crust of earth—and then put a couple of bushels of lime in the space, poured water over it and slackened it, and then put canvas over that and rocks on the canvas so as to keep the wind from getting underneath. Next morning on returning there I found that the frost had been drawn out from the ground for nearly three feet. You can appreciate what an advantage that was, for picking through frozen ground with the thermometer below zero, is no joke. Since then we have tried it several times. It is an excellent plan if you have time enough to let the lime work. In the daytime you cannot afford to waste the time; but if you have a spare night in which to work it is worth while to try it.

MR. SLATER—I presume, Mr. President, you and all the members of the Association have missed Mr. Littlehales at this meeting. I understand he has some trouble from naphthaline in the inlet or outlet of the holder. I move the Secretary be authorized to send a telegram expressing our regret that he is not here, and our sympathy for him in his trouble.

Mr. Pearson—I have a letter from Mr. Gates, the President of the Hamilton Gas Company, regretting his inability to be here on account of some difficulty at the works and wishing me to convey his regards to you.

Mr. A. C. Humphreys—I do not think that in the States generally we experience any such trouble from the cold weather as they do in Canada, but I believe that, scattered all around in New York, New Jersey, and on that line, they do have a great deal of trouble. It has occurred to me a number of times, whether we do not have more trouble, especially from broken pipes and started joints, where the frost line and the pipe keep intersecting. In other words, when the pipe is dipping, going down and then coming up again; it goes first through a piece of frozen ground, and then through a piece of ground not frozen. I would like to ask how Mr. Baxter provides against the expansion and contraction where they have these turned and bored joints; and also how he provides for crossing bridges, where the pipe is absolutely exposed, coming out of the frost line, going into the air, and then back again. We have several means of providing for that in our own works, and I would like to hear how it is done elsewhere.

Mr. Geggie—In passing over bridges, we put our pipe in a box, and try to protect it as well as we can. That is the only thing we can do.

Mr. Scriver—In Montreal we do not happen to cross any bridges, but have to go underneath the canal, and one or two creeks. Instead of running pipes across a bridge we go down underground. The joint that we use is the double joint. We use the turned and bored joint also. We believe it is the best joint we can have.

Mr. Robert Baxter—I can say, in reply to Mr. Humphreys, that we have no trouble at all from the contraction and expansion of the joints. We rarely have a leaking joint. We use no protection against it. We do not run over bridges and have no trouble with joints drawing apart.

MR. STARR—We sometimes have the temperature down as far as 30° below zero, and it is often down to 18° to 25°. I have been frequently troubled by the frost. I used to have a great deal of trouble with my lamp posts. Before I overcame that difficulty I would sometimes have one-half my lamps frozen up every night. In the summer I took them out, dug up the lamp posts, and put in an 1¼ inch pipe. I had a three-quarter inch pipe there before. I run a service pipe around the pipe in the lamp post, four feet high, and since then have rarely had a frozen lamp. With the larger pipe the gas goes through it without any trouble from frost. In regard to frozen holders, I will say I have had trouble of that kind. Our holder is exposed, uncovered; but I put in iron brackets, extending three inches from the holder, and on them I put two inches of plank between the wall and the holder; and that goes within an inch or two of the holder. In the fall of the year I put a little manure around there, and then I have no trouble at all. I build up my wall about three feet above the holder. That may have been another protection. At any rate I am no longer troubled with the frost.

MR. PEARSON—In carrying pipes across a bridge we put them in a box, and pack it with sawdust. It is a very rare thing that any of the pipes freeze. When they do freeze it is generally just where the gas enters the pipe between the ground and the box—just at that particular point. But we have very little difficulty because of the frost. We had one pipe across the bridge all winter (not enclosed at all) that did not freeze. Of course our climate is not as cold as that of Montreal or Quebec. In fact, it is not much colder here than it is in New York State. We have very little trouble of that kind in the street—seldom having a frozen pipe; but we do have a tremendous number of frozen connections in the houses, by reason of neglect. We use methylated spirits for thawing them out, and they very soon yielded to the application. We tried whiskey, but found that about as much whiskey went down one way as the other, and we decided to give that up.

MR. STARR—We have two bridges over which we carry a pipe, and where the pipe goes down perpendicularly two or three feet to the ground, I surround the pipe by an oak box ten inches square, and never had any trouble with frost until last winter. I then discovered that a team had run against the pipe and broken the box. The box was all rotted down to the bottom. The wooden box has always kept the frost from the pipe.

Mr. Lindsley—With reference to the matter of pipes passing an exposed situation, as over bridges and the like, I will say we have a case in our town that may interest some of the members. We have a stone structure on one side of the river, 2,300 feet long, and the pipes which serve the lamps run along that, just inside of the parapet, resting in a ledge or box which had a foot of earth covering it. It was rather a trying situation for a small street pipe. The distribution on each side commenced with an inch and a half, and ended with a one-inch pipe. In that part there are about 28 lamps. Those pipes were laid in a box an inch wider in size that the diameter of the pipe, and the space filled in with ordinary coal tar pitch. During some six years they were in use not a lamp service was frozen in that district—that is, to be frozen out ; and it is a very rare thing, even in what zero weather we get there, to be troubled in that way.

Mr. Nettleton—Mr. Humphreys stated that his company had their own method of dealing with pipes on bridges. A good many of us are interested in that subject and have had trouble from frozen pipes thus exposed ; and so I would like to ask him what his method is.

Mr. A. C. Humphreys—We simply take and expand the pipe before it leaves the ground. If it is an eight-inch pipe we expand it to twelve inches; carry it up to the ground and across the bridge at twelve inches ; if you cover it up with canvas it is so much the better ; but I do not think it would freeze without covering. The degree of expansion must of course be governed by the climate. I will say we were led to that by the experience I had years ago in my first works, where we connected up lamp posts (we had a great deal of trouble with frozen lamp posts) in the same way, with expanded pipes. If it came in with a three-quarter inch we expanded it to an inch and a half. We originally started at two inches, but found that unnecessary. We ran up past the frost line with this inch and a half and then reduced it to one inch pipe. We never had any trouble with those posts after we put in those "anti-freezers," as we call them. We have had the criticism made sometimes that the thing failed, but on investigation we invariably found that the frost was not in the post; it was in the service. We introduced the same thing in all our different works, and had the criticism from some in the West that it did not answer the purpose; but I think there is no one now who does not say it is all right. In Omaha you must have a larger expansion pipe than in New Jersey or Washington.

MR. McMILLIN—What good does the expanded pipe do?

MR. A. C. HUMPHREYS—It gives you greater capacity for freezing before you have trouble.

MR. McMILLIN—That is the chief thing, I suppose?

MR. A. C. HUMPHREYS—No; I do not think it is. If you open the pipe I do not think you will find the frost there; certainly not any depth of it. If you measure it you will not find the same quantity of frost collected in a given time. And, of course, you carry it over in better condition across the bridges. Instead of reducing it or even holding it at the same pressure, we give it a chance to expand wherever the pressure comes, as just at the point of passing through.

MR. DOUGLAS—I think I can give an experience of this kind. We had a pipe extending on top of the rock for about a mile, but before going on the rock it had to cross a bridge for 50 feet. We could not get any gas at all through that pipe for winter after winter, and they had to abandon the gas light. I was not in charge of the works, but was able to assist the man who was, and I suggested to him to expand the pipe, so as to let the water in the gas be deposited in the form of hoar frost; and the remedy was effective. Just make room for that hoar frost to deposit, and there will be no further trouble. They continued supplying gas, carrying the pipes over snow and ice, and never had any further trouble.

MR. McMILLIN—I have two lines of 16 inch pipe crossing bridges 300 feet long, and in one instance, for perhaps 15 or 20 years before I had charge of the works, during cold weather, the men were instructed to go every day with a barrel of hot water and pour it down one of the pipes at the point where the upright pipes rise to cross over the bridge. The difficulty was always there, of course. To avoid that expense, and at the same time to give them a more uniform service across the river, I tried placing an 18 inch pipe on the outside of the 16 inch pipe, filling the space in with felt. That passed up to the top of the bridge girder, 5 or 6 feet above ground, and then I covered it for 10 feet further with sheet iron—the covering getting thinner as it grew in length, so that at the end of it there was no covering at all except the sheet iron. My whole object was to cause the deposition of what moisture there was in the gas, and also of any of the rich hydro-carbons that would not stand the frost, to spread over as much territory as possible, and by doing that we have never had any trouble with the bridges from that time to this. There was one winter when for three weeks it was 25° below zero, but we had no trouble on the bridge where the pipe laid on the top girder, 5 or 6 feet above the floor, exposed to the weather, and covered with nothing except a coat of paint. Although I should not anticipate any trouble from the lamp posts in the case Mr. Lindsley speaks of, yet I might expect the main to be cut off where it comes up out of the ground into the frost. As to passing along that way for some distance, I would not expect any of the lamp services to freeze, as by that time the moisture is all deposited, and the heavy hydro-carbons which will not stand that temperature have gone down before they reach the lamp post. I have in mind another bridge, 180 feet long, which carried over a gas pipe that I never knew to freeze up. There were lamps on both ends of the bridge, and the main, which came out under the bridge in a very cold place, was exposed for 10 or 15 feet, and then ran up above to where there was a meter set; and the supply pipe going across the bridge was three-eighths of an inch, but I never knew it to be frozen up. So that it is not altogether dependent upon the size of the pipe. It it a good deal in dropping your moisture and other material.

MR. STARR—Which of the bridges was the farthest from the works—the one with the small pipe or the one with the large pipe?

MR. McMILLIN—I think they were about equally distant,

1,000 or 1,500 feet; but in either case the gas would have traveled probably 3,000 feet from the works.

MR. SLATER—It is amusing to notice the different conclusions at which we arrive from our experience in the same line of work. I recollect that Mr. Geggie, acting on his experience, has adopted the lead joint altogether; while from our experience at Providence we have pursued exactly the opposite course, as we use the cement joint, for the reason that the continual expansion and contraction of these pipes cause a great many leaky joints. With rigid cement joints we do not have leaky joints at all. If we have anything, we have broken pipes, which are reported immediately after breaking, so we can promptly repair them. If we used lead joints we would have a great many leaky joints, and they would not be reported at all unless they were very bad. In the case of bridges, we always go over them—come up out of the ground and go over the bridge with a boxed pipe. We have quite a number of railroad bridges where the pipe was formerly put underneath, but we found that with the trains running every few minutes we could not readily get at them to make repairs if they happened to spring a leak, whereas by putting the pipe over the bridge, we can take care of it at any time.

The Association then adjourned, to meet on the following day at 10.30 A. M.

———

SECOND DAY—MORNING SESSION.

The Convention was called to order at 10.30 A. M.

The following additional applications for membership were received:

Active Members.

Bell, H. J., Engineer, Camden, N. J.
Chadwick, H. J., Treasurer, Lockport, N. Y.
Higby, W. R., President, Bridgeport, Conn.
———— ————, Superintendent, Toronto, Ont.
Slater, Jr., A. B., Superintendent, Providence, R. I.
Stoddard, C. H., Prest. and Treas., Brooklyn, N. Y.
Thomas, M. B., Manager, Dundas, Ont.

Associate Members.

Van Wie, P. G., Manager, Cleveland, Ohio.

Wright, W. S., Manager, Chicago, Ill.

MR. NETTLETON—I would like to inquire if the gentlemen whose names have just been read as applicants for membership are to be voted for at this session. We have adopted a Constitution, in accordance with which all applications for membership must be received by the Secretary ten days before the meeting. If that Constitution is in force, I would like to inquire how those gentlemen can now be voted for. For one, I shall be glad to see them elected members, but I want them to come in in the proper way; and if the new Constitution is in force, I for one would like to live up to it.

THE SECRETARY—You did not live up to it yesterday in receiving members.

MR. A. C. HUMPHREYS—Yesterday we voted for new members before the new Constitution was adopted.

THE SECRETARY—But there were others voted for afterward.

THE PRESIDENT—I will refer these applicants to the same committee, and let the committee report. We will now take up the paper by Capt. Ross.

CAPT. ROSS—Before proceeding with the paper I intend to submit, I wish to tender my thanks to the gentlemen composing the Executive Committee for their kindness, and for the compliment extended to me in inviting me to address the Association on the subject of the steam stoker. In view of the fact that I am not a professional gas engineer, I esteem it an honor and a privilege to be permitted to address an Association composed of gentlemen of the high order of intellectual and scientific attainments necessary to promote the rapid development of the vast industries confided to your care. I wish to say, Mr. President, that in this paper I have devoted considerable space to the mechanical construction of the machine; but, owing to the courtesy extended to me this morning in allowing me to take precedence in reading the paper, and in view of the fact that a large proportion of the gentlemen constituting this Association have probably seen the machine at work, and of the fact that they have been in a practical working condition for a period of seven years (although under disadvantages to which no other steam machine has ever been subjected), and in view of the further fact that we are willing to give a written guarantee as to their efficiency, I deem it unimportant to go into the details in regard to their construction. But in order to enable those who have never seen the machine to form an intelligent idea of its construction, I have brought here some descriptive pamphlets, with a cut illustrating the machine, taken from a photograph of the machines as they are working in the city of Cincinnati. I will therefore omit the portion of the paper dealing with the mechanical details, to save time.

Capt. Ross then read his paper on

THE ROSS STEAM STOKERS AND IMPROVED CHARGER.

I can hardly claim that the subject-matter of this paper will prove interesting because of its originality, for from the very first practical demonstration of the feasibility of profitably producing and distributing coal gas the desire for some less laborious and expensive method of charging and discharging retorts has apparently been uppermost in the midst of our engineers.

First taking shape in the brain of Brunton over 50 years ago, his ideas were from time to time modified, improved upon, and added to successively by Grafton, Malam, Bouneville, Somerville, Foulis, West, Rowland, and at least 25 others, some of them the brightest and most intelligent men of our day, each in turn hoping and believing that he had at last solved the difficult problem, but each in turn being disappointed over results when called upon to practically demonstrate the correctness of his theories.

So frequent have been such practical failures in the broad field of original conception, that even those most interested in the success of any new invention are not disposed to look upon it with favor until they have been educated up to an understanding of its merits and a thorough and complete comprehension of the principles upon which its operations are based; and hence, even in the most meritorious cases, the inventor has to assume the role of special pleader for a recognition of the benefits which he proposes to confer.

Experience has taught us that there are no exceptions to this rule, no evading these conditions; and, in consequence, the advocate of any change in existing methods must be content with slow and sometimes disheartening progress, until he has not only clearly demonstrated the fallacy of theoretical objections, but has met and conquered other adverse influences and conditions by an actual practical demonstration of the correctness of his views and the capabilities of his invention. Considering the conservative character of the industry affected by mechanical stoking, the requirement of a wide departure from long established methods, and the changes in construction necessary to its profitable operation, *nothing less will be accepted as conclusive, nothing more should be required.*

I shall first, but briefly, refer to these theoretical objections, give a condensed description of the machines and methods of operating, and then submit for your consideration an expression of the views of engineers who have abandoned the " waiting policy."

I am aware that, in the light which up to that time had been shed upon the subject, the theoretical objections to the charging machine were not entirely unreasonable; in fact, one of the most prominent and progressive engineers in this country, and one who has since become an enthusiastic advocate of mechanical stoking and the projector of the most thorough and complete system ever inaugurated, was the first to suggest objections which I have since heard repeated over and over again, but which I have shown, by the long continued and practical operation of the machines, to be utterly groundless.

These objections were in the shape of expressed doubts as to the practicability of evenly distributing the coal; that the concussion incident to the blast might fracture weak retorts, or cause a variation in the seal; that the coal would be packed so as to prevent the free egress of gas generated; that the condensed steam would moisten coal and interfere with the thorough carbonization; that the weight of charge would not be gauged with sufficient accuracy to maintain the desired uniformity of production, etc.

I shall, as briefly as possible, answer these objections. By intelligently directed successive blasts the coal is projected into retorts exactly as it would be by shovels—the first portion, meeting with no resistance, is deposited at the extreme end of the retorts, and each succeeding charge striking that immediately in front causes the whole to be evenly distributed. The conduit of the hopper occupying less than one-half the superficial area of the mouthpiece, it must be evident that no pressure could be maintained within the retort.

A series of tests made at the works of the Cincinnati Gas Company demonstrated the fact that the concussion never occasioned to exceed one-tenth of an inch variation in a pressure gauge placed on nipples screwed into the stand-pipes; and even this slight variation invariably occurred only for an instant during the last blast, after the bulk of the charge had been deposited.

If a charge has been evenly distributed it is evidence that there has been no "packing," for each particle falls into its position on the bottom only by the force of gravity. In no single instance has a retort ever been "blocked;" and while a careless operator might cause irregularity in distribution, the same may be done with either scoop or shovel, but is less likely to occur where all the charging is done by one single individual, and he alone held responsible for its efficiency.

Of the total volume of steam required for a charge, not exceeding 10 cubic feet, could be retained in the retort, representing but 1 cubic inch of water—a volume so small that it would be volatilized and expelled before the lid could be closed.

The hoppers are gauged by ascertaining the number of cubic inches occupied by any given weight of coal to be charged; so that, practically, there can be no variation except that due to a difference in the size of the particles, or variation in the weight of the coal used—it certainly can be no greater than that due to the use of a scoop or any other receptacle gauged by measurement. The actual difference in weight of coal deposited in bins of the East-End works of the Cincinnati Gas Light Company and that theoretically charged during a period of six months varied but 1.33 per cent., and the greatest observed variation in any one month was 2.21 per cent.

The *discharging machine* consists of a carriage composed of longitudinal and transverse eye-beams, supported on journals near ends of axles upon which the flanged wheels are keyed. Upon one side of the carriage are located the upright boiler, water tank, feed pump, propeller, horizontal engine, and water cataract or governor. This engine actuates the traveler to which the drawing rakes are attached, the movement being accomplished by means of a rack connected with engine piston, the rack working into a pinion keyed to a longitudinal shaft, upon the end of which is keyed a drum to which are attached the ends of two chains, coiled in opposite directions and passing over grooved wheels in vertical frame on either end of the carriage ; the other ends of the chain being attached to the opposite ends of the traveler propel the rake attached thereto, back and forth at will of the operator, who handles the lever. The speed of the traveler can be perfectly controlled by a valve adjustment of the cataract.

A counter-weight attached to an adjustable sliding bar, with the grooved rollers supporting the rake beams, can be so adjusted as to hold them in equilibrium at any point during the stroke.

The rake-beams consist of angle iron of suitable dimensions, to the inner ends of which are attached steel rake-heads, of a size and shape suitable to the contour of the retort. The controlling valves and levers are all located within convenient reach of the operator, and at such a distance from the retorts that he is not subjected to any annoyance from the heat and smoke, and can clearly observe and perfectly control the vertical and horizontal play of the rake.

The machines are operated in substantially the following manner:

An assistant opens the lids of three retorts, and, while cleaning the mouthpiece and auguring the stand pipe, the operator having run the discharger into position opposite the retorts to be drawn, with his right hand he controls the vertical movement of the rakes, and with his left the longitudinal motion or length of stroke. He can with the greatest ease retard, stop or reverse the stroke ; elevate, or depress the rake at any desired point, and completely discharge any retort in from 15 to 25 seconds. After a retort has been drawn the rake beam is detached from the traveler and sustained by pin upon vertical frame; and the rake corresponding to the position of the retort to be next drawn is attached to the traveler and the drawing operation repeated. After the open retorts of a bench—usually three on each side— have been discharged the machine is propelled along the track to a point opposite the next retorts to be drawn, and the operation repeated until the round is finished.

It is true that the charging machine, when first introduced to public notice, was not so perfect as it now is; but this was not due to any inherent defect in, or objection to, the principles involved in its construction, but rather to the mechanical arrangement of its parts, necessitating an excessive expenditure of muscular force and delay in its manipulation, incident to a new adjustment for each retort charged, which detracted from its efficiency and seriously interfered with its use as a " running mate " to the discharger—an acknowledged success from the date of its introduction.

The improved charger consists of a rectangular carriage, composed of heavy eye-beams, mounted on axles to which are keyed the flange track-wheels. The vertical boiler, steam reservoir, water-tank, feed-pump and disc-engine for propelling, are all located upon one side of the platform; upon the opposite side are located the charging hoppers, mounted in a vertical frame of wrought iron tubes, with wrought iron top, securely braced and supported upon axles, to which are keyed the wheels running upon rails laid across the platform of main carriage. Between this hopper and the boiler is located a steam cylinder for moving the hopper back and forth, accomplished by a reciprocating movement imparted by a rack attachment to piston gearing, and to the shaft of which is secured a drum over which coils a wire rope in reverse directions. By the movement of the lever the hopper is moved forward to front of benches for the purpose of charging, or backward to the end of traverse rails, for the purpose of refilling the hoppers with coal from the storage bins.

There are now three separate and distinct hoppers varying in forms, but each of the exact dimensions necessary to carry the required weight of charge, so arranged in fixed positions that their conduits will enter the three retorts simultaneously.

The top of the upper hopper and top of conduits leading to

lower ones are on the same level, forming a common receptacle, and these latter so constructed as to contain the exact weight of coal necessary to fill the hoppers for the middle and bottom retorts. To each hopper conduit a door is fitted at the bottom, opened and closed by lever and self-acting catch. From the horizontal blast-pipe at the bottom of each hopper ten ¾-inch horizontal nozzles are connected, through which, when the steam by successive blasts is discharging against the coal projects it into the retort. The blast-pipes at bottom of each hopper are connected with a vertical 3-inch steam stand-pipe, and it is in turn connected to main supply pipe by a swivel-jointed connection, and a full way quick-opening valve, the handle of which is located within easy reach of the operator.

The steam reservoir serves as an accumulator to maintain the volume of steam necessary to give a uniform pressure during the operation of charging, and also serves to retain a uniform water line and relieve the boiler from any sudden strain or shock due to the quick opening of the valve. The working pressure is ordinarily from 60 to 80 pounds, depending upon the length of retort and weight of charge.

The construction and arrangement of the various parts are of so plain and simple a character that any ordinary stoker, after two days' practice, can operate it perfectly. The wearing parts are strong, and seldom need other attention than oiling, packing, etc. These machines have been in constant and continuous operation at the East End station of the Cincinnati Gas Company for the past four years, and are to-day in practically as good a condition as when first placed in position.

I am, therefore, warranted in assuming that under the most unfavorable circumstances the depreciation cannot exceed 5 per cent.

In the practical operation of charging, the machine is moved to its required position opposite the retort previously discharged; the movement causes the hoppers to move back underneath the chute of the storage bins, which are located upon either side of the retort house, the assistant raises the check-gate and the coal slides down until the upper hopper and the conduit leading to the lower ones are all evenly filled; the controlling lever is then changed, and the hoppers move forward until the hopper conduits enter the mouthpieces of the retorts and stops automatically at the proper point. The operator has in the meantime pressed the latch securing the trap at bottom of conduits, and the coal falls into its hopper. The operator then, by three or four times quickly opening and closing the full-way valve, projects the coal into the retort. By the exercise of ordinary intelligence in graduating the duration and force of each blast, he can distribute the charge with as great, if not greater uniformity than is ordinarily accomplished with scoop or shovel—the actual time occupied in charging three retorts seldom exceeds five seconds. The operator again reverses the lever and the hoppers move backward, and, at the same time, starts the propelling motor, which moves the machine to a point opposite the retorts to be next charged, by which time the hoppers are in a position to be again filled—the whole movement occupying not to exceed two minutes.

But the experimental stage having long since been passed, it will, no doubt, prove more satisfactory to herewith submit the testimony of a gentleman who for 20 years has been connected with, and now stands at the head of the manufacturing department of the Cincinnati Gas Light and Coke Company.

OFFICE OF THE SUPT. MANUFACTURE, CINCINNATI GAS LIGHT AND COKE COMPANY, October 8, 1888.

CAPT. A. Q. ROSS, Cincinnati, Ohio :

DEAR SIR :—In response to your request that I briefly state what your stoking machines are doing in the works under my charge, what they are capable of doing, and what observed defects, if any, there are in their practical operation, I have to reply. At the old station, where we are now doing but a limited amount of work, we are using the drawing machines with satisfaction and profit. We are not there using the chargers, because of the impossibility of locating the necessary coal storage bins.

At the East End station, where most of our work is being done, we are using the stokers exclusively.

The maximum duty thus far assigned a pair of machines has been 28 benches of 8's—224 oval retorts, 15 in. by 25 in. by 9 ft. 6 in. long, charged every 5 hours with 333⅓ pounds of coal, consisting of about ¾ Yough. and ¼ W. Va. bituminous coal.

This requires 45 retorts to be drawn and charged every hour, which is usually accomplished in 40 minutes. To perform this duty requires one man on the discharger and two on the charger, together with seven lid men on each watch of 12 hours.

The general arrangement of that house permits of the following described system of work :

If the coal is of suitable size when delivered at the landing it is then loaded into cars, drawn up the incline, thence run over and dumped into storage bins on each side of the retort house. When taken from the yard the coal is elevated to track level by hydraulic elevators and discharged as before. From the storage bins the coal runs down a chute by gravity into the machine's hoppers, charged into the retorts from which the coke is drawn by the discharger—that from the two middle retorts going into the generator furnaces, and the others into cars located in the cellar below, where it is quenched, run out and dumped into the coke bins, from which the supply for public use is drawn. Neither the coal nor resultant coke is touched by hand or shovel from the time it leaves the river until the coke is delivered on the consumer's premises. The average yield is 5.07 cubic feet per pound, representing a production of 908,500 cubic feet of gas in 12 hours.

The following exhibit represents the actual cost of production, as shown by several months' operation with the improved charger :

One operator on discharger...................	$3.12
" " " charger....................	2.82
" assistant	2.32
Seven lid-men, opening lids, etc..............	14.00
One generator furnace man	1.50
Three coke men...............................	4.50
Four coal men................................	6.00
1,750 gals. of water.........................	.14
Cylinder and lubricating oils, packing, etc.....	.37
Renewals of steel rake-heads	.07
" " " chains....................	.07
" " " rake-beams	.04
Fuel, 65 bush. of coke at 5 cts...............	3.25
Total.................................	$38.20

Thus eighteen men in conjunction with the machines produced 908,500 cubic feet in 12 hours at a cost of 4.2 cents per thousand.

During a period of about three months, while the charging machines were being altered to the new form, we made tests to determine the cost of carbonizing the same weight of coal by manual labor; and upon that test the following estimate is based:

21 stokers at $2.50	$52.50
7 helpers " 2.25	15.75
5 coal-men, bringing in coal, at $2.00	10.00
1 weigher	1.25
1 furnace man	1.50
3 coke-cellar men, at $1.50	4.50
Gas used in yard at night	.50
	$86.00

9.47 cents per thousand, or a difference in total expense of $95.60 per day, or 5.27 cents per thousand.

At the West End, or old station, where we have continuously used only the drawing machines and charged with scoop, we last winter discharged 30 benches of sixes (180 retorts) every five hours. The retorts are not on the same vertical line and thus necessitated changing the position of the machine for each retort drawn; but with all this trouble, and only 16½ feet space from mouthpiece to side wall, one man discharged the allotted number of retorts in from 30 to 40 minutes. The charge was 256 lbs., giving a yield of 5.11 cu. ft., or 1,130,000 cu. ft. per day.

The items of expense for 12 hours were as follows:

1 operator on drawing machine	$2.50
8 stokers, charging, etc., etc., at $2.25	18.00
3 coal men, breaking and distributing, at $2.00,	6.00
1 coal weigher	1.25
1 furnace man	2.00
2 coke-cellar men, at $2.00	4.00
700 gals. water for discharger	.05
Renewals of chains, rake-heads, etc.	.17
Cylinder oil, waste, etc.	.11
Fuel, coke 25 bush. at 5 cts.	1.25
Total	$35.33

Thus with 16 men was produced 565,000 cubic feet in 12 hours, at an expense of 6¼ cents per thousand.

The old system of hand labor, in vogue at that works previous to the introduction of the discharger (3 men to 5 benches, or one bench of sixes every hour) called for the following expenditure for 12 hours' work :

18 stokers, at $2.50	$45.00
3 coal men, at $2.00	6.00
3 coke-cellar men, at $2.00	6.00
1 coal weigher, at $2.00	2.00
Total	$59.00

or 10.44 cents per thousand, an increased expense of $47.34 per day.

In my judgment your discharger can be operated with sufficient profit to justify its immediate introduction into any works having not less than eight benches of sixes fired ; in which case the expense of labor for carbonization would be $27.30 per day, while to perform the same labor exclusively by hand would call for an expenditure of $38.00 per day.

We have operated but four benches of eights at our East End station, with a pair of your machines, charging every five hours with 333⅓ lbs. of coal, or 6.4 retorts per hour.

The expenditure in connection therewith for 12 hours was as follows :

1 engineer operating both machines	$2.50
1 lid man	2.00
1 coke-cellar man, clinker, furnaces, etc.	1.50
1 coal man	1.50
Water, 1,250 gallons	.10
Oil, waste and packing	.09
Coke, 25 bush., at 5 cents	1.25
Total	$8.94

To perform same work by hand would involve an expenditure of $12.50, as follows:

3 stokers, at $2.50		$7.50
1 helper, " 2.00		2.00
1 coke-cellar man, at $1.50		1.50
1 coal man, " 1.50		1.50
Total		$12 50

I never observed any defects in their practical operation. The depreciation is mainly confined to the chains actuating rake-carriage, about 4 ft. of the inner end of the beam, and the steel rake-heads ; but in no case exceeds in value the depreciation of the implements used in drawing and charging by hand. Their use has never injuriously affected the retorts, and I have never been able to observe any difference in yield attributable to either system. Very respectfully,

N. G. KEENAN, Engineer.

The following is from a well-known Engineer, whose requirements called for the constant employment of but one machine.

OFFICE OF THE BROOKLYN GAS LT. CO., }
BROOKLYN, N. Y., Sept., 20, 1888. }

CAPT. A. Q. ROSS:

MY DEAR CAPTAIN :—I have yours of 19th inst. in regard to a further expression of my experience in the operation of your steam stoker, and have simply to add, to what I have already written you, that during the past summer we have been making certain changes in our works, by which we have been temporarily deprived of the use of the machine, and an increase in our pay-roll for the additional number of men employed shows plainly the value of the steam stoker.

Respectfully yours,

JAS. H. ARMINGTON, Prest. and Engineer.

The following certificate is from the President of the New York Consolidated Gas Company, whose works are without the advantages of a stage flooring :

CONSOLIDATED GAS COMPANY OF NEW YORK, }
NEW YORK, October 12, 1888. }

DEAR SIR:—The eight drawing machines supplied by you to the Fourteenth and Eighteenth St. stations of this Company have been in constant use in these two stations for several years past, working to our entire satisfaction. The saving in time and labor by their use is considerable, and the comfort of the workmen greatly promoted. They are a valuable improvement on the old method of drawing by hand. Yours truly,

JAS. W. SMITH, President.

To CAPT. A. Q. ROSS, Gen'l Manager U. S. Steam Stoking Co.

And this from the Vice-President and General Manager of the Boston Gas Light Company—a gentleman who has, to a greater extent than any other American engineer, had an opportunity of observing the various systems of retort house labor throughout Europe as well as in this country :

THE RICHELIEU, MICHIGAN AVE. BOULEVARD, }
CHICAGO, October 14, 1888. }

A. Q. ROSS, Esq.:

DEAR SIR:—I regret that I am prevented from attending the Toronto meeting, as I had intended to be present and to have taken part in the discussion which might naturally follow your paper. My views as to the value of your discharging machine are well known and unchanged. No large gas company can afford to draw its retorts by hand, provided they can introduce your machines into the retort house ; and your experiments in the direction of shortening the drawing machine have now made it available in places where it could not formerly be used. The Boston Gas Company has recently bought two more machines from your Company, and hopes next year to introduce a third. As to your charger, which has just been introduced, I am not yet prepared to speak with that decision which can come only from experience. I can, however, say this—that we are using one in our Commercial Point works, though not yet to the extent of its full capacity, and that it promises to do extremely well. It certainly charges the retorts with wonderful quickness; but whether it will fulfill every other requirement upon it I cannot of course speak with assurance yet. I will say, however, that I shall be greatly disappointed if it does not work with sufficient accuracy and reliability to make it a very valuable complement to the discharger.　　　　　　　　　　Yours truly,

M. S. GREENOUGH.

And this from a gentleman who will be at once recognized as one of the leading engineers of this country, and now the honored President of the Chicago Gas Light Company:

CHICAGO, ILLS., Sept. 26, 1888.

A. Q. ROSS, Esq.:

DEAR SIR:—The drawing machines which were placed in our South Station about a year ago, have been working *continuously*, and have fully come up to our expectations. The saving of labor from their use has been quite four cents per thousand cubic feet on gas manufactured at that station.

Yours truly,　　　　　　THEOB. FORSTALL, Prest.

These statements are so full, complete and comprehensive that it leaves little or nothing more to be added in the way of details.

As the world grows older and material wealth increases there is a natural and very proper demand for additional comforts and conveniences; and in no direction is this more apparent than in the ever increasing demand for the more brilliant illumination of our homes and highways. In fact this increase of light is now regarded as one of the prime necessities of our advanced civilization.

These conditions have been realized and promptly met by the manufacturers of oil lamps, placing *those* wares upon the market in the most beautiful and attractive form; by the oil producers in the improvement of their refining processes, until their product is now absolutely safe—if properly handled; by the advocates of electric lighting, lavishly expending both time and money in efforts to secure for their favorites public approval; and last, but by no means least, the water gas promoters are bidding high for public patronage by increasing the light giving properties of their product beyond the coal gas range.

There appears to be but one direction in which coal gas engineers can turn with the hope of successfully competing with these formidable rivals, and that is to supply the equivalent of an equal volume of light for less money.

To accomplish this result the cost of production must be reduced, and it now only remains to determine in what direction this can be best and most expeditiously effected. These machines having been subjected to the crucial test of practical experience and the results laid before you, I need not encroach upon your time and patience by giving further expression to my own judgment and belief in the future possibilities of steam stoking; but I do feel that if I have clearly shown you that the price of the machines can be saved by working them for less than six months—up to their maximum capacity, and that the cost of labor expended in placing gas in the holder can be reduced—as it has already been—to less than four cents per thousand, no apology is necessary from me for having advocated their adoption as the means of producing an improvement in the hygienic conditions of your works; the acquirement of steadier and more reliable service, and the attainment of an economy in production never before equaled.

Discussion.

The Secretary read the following letter:

The Cincinnati Gas Light and Coke Co., }
Cincinnati, O., Oct. 16, 1888. }

C. J. R. Humphreys, Secy. American Gas Light Association,
Rossin House, Toronto, Canada:

Dear Sir:—I have delayed until the last moment, hoping that I might be able to attend this meeting and, as you requested, take a hand in the discussion of the paper on "Steam Stoking;" but important business engagements here will prevent this anticipated pleasure. As to my personal views upon this subject "the proof of the pudding is in the eating." By their use we are to-day saving this Company nearly $50,000 per year, and putting gas into the holders at a figure that would astonish any engineer who may think he has struck "bed-rock."

Yours truly, A. Hickenlooper, Prest.

The President—Does any member wish to make any remarks upon the Ross Stoker, or to make any inquiry?

MR. HARBISON—I was quite interested in listening to the paper read by Capt. Ross. I would like to inquire what advance he has made within the past year, if any, with regard to being able to put the steam stoker into works that are sending out, say, a hundred million cubic feet per year? What prospect is there of its being introduced into works of that size?

CAPT. ROSS—I am glad to answer the question of the gentleman. The statements embodied in this paper relate to the practicability of making it profitable to put the machine into works running eight benches of 6's. The paper gives you the exact cost of charging and discharging that number of benches, and the labor incident thereto, including the investment on the machine. Of course we assume that every gentleman present understands the cost of the present method. The only change that I refer to as having been made is in reducing the length of the discharger to admit of its successfully working in a retort house with but 16½ feet between the face of the benches and the retort house wall. I would be pleased to submit to the gentlemen these figures. Of course, I am not, as I have stated, a professional gas engineer, but the testimony as to its use that I have read comes from practical engineers, and is the result of their experience based upon actual use. So far as the working of the machines is concerned, I will say that we will guarantee them to do precisely what we represent, so that any company contemplating their purchase can run no risk, so far as that is concerned. I know there are a number of companies in the United States which would be very glad to adopt them if their sendout would warrant the investment. Of course, those are questions that should be carefully considered, as local circumstances might determine the utility of introducing them. I know one gentlemen (I believe he is present) who has a sufficient output to warrant the introduction of the stoker, but unfortunately the output is divided between two works. There are, of course, disadvantages of that kind to be considered.

MR. A. C. WOOD—I would like to ask Mr. Ross if the charging machine is being used in any gas works excepting Cincinnati?

CAPT. ROSS—Yes; it is being used now in Boston. Mr.

Greenough visited Cincinnati in company with Mr. Lamson, and saw the charger at work, and made a contract with us to put the machine into his works to charge the entire 90 retorts with one man. The method of delivery of coal now is temporarily through wooden tubes. The time of charging is from 5 to 10 seconds. The charging can be done much more rapidly than the discharging men can discharge.

MR. A. C. WOOD—Has not the charging machine been introduced into various works heretofore?

CAPT. ROSS—No; it has never been introduced in any works, excepting the Manhattan in New York.

MR. A. C. WOOD—Was it not discontinued there?

CAPT. ROSS—It was discontinued there for the reason that it was not perfect at that time, and if the gentlemen who managed the gas works had owned the machine they could not have done more to make it work. They were faithful to their trust and did all they could to facilitate its working. Now, however, it is perfect; it is a practical and demonstrative success. Of course, there are always difficulties that may be encountered in the introduction of any new process or system of making gas, and I beg to call your attention to the fact that these machines are without exception subjected to the worst possible character of labor that ever a piece of steam machinery was ever subjected to. We have represented to you that you can employ an ordinary stoker to run the machine, but I ask you to go into the retort house and examine the conditions there. Remember that this machine does not stop with the bell, but works from 18 to 24 hours each of the 365 days in the year. You can take an ordinary laborer from your benches and put him on the machine, and while it is subject to the grit, coal, soot, dirt and everything of that kind, yet absolute experience as demonstrated according to the statements of gentlemen in whom you must all have confidence, that those machines have worked at the Manhattan Gas Works for nearly six years, and have also been working in Cincinnati for the same period of time, and yet are as good to-day as the day they were adopted, with the exception of the wearing parts, which necessarily have to be replaced when worn out. You can use ordinary laborers for operating them, but of course some intelligent mechanic should be detailed to see that they are properly lubricated and cared for.

MR. SMEDBERG—In San Francisco, while we were sending out of the retort house about 1,200,000 cubic feet, our retort house labor, including all classes of labor contemplated in Mr. Ross' statement, was eleven cents; but we were, of course, paying higher prices for our stokers and helpers than those paid in the East.

CAPT. ROSS—But if you can dispense with one-half of the labor it would certainly effect a saving?

MR. SMEDBERG—Undoubtedly.

MR. LINDSLEY—Can the stoker be used in one-story retort houses, where there is no cellar?

CAPT. ROSS—Certainly. In the Manhattan works there were no cellars. We are now putting them in the Philadelphia works where there is no cellar, and also in the Cleveland works, where like conditions prevail; also, at the old works in Boston, at the north end station, where the same remark would hold good.

MR. LINDSLEY—Does the distance mentioned (16 feet between the bench and the outer wall), suffice in that case?

CAPT. ROSS—16 feet 6 inches is sufficient. It would depend somewhat upon the distance from the height of the lower retort from the floor. If we can get the height so that the coke barrow will pass under the mouthpiece it will be practicable.

MR. SCRIVER—Is it necessary to elevate the coal to the height shown here, so as to run it down the chutes?

CAPT. ROSS—It would only be necessary to raise the coal to the height of the top of the charger. The design which you see here was for the original charger, and the photograph is taken from that.

MR. SCRIVER—Can the coals be thrown into the charger without elevating them?

CAPT. ROSS—Yes; but I believe it is more economical to elevate them. They can be elevated cheaper by machinery than thrown in by hand.

MR. SCRIVER—In that case most of us would have to build our retort houses to suit the machines.

CAPT. ROSS—In a small house, of 10 or 12 benches, you can build one elevator at the end of the house.

MR. SCRIVER—In our case at Montreal, where the coal sheds are on each side of our retort house, that would not be practicable.

CAPT. ROSS—I mean by that that one point of delivery for the coal, instead of having a series of bins, would be quite sufficient for a small house.

MR. SCRIVER—Do you charge three retorts at a time ?

CAPT. ROSS—Yes, practically. For instance, three conduits enter three retorts to be charged simultaneously—all being on one bench. Then the operator opens the valve of one of them, then of the second, and then the third. The charging time required is only from 5 to 10 seconds.

MR. SCRIVER—At our works we are putting in nine retorts to the bench. I would like to know if a machine can be adapted to charge three retorts, one above the other, as we are setting them ?

CAPT. ROSS—Yes; we are now charging nines in Cincinnati in the same way.

MR. SCRIVER—I suppose Capt. Ross has no objection to hear the cons as well as the pros ?

CAPT. ROSS—Certainly not.

MR. SCRIVER—We have had no experience in running either the charger or the drawer; but from the testimonials read it would seem that the dischargers are giving very great satisfaction, while perhaps it is still a question whether the chargers are doing so well. I do not wish to say anything against the charger—personally I cannot, as I have not had any experience with it; but when we are discussing a question we have to argue from all standpoints.

CAPT. ROSS—That is perfectly proper. Of course I could not consistently, under the circumstances, ask Mr. Greenough to give me a recommendation of the charger. We prefer to wait, and after two or three months of trial we will know the results as far as Mr. Greenough is concerned. I would like to call the attention of the members to the certificate attached to the circular from Mr. Hunt, of Birmingham, England, in which that gentleman states he is paying 5 shillings per day for labor; but he is not, as he states, working the machines to their maximum capacity—he is only working 200 days in a year—yet he states that his saving is $2,500 on each machine.

Mr. SCRIVER—No one present would more gladly hail the advent of a successful charger than I would. The Company I represent would be glad to introduce such a machine. Unfortunately, strikes have occurred at our place on one or two occasions, and we find that stokers are the worst strikers that we have to deal with. If it were possible by the use of machinery to dispense with their services, we would be glad to use the machine. As I said yesterday, I enjoyed a somewhat extended trip on the other side of the water, and saw at the Beckton Station, London, a couple of stoking machines laid up high and dry in the works. I do not wish to say anything against the Ross machine; still, as I said before, it is necessary to argue this question from all points in order to get at all the facts. It is well for us to know what can be said against a machine as well as what be said in favor of it, if we want to arrive at an intelligent decision. As I say, there were objections to machines, and they were not at work; and if there is any place in the world where stoking machines should or ought to be used, I should say it was there, for they are turning out a great quantity of gas. When I was there they were putting out 39 million cubic feet per day at one station alone. I expressed some little surprise, to the engineer who conducted me about the works, that they were not using the machine stoker, and he said that those machines cost more than they were worth to keep them in running order.

CAPT. ROSS—May I ask you do you not know they were the West machine?

MR. SCRIVER—I cannot tell you.

CAPT. ROSS—Our machines are not there and never have been; but they are working in Birmingham, England, and the Nine Elms, London.

MR. SCRIVER—I do not think that they are your machine;

but if they are such very tender machines as they apparently were there, I think it would prove a very expensive machine for any of us to adopt. For my part I would rather put up with the strikers.

Mr. PAGE—The subject of this paper presents three aspects—philanthropic, prudential and financial; but I believe that every gas manager is influenced by the first, because the hardest work, it seems to me, that is done by the men, is stoking—particularly in the summer time—whether it be in Canada, in the South, or in the Middle States. Therefore, any means by which labor-saving machinery can be substituted for the hardest manual labor ought to receive our earnest attention. I am told that in some works the average time that the stoker is employed is not over five years. Therefore a machine that can do his work is something to be hailed with joy. Next, prudential. I suppose most gas works are subject to strikes, and therefore a great industry is left to the mercy of men who, generally speaking, do not care for the company which employs them. Hence a machine that will take the place of the striker is something to be considered carefully and seriously. Third, financially. The statements made by Capt. Ross and the names read by him must be accepted by us all as substantial. We certainly cannot go back of them as to results. Capt. Ross has referred to the use of the machine at Birmingham. In England, in June last, at the meeting of the Gas Institute, I asked specially about the " Ross Steam Stoker." I was interested in learning (perhaps from patriotic motives, because I know it is a chief competitor of the West mechanical stoker) with what success it had been used. I was told that the discharging machine had been a success from the first, but that the charging machine was a failure. I was also assured by an official of the Gas Light and Coke Company that the discharging machine at the Nine Elms station, London, was an absolute success; that they could not get along without it; that they saved 60 per cent. of the cost of stoking by the use of the Ross discharger. During the present summer one of our honorary members (Mr. R. P. Spice) was in this country, and he, in company with Mr. Samuel Cutler, of London (who is largely interested in gas matters), made a special examination of the stoker at Cincinnati. Gen. Hickenlooper, the President of the

Company and the engineer of the works, gave them ample opportunity to examine the machines. They saw the plant in operation. Their decision was that the charging machine was as thoroughly a success as the discharging machine. They saw, time and again, the charges put in and evenly distributed. They saw them make on the days that they were there 1,400,000 cubic feet with only nine men. The stoking work of that great retort house was being done by these machines. We saw the discharging machine, in nine minutes and fourteen seconds, take up every particle of coke cleaner than the average stoker takes it out with his hand apparatus. The charger deposited 300 pounds of coal promptly and evenly. Reference has been made to the stoker at work at the Beckton station. I had an opportunity of seeing it last June in company with members of the Institute who visited the works to inspect that station. The charging machine was not in operation in consequence of breakdown. It is the West mechanical stoker—the compressed air machine. Its use is attended with many difficulties. It often breaks down. But you could not take it out of that works. You could not buy it out of that works, for two reasons. The first is that while it is working it has an effect upon labor, at $1.25 per day for stokers. Second, it makes a large saving in labor. The West Company have, I believe, 130 machines in operation in large and small works. You know that Mr. West was formerly engineer of the Manchester gas works, but now he gives his entire time to the large Company which is building and putting up that apparatus. The comparative cost of the two is largely in favor of the Ross steam stoker. The comparative efficiency of the two is also largely in favor of the Ross steam stoker. There is no question about that. The Ross steam stoker is one of several which have been invented in this country; and the West one of many invented on the other side. I saw, in 1870, the Somerville steam stoker in operation at the Dublin works. If it had been pursued as thoroughly as Capt. Ross has pursued this and a success made of it, doubtless it would have been in general use. I think the fraternity owe Capt. Ross thanks as well as substantial support for his persistency in making a success of this stoker. Labor-saving machines in the retort house, and purification in closed vessels at the other end, will reduce coal gas making very quickly to the point which I have previously prophesied—when gas shall be put into the holder at *nil.*

MR. SCRIVER—Mr. Page has spoken of the financial question. Would Capt. Ross have any objection to tell us about the cost of this machine—say for one stoker and one drawer, set up complete in the works?

CAPT. ROSS—You will observe we have advertised the price. The established price is $7,000 for the discharger and $6,000 for the charger; but there are certain additions. Modifications or radical changes are sometimes made necessary, and we have to charge the cost of making them, which is added to the price named. A standard machine, as delivered in the works, with the steam up and with the services of an expert to thoroughly instruct your employees as to its operation, is $7,000, provided no radical change in the design is made necessary by the location.

MR. HARBISON—What will the machine weigh?

CAPT. ROSS—The discharger will weigh 8½ tons, and the charger about 7 tons.

MR. SCRIVER—Are the chargers and drawers suitable for through retorts? Our retorts are of that description, 20 feet long.

CAPT. ROSS—Yes. That would necessitate a 10 ft. stroke.

On motion of Mr. White, a vote of thanks was tendered to Capt. Ross for his paper.

THE PRESIDENT—Is the Committee on Nominations ready to report?

MR. STINESS—I am instructed by the Committee on Nominations to make the following unanimous report. Before I read the name which has been decided upon for President of this Association, I may perhaps be pardoned at an expression of the pride which is natural and inborn to me. Within a few years the State which I represent has been honored by this Association, and one who occupied the position which you now fill, Mr. President, equally honored the Association. I name to-day for President of this American Association of Gas Engineers, one who has been to me for more than a quarter of a century a friend and a brother. I give to you the name of Alpheus B. Slater, of Providence, Rhode Island, as the nominee for the office of President. (Applause.)

For Vice-Presidents—Emerson McMillin, Columbus, Ohio ; John P. Harbison, Hartford, Conn. ; William Henry White, New York.

For Secretary and Treasurer—C. J. R. Humphreys, Lawrence, Mass.

By the amended Constitution we were directed to bring in the names of eight active members as nominees for the Council. As four members of the Council are to retire annually, it will be necessary to elect at this meeting four members for the term of two years, and four others for one year. We therefore give you for the long term the names of—

For Two Years.

W. H. Pearson, Toronto, Canada ; Chas. W. Blodget, Brooklyn, N. Y.; G. G. Ramsdell, Vincennes. Ind. ; A. E. Boardman, Macon, Ga.

For One Year.

Matt. Cartwright, Rochester, N. Y.; Thomas Curley, Wilmington, Del.; B. E. Chollar, Topeka, Kansas ; Wm. H. Baxter, Petersburgh, Va.

MR. STINESS—I move that the Chair appoint a committee of one to cast a ballot of the Association for the election of the nominees.

The motion prevailed; the President appointed A. C. Humphreys as such committee. The ballot was cast accordingly, and the nominees were declared duly elected officers of the Association for the ensuing year.

The President appointed Mr. White and Mr. Harbison a committee to present the newly elected President.

MR. WHITE —Mr. President, I have pleasure in presenting to you Mr. A. B. Slater, the President-elect of this Association.

THE PRESIDENT—Gentlemen, I take great pleasure in presenting to you Mr. Alpheus B. Slater, of Providence, R. I., as your President for the ensuing year.

MR. SLATER—Gentlemen of the Association, for the distinguished honor you have conferred upon me in electing me to this office you have my grateful appreciation. Remembering whom my predecessors have been, I can but have a realizing sense of what you have a right to expect from me. It is fortunate, perhaps, that the success of this Association does not depend upon the President alone, but upon the united efforts of individual members. I class myself with the workers rather than with the talkers; and whatever I can do to promote the interests and welfare of the Association I shall endeavor to do to the best of my ability. (Applause.)

THE PRESIDENT—Is the Committee on applications for membership ready to make a report?

MR. RAMSDELL—The Committee beg leave to report as follows: We find, because of the adoption of the new Constitution, there is some conflict in the election of associate members, and we ask for instructions from the Association as to our duties. According to the new Constitution which has been adopted, it will be necessary that applications for membership be received ten days before being acted upon. It says:

"Application for Active Membership, or for Associate Membership, or for transfer from Associate to Active Membership, must be received by the Secretary at least ten days prior to the meeting at which the application is acted on."

MR. STINESS—As we have just adopted a new Constitution I hope that we shall live up to it. I take a little pride to-day, as being one of the movers in the matter of the forming of a new Constitution for this Association. The new Constitution may prove in course of time to have defects; but as it is, let us stand by it. The thought that actuated me in my efforts to secure amendments to the old Constitution, was that in an Association of this character there should not be the hasty action which was taken at the Philadelphia meeting in making members of this Association—not, as you well know, that I had the least objection to any one of them; but I did object to the rushing of the names through in the way it was done there, and without the consideration which is due to the Association, and to that class of membership. As we have adopted a new Constitution, I for one do most earnestly hope that its provisions will be strictly adhered to. I hope no amendments to it will be offered before the ink is hardly dry upon the document. I do hope that we will conform to the Constitution, to-day and hereafter.

MR. WHITE —I move that the matter be referred again to the Committee, with instructions to report these names for ballot. I make that motion for this reason. When that constitution was presented in the Executive Committee night before last, and discussed, its bearing upon this very subject was one of the topics of discussion; and it was unanimously agreed there that it should have no effect upon gentlemen who are present at this time and soliciting membership here. That after the adoption of this Constitution, at subsequent meetings members should be divided into the new classes of active and associate members; but that anybody present at this meeting, coming here under the old Constitution, and coming here with the expectation of joining this Association, should not be debarred from that privilege. It will be a great mistake to enforce that provision of the new Constitution at this meeting. While this Association has the right to adopt this new Constitution, it has no right to pass any *ex post facto* law of that kind. It is not good judgment. It is not good taste. It is not courteous to those gentlemen who have applied for membership at this meeting. I stated yesterday, in presenting the Constitution, and as the expression of opinion upon the part of your Executive Committee, that the gentlemen who at this meeting presented applications should be treated just the same as at past meetings, except that those gentlemen should be divided into the two new classes. I, therefore, press my motion for the consideration of this body, that these names may be again submitted to your committee, with instructions to the committee to report upon them favorably.

MR. McMILLIN—I had risen to say about what Captain White has said, and he said it so much better than I could that I am glad he got the floor. It was the understanding of the Executive Committee that the adoption of the new Constitution should not interfere with the presentation of names at this meeting. It was so understood yesterday, I think, when the Constitution was adopted; and it was certainly violated yesterday. We voted in members yesterday, and in that way the Constitution was violated, and the precedent was established. It would be impossible for gentlemen who came here expecting to be made members to know that they would have to present their names ten days beforehand; and I think it would be decidedly unfair to have them wait for another year. No harm can be done by admitting them now. The Committee will examine the names with the greatest care. We all know that Mr. Ramsdell always attends to his work very carefully. I am also a member of the Committee, and I sure that no harm can be done by following the precedent established yesterday; whereas great injustice may be done by ignoring the rule as it was understood in the Executive Committee, and it was understood when the Constitution was adopted and as was practiced yesterday after the Constitution was adopted.

MR. HARBISON—I heartily advocate the view taken by Captain White. It was the distinct understanding before the adoption of the Constitution yesterday, and was so distinctly stated in respect to the question bearing upon that particular point, that the new Constitution should not apply to applicants for membership at this meeting. But there it should end. At the adjournment of this meeting the provisions of the new Constitution will come into force; but as to those who applied for membership at this meeting the ten days' provision should not apply, but that they should have the right to come in and be divided among the two classes of members.

MR. CLARK—I would like to inquire under what clause of the Constitution under which we are now acting this Association has any right to appoint a committee to examine the names of applicants. Hereafter such applications will come into the hands of the Council, and without a violation of the Constitution the President cannot appoint a committee, nor can the Association, even by unanimous consent, instruct the committee to return any names. If we open the door to a violation of the provisions of the Constitution we do not know where it will end. If there is any good in the Constitution it should be lived up to to the very letter.

MR. A. C. HUMPHREYS—I think it does not concern this meeting to learn what the agreement was in the Executive Committee. The Executive Committee were privileged to come in here and make arrangements which would carry out their ideas; if they failed to do so, we have nothing to do with it, so far as I can see. The Constitution has been adop'ed, and we should be governed by it. If the Executive Committee had brought in a provision making it take effect immediately upon the adjournment of this meeting of the Association, that would have been proper enough; but as they failed to do so, I think that we should carry out the Constitution just as it has been adopted.

MR. HARBISON—I will suggest that it has been strictly adhered to, in that it was verbally stated that the Constitution was to take effect at the close of this meeting.

MR. McMILLIN—Except as to making the two classes of members.

MR. HARBISON—Yes; that was distinctly stated as one of the provisions—not in the printed Constitution, but verbally. Further, in reply to the suggestion that the Peesident has no right to appoint the committee under the Constitution, I beg leave to differ. A committee was appointed by the President before the new Constitution was adopted. The committee is still in session, and has made a partial report; and now comes in with an additional one.

MR. WHITE, W. H.—In reply to Mr. Humphreys I would say it was very distinctly stated what were the wishes or views of the Executive Committee on this subject, and the Association then showed its appreciation of that fact by adopting unanimously the report of the Executive Committee, and by proceeding immediately to take the very action we now ask for. The Association did elect three or four gentlemen here yesterday, who had not given the ten days' notice required by the new Constitution; and I say it is an outrage upon the gentlemen who have paid out their money to come here with the expectation of being made members of this Association. It is all a farce to talk about this matter as being a precedent which would open the doors hereafter to all applicants. It is a matter which has been thoroughly well discussed here. It is a matter of courtesy that we cannot fail to extend to these gentlemen without stultifying ourselves.

MR. HUMPHREYS, A. C.—I think if the record is searched you

will find that the intimation referred to by Mr. Harbison and Mr. White was that we were to act upon those three names that were offered as associate members; that the action on those was delayed on account of not being able to act upon them under the old Constitution, because under that there were no associate members. It was distinctly stated that this action referred to those three applications. I think if the record is searched you will fail to find there was any intimation that the law was to be broken afterward. Of course the committee was appointed before that action, because there was no Council then to act upon the applications. We were still acting under the old Constitution when the committee on membership was appointed; but the moment that Constitution went into effect that committee was discharged.

Mr. Harbison—The report of the Executive Committee was two-fold—part verbal and part printed. The verbal part was that the action of the Committee should not affect the applications which might be received at this meeting, except so far as classification was concerned. The printed report also classified the applicants. The entire report was adopted by the Association—the verbal portion as well as the printed; the verbal portion being that it would not apply to applications received at this meeting except as to classification. That was adopted in conjunction with the printed report making the classification. So that in strict parliamentary law you cannot shut out these applicants, if they are eligible, because you adopted the report of the Committee, which was two-fold.

Mr. Clark — I will ask if in strict parliamentary law any man who is elected to his office outside of the Constitution is legally entitled to that office or is legally a member? It is not so held in State, municipal or national elections. I think any man who is now elected outside of that Constitution is not a member of the Association. There is no objection to any man who has applied for admission; and they would have been reported favorably upon and immediately if the Constitution had not stood in the way. But as it is, if I know anything of parliamentary law, we cannot now elect those members. We have a Constitution, and whatever the verbal arrangement or understanding of the Executive Committee may have been, we have nothing to do with it. This Association now stands upon this printed Constitution which it has adopted.

MR. WHITE—I maintain that the Constitution is practically not in effect until after the adjournment of this meeting. The officers elected under that Constitution do not take office until after we have adjourned ; and the general understanding was, in the discussion of that subject, that the Constitution did not go into effect, and did not practically affect this meeting, except that we all agreed that the classification of members therein provided for should take effect as quickly as possible. It seems to me that our quibbling on technicalities will belittle us considerably, and will amount to nothing as a protection of this Association. This Association is big enough and ugly enough to take care of itself.

THE PRESIDENT—You have heard the motion as offered by Mr. White. It is that the applications of these gentlemen be referred back to the committee, with instructions to report at this meeting. Are you ready for the question ?

The motion prevailed.

Mr. Jas. D. Perkins, of New York city, read his paper on—

GAS COALS, WITH SPECIAL REFERENCE TO PROVINCIAL COAL.

Mr. President and Gentlemen of the American Gas Light Association :—The invitation of your Committee to submit a paper to the Association at the present session was not only unsolicited but entirely unexpected. The subject assigned to me was one with which I have been somewhat familiar for nearly forty years, although I can hardly expect to add anything to the general fund of information already in the possession of the members of the Association.

The subject assigned to me by your Committee was, "Gas Coals, with Special Reference to Provincial Coal." I shall make no attempt to separate the special from the general subject, as during a large part of the time to which reference will be made the two have been so closely interwoven as to render such division impracticable.

For a period of nearly 60 years prior to 1880, Provincial coals occupied a most important relation to the gas industry of the United States; and a brief sketch of their early history may find appropriate record within the limits of this paper, and not prove entirely uninteresting to the members of the Association.

It is a matter worthy of note that the first recorded mention of the existence of coal in North America had reference to the coal deposits of Cape Breton. This occurs in a French work published in 1672 by one Nicholas Denys, who was appointed Governor of that island by Louis XIV., in 1637. In 1654 he secured from the French government a concession to "search for and work all mineral deposits of the Island." By virtue of this grant he made some trial shipments of coal to France, where it was highly esteemed; but Denys was more interested in fishing than in coal mining, and when his patent was revoked, in 1690, no organized effort had been made to develop these valuable deposits.

Following the above in chronological order appears the first record of the existence of coal within the present limits of the United States. This occurs in a report made by Father Hennepin, the Jesuit, in 1698, wherein he speaks of coal deposits on the Illinois River, near what is now Peoria.

Returning to Provincial coal, the first attempt at regular mining in Cape Breton was made in 1720, when the celebrated fortress at Louisburg was constructed by the French Government. The fuel necessary for the large force employed in this work was obtained from a coal seam on the north side of Cow Bay. A considerable trade had sprung up about this time between Cape Breton and New England, and in 1724 mention is made of a vessel having "*loaded coal at Cow Bay for Boston.*" The records are silent as to further shipments down to 1745, when the island passed into the hands of the English, who held it for four years, when the French again came into possession. From this time forward until the reduction of Louisburg by the English in 1758, the mining of coal at Cow Bay appears to have been limited to the wants of the forts at Louisburg and Halifax; but between 1763 and 1767 applications for leases to work the Cape Breton coal mines were made to the British Government. These applications met the approval of the Governor of Nova Scotia, under whose directions an accurate survey of the island was made in 1766. In his letter to the Home Government the Governor refers to the *only coal mine then open;* viz., that on the north side of Cow Bay, where there was a block-house located upon the site of what has since been known as the *Block House Mine.*

It was about this time that further evidence of the existence of coal in the United States was furnished by Colonel Cregan, a prisoner in the hands of the Indians in 1763. The coal was located on the banks of the Wabash, in Indiana. This was followed in 1770 by the discovery of coal in Western Pennsylvania.

In April, 1767, in accordance with the recommendation of the Governor of Nova Scotia referred to above, a coal-mining lease was granted to certain Halifax merchants, under which they guaranteed to produce and ship not less than 3,000 chaldrons of coal within eight months. This undertaking they failed to carry out, their shipments within the time specified amounting to not quite 2,300 chaldrons.

It is interesting to note the points to which a portion of this coal was sent, as bearing upon the operations of the Cape Breton collieries in later years, and also to contrast the capacity of the vessels employed in its transportation with those of the present day.

Of the 2,300 chaldrons named, there were shipped to New York 60 tons; Providence, 54 tons; Boston, 44 tons; Philadelphia, 45 tons.

From this time forward, until 1826, continued attempts were made to extend the operations of the Cape Breton collieries, alternately by lease to private parties, and by Government itself, but with apparently little profit to either. Lack of facilities for preparing the coal properly for market, and the uncertain tenure of the leases under which some of these efforts were made, were the main obstacles in the way of success. The quantity mined in any one year prior to 1826 does not appear to have exceeded 10,000 chaldrons, while the average for the 40 years preceding that date was but little over 7,000 tons. Such was the condition of the Provincial coal trade in 1826, and a more discouraging one could scarcely be imagined.

In the exercise of his royal prerogative, and in one of those freaks of liberality which characterized royalty at that time, George IV. had granted to his impecunious brother, the Duke of York, a lease of all the mines and minerals of Nova Scotia (the island of Cape Breton having been annexed to Nova Scotia in 1820), with certain exceptions, for a term of 60 years. This grant was dated August 26, 1826. As the Duke of York had no means of working the mines on his own account, even if he had possessed the ability, he transferred the lease in 1827 to a company which had then been recently organized in London under the name of "The General Mining Association," and in 1828 this association secured the control of the Albion Mines in Pictou, which, up to that time, had been held by private parties, and not covered by the royal grant. This gave to the association the exclusive working of all the mineral properties in Nova Scotia and Cape Breton belonging to the Crown. The efforts of the management of the association were directed mainly toward placing upon the market such coals as were best adapted to domestic and general steam purposes. Anthracite coal had only recently come into the market, and there was a large demand for bituminous coal of such a character as the association could supply; hence the rapid increase in the sale of Sydney coal in the New England States, and for many years this coal enjoyed the highest reputation for house use in open grates as well as for steam purposes. But as the present paper has reference to *gas coals* mainly, I turn to the consideration of that portion of the business of the association specially connected with such coals.*

At the period referred to (about 1830) the gas industry of the United States was in its infancy; it had scarcely assumed the proportions of a distinctive feature in the manufacturing enterprises of the times. The requirements for coal were insignificant, and no special efforts were made to meet them. Newcastle coal was the standard gas coal in England, and formed the larger part of the supplies of the gas companies then in operation in New York and New England.

---

*For the historical facts given above I am indebted to the admirable work entitled, "The Coal Fields and Coal Trade of Cape Breton," by Richard Brown, Esq., published in 1871.

Some idea of the limited character of the business may be gathered from the following item, which I quote from the Boston Almanac of 1837. Speaking of the city gas works, it says: " The gas made at this establishment is a compound of coal and resin, and is esteemed for its brilliancy and illuminating power. There are three gasometers connected with the company's works —two in Hull street, each 40 feet in diameter, and one in Washington street, at the extreme south part of the city, of 80 feet. This is the largest gasometer in the United States, and contains 15,000 cubic feet of gas. The roof over this building spans 102 feet, and rests entirely upon the walls, without any support in the center."

I venture the assertion that no better illustration of the progress of gas manufacture during the past fifty years can be presented than is found in comparing this description of the Boston gas works in 1837 with the present complete and perfectly appointed establishment of that company, representing every department of modern improvement in the science of coal gas manufacture, embodying the results of nearly forty years of the personal experience of its present executive head.

Enquiry as to the description of coal referred to in the above extract leads to the conclusion, that it was from the Albion mines, Pictou, as it was supplied by Mr. Samuel Cunard, who represented the General Mining Association at that time.

The only gas coals available to the General Mining Association were those from the Albion Mines at Pictou, and the Lingan Mines in Cape Breton ; as the latter was not operated until 1855, the Albion was the only Provincial gas coal obtainable prior to that date.

The records of the association give the annual shipments of this coal to the States ; but, as a large percentage of the quantity reported was used for iron manufacture and foundry purposes, it is difficult to form any reliable estimate of that which entered into the manufacture of gas. It was used in the Boston works in 1838, and no doubt continued to form a part of their supplies from that time forward until 1875, when its use by that company was abandoned.

My own personal recollection of this coal dates back to 1845, when the house with which I was connected commenced the importation and sale of this coal. The facilities for the conduct of the business at that time were extremely limited ; navigation was only possible between May and December, the straits of Canso being closed by ice during the remainder of the year ; the vessels employed in carrying the coal were small, varying from 80 to 120 tons capacity, and mainly owned by the maritime interests of the Province. While these benefits were generally acknowledged and appreciated, there had been gradually developed a feeling of dissatisfaction that such important interests were restricted to one company.

It was felt that the continued existence of such a monopoly was an obstacle in the way of a larger development of the immense mineral resources of the Province. The management of the association realized the importance of meeting the situation thus presented to them, and negotiations were commenced in 1855 looking to some modification of the lease under which they had for nearly 30 years been working.

In 1858 an agreement was entered into with the Colonial Government by which the lease of 1828 was abrogated. The association was confirmed in the possession of the collieries which it was then operating, with the exclusive right to further territory adjacent thereto, and an additional consideration in a material reduction of the royalties which had hitherto been paid by them.

This arrangement threw open at once to private enterprise a large area of mineral property which otherwise must have remained for many years undeveloped. The local government at once received numerous applications for leases to work some of the most promising of these deposits, and it was under the management of the parties receiving these grants that some of of the most successful collieries in the Province have been conducted. These new enterprises had scarcely been placed in working condition when the events of 1861, suspending for several years the operations of some of the larger collieries in the States, gave to the Provincial coal trade an impetus which called for the exercise of all the resources at the command of its managers. From 1861 down to 1870 it was not so much a question of price as it was of ability of the companies to meet the pressing demands for coal—not alone from gas companies, but for general steam and manufacturing purposes.

In addition to the Albion and Lingan Collieries, to which reference has already been made, there were five collieries in the Provinces opened up by private enterprise, from which the gas companies in the States drew a large part of their supplies during the twelve years named.

A brief sketch of the organization of these collieries, and of their operations during this period may not be entirely without interest. I shall refer to these new enterprises in the order in which the applications were granted. Commencing with the lease for the working of the Little Glace Bay Mines, Little Glace Bay, C. B.

This was given to Mr. E. P. Archbold in 1858. A company was formed in 1861, and a harbor constructed giving excellent facilities for loading vessels of the largest class.

Block House Mines, Cow Bay, C. B.—Lease granted to Marshal Bourinot in 1859. Operations commenced in 1860 upon the site from which coal had been mined in 1766, nearly one hundred years previous.

Gowrie Mines, Cow Bay, C. B.—Lease granted to Messrs. Archibald & Co., 1861.

Caledonia Mines, Port Caledonia, C. B.—Mining operations commenced in 1865, under the management of Messrs. J. H. Converse, Estes Howe, and others of Massachusetts; but shipments were delayed until 1868, when the present harbor at Port Caledonia was completed, and a railway constructed to connect with the colliery.

International Mines, Bridgeport, C. B.—Leases for the working of these mines were granted in 1858. There being no suitable harbor for the loading of vessels, the first shipments of coal were lightered to vessels at anchor in the open bay. The mine was transferred to a New York company in 1863, when arrangements were made to connect the colliery with Sydney by rail; but this project was not carried out until 1870. The delay in the completion of this work prevented the company from availing of the active demand for coal in the States up to that time.

The coal from the Glace Bay and Block House Mines came into the market at a time when the demand for gas coal was very active. No difficulty was experienced in finding sale for all these collieries could then produce. *The Glace Bay* was distributed among the leading gas companies between Portland, Maine, and Washington, D. C., the capital being lighted by gas from that coal in 1863. It was also used at Fortress Monroe while General Butler was in command at that station. The Northern Liberties Gas Company, Philadelphia, purchased a large part of their supplies from Glace Bay during the war and immediately thereafter. The price during the early years of its operations was $2.40 gold per ton 2,240 lbs., f. o. b. vessel at the mines; and in 1863 the company sold its entire product at the opening of the season at that price. This coal was a favorite one with the New York companies, and shared the trade in that market in nearly equal proportion with the Block House, supplying at the same time a larger part of the gas coals required in New England.

Block House—In spite of the difficulties attending the loading of vessels at Cow Bay, owing to the exposed condition of the harbor, this colliery enjoyed a most prosperous trade with the States from 1861 down to 1873; the bulk of its product went to New York, where it easily commanded $2.60 gold per ton f. o. b. vessel during the early years of its operations.

About 1880 indications of an early exhaustion of the mine were apparent, and from that time forward, the bulk of the coal shipped was obtained from the pillars. This work was completed in 1885, when the mine was abandoned.

The Caledonian Mines, which went into active operations in 1868, were managed by gentlemen who had been largely interested in the Glace Bay Colliery, and a somewhat sharp competition sprung up between the two interests for the United States trade, and in the active demand for coal following the opening of the colliery, it succeeded in getting a strong footing in the market. It reached a maximum output of over 75,000 tons in 1873. From that date forward it shared in the general decline of all Cape Breton coals; its export in 1874 being less than one-half of that of the previous year, and again in 1875 falling off to 16,000 tons. The larger part of the product of this colliery in its most prosperous days was sent to New York. When the competition for the gas coal trade became the sharpest, this coal was one of the first to yield to the pressure, its quality for that purpose not being considered equal to the Block House or Little

Glace Bay. It can hardly be rated in the catalogue of gas coals at the present time.

International—As noted above, this coal did not come on the market to any extent until 1870. It found temporary foothold in the New York market during the three years following, over 100,000 tons having been disposed of there for gas purposes. Various causes, partly incident to the management and in part to the value of the coal, as compared with other Provincial coals, led to its early abandonment by the gas companies in the States, and its operations subsequent to 1873 were upon a very limited scale. In 1877 financial difficulties led to a sale of the property. Since that date the colliery has been successfully worked by the new management, finding sale for its product mainly in the Provincial market.

The Gowrie coal came into the market as a gas coal, and found limited sale for that purpose in the early days of its operations. The peculiar character of this coal did not warrant its being screened at point of shipment, and the condition in which it came to market soon led to its abandonment for gas purposes.

The proper limit of this paper has not warranted a more detailed sketch than is here presented of the important part which the Provincial gas coals assumed in the United States market down to 1880. A large degree of their prosperity was no doubt due to the existence of the Reciprocity Treaty, which continued in force until 1867, giving these coals free admission into the States for over five years. The abrogation of that Treaty in 1866 subjected Provincial coals to a duty of $1.25 per ton, payable in gold, which was still held at a premium. The effect of this tax was seen in a decrease of importations in 1868, of nearly 100,000 tons, or about twenty per cent. less than the previous year. I have annexed a table showing the shipments of Provincial coal to the States from 1850 down to 1886, inclusive; the quantities named therein include shipment for other purposes as well as for gas, but the changes indicated from year to year may be taken to fairly represent fluctuations in the gas coal trade for those years. I also append a table showing comparative results obtained from the best-known American and Provincial gas coals. This table was prepared from the records of a leading gas company, in whose works both descriptions of coal had been largely used prior to 1876.

I have not attempted to give the cost of these coals in detail at the points of consumption during the period of their most active sales. The purchaser paid for the coal in gold at the mines, and assumed all the additional items entering into its transportation to the point where it was required; the fluctuations in the premium on gold varying at times from 5 to 20 per cent. in one day, and from 20 to 50 per cent. during the year, renders it impracticable to give any reliable quotations for these coals in the States prior to the resumption of specie payments. Sales were occasionally made in 1865 at $14 U. S. currency per ton delivered in New York, and these figures no doubt represent the maximum cost of any of the Cape Breton coals in the States at any one time; this item represented say $2.50 gold per ton for the cost of the coal at the mines, and a vessel freight varying from $6 to $8 per ton U. S. currency. These high freights were caused partly by the heavy demand for tonnage necessary for the delivery of the large quantities of Provincial coal required during the war and the few years subsequent thereto. A large per cent. of the vessels employed were under the American flag, necessitating extra marine insurance to cover the war risks attending such voyages. So heavy was the strain upon the capacity of the collieries during that period, that it was no uncommon event for vessels to wait four or five weeks for their turn to load; this delay in securing cargo had much to do with the high freight demanded at that time. The close of the war and the removal of the disabilities which had during that time rested upon American vessels, the opening up of other sources of coal supplies and consequent decrease in the demand for Provincial coal, caused a gradual decline in these freights, reaching a nominal rate of $1.75 during the later years of the importation of these coals.

Albertite—Any presentation of the subject of Provincial gas coals which did not include some consideration of the celebrated Albertite of New Brunswick would necessarily be incomplete.

For a period of nearly thirty years from 1852 down to 1881 this mineral stood at the head of all the then known materials for the enrichment of coal gas. Immediately upon the discovery of this valuable deposit a company was organized to develop it, and the first shipments were made to the States in 1852. As the lease of the General Mining Association covered all the mineral deposits in the Provinces, its managers at once laid claim to the property. This claim was resisted upon the ground that the article was not a mineral, and therefore not covered by the Association lease. Protracted litigation ensued, involving the the testimony of some of the most expert scientists in the States and Canada. These gentlemen differed materially as to the true name of the deposit and of its geological formation. Professor Dawson, in his admirable work on Acadian Geology, thus comments upon these divergences of opinion : " This was not wonderful in the circumstances ; for the substance was really a new material, intermediate between the most bituminous coals and and the asphalts, and the geologists examined had enjoyed very few opportunities of studying that very remarkable group of rocks to which the deposit belongs. Consequently some, in all sincerity, called the material ' coal,' others, ' asphalt.' "

The same eminent writer thus describes the appearance of this material, which he characterizes as " asphaltite mineral : "——

" The substance has externally an appearance not dissimilar from ordinary asphalt of commerce in its purest forms ; but it is very much less fusible, and differs in chemical composition. Its lustre resinous, and splendent or shining. Its color and the powder and streak on porcelain, black ; and it is perfectly opaque. It is very brittle and disposed to fly int fragments. It emits a bituminous odor, and when rubbed becomes electric. In the flame of a spirit-lamp it intumesces and emits jets of gas, but does not melt like asphalt."

The decision as to the ownership of this valuable deposit was adverse to the claim of the General Mining Association, and the rights of the company originally in power were confirmed.

The earlier shipments of this mineral were used in the gas works at Boston and New York ; but upon the introduction of kerosene oil manufactured from shale and cannel coal a large portion of the product of this mineral was devoted to that purpose. The discovery of petroleum in 1859, however, put an end to the distillation of oil from cannel and similar material, and albertite took its place for many years as an enricher of coal gas. Its use in later years was almost entirely confined to the Boston gas works; the limited production only allowed an occasional cargo to be placed in other markets.

Its value for gas purposes had been variously estimated at $22 to $25 per ton. The deposit was exhausted in 1881, and all attempts to locate other deposits of a similar character have so far been unsuccessful.

It is scarcely probable that Provincial gas coals will ever regain the position occupied by them during their most prosperous years. Their geographical position places them at a great disadvantage, even under the most favorable circumstances, when competing with American coals; being restricted to about seven months in the year, during which vessels can be secured at favorable freights, and it is at this period that the requirements of gas companies are the lightest.

Neither party to a contract for any large quantity of these coals for delivery in the States would be justified in estimating the cost of such delivery, say at New York, under $4 per ton of 2,240 lbs. This estimate is based upon the following figures:

Cost of the best screened gas coals f. o. b. vessel at shipping point... $1 50
Average freight on same from *May* to *November* 1 75
Duty under present tariff.................................... 75

$4 00

which is the contract price for the best American gas coals for the present year, covering continuous delivery in New York through the entire season from April to April.

American Gas Coals.

The records of the early gas companies in the States do not indicate clearly the period when the American coals were first used in the manufacture of gas, or from what particular mines they were received. It is well known that illuminating gas has been made from various materials before coal came into use. As early as 1802, the city of Richmond, Va., had been lighted by gas from wood. Whale oil was first used about 1825, in the New York works, to be substituted for resin soon after; and the latter article found a place in all the older gas works down to 1850, being used not only alone, but also as an enricher for coal gas. In the early days of the Baltimore works, which were incorporated in 1817, resin and foreign coals were used, and it was in these works without doubt that American gas coals were first used. It came from the Midlothian region near Richmond, Va. The date of its introduction is not stated, and it was probably the coal later known as Clover Hill.

Coal was first used in the gas works in Philadelphia in 1836. This was domestic coal from the Pittsburgh region, and was no doubt of the same general character as that now procured from that region.

Resin and foreign coals were the materials used in the early days of the Manhattan gas works of New York in 1835 and 1837. American coal first appeared upon their records in 1850, under the general name of Virginia coal; this was without doubt the Midlothian coal, which had been in use for some time in the Baltimore works. In 1855 the so-called West Virginia coal came into the market, the first shipment being from the Newburg Orrel Mine to the Baltimore works. This coal and others of a similar character from the same region formed a large part of the gas coal supplies in the New York market down to 1861, when operations were interrupted, not to be resumed until after the close of the war. In the meantime the rapid development of the gas coal mines in Western Pennsylvania had been going on, and when the West Virginia coals were again available, the market, which they had formerly controlled to a large extent, had been secured by the various Pennsylvania companies.

The operations of these gas coal companies from 1865 down to the present time, with the extension of the Baltimore and Ohio R. R. into the Youghiogheny coal district, opening up the valuable gas coal of that region to the market on the Atlantic seaboard, and more recently the development of the gas coal deposit on the line of the Chesapeake and Ohio R. R. are events all familiar to the members of this Association, and do not call for comment from me at this time.

I desire, Mr. President, to express to you, and through you to the gentlemen of the Association, my appreciation of the courtesy extended to me by your committee in the invitation to address you on this occasion, and to thank the members present for their patient attention to what I have had to say.

PROVINCIAL COAL EXPORTED TO THE UNITED STATES.

YEARS.	TONS.	DUTY.	YEARS.	TONS.	DUTY.
1850	118,173	24 ad.	1869	257,485	$1 25
1851	116,274	"	1870	168,180	1 25
1852	87,542	"	1871	165,431	1 25
1853	120,764	"	1872	154,092	75
1854	139,125	Free	1873	264,760	75
1855	103,222	"	1874	138,335	75
1856	126,152	"	1875	89,746	75
1857	123,335	"	1876	71,634	75
1858	186,743	"	1877	118,216	75
1859	122,720	"	1878	88,495	75
1860	149,289	"	1879	51,641	75
1861	204,457	"	1880	123,423	75
1862	192,612	"	1881	113,728	75
1863	282,775	"	1882	99,302	75
1864	347,594	"	1883	102,755	75
1865	465,194	"	1884	64,515	75
1866	404,252	"	1885	34,483	75
1867	338,492	$1 25	1886	60,646	75
1868	228,132	1 25			

The above table is from the "Report of the Department of Mines, Nova Scotia, for the year 1886."

NAME AND LOCATION OF MINE.	GAS.				COKE.			ANALYSIS OF COAL.				
	Feet per Ton, 2240 Standard.	Maximum yield per ton of 2240.	Candle Power.	Specific Gravity. Air 1000.	Bushels of Coke per Ton of 2240 Coal.	Pounds of Coke per Ton of Coal.	Specific Gravity of Coal.	Per cent. of Volatile Matter.	Per cent. of Fixed Carbon.	Per cent. of Ash.	Per cent. of Sulphur.	Per cent. of Water.
Average result obtained from the Standard American Gas Coals from Western Pennsylvania, viz.: Westmoreland, Penn., and Youghiogheny.	9500	11800	16.50	0.450	42	1600	1300	33.80	56.99	6.52	1.19	1.50
Average result obtained from the leading Cape Breton Gas Coals, viz.: Block House, Glace Bay, Caledonia.	9500	10800	15.60	0.447	34	1570	1285	35.25	53.18	5.50	3.01	3.06

The coke produced from the American gas coals herein named is a most excellent article for house and general use, but *not so strong* for use *under the retort* as that obtained from the Cape Breton coals, or from some of the *sulphurous* gas coals obtained from Western Virginia. Those gas companies whose facilities for *purifying* are *ample* prefer to have from *one-fourth to one-third* of their coal from either Cape Breton or Western Virginia, in order to get a *stronger* coke than the standard Pennsylvania coals afford.

It will be noticed that the *American coals* produce 20 *per cent. more coke* than the Provincial coals—a very important item when it is considered that from 50 *per cent.* to 60 *per cent.* of the coke made is *sold by the bushel* for house use.

Sulphur—One bushel of hydrate of lime will purify about

5,000 cubic feet of gas made from American coal, and about 2,500 cubic feet of gas made from Provincial coal.

On motion of Mr. Page, a vote of thanks was passed to Mr. Perkins.

The President announced that as the hour for adjournment had arrived, the discussion on the paper would be postponed until the afternoon session.

REPORT OF COMMITTEE ON APPLICATIONS FOR MEMBERSHIP.

MR. RAMSDELL—In behalf of the committee on applications, I make a favorable report upon the names of William R. Higby, A. B. Slater, Jr., Charles H. Stoddard, Mark B. Thomas, H. J. Bell and H. J. Chadwick for Active Members; and Peter G. Van Wie and W. S. Wright for Associate Members.

MR. HARBISON—I move that the report of the committee be accepted, and that the chairman of the committee cast the ballot of the Association for the election of the applicants named.

The motion prevailed.

MR. RAMSDELL—Hearing no objection to the names read, I cast the ballot of the Association for their election as members in accordance with the instructions.

MR. HARBISON—I want to offer a resolution at this time, if the Association will bear with me. Before offering it I will give a word of explanation as to why I offer it. In reporting the Constitution yesterday, and in our action upon it, there is in the minds of some gentlemen an opinion, to which they are well entitled—for I have no question about its honesty—that we were not acting yesterday in a strictly parliamentary way in the election of these gentlemen as members, after the Constitution was adopted, and to-day; on the other hand, those of us who have advocated their election are equally conscientious in our position. I think I see a way in which all can come to the same conclusion—doing no injustice to the gentlemen who have been elected, and at the same time doing credit to ourselves by doing business in a strictly orderly manner. I, therefore, desire to offer this resolution for the purpose of clearing away whatever mist there may be with respect to this matter:

" *Resolved*, That the Council of this Association be, and they are hereby instructed to report the names of gentlemen who were elected on the 17th and 18th of October, 1888, as members of this Association, after the adoption of the Constitution, for election at the next annual meeting of this Association to be holden in the city of Baltimore, Maryland."

If we adopt that resolution the gentlemen whom we elected yesterday, and those who have been elected to-day, will in honor consider themselves, and the members of this Association will consider them as brothers and members of the Association, having had the honor of an election by unanimous vote of the Association.   By instructing our Council to report their names for election we put ourselves again on record under the Constitution as favoring their election at the next annual meeting, which will be done in a strictly constitutional way, as they will then come in under the ten days' provision of the Constitution. This proposed vote meets the hearty approval of one of the gentlemen who earnestly and conscientiously opposed our action in this matter, and who has served as a member of the committee on applications; and I trust that it will meet the concurrence and approval of the gentlemen who were as conscientious as he is in opposing our action.   I think that the passage of the resolution which I now offer will clear away all the mist that surrounds the whole matter; and I, therefore, ask for a vote of the Association upon the resolution.

MR. STINESS—I would like to ask one question of my brother Harbison: Are not these gentlemen already at this moment, according to the general understanding of this Association, members of this body?

MR. HARBISON—Yes, I believe they are members according to the understanding, but according to the interpretation of the Constitution which others put upon it they are not, and it is to harmonize the views of the entire Association, and so to prevent the possibility of this question coming up again, and also to prevent our action on this occasion being cited as a precedent in future cases as a waiver of the ten days' provision of the Constitution, that I offer this resolution.

Mr. Stiness—I have no objection to the adoption of the resolution. The point that I raised was whether there was any general understanding among all the members of the Association that all the names presented at this meeting would be considered as properly presented, or only those that were presented yesterday before the adoption of the Constitution. Had I understood as clearly as I believe some other gentlemen of the Association did understand, that all the names presented at this meeting were to come in under that general head, I would have acquiesced in it. But I did not so understand it. I do not think that this resolution can do any harm, and I do not really see that it is going to do away with any precedent that has been already established. It is like a good many other things—it don't do much good, and cannot do much harm.

Mr. Harbison—After the adoption of this resolution there will be no question, at the meeting of next year, as to the right of these gentlemen to be considered by everybody as members of this Association, in equal standing with every other member; whereas now their standing is in doubt in the minds of some of the gentlemen in this room.

Mr. Stiness—If there were a preamble put to that resolution, that whereas certain names having been presented under a misapprehension, or a misunderstanding of the Constitution, it then would explain why the resolution was presented.

Mr. Harbison—I will accept the suggestion as to a preamble.

Mr. A. C. Humphreys—I would like to ask Mr. Harbison under which Constitution these gentlemen were elected associate members?

Mr. Harbison—They were elected as associate members under the provisions of the new Constitution, as the old Constitution did not provide for them, and I think that the gentlemen who voted for them did so with that understanding.

The President—Are you ready for the question on the resolution offered by Mr. Harbison, with the preamble suggested by Mr. Stiness?

Mr. Harbison amended the resolution so as to read as follows :

" *Whereas*, There is doubt in the minds of some of the members as to the legality of the election of certain members since the adoption of the Constitution : therefore,

" *Resolved*, That the council of this Association be, and they are hereby instructed to report the names of gentlemen, who were elected on the 17th and 18th of October, 1888, as members of this Association, after the adoption of the Constitution, for election at the next annual meeting of this Association, to be holden in the city of Baltimore, Maryland." This resolution was adopted.

The Association then took a recess until 2 o'clock P. M.

SECOND DAY—AFTERNOON SESSION.

The Association met at two o'clock P. M.

THE PRESIDENT—The last paper read was that of Mr. Perkins, on gas coals. I do not see that Mr. Perkins is present now, but if any member has any remarks to make upon that paper we are ready to hear them.

MR. NETTLETON—May I be allowed to say a word. I think we all feel very much in debt to Mr. Perkins for having prepared this paper. It is hardly one that can be discussed, and yet it is a paper that I am sure we are all glad has been written. It gives us a history of the development of the coal mines in the Provinces, and gives us facts with which very few of us have been familiar. I hope at the next meeting of the Association this paper will be followed by another, giving the history of the development of the American coals. I am certainly very greatly indebted to Mr. Perkins for the labor he has spent on this paper, and I think all the members must feel in the same way.

THE PRESIDENT—If there are no further remarks on the paper of Mr. Perkins, we will now listen to that of Mr. Smedberg.

Mr. James R. Smedberg then read a paper entitled :

OBSERVATIONS DURING MANY YEARS' EXPE- RIENCE IN THE GAS BUSINESS.

Mr. President and Gentlemen of the American Gas Light Associa-

tion :—In the early part of the year 1853, John Jeffrey was engineer of the Cincinnati Gas Light and Coke Company; and the lamented Thomas Butterworth, Joseph Light and myself were among his young subordinates.

The exhauster was matter of debate—the clay retorts (even of Cliff or Keller) were unknown, and the public regarded gas maker and plumber alike as queer monsters, full of "ethereal hydrocarbons" and solid diamonds.

A favorite Cincinnati setting was one of three iron retorts—the upper being carried on iron bridges from the two lower ones, the arch being a Gothic or pointed one of 5 feet 4 inches span, and fire-stone slabs being used indifferently with Kreischer's tile for the flue-covers. From the crude photometric appliances of those days, Mr. Jeffrey decided that coal gas had a higher illuminating value where he used a box washer than where the jet washer was employed. The washer was invariably set next in sequence of apparatus to the hydraulic main; the trustees of the Philadelphia Gas Works stating in their report to Councils for 1857, however, that those works "first introduced the system of giving increased purity to their gas by means of refrigerating jets thrown into the gas while hot."

The immersed Multitubular Condenser had not been developed by the distinguished Joseph A. Sabbaton from John Peck's British patent of 1817; nor had Pelouze & Audouin deduced the condensation of the difficult tar vapors from Halley's vesicular theory. The great coke columns of Mann and Livesey had not arisen to give place in turn to the noble Kirkham Hulett Scrubber, and to the other implements which logically feed the surface to the water, instead of feeding the water to the surface. The guide-columns of Jeffrey's great single-lift gasholder were handsome Corinthian shafts, arranged in groups of three, as atmospheric condensers; while another successful contractor connected his suspension frames by curved girders at top. In small works, the center-mast gasholder was not uncommon; and it still survives and does good work in some sequestered villages.

Four feet from the pound of coal was considered good work; the regenerative furnace and the whole modern pursuit of high heats were not; and stoppages by naphthaline were exceedingly rare.

Kerosene was no competitor; and that vigorous intellect to which is due the entire growth of American water gas was ineffectual and among the clouds for want of petroleum. There were no regenerative nor incandescent burners. Carburetting, whether by liquid hydrocarbons or by Bowditch's valuable use of residuary naphthaline, was not thought out. Apart from the nearly obsolete wet lime purifier, there was no idea of purification by liquids or in closed vessels. We had neither natural gas nor electric lighting nor Laming's mass; and the apostle of the commercial value of our by-products was silent. The dry valve, the automatic station governor, the jet photometer, the dry meter and the coal-liming process, for which has been claimed the remarkable saving of 700 per cent., were all uncreated.

In fine, the gasman was "dim, remote like Sirius." He was not eternally engaged in some tilt or other with buccaneering capital; nor were there any quirks of legislation, or "comet-like return" of patents, to vex his calm, judicial notions of price and purity and candle power.

This sketch of gas lighting in 1853 shows that 35 elaborate monographs would be required to contemplate the industrial progress of 35 years, and thus comply fairly with the title assigned by the courtesy of your committee. You must, therefore, bear with the risky flavor of personal anecdote.

In Norwich, Connecticut, the construction of the hydraulic center-valve was taught by the corrosion of the vertical divisions of the cover, and a consequent passage of foul gas to the burner. Curiously enough, the same unfortunate result occurred 30 years later, in Lancaster, Pennsylvania; but in the latter case the centre-valve—a dry one—was not in fault. By over precaution of design, the centre-valve itself had been provided with a four-way dry by-pass, having wrought iron drip-tubes entering a common seal-pot from each quadrant of the valve-box. The tubes were cut off by the corrosion at the water line; the by-pass was in a forgotten corner of the cellar—there was no plan of the works; and, to conclude, the gas showed clean at the third lime box, but stained at the station meter inlet, to which it passed around the lime by preference.

In Knoxville, Tennessee, a Worthington pump had been set on the yard level, 28 feet above the Holston River, and without a foot-valve. It was made effectual by placing the pump at the bottom of a pit sunk 20 feet deep in the tenacious clay, and providing its suction with a strainer and foot-valve.

It next became necessary to change the grade of an 8-inch main from an arc of 15 feet rise to its chord of 150 feet in length. Beyond cutting out at the centre the difference in length between the old profile and the new, no joint was broken ; and after connecting with a sleeve and recaulking, the pipe was perfectly tight—a sufficient lesson as to the capabilities of the lead joint.

Then the station meter stopped registering. Like many others, I knew the generous skill of Joseph A. Sabbaton, but was ashamed to confess that this meter was too much for me; I wrote in what appeared to be an airy and professional way that the meter "required looking at." His prompt advice, as a brother and an engineer, was to "buy a table, a pipe and some canaster, an arm-chair and a lemonade, and then to sit down in the meter room and look the thing out of countenance." This *was* a settler, to be sure. The trouble was found within 20 minutes to be that the main driving pinion was split, allowing the drum shaft to turn loosely inside of it.

These incidents, trivial as they now appear, were interesting enough at the time.

When appointed superintendent of the Savannah works the leakage was large, with a ton yield of 8,000 cubic feet from iron retorts, without an exhauster. It was some years before the firing on Sumpter, and excepting an occasional cargo of Fairmont the coals were imported. Our material was Pelton, New Pelton, Silkstone and Arley ; Ince Hall and other Wigan cannels—with some Lesmahagow, less Boghead and a trifle of Albertite. The Company's capital was unwatered, the product being 60,000 or 70,000 feet per day through 14 miles of mains to 1,200 consumers and 450 street lamps. Our lime was derived from the abundant oyster beds of the river delta.

The city occupies a sandy plateau ; and close to the outlying residences were, then, forests of pine and live-oak, with here and there a magnolia nearly dead in the clasp of misletoe, trailing moss and yellow jasmine.

Most of the streets were unpaved; and Broad street, in particular, was often flooded from curb to curb by semi-tropical rain. The street had neither declivity nor sewer; but presently a little mule, an ebony bare-legged boy, and a primitive plow ran one or two furrows lengthwise through this Venice, and in a few minutes the water subsided on edge to the thirsty, hospitable sands below. It was, therefore, an easy matter to strip the mains and a few of the services, the leakage falling from an old figure of 22 to a new one of between 7 and 8 per cent.

The consumers' meters were mainly " wet," of the make of Colton, Code & Co., with about 300 of the imported " dry " ones of Croll & Glover. They were all taken out and proved—50 condemned and the rest replaced; the average registration of the entire list being between 1 and 2 per cent. slow. In 1859 the Company adopted Keller's Belgian clay retorts.

A valuable guide, then and through the stormy years that followed, was a special system of monthly statements. The book containing them was ruled and printed in blanks comprising 4 pages for each consecutive month.

It gave the profit and loss account in every detail for the month just completed, for the current year as far as completed and for the corresponding periods of the preceding year. It similarly included all the working averages, the disposition of all gas registered, the financial condition of the Company, the number of consumers and public lamps, and, in brief, was as elaborate as any formal yearly report. This last must be qualified by the exception of bad debts, the underrun or overrun of coals, and the variation of estimated from actual wear and tear, which was rigorously written off, instead of running on to swell the *apparent* profits and the *apparent* value of permanent accounts. These three elements of doubt were adjusted by closing entries in December of each year, the aggregate of final corrections being represented by a purely trifling figure. The proposition was carefully passed upon by Dr. Francis T. Willis, the President of the Company, before adoption by the Board.

It is unsafe to say that the method can be availed of by companies having over 3,000 or 4,000 meter accounts; but below those limits it establishes certainty of programme, and equal and exact confidence between directors and superintendent, both of which are desirable.

Soon after the establishment of the blockade, we were asked to inflate a balloon, from which Mr. Steiner, a well-known aeronaut, and Captain Lawton, of the Confederate staff, were to take a bird's-eye view of the Union batteries, then being placed by General Q. A. Gillmore, for the reduction of Fort Pulaski.

All arrangements had been made over-night, benches arranged for selected spectators, and the foreman ordered to touch nothing.

On reaching the works at 4 o'clock the next morning (a full half-hour before appointment), I found that he had removed a closing flange from the blank end of a 6 inch pipe, and had led a forlorn hope, by way of magnifying his own office, to the task of tying on the duct against 22-tenths pressure.

All this, beginning in disobedience and ending in murder and almost suicide, while there was a closing valve within two feet of the deadly muzzle of the pipe.

There were several men badly asphyxiated; one man dead, with a broken neck, at the bottom of a 24-foot dry-well; another hung dead by the jaws, between a flange on one side and the brick-work of the well on the other, and the stokers of both watches nearly mad with panic.

The flooring of the little valve house had been taken up the day before, so that it was an easy thing for me, after knocking off the lids, to kneel on the beams and close the valve. As I reached out vaguely for support against the intolerable gas-flow, my hand rested on the still face of the suspended man. He was extricated; and a big-hearted Irishman, whom I had discharged a day or two before, took the slings from under my own arms, and went down into the fatal well and retrieved the other body, myself of course, watching his signal rope. Three or four men sprawling about the yard in idiotic attitudes, with bloodshot eyes, were revived by heroic doses of the standard remedy; and the balloon was filled, went up, and presently came comfortably down in the tender mud of a neighboring rice field.

The tragedy teaches the common mind that discipline is good; but Mr. Steiner (tall, muscular, and the last to be suspected of superstition), told me, "all tears like Niobe," that it happened at all because it happened on Friday. Observe, however, as an attaché who married a Georgia heiress put it, that "finance is conservative." My peremptory discharge of the culprit was commuted by higher authority, for fear that the two widows might enforce exemplary pensions from the Company.

Our stock of coals ran low; the railroads were occupied by troops and ordnance stores and commissariat; and the block-ade was impenetrable. We were in what a bishop styled as a "dilemna," which could never have been solved but for an humble German named Breisach, who had previously brought Pettenkoffer's wood gas to the attention of Philadelphia gas officials.

In his report for 1854, Mr. John C. Cresson stated "as a matter of official record, that a cord of ordinary fire wood, of any of the varieties brought to our market, will furnish nearly twice as much illuminating material as is obtained from a ton of the best Pitts-burg coal;" and he mentioned, on the same page, that this wood gas was "not only as cheap but much cheaper than that made from coal."

In his report for 1855, he claimed a yield of 15,000 to 17,000 cubic feet of 27¾ candle gas from a cord of dry oak—the candle being Judd's patent sperm.

His report for 1856 gave the following analysis of wood gas by Doctors Wolcott Gibbs and F. A. Genth :

	Gas from Pine.	Gas from Oak.
Specific Gravity................	0.663	0.580
COMPARISON :		
Hydrogen.....................	32.71	30.44
Light carburetted hydrogen......	21.50	33.12
Olefiant and hydrocarbon vapors.	10.57	6.46
Carbonic oxide.................	27.11	26.11
Carbonic acid.................	4.90	0.48
Oxygen......................	0.66	none.
Nitrogen.....................	2.55	3.39
	100.00	100.00

These gases were taken to New York for analysis, and the reported illuminating power was 26 candles.

Early in the Philadelphia experiment, a cellular form of iron retort was devised by Dr. Charles M. Cresson ; and prior to the opening of the war the gas companies in Charleston and other

Southern cities had been making wood gas in settings of these retorts.

With these precedents, and no gas literature beyond early numbers of the *London* and *American Gas Journals* and a copy of Hughes' valuable but unpretending work on coal gas, we began making wood gas from the splendid light-wood of Southern Georgia—our type gasholder at once showing 24-tenths pressure instead of 22. Our burners had metal tips ; so it was easy to bore out the fishtails and saw out the batswings to accommodate the higher specific gravity of the new product. The percentage of carbonic oxide in the purified gas varied from 18 to 35 per cent.

For a few weeks all was well ; but the cementing carbon burnt out of our clays, and we were compelled to replace them with iron retorts 20 in. x 12 in. x 8 ft. 0 in., at a cost of 12½ cents per pound. Then the ash swept out of the fire-bags (for we had to fire with wood) and the flue setting of the elder Sabbaton had to be modified by flues larger at back than at front, so as to give the flue-rakes control of this difficulty. All the time, the furnaces proper formed a peculiar wood clinker.

Finally, we found that the wood ought not to be split too small, and that 1½ hour charges were most advantageous.

After this we had no manufacturing trouble throughout. The consumers were satisfied, because the illuminating power was as high or higher than before ; and the Directors were naturally pleased, because the Company's whole investment was saved. We made 10,000 cubic feet per day per retort, the yield being from 8 to 12 feet per pound, or from 24,000 to 36,000 feet per cord of wood, according to the relative percentages of resin, fibre, and water composing it. These averages refer to the wood actually carbonized—about an equal quantity being additionally used for firing. There was local demand for far more of the wood-tar than we could supply. We quenched with water the residuary charcoal, which though of poor quality enough, found ready sale. We had no standard candles ; but I am thoroughly satisfied that the gas had a value of not less than 18 candles.

It so happens that Mr. Thomas Turner, President of this Association, was connected with the late B. P. Brunner in the conduct of the Charleston gas works for some years preceding the war, and throughout its course ; and he will probably agree as to the singular beauty of the wood gas flame.

Reissig has given us a valuable work on wood gas and peat gas; Wagner's Technology contains a brief and reliable resumé of the subject; and King's Treatise, while through a clerical error confounding a cubic inch with a cubic meter, gives a page or two to German facts—to some English experiments—and to the methods applied by Dr. A. W. Wilkinson in the Mutual gas works of New York City.

All these, however, differ widely between themselves, and, at best, have little value as criteria of the Savannah results.   In Red Bluff, California, many years later, I found the average cord of Sierra Nevada pitch pine to weigh 3,139 lbs.; its yield being 21,000 feet of nearly 17-candle gas.

The volume, character, and behavior of the product are largely modified by the amount of moisture in the wood, by the form and temperature of the retort, by the weight and duration of the charge, and by the nature and size of the burner employed.

As against Mr. John C. Cresson's figures, quoted above, *King's Treatise* says that " old oak has been found to yield 4,500 cubic feet of 5-candle gas per ton."   This is about equal to 6,000 feet per cord ; assigning a joint cord value of about one-sixteenth of that given by Cresson.

In 1868 a correspondent who suitably signed himself " Ignoramus," wrote to the London *Journal of Gas Lighting* as follows :—

" My gasholder, 52 feet high, gives 6 inches pressure.   .   .   . And again, why does a gasholder 52 feet high not give 6 5-10 inches pressure on top, instead of six inches ?"

As a fact, an inflated gasholder *does* give uniformly more pressure at the top than at the water line ; and " Ignoramus " might as well have tried the experiment before rushing into print.

My motive in quoting him is to offer a paradoxical fact, which has not been completely accounted for.   The process to your verdict will, therefore, be precisely the reverse of that followed by the critics of the bothered Englishman.

In 1878 I was employed to connect the mains of the Vallejo (California) Gas Company with the government gasholder in the Mare Island Navy Yard, the impediment being a tidal strait some 1,400 feet wide and 30 feet deep. The fee was a fair one, but conditioned upon the success of the work.

At the end of the Georgia street wharf, on the Vallejo side, I placed an Otto engine, a piston gas pump, and a tension cylinder, with quick motion gates to act like a fitter's pump in blowing out any water condensed from the gas in the droop of the traversing-pipe. The inlet to the gas engine was, of course, provided with a little gasholder to ensure regularity of explosion.

The next task was to get a 2-inch galvanized wrought iron pipe across the strait. A series of barges were moored, and the pipe jointed on them ready for lowering; but some tipsy sailors found an obstacle in the way of their evening expedition, and cut the mooring ropes, so that the whole flotilla swung with the tide, and twisted the pipe almost into a knot.

We then decided, on the hint of Mr. Fagan, the Vallejo Company's superintendent, to place a capstan on the Mare Island side, and pull the pipe across by sheer strength. So this was done, with a beveled chair under the leading end of the pipe, and a buoy tied to it in case of accident, coupling on length after length from the Vallejo wharf. The completed pipe, laid like a hollow rope on the bottom of the strait, was connected at both ends, the engine and pump were started, and the navy yard was, for the first time, lighted with coal gas instead of gasoline.

Then it was the unexpected which happened, or rather the expected which did not happen. During three years the pipe was never tapped off—there was no condensation of water vapor in 1,400 feet of pipe laid in water, with a drop of 30 feet in the center—the tension cylinder was never used.

It occurs that the gas may have left the pump under so high a temperature, due to compression, as to retain its carrying power of the vapor through the long conduit, because the linear velocity through that conduit was so high; in other words, that a larger pipe would infallibly have been trapped. The friction developed by high velocity against the interior surface of so small a tube must also have tended to keep up the temperature of the gas flow. The gas left the pump at 100° Fahrenheit, and went across at the rate of 2,250 cubic feet per hour. The linear velocity was, therefore, nearly 20 miles per hour, and the time of transit about 50 seconds.

While on the subject, D'Hurcourt gives the following in his French work on gas lighting, in reference to atmospheric and immersed condensers :—

"The tubes can only release the quantity of heat lost from their exterior surfaces, whether those surfaces radiate into space, or are cooled by contact with water.

"Where the cooling tubes radiate freely into space (representing the excess of temperature) the quantity of heat given off per hour per square meter, expressed in calories, supposing the difference of temperature to be constant, is given by the formula $K(1+o, oo66\ t)\ t$. K is a co-efficient which varies according to the nature of the surface. For cast iron, Peclet has found K to be 7.70; but as for lamp black, K is equal to 9, and as the tube surface is more nearly that of lamp black, we will asume the value 8, modifying the above formula to $8(1+o, oo66\ t)\ t$.

"The heat lost per square metre per hour, where the tubes are entirely submerged in water, and supposing that the water has no current except that due to its heating, is independent of the nature of the enclosures, and is closely stated, according to Peclet, by the formula $43(1+o, 105\ t)\ t$. This formula is found to be exact, so long as t, representing the excess of temperature of tube above liquid remains below 40°."

It is for two reasons that I quote these formulas, which are of easy reduction from Centigrade to Fahrenheit, and from square metres to square feet.

The first is that Peclet's formulas do not seem to be given in any of the gas books published in our language.

The second is that D'Hurcourt proceeds in his really delightful work, abounding in technical mathematics, to calculate in a parallel table the relative powers of the two systems, and *misplaces several of his decimal points*. The errors, flagrant as they are, were copied and recopied through several editions of his own work—of Hughes—and of Clegg; and were first pointed to in an ephemeral letter to the AMERICAN GAS LIGHT JOURNAL as late, or later than the year 1868. The offender would have had short shrift in these later and better days of analytic study.

I found the Hartley shale, Wollongongite, of Australia, to yield 14,000 cubic feet of 80-candle gas to the ton, the figure of illuminating value being assured by many tests made of dilutions of the rich gas with coal gas of known character, and with air. The dilution tests were calculated by direct proportion, and were practically coincident. The Manhattan Gas Company found 13,716 cubic feet of 133-candle gas from the same material, also by dilution; but employing the theorem of squares, the authorship of which is claimed both by William Farmer and Henry H. Edgerton. One of Mr. Farmer's letters of 1874 closes as follows :—

" This new law shows what an intense light might be obtained if we only had a burner that could consume 100,000 or 200,000 cubic feet of gas per hour, with as perfect combustion as Suggs' London Argand."

Mr. Farmer might well say so, for

$$\frac{(200,000)^2}{(5)^2} \times 16 = 25,600,000,000.$$

That is according to the theorem of squares, and with a suitable burner 200,000 feet of 16-candle gas would give as much light as 25,600,000,000 of standard sperm candles ; being at the rate of 128,000 candles to the foot; or to express it differently, each cubic foot of gas burnt according to the new theory would do the work of 1,600,000,000 feet under the present system.

Some of us, however, have seen 16-candle gas commanding $5 per thousand; and many of us now see 30-candle gas selling at $1.25—a clean drop from $7.50 to $1.00 for equal light. It is not safe, therefore, to assert that anything is impossible.

We owe to Mr. Farmer the Kindergarten chemical blocks, and a formula for air-dilution which agrees with the observations of Dr. Carl Schultz, and is a far more accurate guide than the nearly forgotten Erdmann gas-power.

We are all aware that our Bunsen photometer varies in its accuracy according to the burner and quality of gas employed; but it cannot be too positively added that its verdict, when the blue light of an incandescent burner is to be compared with the red light of a candle, is absolutely worthless for the purposes of the human eye.

In spite of the many and important topics omitted from this paper, it is already long enough.

Even in regard to the burning subject of water gas, it is well only to remind you that it acted on a service layer in Lancaster precisely like nitrous-oxide. Let the why and wherefore of his capers be relegated to the " question box."

On motion of Mr. Slater, a vote of thanks was tendered Mr. Smedburg.

IN MEMORIAM.

Mr. W. H. White—Mr. President, if there is to be no discussion upon the very interesting paper read by Mr. Smedburg, there is a matter upon which I would like to occupy the attention of the Association for a few minutes.

Our action of yesterday, in receiving the report upon our deceased members, while it was in strict comformity with our usage for a number of years—a custom best, perhaps, in most cases in view of the pressure upon our time—seems insufficient, now that I recall one of the names then presented to us. It is unjust to ourselves, and to the memory of " a good man and true " to thus, in the hurry of business, pass with no more fitting notice than the record in our sadly lengthening necrology of the death of such a member as was Wm. Helme.

I am lacking in no respect, nor do I intend any injustice to the memory of the other members who, with him, have passed beyond the scenes of human endeavor. I recall them all with pleasant recollections : T. F. White and Mr. Pratt, of our older members, were men who gave to the Association the dignity of their years and the benefit of their exprerience secured in widely separated fields of labor ; and no one can more sincerely regret the untimely ending of the promising career of our late talented associate, Mr. Collins ; or recall with sadder memory the merry and genial Murphy. Yet there is a fitness in our pausing for the moment to call again into our midst, if only in recollection, the person of Wm. Helme.

For this purpose I ask your patience. You who began with him in this Association in its first or its earlier days, and have borne, with him, the heat and burden of sustaining this society when doubters were many, and zealous friends were but few. While I recall the name of your dead comrade of those days, who, faltering upon the highway of life has lain down by the roadside in peaceful rest, and ask of you that this dead man's name may not be coldly and formally passed to the records of this meeting.

From the first Mr. Helme was present at our meetings, taking active and zealous part in furthering the work which had called us together. With ripened judgment, kindly heart and manly dealings with all, he has left an enduring memory in the hearts of young and old among us. No member ever called on him to share his vast fund of information, but found ready welcome to any aid he could extend. To no one, more fitly than to our dead friend, could be applied Emerson's lines:

"July was in his sunny heart;
October in his liberal hand."

In noting the character of the new and younger element coming into the Association, we, older members, cannot fail to be impressed with the fact, that stronger men and truer methods are pressing behind our lingering feet as we approach the Western gateway of life. Their business will be more carefully transacted; their work bear the impress of greater scientific attainments than ours, and doubtless, a broader field of usefulness will mark the future of this Association under their guidance. But, I question, Mr. President, if any action taken by us will so challenge their consideration in days to come, or be a more fitting example to them of kindly human nature than this very service of tender recollection, in holding which we have checked the prosaic wheels of business with the tender touch of sentiment.

Mr. President, we have with us to-day a member who was bound to Mr. Helme by the closest ties; who was his business partner and life-long friend, and I ask for Mr. John McIlhenny the privilege of speaking to us of this warm hearted friend of his, and ours, who is no longer able to speak for himself.

" Dead upon the field of honor," was the response at roll-calls
of Napoleon's old guard, by living comrade answering to the
name of a dead hero ; and I ask that this comrade of our dead
friend be permitted to lay upon his grave the tribute of a flower
of his recollections of him and thus enable us all to feel that a
becoming farewell has been spoken to our dead.

MR. JOHN MCILHENNY—Mr. President and gentlemen of the
Gas Light Association, the words that have just fallen from the
lips of our friend, Captain White, express far more eloquently
than I can, the praises of our departed friend, William Helme.
I am very highly gratified in coming to this meeting to hear
expressions of regret from every one who has spoken to me
about him, to hear his virtues extolled, and to listen to sentiments
of good will from every member who has mentioned his name.
I can say that he was entirely worthy of all commendation and
praise from those who knew him. When this Association met
last year in New York City and it was announced that the next
meeting would be held in the city of Toronto, Mr. Helme said to
me, " We will have to be there," but alas! how many of us are
mistaken in our expectations. He is not here to answer to his
name and we will no more hear his voice in our deliberations.
He has passed beyond the Western gate whither we are all
tending, and especially those of us who have passed fifty ; to us
the door only opens outward, and the loss of our old time friends
is irreparable.

As you all know, Mr. Helme felt an exceedingly deep interest
in the welfare of this Association. He was present at its very
beginning, and he lived long enough to see it become a large
and prosperous Association, and to see the gas business, from its
small beginning, grow to the second in importance of the industries of the country.

For several years Mr. Helme had been in rather poor health.
although at these meetings, in his business life, and at his home,
he appeared always to be hopeful and cheerful. On the third
day of last June, a bright Sunday morning, when everything
was peaceful and quiet, and when he was in unusually good spirits,
he was going to church with his family. While walking along
the road he stooped to pick up a daisy and hand it to a little
child ; just at that moment he was stricken by the hand of

death. He lingered for a while and on the 12th of June he went to fairer skies, and a happier home, as I firmly believe.

I have known him for many years; I was his business partner, and also very closely associated with him as his friend. When young we were employed by the same firm in building gas works, and during all that time I have only known him as a correct, upright, honorable, high-toned man. I have never known him in his private conversation to use an expression which he would be unwilling to use anywhere. He was a man of remarkable purity of character, and was also a man of great liberality. He took a deep interest in many things outside of the gas business, and was an ardent member of the Franklin Institute, for the promotion of science. In every department of business enterprise, as well as in everything he took up, he was at all times earnest and sincere. You all know that he was upon one side or the other of every question that came before this body for consideration; a generous opponent, and a staunch advocate.

I believe this is all I would say; I thank Captain White most sincerely for this opportunity of giving expression to my kindly regard for Mr. Helme, and my deep regret that he has been taken from us.

MR. FODELL—It was my good fortune to be intimately acquainted with Mr. Helme, in this and in other associations. What has already been said of him is true indeed. He was a man endowed with more than ordinary talent and ability of the faculties necessary in his profession; and was always willing and pleased to impart his knowledge, gained by long experience in business, to those asking his advice. I desire to add this, my feeble tribute to his memory. In all his relations and intercourse, whether in business or in social life, he ever exhibited in himself the characteristics of the gentleman. The death of such a man as Mr. Helme is a loss to this Association.

MR. W. H. WHITE—The home life of Mr. Helme was probably the most tender and beautiful feature of his manly career. It is one of the charming evidences of his nature left us that his widow mourns for a tender lover lost, rather than for a husband dead.

The loving regard of Mr. Helme for his wife was always beautiful in its frank expression. This Association would be lacking in proper respect if there was not conveyed to that mourning woman something from us, his life's associates in business, that she could treasure as the evidence of the esteem in which we held her partner in life. I therefore move that the Secretary be directed to write a letter to Mrs. William Helme, expressive of our sympathy, our sense of loss and our sincere regret at her husband's death.

The motion was seconded by Mr. Stiness and adopted by a rising vote.

THE QUESTION BOX.

THE PRESIDENT—We will now take up the question box. The first question is :

" *What is the extra cost on wear and tear of meters where iron purification is used ?* "

MR. SOMERVILLE—I do not know' what the extra cost is; but I believe it is something. I am very sure that oxide of iron does injuriously affect the meter, because I noticed that when I used it the diaphragms for some cause or other become stiffened. That was one trouble. There was a kind of deposit that I never before witnessed in the meter, that appeared after I began to use the oxide of iron. How it came there I cannot tell; but I am firmly convinced that oxide of iron purification does injuriously affect dry meters.

MR. SCRIVER—We use oxide of iron to a very large extent in the purification of our gas, but we do not notice that its use is in any way injurious to our meters. It may be owing to the fact that we do not allow our meters to run over five years without overhauling—the law of this country is such that we have to take our meters out every five years. I feel warranted in saying that the oxide of iron purification does not injure either the consumer's meter or the station meter at the works.

MR. SOMERVILLE—Your meters are all wet; are they not?

MR. SCRIVER—No, sir; they are all dry.

MR. YOUNG—Do I understand you to say that they are required to be taken out and not used again? The law, as I recollect it, is that they háve to be tested every five years, and if found incorrect they have to be made correct.

MR. SCRIVER—That is it, certainly; they have to be tested every five years.

MR. YOUNG—I have been using oxide of iron for ten or twelve years; and I was not aware of any injurious effect upon the meters, or on the illuminating power of the gas, until we put in our Standard scrubber. After that we discovered a little deterioration in the illumininating power. Before that time we used exclusively the oxide of iron for purification, and had no trouble with the meters nor with the illuminating power.

MR. PRICHARD—We have been using oxide of iron for quite a number of years and on receiving this question from the Secretary, I inquired of the man who examines our meters as to its effect upon the meters, and he said he could tell no difference between them and those in Massachusetts, where they are using lime exclusively. He said it was impossible to tell the difference. In fact, he seemed to think that a small amount of ammonia in the gas, purified by iron oxide would be rather a help to the diaphragm than an injury to it. But the last week before I came away we had occasion to go into the station meter, and found that the inlet pipe had been entirely corroded from the oxide. It had not rusted from the outside, but we found a deposit of matter there which smelled like naphthaline, and looked like a cross between iron rust and iron sponge. That material, whatever it was, had eaten clear through the galvanized iron of the meter.

" *What is the best way to treat men who, while working in the trench, are overcome by gas ?* "

MR. CLARK—I have a recipe given to us by a prominent physician, which seems to be a very good one. The rules are as follows :

1, take the man at once into fresh air. *Don't* crowd around him ; 2, keep him on his back. *Don't* raise his head, nor turn him on his side ; 3, loosen his clothing at his neck and waist ; 4, give a little brandy and water; not more than four tablespoonfuls of brandy in all. Give the ammonia mixture (one part aromatic ammonia to sixteen parts water) in small quantities, at short intervals, a teaspoonful every two or three minutes; 5, slap the face and chest with the wet end of a towel; 6, apply warmth and friction, if the body or limbs are cold; 7, if the breathing is feeble or irregular, artificial respiration should be used, and kept up until there is no doubt that it can no longer be of use; 8, administer oxygen.

Some of these rules I have myself used, and I think very successfully.

MR. A. C. HUMPHREYS—I will add to what Mr. Clark has said, that these rules were not prepared hastily, but were obtained from a physician who was familiar with the subject from personal investigation.

MR. HARBISON—I would like to inquire whether he experimented with the same man or not.

MR. CLARK—The experiments were made on animals.

MR. WHITE— I have been told by a physician who has had considerable experience in the treatment of those overcome by gas, that there is no more direct or certain way to overcome the effects of gas, if a man is sensible enough to swallow, than to give him a tablespoonful of olive oil, or of common sweet-oil. If he can swallow it, give him a tablespoonful of oil, and then give him a little milk, or some brandy, or whiskey, or whatever stimulant may be at hand. Of course you should loosen his garments, and place the man in easy position to breathe freely, and if you can, create a circulation of air by fanning, or by placing him in a draught. The handiest thing usually for gas men to get, when a man is overcome in the trenches, is to get at a neighboring drug or grocery store, a bottle of sweet oil and some milk, and it is my experience that, whether the man is overcome with water gas or coal gas, nothing acts so quickly in restoring his breathing as sweet oil. It is not unpleasant to take, it lubricates his breathing apparatus, and the man will recover very much more quickly. It is founded upon many years' experience with men who have been overcome with gas, and I have used it myself when suffering from the same cause.

MR. SOMERVILLE—I was once engaged in taking off the top

of a station meter, inhaled too much gas, toppled over, and was carried out insensible. I understand that I was taken to the open air, my collar and waist-coat were loosened, and I soon recovered consciousness; but I did not get well until the contents of my stomach were ejected. The whole system seemed to be affected by the gas. A few weeks ago I had to take my foreman out of a hole. It was a very serious matter—he was a nice man, and I was sorry to see him tumble off like that. We dragged him out as quickly as we could, unbuttoned his vest, fanned him, and he soon recovered. That was with coal gas, Still he felt the effects the balance of the day. With water gas it is entirely different. Then it is a very serious matter, indeed. We always take extra precautions in dealing with water gas. It does not seem to produce the same effect as coal gas. It seems to touch the blood, and it takes men some weeks to get over its effects. In fact, I know a man who has never gotten over it. If anything can be devised which will overcome the effects of the inhalation of water gas it is very important that we should know it. I have no doubt but that some one is asking this question in all sincerity, and if we can think of anything which would be an effectual remedy it will be a good thing to come before the meeting.

Mr. Scriver—I believe that very recently an inspirator has been invented, which fits over the nose and mouth, and enables the man to remain in an atmosphere where gas is escaping for a great length of time.

Mr. Harbison—Two or three years ago I had some experience in this matter, and it was a little different from anything which has been stated here—I was not within reach of physicians at the time, and so could not avail myself of their services. Some workmen were laying a large main, connected with two six-inch pipes, and had to make a temporary connection over night in order to maintain the supply of gas in one section of the city. The gas escaped, and within ten minutes seven men became insensible in the ditch. We took the pressure off as soon as we could, removed the men to the open air, put water upon their faces and necks, gave them a mixture of whiskey and water, and, as soon as they could swallow anything, I gave them apples to eat, and the acid of the apples immediately started the gas out of the stomach. Just as soon as I could reach it I gave them some strong, hot coffee, and very soon they were ready to take their supper pails and walk home.

MR. WATSON—I have had men in the same condition, but I administered vinegar to them, which I suppose acted in the same way as the apples. I gave them vinegar with eggs in it—breaking the eggs in the vinegar and letting them drink it. I find it very effectual.

MR. KUEHN—On two different occasions when one of my men was overcome with gas I called a physician, who injected the carbonate of ammonia. The man was ill eight or ten days after from the effects of it. He became so bad the second time that I did not put him back to that kind of work again.

"What advantages are gained by using high gravity naphtha for water gas?"

THE PRESIDENT—I will call on Mr. Humphreys to answer that question.

MR. A. C. HUMPHREYS—I will say, very briefly, that one of the advantages of high grade naphtha for water gas is that it will allow you to make the gas from the old style apparatus. If you will think of all that means, that about answers the question. There are a great many disadvantages in the use of high grade naphtha. Its increased danger specially. I should not advocate the use of high grade naphtha in making water gas. It is unnecessary.

MR. SCRIVER—I would like to ask this question : Is there any gentleman present who can give any information with regard to the reduction of Sunday work in our gas works? How can Sunday labor in our gas works be reduced—especially with reference to the working of the retorts?

MR. HARBISON—I would say it can be done by striking off the lids from the charges that are burned off, and slacking the fires and not charging them again. We ought to be able to do that, and still keep a sufficient supply. It may in some cases be thought insufficient; but if you have storage room enough, work the retorts well, and have enough of them running during the week, there would be no difficulty at all in doing away with Sunday work in the retort house—except so far as taking the lids off, which is a very slight work if you do not draw the charge.

Mr. Smedberg—Is there any injury to the retorts?

Mr. Harbison—Not at all. You leave the charge in the retorts and strike the lids. We have made a practice of it for over 15 years.

Mr. Scriver—Do you find any difficulty with the purifiers?

Mr. Harbison—Not a particle.

Mr. Smedberg—I suppose that on 500 occasions I have had to lay off two or three benches at a time; and I have never yet charged one of those benches after an expiration of twenty-four hours without having at least one-half of the retorts leak.

Mr. Robert Baxter—I will give you a little of my experience with regard to Sunday labor. When I came to our present works our retort men worked Sunday and Saturday, both alike —at least they worked on Sunday the same as on Saturday or Monday, but they knocked off about two or three o'clock on Monday morning, and remained off until early in the forenoon. That was while I was Assistant Manager of the works. On my appointment as Manager I at once changed the order of procedure. We knocked off Sunday work on Sunday morning, at seven or nine o'clock, just as the quantity of gas in our holders enabled us to do. We quit as early Sunday morning as possible. We have never had a crack in our retorts. We never slack the doors. We have a three-inch pipe to the hydraulic main, with a valve on it, and about half an hour before the charge is worked off we open that valve and shut the outlet valve, and never a particle of air gets in. The retorts are just as tight when we start work again as they are on Sunday morning when we stop. We never slacken the doors. Our men get full pay. If something happens in the winter so that they need to work the whole 24 hours of Sunday, they do it; but otherwise the men get off on Sunday morning as early as they can.

Mr. Harbison—We have no valve on the hydraulic main,

but we slacken the lids. Our men are paid in full for seven days' work, but if the necessity occurs for doing any work on the Sabbath they are notified, and they come and work without extra pay, for they are already paid for it. We were led to try this way of doing it because our experience showed us a good many years ago that the retorts were not injured by being out of use a portion of the time. We were at one time situated where we had to furnish, night by night, between 80,000 and 90,000 cubic feet from a 60,000 foot holder; and we were obliged to keep two benches extra to use from dark until 12 o'clock, and then have them off during the rest of the 24 hours, because the holder would be full. We found those benches were not injured, and that was the reason why we saw that we could (if we provided more storage room) do away with Sunday labor ; so we at once built a new holder, and now have a storage capacity for 33 per cent. more than the consumption, and have no difficulty at all. Many members will remember that this subject has been frequently discussed before the Association during the past 10 years ; and I can only add to what I have before said, that continued practice in this line confirms us in the experience and opinion that it is wholly unnecessary, as far as the working of the retorts is concerned, to do work on the Sabbath in the retort house, if you have sufficient benches, and storage capacity for the gas without it. We do not work, as some engineers do, on the Sabbath to make up whatever deficiency there may be in the other six days of the week.

MR. SCRIVER—Does Mr. Harbison leave the coke in the retorts over Sunday ?

MR. HARBISON—Yes; we leave the coke in until we charge up again. I will add to what I have already said, that we had had no experience at all with regenerative furnaces until last Sabbath. That was the first time. We had only been charging our new house ten days, and last Sabbath we treated the regenerative furnaces in the same way precisely. I was careful to note on Monday morning what the effect on the retorts was, and I could not observe that there was any indication of injury. When we started our gas was quite as good as at any other time, showing that the retorts had not sustained any fracture, as no air had been drawn in.

Mr. Watson—At what time do you start on Monday morning.

Mr. Harbison—We start up on Sunday evening.

" Is there any way to prevent naphthaline from getting into street mains and services ? It does not show itself in the works, but in the inlet drip of the holder it causes me many restless nights."

Walton Clark—I have tried many ways of keeping naphthaline out of the inlet pipes of gas holders, but from my present knowledge the only way I can recommend in answer to this question is to stop making gas at that works.

Mr. Cole—In answer to the last question I will state that to prevent trouble from naphthaline, I purchased an old tank, similar to those used under cars for conveying gas for illuminating the cars on a railroad, stationed it in the cellar, and attached to it a steam pipe, and filled this tank two-thirds full of ordinary naphtha, or raw benzine, and at stated times (once or twice a week) I turned on the steam and vaporized that naphtha into the gas—either before it goes through the center seal, or beyond. I have it so connected with steam pipes that I can take it directly from the pipe into the holder, or through the center seal or scrubber, or any way whatever. In that way I have been able to keep down naphthaline and have had no trouble on the street with any of the services.

VOTE OF THANKS.

Mr. White—Is there any further business before us, Mr. President?

The President—There is no further business. There is a paper here, but under the ruling of the Association we cannot read it, as the author is not present.

Mr. White—Then I move you, Mr. Slater, as the incoming President, that the thanks of this Association be tendered to our retiring President, Mr. Turner, for the courteous manner in which he has presided over this meeting; and that we express our sympathy with him in the accident which recently befell him, as well as our appreciation of his sense of the duty which he owed to this body and which prompted him to come thus far from his home, while suffering so severely, in order to preside at our deliberations.

MR. HARBISON—I second that motion.

The motion was put by Mr. Slater and unanimously adopted by a rising vote.

PRESIDENT TURNER—Gentlemen, I can only thank you for your expression of sympathy, and for your courtesy and indulgence during my term of office.

MR. SCRIVER—I believe that some of the gentlemen present intend returning to their homes by way of Montreal; and I would like to extend an invitation to any who are going that way to favor us with a visit. We are carrying forward very large extensions in our works this year, and we shall be delighted not only to show them to any of the gentlemen who may visit us at our works, but also to take them driving around and on top of our beautiful mountain, and around the city, and to show them all the sights of the city of Montreal that may interest them.

On motion of Mr. A. C. Wood, seconded by Mr. White, the thanks of the Association were voted to the Secretary, Mr. C. J. R. Humphreys, for the very able manner in which he had conducted the business of the Association during the past year.

THE SECRETARY—Mr. President and Gentlemen : I am very greatly indebted to you for this kind expression of your appreciation.

On motion of Mr. Lindsey, seconded by Mr. Graeff, a vote of thanks was given to the Executive Committee for the faithful way in which they had performed the duties of that office.

MR. SOMERVILLE—I move a vote of thanks to Mr. Friedrich Lux for his kindness in leaving that beautiful instrument—the Lux balance—here for our examination.

The motion was adopted.

MR. STEDMAN—It occurs to me that we have overlooked the Committee of Arrangements in the expression of our gratitude. I, therefore, move you that we offer a vote of thanks to the Committee of Arrangements for the very efficient manner in which they have made the arrangements for the comfort and well being of the members here, and for the very interesting meeting that we have had.

The motion was adopted.

MR. PAGE—I offer a resolution of thanks to the local press for their able reports in the daily papers.

The motion was adopted.

MR. STEDMAN—I move that we tender a very hearty vote of thanks to the local Gas Company for what they have done for us, and for what we are about to receive.

The motion was adopted.

The Association then adjourned.

In Memoriam.

There is no Death. What seems so is transition;
This life of Mortal breath
Is but a suburb of the Life elysian,
Whose portal we call Death.

WILLIAM HELME,
President Atlanta, (Ga.) Gas-Light Company,
Died June 12th, 1888.

JOHN C. PRATT,
President Jamaica Plain Gas-Light Co.,
Died June 7th, 1888.

JOSEPH H. COLLINS,
*Assistant Gen'l Superintendent United Gas
Improvement Co. of Philadelphia,*
Died June 26th, 1888.

JOHN M. MURPHY,
*General Manager Maryland Meter and
Manufacturing Company, Baltimore,*
Died September, 1888.

T. F. WHITE,
*Secretary and Treasurer Houston (Texas)
Gas-Light Company,*
Died February 28th, 1888.

JOHN McDOUGALL,
President Hornellsville Gas-Light Co.,
Died November 2d, 1888.

His voice is silent in your Council Hall forever.

OBITUARY.

WILLIAM HELME.

Born April 25, 1824.   Died June 12, 1888.

> July was in his sunny heart,
> . October in his liberal hand.

With what perfect truthfulness do these lines apply to our late member William Helme. Always bright, cheerful and cordial toward all with whom he came in contact; always ready to give from his ample storehouse of knowledge and experience such information as his younger brethren stood in need of, and always forward in giving from his purse amply toward every worthy cause presented to him. That his was a busy life only a brief recital of his many labors is necessary to prove.

Born at Dumfries, Scotland, on the 25th of April, 1824, he accompanied his parents to Philadelphia, Pa., while in childhood, and acquired in this, the city of adoption of his parents, his education in the public schools. The trade he adopted was that of a machinist, serving his time at the works of the Baldwin Locotive Company. While he was still in the employ of that company, he was tendered the position of Superintendent of the Trenton, N. J., Gas Company; he accepted the office. After remaining in New Jersey a while, he went to Augusta, Ga., to erect gas works at that place. After completing the works he assumed the management of them, remaining in charge for some while. In 1853 he resigned this position, and engaged in the lumber and saw mill business. This business not proving successful, he returned to his former business and we soon find him erecting gas works at Winchester, Va., and later he put up the works at Atlanta, Ga., and he remained connected with this company to the time of his death. His management of this enterprise during most trying and troublesome times, was most successful and reflects great credit upon his business career and sound judgment.

Prior to the war we find Mr. Helme engaged in the business of refining oil, in the City of Philadelphia; and later he became interested in a mining venture in Arizona Territory. In 1872 Mr. Helme entered the firm of Harris & Brother, meter manufacturers, the style of the firm being changed later to that of Helme & McIlhenny; Mr. Helme remaining the senior member of that firm to the time of his death.

Mr. Helme was one of the original members of our Association, being present at the roll call at the Knickerbocker Cottage in New York City on the occasion of the organization meeting held April 16, 1873. There have been few meetings of our body where Mr. Helme has not taken a prominent part. His recognized good judgment always making his advice and counsel very welcome to his associates.

Mr. Helme had been in poor health for some time prior to his death, but the final blow came while on his way to church, June 3, when he was attacked by a stroke of paralysis. He lingered for nine days, when he finally passed away in the quiet village of Stratford.

JOHN C. PRATT.

Born March, 1813.   Died June 7, 1888.

Mr. Pratt was in every sense of the word a Bostonian, having been born, brought up, educated within the Capital of Massachusetts, and there it was he passed all of his busy life, and there it was he breathed his last. It was in 1813 that the subject of this sketch first saw the light of day, and after receiving the education which so many Boston boys received, he, in 1833, entered the office of H. H. Hunnewell, of Wellesley. On the death of Mr. Hunnewell, Mr. Pratt became manager of both the Hunnewell and Weld estates, continuing in this position to the time of his death.

Mr. Pratt considered himself more of a railroad man than a gas man, having been connected as President with several prominent railroads; at the time of his death he held the position of

President of the Granite Railway Company. The gas fraternity know him best as President of the Jamaica Plain Gas Company. This company was formed in 1853, Mr. Pratt being elected the first President and continued in that position to the time of his death, having been re-elected for thirty-five successive terms. Mr. Pratt was a pronounced believer in telling the gas consumer all he knew in regard to the business of the company over which he presided; the annual report of the Jamaica Plain Gas Company being sent alike to gas consumer and gas share-holder.

Mr. Pratt joined our Association in 1879, and always took an interest in our work. He contributed many papers at our meetings and took an active part in the discussion of the many topics.

Mr. Pratt passed away, after a lingering illness, on the seventh of June, 1888.

JOSEPH H. COLLINS, Jr.

Died June 26, 1888.

Jos. H. Collins, Jr. was thirty-six years of age at the time of his death, Tuesday, June 26th, 1888. He was a native of Philadelphia, and spent nearly his whole life in that city. His parents were Friends, well known in his city.

After completing a regular school course, he entered the machine shop of Pusey, Jones & Co., and served there a full apprenticeship of five years, becoming unusually proficient in his chosen calling. Returning home he spent the three succeeding years in the lumber business with his father's concern, Jos. H. Collins & Son. Here he acquired a business training which was afterward of great value to him.

Giving way to his natural bent, he then entered into partnership with Arthur O. Granger, under the firm name of A. O. Granger & Co. This concern built up an enviable reputation as engineers and dealers in machinery. Gradually the firm's business drifted almost entirely into the line of Water Gas Works construction, and thus Mr. Collins became identified with the gas industry. When the firm of A. O. Granger was merged into the United Gas Improvement Co., Mr. Collins became Assistant General Superintendent of that Company. Mr. Collins held this position up to the time of his death.

It is thought by some that the exacting nature of his duties in that position reduced the tone of his system, so that he more readily gave way under an illness which was not considered serious until almost the last day. He had been suffering from a catarrhal trouble, and on Saturday, the 23d of June, one of the most oppressively hot days of the summer, he left his office, for the last time, early in the afternoon, to submit to a close examination at his physician's hands. He was greatly prostrated after this examination, and by Monday his condition was regarded with some alarm. From this on he rapidly grew worse, and finally sank to rest the next Tuesday evening.

From Mr. Collins' almost peculiar family relations, his sudden removal was more than usually sad. His parents were both alive, and no death had occurred in the family in forty years— the family circle had been so far complete, held together by a bond strong, but most tender.

Mr. Collins left a widow (daughter of Y. M. Delaney, Philadelphia), and two little girls, and only those who had the opportunity to know him as an upright, manly, Christian gentleman, can appreciate what a terrible loss this family suffered, and will suffer from his—as it seems to our limited vision—untimely end.

In his business relations Mr. Collins was universally respected. "Justice tempered with mercy," seemed to be his motto. It speaks volumes when we find that the business associates most earnest in his praises, are those that were most closely connected with him. Mr. Collins was quite largely interested in some business concerns outside of the gas business. He was a member of the Union League and the Franklin Institute.

He was also a trustee of the Second Reformed Church of Philadelphia, and was an earnest and unostentatious worker in that Church.

This is the brief record of an honorable, busy life—a record which his family may in the future look back upon with honest pride.

What was there more to win?

JNO. M. MURPHY.

Born September 11, 1860.   Died August 25, 1888.

The subject of this brief obituary was the eldest son of Mr. and Mrs. Murphy, of Ironton, Ohio, where he was born September 11, 1860. His early education was had at the local schools of his native town, afterward entering St. Mary's College, of Cincinnati, from which institution he graduated in due course. For a while Mr. Murphy, on his return to Ironton, acted as an assistant to his father, but after a few years we find him connected with the New York and Ohio Iron and Steel Company, a concern in which Emerson McMillin, Esq., was interested. In the latter part of 1884, Mr. Murphy was appointed Treasurer of the Sioux City Gas Company, but after a short time resigned to accept a more lucrative position with the Nebraska City Gas Company. Early in 1887 we find him in charge of the western business of the Maryland Meter and Manufacturing Company; that he rendered this Company valuable service and that his work was appreciated is evidenced by the fact that when he had been with them less than a year, he was made the General Manager of the Company's Agencies. The subject of this memoir was elected a member of our Association at the meeting held at New York City in 1887; he was also a member of the Western Gas Association and the Ohio Gas Association.

Mr. Murphy was one of those men who are liked wherever they are known; genial, kind, warm-hearted, he made hosts of friends, friends who will ever hold him in happy remembrance for his sunny disposition and his strict integrity.

———

T. F. WHITE.

Died February 28, 1888.

Though most of the life of Mr. White was passed in the south and southwestern portion of our country, it was in the solid old Commonwealth of Massachusetts that he was born—the part of the State or the year in which he first saw the light of day are not included in the brief data at our command. We know, however, that early in life he removed, with his parents, to South Carolina, and there it was that he received his early education. Evincing a liking for a military life, his parents consented to his adopting this profession, and we find him at West Point in early life. Graduating from there he joined the regular army, and his services at many frontier outposts bear evidence of his bravery and good judgment. During the Civil War the subject of this brief notice was connected with the Quartermaster's Department; when peace again reigned in the land he settled in Texas, where he became interested in the cotton business. In 1872 Mr. White, or more properly, Major White, accepted the position of Secretary and Treasurer of the Houston Gas Light Company, and much of the after success of that company is due the executive ability and good judgment of Major White.

Major White joined our Association at its Fourth Annual Meeting, held in New York City in 1876. Circumstances were such that he was prevented from attending many of our meetings, but he always took a warm interest in the work of the Associaion. At the time when our annual meetings are held—namely October—the yearly meeting of the stockholders of the Houston Gas Company takes place; this fact sufficiently explains why Mr. White so seldom met with us, but the many letters the Secretary received from him in regard to Association matters are ample evidence of the warm interest he took in the affairs of the Association.

JOHN McDOUGALL.

Born 1833.   Died November 2, 1888.

The Hon. John McDougall was born at Paisley, Scotland, in 1833, and when eighteen years of age arrived in this country, an almost penniless and inexperienced lad. Upon his arrival he became a resident of New York State, spending his first year in Brooklyn, and then removing to Syracuse. Subsequently he took up his abode at Oswego, where he went into partnership with

Mr. Avery, a partnership which was severed only by the death of Mr. McDougall, after a lapse of thirty-two years. The firm built many Gas Works, among them those at Hornellsville, which were erected in 1861, since which date Mr. McDougall had been a resident of that city, leaving, as is remarked by a local paper, " the impress of his energy and intellect upon the record of every year's growth since that time."

Mr. McDougall was interested in several chemical works, being interested with Messrs. Hilton & Sherwood in a large plant at Hiltonville, and also in conjunction with another gentleman, erected at Hancock, one of the largest acids works in the country.

Mr. McDougall was an influential citizen of Hornellsville, where many enterprises, faltering for a time, were taken up and pushed to a happy completion by his energy and determination. He was a prominent member of the Masonic Order.

Mr. McDougall attended very many of the meetings of our Association, and by his happy, open-hearted manner, endeared himself to all with whom he came in contact.

Mr. McDougall passed away on November 2, 1888, after an illness or several months. The whole city turned out on the occasion of his funeral, Sunday, November 4.

AMERICAN GAS LIGHT ASSOCIATION.

OFFICERS 1887–88.

President.

Thomas Turner, - - Charleston, S. C.

Vice-Presidents.

A. B. Slater, - - Providence, R. I.
Emerson McMillin, - - Columbus, Ohio.
J. P. Harbison, - - Hartford, Conn.

Secretary and Treasurer.

C. J. R. Humphreys, - - Lawrence, Mass.

Finance Committee.

C. H. Nettleton, - - Birmingham, Conn.
A. E. Boardman, - - Macon, Ga.
W. H. Pearson, - - Toronto, Ont.

Executive Committee.

William Henry White, - New York City.
G. G. Ramsdell, - - Vincennes. Ind.
H. B. Leach, - - - Taunton, Mass.
D. H. Geggie, - - Quebec, Canada.
T. G. Lansden, - - Washington, D. C.
F. S. Benson, - - Brooklyn, N, Y.

Past Presidents.

Charles Roome,   A. Hickenlooper,
Theobald Forstall,   Wm. A. Stedman,
Eugene Vanderpool,   A. C. Wood,
*William H. Price,   M. S. Greenough.

Deceased.

AMERICAN GAS LIGHT ASSOCIATION.

OFFICERS, 1888-89.

President.

Alpheus B. Slater, - -	Providence, R. I.

Vice-Presidents.

Emerson McMillin, - -	Columbus, Ohio.
John P. Harbison, -	Hartford, Conn.
Wm. Henry White, - -	New York City.

Secretary and Treasurer.

C. J. R. Humphreys, - -	Lawrence, Mass.

Members of Council—For Two Years.

W. H. Pearson, - -	Toronto, Canada.
G. G. Ramsdell, - -	Vincennes, Ind.
Chas. W. Blodgett, - -	Brooklyn, N. Y.
A. E. Boardman, -	Macon, Ga.

For One Year.

Matt Cartwright, - · –	Rochester, N. Y.
B. E. Chollar, - -	Topeka, Kansas.
Thomas Curley, - –	Wilmington, Del.
Wm. H. Baxter, - -	Petersburg, Va.

Past Presidents.

Chas. Roome,	A. Hickenlooper,
Theobald Forstall,	W. A. Stedman,
Eugene Vanderpool,	A. C. Wood,
* Wm. H. Price,	M. S. Greenough.

Thomas Turner.

*Deceased.

LIST OF MEMBERS,
—1889.—

The date following each name in this list indicate the date of the election of the person to membership in the Association.

HONORARY MEMBERS.

Prof. C. F. CHANDLER, of Columbia School of Mines, N. Y.   Oct., '75.

WILLIAM KING, Engineer Gas Co., Liverpool, England.   Oct., '77.

W. W. GREENOUGH, Treasurer and Agent Boston Gas Light Co., Boston, Mass.   Oct., '78.

Gen. CHARLES ROOME, Ex-President Consolidated Gas Co., New York, N. Y.   Oct., '79.

Prof. HENRY MORTON, Ph. D., President Stevens Institute of Technology, Hoboken, N. J.   Oct., '78.

ROBERT P. SPICE. M. Inst. C. E., 21 Parliament Street, London, S. W., England.   Oct., '85.

Prof. E. G. LOVE, Ph. D., Gas Examiner of New York City, 122 Bowery, New York City.   Oct., '86.

ACTIVE MEMBERS.

Abel, W. G	Atlanta, Ga	Oct.	'86
Adams, H. C	Philadelphia, Pa	Oct.	'86
Adams, Wm. C	Richmond, Va	Oct.	'84
Addicks, J. Edward	Philadelphia, Pa	Oct.	'86
Africa, J. Simpson	Huntingdon, Pa	Oct.	'74
Allen, Augustus L	Poughkeepsie, N. Y	Oct.	'75
Amory, Dr. Robert	Brookline, Mass	Oct.	'86
Andrew, Jno	Chelsea, Mass	Oct.	'76
Archer, Benj. F	Camden, N. J	Oct.	'79
Armington, James H	Brooklyn, N. Y	Oct.	'81
Atwood, H. A	Plymouth, Mass	Oct.	'83
Averill, A. T	Cedar Rapids, Iowa	Oct.	'81
Axworthy, Thomas	Cleveland, Ohio	Oct.	'82

Balmore, John	New York, N. Y	Apr.	'73
Barret, A. H	Louisville, Ky	Oct.	'78
Bartlett, E. L	Baltimore, Md	Oct.	'89
Bates, Jno. W	Hoboken, N. J	Oct.	'74
Battin, Isaac	Omaha, Neb	Oct.	'74
Bauer, P	Texarkana, Texas	Oct.	'83
Baumgardner, John H	Lancaster, Pa	Oct.	'79
Baxter, Isaac C	Detroit, Mich	Oct.	'82
Baxter, Robert	Halifax, Nova Scotia	Oct.	'81
Baxter, Wm. H	Petersburg, Va	Apr.	'73
Beal, Wm. R	New York City	Oct.	'74
Bell, H. J	Camden, N. J	Oct.	'88
Benson, Fred. S	Brooklyn, E. D., N. Y	Oct.	'75
Betts, Edward	Wilmington, Del	Oct.	'88
Bierce, Frank	Memphis, Tenn	Oct.	'87
Bigelow, Henry N	Clinton, Mass	Oct.	'88
Bill, George D	Malden, Mass	Oct.	'78
Blodget, Chas. W	Brooklyn, E. D., N. Y	Oct.	'84
Boardman, A. E	Macon, Ga	Oct.	'84
Boardman, Henry	Bangor, Me	Oct.	'88
Bodine, Samuel T	Philadelphia, Pa	Oct.	'86
Booth, Chas. E	Chicago, Ill	Oct.	'83
Borgner, Cyrus	Philadelphia, Pa	Oct.	'80
Bradley, Wm. H	New York, N. Y	May	'75
Bredel, Frederick	New York, N. Y	Oct.	'85
Breeze, E. M	Rock Ledge, Florida	May	'75
Brown, E. C	New York, N. Y	Oct.	'87
Brown, Thos. R	Philadelphia, Pa	Apr.	'73
Burtis, Peter T	Mount Holly, N. J	Oct.	'79
Bush, Jno. S	New York, N. Y	Oct.	'83
Butterworth, Wm. C	Rockford, Ill	Oct.	'83
Byrne, Thos. E	Brooklyn, N. Y	Oct.	'82
Cabot, George D	Lawrence, Mass	Oct.	'74
Cabot, John	New York, N. Y	Oct.	'81
Capelle, George S	Wilmington, Del	Oct.	'88
Cartwright, Matt	Rochester, N. Y	Oct.	'74
Cartwright, William	Oswego, N. Y	Oct.	'83
Callahan. W. P	Dayton, Ohio	Oct.	'81
Chadwick, H. J	Lockport, N. Y	Oct.	'88
Chambers, John S	Trenton, N. J	Oct.	'73
Chollar, Byron E	Topeka, Kansas	Oct.	'88
Clark, Geo. S	Kansas City, Mo	Oct.	'88
Clark, Walton	Philadelphia, Pa	Oct.	'84
Clifford, James B	Lockport, Pa	Oct.	'86
Coffin, John A	Gloucester, Mass	Oct.	'86
Coggshall, H. F	Fitchburg, Mass	Oct.	'74
Cole, T. W	Altoona, Pa	Oct.	'82

Collins, A. P	New Britain, Conn	Oct. '81
Connelly, J. S	New York, N. Y	Oct. '84
Connelly, T. E	New York, N. Y	Oct. '83
Cooper, Arthur F	Exeter, N. H	Oct. '83
Copp, Austin M	Boston, Mass	Oct. '81
Corbett, Charles H	Brooklyn, N. Y	Oct. '82
Cornell, Thos. C	Yonkers, N. Y	Oct. '73
Cornelius, Robert C	Philadelphia, Pa	Oct. '86
Cosgrove, W. L	Evanston, Ill	Oct. '86
Cowdery, Ed. G	Milwaukee, Wis	Oct. '85
Cowing, Jno. H	Buffalo, N. Y	Oct. '74
Coyle, Patrick	Boston, Mass	Oct. '81
Crafts, David W	Northampton, Mass	Oct. '75
Cressler, A. D	Fort Wayne, Ind	Oct. '82
Crockett, Joseph B	San Francisco, Cal	Oct. '83
Curley, Thomas	Wilmington, Del	Oct. '79
Cushing, Oliver E	Lowell, Mass	Oct. '74
Daly, David	Jersey City, N. J	Oct. '85
Davis, Frederick J	Waltham, Mass	Oct. '75
Davis, Frederick R	Athol, Mass	Oct. '83
Dell, Jno	St. Louis, Mo	Oct. '85
Denniston, W. H	Pittsburg, Pa	Oct. '73
Diall, M. N	Terre Haute, Ind	Oct. '76
Dickey, Charles H	Baltimore, Md	Oct. '83
Dickey, R. R	Dayton, Ohio	Oct. '81
Dingee, F. A	Philadelphia, Pa	Oct. '82
Doty, Albert J	Philadelphia, Pa	Oct. '86
Douglass, David	Savannah, Ga	Oct. '88
Douglas, S. H	Ann Arbor, Mich	Oct. '85
Down, Wm. H	New York, N. Y	Oct. '81
Edgerton, H. H	Philadelphia, Pa	Oct. '74
Edwards, George B	New York, N. Y	Oct. '82
Elkins, George W	Philadelphia, Pa	Oct. '86
Elkins, William L., Jr	Philadelphia, Pa	Oct. '86
Enfield, William	Dallas, Texas	Oct. '85
Ensley, Enoch	Memphis, Tenn	Oct. '85
Faben, Charles R., Jr	Toledo, Ohio	Oct. '85
Fay, Wm. J	Denver, Col	Oct. '84
Ferrell, Joseph L	Philadelphia, Pa	Oct. '86
Findlay, J. H	Ogdensburg, N. Y	Oct. '82
Flanigen, C. D	Athens, Ga	Oct. '84
Flemming, Dudley D	Jersey City, N. J	Oct. '80
Fletcher, A. M	Indianapolis, Ind	Oct. '81
Floyd, Fred W	New York, N. Y	Oct. '82
Floyd, Henry E	New York, N. Y	Oct. '82
Floyd. James R	New York, N. Y	Apr. '73
Fodell, Wm. P	Philadelphia, Pa	Oct. '79
Fogarty, Thomas B	Astoria, N. Y	Oct. '81

Forstall, Alfred E	Chicago, Ill	Oct. '88
Forstall, Theobald	Chicago, Ill	Oct. '74
Foster, T. G	Montgomery, Ala	Oct. '86
Fowler, John	Philadelphia, Pa	Oct. '79
Frost, Edward I	St. Paul, Minn	Oct. '87
Frost, W. H	New York, N. Y	Oct. '79
Fry, Chas. C	Lynn, Mass	Oct. '83
Fullager, John	Napa City, Cal	Oct. '83
Gardner, James, Jr	P. O. Box 373, Pittsburg, Pa	Oct. '83
Gardner, William	P. O. Box 373, Pittsburg, Pa	May '75
Gartley, Wm. H	Chicago, Ill	Oct. '85
Gates, Frederick Wm	Hamilton, Ontaria, Canada	Oct. '73
Geggie, David H	Quebec, Canada	Oct. '81
Gerould, Chas. L	Brooklyn, E. D., N. Y	Oct. '83
Gerould, L. P	Mendota, Ill	May '75
Gibbs, W. W	Philadelphia, Pa	Oct. '86
Gibson, W. H	Lima, Ohio	Oct. '85
Gilbert, Thomas D	Grand Rapids, Mich	Oct. '74
Glasgow, Arthur G	Kansas City, Mo	Oct. '87
Goodwin, W. W	Philadelphia, Pa	Apr. '73
Gordon, J. J	Cincinnati, Ohio	Oct. '85
Graeff, Geo. W., Jr	Philadelphia, Pa	Oct. '83
Graves, Henry C	Dayton, Ohio	Oct. '83
Greenough, Malcolm S	Boston, Mass	Oct. '78
Green, James	St. Louis, Mo	Oct. '85
Gribbel, John	New York, N. Y	Oct. '83
Griffin, John J	Philadelphia, Pa	Oct. '79
Hall, Richard F	Troy, N. Y	Oct. '83
Hallett, J. L	Springfield, Mass	Oct. '82
Hambleton, F. H	Baltimore, Md	Oct. '88
Hanford, L. C	Norwalk, Conn	Oct. '74
Harbison, John P	Hartford, Conn	Oct. '74
Harris, J. A	Philadelphia, Pa	Oct. '86
Hauk, Charles D	Chicago, Ill	Oct. '85
Hayward, Thos. J	Baltimore, Md	Oct. '84
Helme, Wm. E	Philadelphia, Pa	Oct. '86
Hequembourg, C. E	Bradford, Pa	Oct. '81
Hickenlooper, A	Cincinnati, Ohio	Oct. '73
Higby, Wm. R	Bridgeport, Conn	Oct. '88
Hookey, George S	Augusta, Ga	Oct. '73
Hoover, C. E	Winchester, Va	Oct. '84
Hopper, Thos. C	Germantown, Pa	Oct. '76
Hopper, Wm. H	Germantown, Pa	Oct. '82
Horry, Wm. Smith	Philadelphia, Pa	Oct. '86
Houston, Walter B	Rahway, N. J	Oct. '87
Howard, Eugene	New York City	Oct. '87
Howard, Laclede J	St. Louis, Mo	Oct. '80
Humphreys, Alex. C	Philadelphia, Pa	Oct. '75

Humphreys, C. J. R	Lawrence, Mass	Oct. '81
Humphreys, William	Dansville, N. Y	Oct. '75
Huntington, P. W	Columbus, Ohio	Oct. '83
Hyde, Gustavus A., Sr	Cleveland, Ohio	Oct. '82
Isbell, Chas. W	New York, N. Y	May '75
Jackson, Walter M	New York, N. Y	Oct. '87
Jones, Edward	So. Boston, Mass	Oct. '75
Jones, Edward C	So. Boston, Mass	Oct. '79
Jones, Lewis S	Philadelphia, Pa	Oct. '83
Judson, C. E	Chicago, Ill	Oct. '83
King, E. J	Jacksonville, Ill	Oct. '86
Kingsbury, F. D	Corning, N. Y	Oct. '73
Kitson, Arthur	Philadelphia, Pa	Oct. '86
Knowles, John H	Richmond, Va	Oct. '79
Kraft, Geo. W., Jr	Philadelphia, Pa	Oct. '86
Kraft, Geo. W	Philadelphia, Pa	Oct. '79
Kreischer, Geo. F	New York, N. Y	Oct. '85
Krumholz, Joseph	Buffalo, N. Y	Oct. '87
Kuehn, Jacob L	York, Pa	Oct. '81
Lamson, Charles D	Worcester, Mass	Oct. '81
Lane, Wm. M	Lancaster, Penn	Oct. '84
Landsen, Thomas G	Washington, D. C	Oct. '85
Langford, John T	Boston, Mass	Oct. '83
Leach, Henry B	Taunton, Mass	Oct. '82
Leadley, James E	Philadelphia, Pa	Oct. '86
Learned, E. C	New Britain, Conn	Oct. '81
Learned, Waldo A	Newton, Mass	Oct. '82
Leavitt, Heyward G	New York, N. Y	Oct. '84
Lee, Edward C	Philadelphia, Pa	Oct. '86
Lenz, Emil	New York, N. Y	Oct. '87
Light, Joseph	Dayton, Ohio	Oct. '85
Lindsley, Edward	Cleveland, Ohio	Oct. '76
Linton, I	Ravenna, Ohio	Oct. '75
Littlehales, T	Hamilton, Ontario	Oct. '74
Loomis, Burdett	Hartford, Conn	Oct. '84
Lowe, T. S. C	Norristown, Pa	Oct. '86
Lowe, L. P	Norristown, Pa	Oct. '83
Lucas, Philip	Mt. Vernon, N. Y	Oct. '87
Ludlam, Edwin	Brooklyn, N. Y	Oct. '74
Mayer, Frederick	Baltimore, Md	Oct. '84
McCleary, Alex. J	Philadelphia, Pa	Oct. '88
McCullough, Edmund H	Philadelphia, Pa	Oct. '82
McDonald, Wm	Albany, N. Y	Oct. '79
McElroy, Jno. H	Pittsburg, Pa	Oct. '77
McIlhenny, Jno	Philadelphia, Pa	May '75
McIlhenny, Geo. A	Washington, D. C	Apr. '73
McMillin, Emerson	Columbus, Ohio	Oct. '73
Merrill, Hiram	Janesville, Wis	Oct. '74

Merrifield, Paul S	New York, N. Y	Oct. '79
Merrick, Samuel V	Philadelphia, Pa	Oct. '83
Merritt, Charles H	Danbury, Conn	Oct. '79
Milsted, Wm. N	New York City	Oct. '87
Monks, Richard J	Boston, Mass	Oct. '75
Mooney, William	New York, N. Y	Oct. '87
Moore, David	Salem, Mass	Oct. '81
Morgans, W. H	Pontiac, Mich	Oct. '87
Morris, Henry G	Philadelphia, Pa	Oct. '79
Moses, G. W	Chelsea, Mass	Oct '80
Murphy, Hugh	Sing Sing, N. Y	Oct. '77
Nash, C. H	St. Louis, Mo	Oct. '81
Neal, George B	Boston, Mass	Oct. '74
Nettleton, Charles	New York, N. Y	Oct. '73
Nettleton, Chas. H	Birmingham, Conn	Oct. '75
Newell, Jno. W	New Brunswick, N. J	Oct. '75
Norton, A. M	Nashua, N. H	Oct. '79
Nute, Jos. E	Jersey City, N. J	Oct. '88
O'Brien, Wm. Jno	Philadelphia, Pa	Oct. '84
Odiorne, Fred H	Boston, Mass	May '75
Page, George Shephard	New York, N. Y	Oct. '80
Park, William K	Philadelphia, Pa	Oct. '84
Parkhurst, J. G	Coldwater, Mich	Oct. '73
Parrish, William	Seneca Falls, N. Y	Oct. '81
Parritt, Willard	Bloomington, Ill	Oct. '73
Payne, M. J	Kansas City, Mo	Oct. '85
Pearson, Wm. H	Toronto, Ont	Oct. '75
Pearson, Wm. H., Jr	Toronto, Ont	Oct. '88
Perkins, James D	New York, N. Y	Oct. '82
Perry, Albert D	Schenectady, N. Y	May '75
Peters, Malcolm	Brockton, Mass	Oct. '87
Pratt, Edward G	Des Moines, Iowa	Oct. '86
Prichard, Chas. F	Lynn, Mass	Oct. '83
Prichett, Samuel	Nashville, Tenn	May '75
Printz, Eugene	Zanesville, Ohio	Oct. '75
Quinn, A. K	Newport, R. I	Oct. '87
Ramsdell, George G	Vincennes, Ind	Oct. '79
Raynor, Charles H	Adrian, Mich	May '74
Read, John	Stratford, Ont	Oct. '88
Reed, J. Covode	Greensburg, Pa	Oct. '86
Reinmund, Henry J	Lancaster, Ohio	Oct. '74
Rider, Geo	Norwich, N. Y	Oct. '83
Ridgely, William	Springfield, Ill	Oct. '85
Richardson, Frank S	North Adams, Mass	Oct. '81
Robinson, Wm. L	Uniontown, Pa	Oct. '82
Rogers, James F	Jamaica Plain, Mass	Oct. '76
Roots, D. T	Connersville, Ind	Oct. '83
Rollins, J. H	Worcester, Mass	Oct. '73

Ross, A. Q.	Cincinnati, Ohio	Oct.	'82
Rowland, Chas. L	Brooklyn, N. Y	Oct.	'88
Rowland, T. F.	Brooklyn, N. Y	Oct.	'74
Rowland, T. F., Jr	Brooklyn, N. Y	Oct.	'81
Rowland, Wm. L	Philadelphia, Pa	Oct.	'86
Rusby, Jno. M	Jersey City, N. J	Oct.	'88
Russell, D. R	St. Louis, Mo	Oct.	'87
Sabbaton, F. A	Troy, N. Y	Oct.	'74
Salter, James E	Philadelphia, Pa	Oct.	'86
Scrafford, Wm. H	Bath, N. Y	Oct.	'87
Seaverns, F	New York, N. Y	Oct.	'83
Scriver, J. F	Montreal, Canada	Oct.	'87
Shelton, Frederick H	Philadelphia, Pa	Oct.	'88
Sherman, B. F	Boston, Mass	Oct.	'86
Sherman, F. C	New Haven, Conn	Oct.	'75
Simpkin, Wm. E	Richmond, Va	Oct.	'84
Sisson, Frank N	Albany, N. Y	Oct.	'86
Slade, James	Yonkers, N. Y	Oct.	'83
Slater, A. B	Providence, R. I	Oct.	'74
Slater, A. B., Jr	Providence, R. I	Oct.	'88
Smallwood, James B	Baltimore, Md	Oct.	'83
Smedburg, James R	Baltimore, Md	Oct.	'82
Smith, Chas. F	Fitchburg, Mass	Oct.	'75
Smith, James H	Newark, Ohio	Oct.	'75
Smith, Jno. W	Philadelphia, Pa	Oct.	'86
Smith, Marcus	Wilkes Barre, Pa	Oct.	'74
Smith, Orlando F	Washington, D. C	Oct.	'86
Smith, Robert A. C	New York City	Oct.	'83
Snow, W. H	Holyoke, Mass	Oct.	'87
Somerville, James	Indianapolis, Ind	Oct.	'75
Spaulding, Chas. F	Waltham, Mass	Oct.	'78
Spaulding, Chas. S	Brookline, Mass	Oct.	'86
Spear, Jno. Q. A	Boston, Mass	Oct.	'73
Sprague, Charles Hill	Boston, Mass	Oct.	'82
Stacey, Wm	Cincinnati, Ohio	Oct.	'87
Stafford, Jno. W	Meridian, Miss	Oct.	'85
Stanley, Ira N	Brooklyn, N. Y	May	'75
Stannard, A. B	Philadelphia, Pa	Oct.	'85
Starr, James M	Richmond, Ind	Oct.	'75
Stedman, Wm. A	Newport, R. I	Oct.	'77
Stein, E	Philadelphia, Pa	Oct.	'82
Stephens, Geo. W	Tarrytown, N. Y	Oct.	'87
Sterling, J. M	Monroe, Mich	Oct.	'74
Stiness, Samuel G	Pawtucket, R. I	Oct.	'79
Stoddard, C. H	Brooklyn, N. Y	Oct.	'74
Stratton, Rodney J	Decatur, Ill	Oct.	'86
Taber, Robert B	New Bedford, Mass	Oct.	'81
Tayler, George H	Warren, Ohio	Oct.	'82

Thomas, Joseph R	New York, N. Y	Oct. '83
Thomas, Mark B	Dundas, Ont	Oct. '88
Thompson, James D	St. Louis, Mo	Oct. '85
Tilden, William D	New York City	Oct. '87
Townsend, S. S	New York, N. Y	Oct. '84
Tufts, Nathaniel	Boston, Mass	Oct. '81
Turner, Thomas	Charleston, S. C	Oct. '73
Twining, E. H. B	Chicago, Ill	Oct. '86
Van Benschoten, Chas. C	New Rochelle, N. Y	Oct. '76
Vanderpool, Eugene	Newark, N. J	Oct. '73
Wagner, H. D	Philadelphia, Pa	Oct. '86
Wagner, Louis	Philadelphia, Pa	Oct. '87
Waldo, Chas. S	Boston, Mass	Oct. '86
Waldo, John A	Boston, Mass	Oct. '87
Walker, James H	Pittsburg, Pa	Oct. '83
Warmington, G. H	Cleveland, Ohio	Oct. '73
Watrous, V. S	Little Falls, N. Y	Oct. '86
Watkins, Elias T	Chicago, Ill	Oct. '73
Watson, Charles	Camden, N. J	Oct. '81
Ward, George M	New York City	Oct. '87
Weber, Adam	New York, N. Y	Oct. '80
Weber, Oscar B	New York City	Oct. '83
Wells, George Henry	Nashville, Tenn	Oct. '76
White, C. A	Schenectady, N. Y	Oct. '74
White, Ed. D	Brooklyn, N. Y	Oct. '83
White, Wm. Henry	New York, N. Y	Oct. '73
Whittier, Charles R	New York, N. Y	Oct. '87
Wilcox, H. K	Middletown, N. Y	Oct. '87
Williams, E. H	Waterbury, Conn	Oct. '88
Williams, James	Johnstown, Pa	Oct. '76
Willets, Chas. A	Flushing, N. Y	Oct. '83
Wood, Austin C	Syracuse, N. Y	Oct. '73
Wood, Gideon	New Bedford, Mass	Oct. '75
Wood, Walter	Philadelphia, Pa	Oct. '81
York, Eugene H	Augusta, Me	Oct. '81
Young, John	Allegheny City, Pa	Oct. '82
Young, Peter	Knoxville, Tenn	Oct. '85
Young, Robert	Allegheny, Pa	Oct. '75
Zimmermann, W. F	Pittsburg, Pa	Oct. '87
Zollikoffer, Oscar	New York, N. Y	Apr. '73

ASSOCIATE MEMBERS.

Norton, H. A	Boston, Mass	Oct. '88
Persons, F. R	Chicago, Ill	Oct. '88
Wilson, W. J	New York, N. Y	Oct. '88
Wright, W. S	Chicago, Ill	Oct. '88
Van Wie, Peter G	Cleveland, Ohio	Oct. '88

(**A.**)

FORM OF APPLICATION

For Active Membership to the American Gas Light Association.

I desire to become an active member of your Association, and respect
fully submit this application therefor. And agree, if elected, to conform to
the requirements of the Constitution.

....

(Name of Applicant.)

....

(Position held by Applicant.)

....

(Name of Comp'y Applicant is with.)

....

(Address of Applicant.)

....

Date...188

We hereby approve and endorse the above application for active
membership.

.... } Active

.... } Members.

Passed by the Council.. ....

Date of Election...

....*Secretary.*

(C.)

FORM OF APPLICATION

FOR TRANSFERENCE FROM ASSOCIATE TO

Active Membership to the American Gas Light Association.

The undersigned associate member of the Association respectfully asks to be transferred to the class of active members.

_____

(Name of Applicant)

_____

(Position held by Applicant.)

_____

(Name of Comp'y Applicant is with.)

_____

(Address of Applicant.)

Date _____ 188

We hereby approve and endorse the above application for active membership.

.... ⎫
.... ⎬ Active Members.
.... ⎭

Passed by the Council ....

Date of Election ....

.... *Secretary.*

CPSIA information can be obtained
at www.ICGtesting.com
Printed in the USA
BVHW041102150819

555975BV00017B/1478/P